* 87 new exceptionalism?
   Right by _virtue_?
     (Commerce, peaceful)

* (79.) level of self-awareness!
   reluctance of "conquest"
    - more symptomatic of
     fragility of Europe ...

* imagination/narrative DOES change
  how people act on ground, ... concede
facts

* chronology is a bit jumpy

Lords of all the World

✱ effort in 'empires' self-perception, self-understanding

✱ the need to self-express
eg. Rome - winter

1), language - actors' categories

✱ 'empire' ∴ internal'?
role of foreign 'within'?

✱ evangelization : imperium + rel : Christianity
(orbis)

✱ Brit. civ. > rel. abroad
NB - culturally - vvv classical!
∴ no 'empire'??
(dependant on Cath. stepping
stone?)

✱ pg 66 → Jesuit Relations??

✱ pg 78 - power dynamic of knowledge, "best interest,"
97   & eur. sci/reason affirming this

✱ 83 - idea of land's telos.

Lords of all the World

*Ideologies of Empire in
Spain, Britain and France
c.1500–c.1800*

Anthony Pagden

Yale University Press · New Haven & London

Set in Bembo
Printed in the United States of America by Lightning Source

Library of Congress Cataloging-in-Publication Data

Pagden, Anthony.
    Lords of all the worlds: ideologies of empire in Spain, Britain and France
   c. 1500–*c.*1850/Anthony Pagden.
      p. cm.
    Includes bibliographical references and index.
    ISBN 0–300–06415–2
    ISBN 13: 978-0-300-07449-9

    1. Imperialism—History. 2. Spain—Colonies—History. 3. Great Britain—
Colonies—History. 4. France—Colonies—History.
    I. Title.
    JC359.P278   1995
    325'.32'0903—dc20   95–13867
                                                        CIP

A catalogue record for this book is available from the British Library.

For John Elliott
il miglior fabbro

We need history, certainly, but we need it for reasons different from those which the idler in the garden of knowledge needs it, even though he may look nobly down on our rough and charmless needs and requirements. We need it, that is to say, for the sake of life and action, not so as to turn comfortably away from life and action. . . . We want to serve history only to the extent that history serves life.

Friedrich Nietzsche,
On the Uses and Disadvantages of History for Life

Contents

Acknowledgements

This is a greatly expanded and much revised version of the Carlyle Lectures delivered at Oxford University in the Hilary Term of 1993. I would like to thank the electors to the Carlyle Lectureship for the honour of the appointment, and particularly their chairman Larry Siedentop, who made my stay in Oxford so agreeable. I would also like to thank the Warden and Fellows of Nuffield College for their hospitality, and David Miller for having made me feel so welcome. As with every work which trespasses so unashamedly on the well-preserved gardens of a number of different disciplines, I owe more than I am now able to recognize to the kindness and forbearance of many, many people in a dozen different countries. Special gratitude, however, is due to Annabel Brett who introduced me to the writings of Vázquez de Menchaca and greatly refined my understanding of neo-Thomist natural law. She generously gave me a free hand with a doctoral thesis which, when it is published, will change the way we think about the early history of rights. Richard Tuck lent me a draft of his own Carlyle Lectures which helped me to see parallels between British and Spanish arguments for conquest, and their classical sources, which I would never have seen for myself. Anthony Black put me right about the political and legal thought of the Middle Ages. James Tully read Chapter 3 and guided me though the disputes over the status of the Aboriginal peoples of Canada. María Angeles Pérez Samper taught me about the Conde de Aranda. An anonymous reader of an early draft of the manuscript made a number of suggestions which persuaded me to re-shape the entire work, and to add what has now become the final chapter.

My greatest single debt, however, is to David Armitage and Peter Miller who read the entire manuscript in draft and with characteristic perceptiveness suggested many changes in the balance of the work, as well as providing me with endless bibliographical assistance.

Finally my gratitude, once again, to those at Yale who conferred upon this book whatever shape it now has, and in particular to John Nicoll, Candida Brazil, and to Beth Humphries whose painstaking copy-editing saved me from many unnoticed blunders. No author could hope for more.

This book is dedicated to John Elliott. To him I owe a debt which goes back more than twenty years, and which I can never now repay. I can only hope that this may, at least, be some small measure of my gratitude.

Introduction

I

The rise and fall of the modern colonial empires have changed dramatically the human geography of the planet. The 'expansion of Europe' which began in the late fifteenth century resulted in massive migrations, many of them forced. It led, sometimes intentionally sometimes not, to the destruction of entire peoples. And it produced new nations, Creoles and mixed races, peoples who had been born and reared in colonies and whose futures, and sense of identity, were markedly divergent from those of either the European invaders or the societies of the Aboriginal populations. In its final phase it also created new states, and new political forms, or renewed and transformed versions of older political types, one of which – democratic republicanism – was to become the dominant ideology of the modern industrialized world. Colonialism also created the trade routes and lines of communication which have been responsible for a slow erosion of the ancient divisions, natural and cultural, between peoples. For those routes which once carried, often indigent, Europeans out, have more recently carried ever-increasing numbers of non-Europeans back.

The modern world has been shaped by these changes. Today we live with cultures which are porous and unstable in ways which few cultures, including most of those of western Europe, were before the early sixteenth century. We live, and are increasingly aware of so doing, in societies which are in the process of becoming plural and multicultural, in which 'English' is no longer predominantly the language of the English, or Spanish of the Spanish, in which the choices, cultural, political and linguistic, which we make are shaped by the choices and the needs of others about whom we may know very little. We live too, in a world in which the nation is in prolonged and often violent conflict with the confederation for the right to become the dominant mode of political association of the next century. And this struggle is also a legacy of Europe's colonial past. Understanding how this has come to be is an important part of what it is to be a citizen of any one place – for that, as David Hume recognized over 200 years ago, is also to be a citizen of the world.

The European empires have two distinct, but interdependent histories. The first, with which this book is concerned, is the history of the

European discovery and colonization of America. It begins with Columbus's first voyage in 1492 and ends somewhat less precisely in the 1830s with the final defeat of the royalist armies in South America. The second is the history of the European occupation of Asia, of Africa and of the Pacific. It begins in the 1730s, but only takes hold in the 1780s as European hegemony in the Atlantic is coming to an end. These 'Second European Empires'[1] have only recently been dissolved, a process which for most of their inhabitants has been a slow and murderous one. Indeed some might argue that while the French still rule in Martinique and Guadeloupe, the British occupy Gibraltar and more notoriously the islands of the South Atlantic, and the Spanish fragments of North Africa, that process is still incomplete. The more indeterminate legacies of these empires − the British Commonwealth, the informal French tutelage over parts of Africa − remain a significant feature of the relationship between the 'First' and the 'Third' worlds.

This book is concerned with the first of these two imperial phases. The discovery by the peoples of Europe that between their continent and Asia there existed another of which, prior to 1492, they had had no knowledge, nor any recorded contact, has been described as an event of world historical significance almost from the day Columbus returned from his first voyage. It was, said David Hume in 1757, 'really the commencement of modern History'.[2] The late fifteenth century, he wrote, had been a time in which 'America was discovered: Commerce extended: the Arts cultivated: Printing invented: Religion reform'd; And all the Governments and Empire almost chang'd'.[3] The discovery had devastated the intellectual world of Europe and had exposed Europeans, if not for the first time at least in uniquely dramatic ways, to a number of non-European cultures. It had also made possible the creation of the first large European overseas empires. Since the first decades of the sixteenth century, the modern world, much as Hume and most of his contemporaries might have lamented the fact, had been dominated by a struggle between the three major European powers − Spain, France and Britain − for control of the non-European world. And the main theatre for that struggle had been America.

Because of this perception of the New World as, in Voltaire's words, a 'species of new creation',[4] the European empires in America became by the second half of the eighteenth century a subject of intense historical scrutiny. Some of this attention, like the Spanish chronicles of conquest or the French and English histories of exploration and settlement which had preceded them, was openly triumphalist, and explicitly nationalist in inspiration. As the competition between the three major powers intensified, discovery, exploration and conquest became a crucial location for the display of national pride. There were those, intellectuals for the most part with increasingly cosmopolitan concerns, who, during the eighteenth century, attempted to find something like a common purpose behind the colonizing process. For them comparison between the differing histories and objectives of the European empires could be the only possible route to an understanding of their true significance. 'In a subject as new and as little thought about as that of colonial theory', a certain Monsieur Blin, a *député* in the National Assembly, in March 1790 advised his colleagues that, in their efforts to understand the place of the old colonial system within the new French state, 'nothing is more likely to open the way to new ideas, nothing more likely to provide a more advantageous grip on one's judgement than a method of comparison'.[5]

Works such as Edmund and William Burke's *An Account of the European Settlements in America (1757)* or Anquetil-Duperon's *Considérations philosophiques et géographiques sur les deux mondes*[6] or, as it was originally planned, William Robertson's *History of America*,[7] had all attempted the kind of comparison which M. Blin called for. The most remarkable of them, however, far the most wide-ranging, and the one which Blin may have had in mind, was the abbé Guillaume Raynal's *Histoire philosophique et politique des deux Indes* which first appeared in 1772. This sought to compare not only Spain, Britain and France, but also Portugal, Holland, Sweden, Prussia, Russia and Denmark. Raynal's work (to which I shall return in Chapter 6) has for long been neglected, but until the mid-nineteenth century it was the most widely read account, as well as the fiercest indictment, of the first European overseas empires.

The *Histoire* is an attempt, as its title suggests, to bring together the two main spheres of European expansion into one text. It was also the first work to offer, however difficult it might be to recognize it as such today, a theory of imperialism. This, Raynal hoped, would transform the data he had amassed into some prevailing theme, some lesson, from which future Europeans might benefit. But such a theory could only, he knew, be fully understood in a global, and comparative, idiom and fully realized only by one who was, as he claimed to be, 'disengaged from all passions and prejudices'.[8]

The *Histoire*, however, was not only the most ambitious of such projects, it was also the last. Both the theorists of empire and its historians have remained curiously indifferent to the possibilities offered by comparison ever since. There have, of course, been many studies which have compared the political formation, the economies, or the institutional structures of more than one European empire. There have also been attempts to compare the developing cultures of the European colonies in America.[9] But there has been little sustained effort to examine the extended, theoretically complex, debates over the nature and the purpose of empire. Yet, in their several ways, these debates changed the whole course of European political thinking, and, in radically transformed but still identifiable idioms, continue to have a massive impact upon modern thinking about the relationship between states.

This book is not an attempt to emulate Raynal. It is concerned with a far shorter span of time – from the establishment of the first true settlements in America in the sixteenth century to independence in the nineteenth – and is restricted to three of the European empires, and only to those in America. There are obvious reasons for these limitations. Throughout this period, the British, the French and the Spanish watched each other constantly. They measured their behaviour against each other, and, far more frequently than has been supposed, borrowed from each other in their continuing attempts to understand the evolving shape of the empires which they had created. The Scandinavian, German and Russian settlements in America were too transitory to arouse much interest. The Portuguese presence in Brazil, although of more lasting importance, was overshadowed by the Portuguese empire in India. There are certainly important Portuguese theoreticians of empire (one of them, Serafim de Freitas, I discuss in Chapter 2) and writers from France, Britain and Spain who were keenly interested in the Portuguese imperial venture. But few of these have much to say on Brazil, if only because in most outward respects Brazil too closely resembled a Spanish colony to be of much theoretical significance. The Dutch, although they became the object of intense scrutiny by the British, were never until the nineteenth century an imperial power in any meaningful sense, nor ever regarded themselves as such. The claim by English royalists in the 1660s that the Republic of Holland was seeking a Universal Monarchy of the sea was an oxymoron. As every imperialist knew, 'empire' implied rulership, and that, on the British and Dutch understanding of the law of nations, could not be exercised at sea.

Any attempt to compare the ideologies of even the British, French and Spanish empires in America presents structural and thematic difficulties which, as with all comparative enterprises, can only ever be partially resolved. Although the topics I have chosen are those which dominated the various discourses of empire during this period, they were not all of equal significance, nor significant at the same time for all three empires. To attempt to recover the responses of the theorists from all three nations in equal measure would have been like attempting to reconstruct a tennis game with three players. Some of my chapters, therefore, focus on one national culture at the expense of the other two. The preoccupation with true 'lordship of all the world', for instance, began in Spain, and remained very largely a Spanish concern. In the late seventeenth century there were many Europeans who accused Louis XIV of harbouring designs of Universal Monarchy. But by this they meant, as Leibniz's satire *Mars Christianissimus* of 1683 made clear, little more than political hegemony in Europe. The ideologues of the Spanish empire, however, actually considered, if only briefly in the mid-sixteenth century, the possibility that their king might become ruler of a world state. Because of this, and because even those with more modest ambitions recognized that the

won't perhaps [handwritten]
(or perhaps because of ...) [handwritten]
least dependent on slaves [handwritten]

identity of the Spanish monarchy was linked to the older Roman imperial vision of the single 'orbis terrarum', Chapter 2 is largely concerned with Spain.

Similarly the question of slavery became a subject of moral and political anxiety in Spanish and in British America only after independence. In France, however, it figured pre-eminently in anti-monarchical and anti-imperial literature from the 1730s on, and by the 1790s had been placed firmly on the Revolutionary agenda. Slavery was also seen – in ways which were not replicated in either of the other two empires – as a direct consequence of the European Atlantic empires. For this reason, in Chapter 6 the question of slavery is discussed entirely in its French context, and as part of a critique whose target was, in effect, the entire colonial culture of the *ancien régime*.[10]

slavery [handwritten margin note]

Neither can any comparative study make any pretence to inclusivity. The apparatus of scholarship on all three empires has grown so large since Raynal's day that any attempt to master all of it would take half a lifetime. There are obvious themes – population decline, the effect of the growth of the American trade on world markets, above all, perhaps, the whole question of the relationship between the European colonizers and the colonized – which I have either not discussed, or discussed only in passing. This is inescapably a Eurocentric study. It is an attempt to understand how Europeans thought about the empires which they had created and with the consequences of which they were compelled to live. It is also an attempt to show how that thinking changed over time, so that by the first decades of the nineteenth century a pattern of expectation – and of anxiety – had been established which would determine much of what subsequently transpired between Europe and almost the rest of the entire world.

∗agency of empires? nations? [handwritten]

II

With the collapse of the European empires in America, the first phase of European expansion came to an end. These empires had all been, in their different ways and despite their sometimes self-conscious modernism, attempts to perpetuate the traditions and the values of the empires of the ancient world. 'Empire' and 'imperialism', however, are terms which have subsequently become associated not with this early period of expansion, but with the global European empires of the nineteenth century, empires which, with the exception of the lingering British presence in Canada and the Caribbean and of the French in Martinique and Guadeloupe, excluded America.[11] The invasions of India and later Africa, the settlement of Australia and the Pacific, the seizure of parts of China and the economic domination of the Persian Gulf, were all to be of far greater economic, and possibly more lasting political and human, significance than the colonization of America had ever been. But what have often been called the 'First European empires'[12] cannot so easily be distinguished from these later developments. The language of empire, and many of its fundamental anthropological assumptions, persisted from the sixteenth into the nineteenth century, and in many cases into the twentieth. The centres of imperial power shifted from the south of Europe to the north. But two of the major states involved in colonizing the Americas, Britain and France, were also engaged in colonizing other parts of the globe in the nineteenth century. The American experience, furthermore, demonstrated that overseas settlement, despite massive logistical and technical problems, was both possible and potentially vastly profitable.

Yet the real intellectual significance for Europeans of their several experiences in America was that these had demonstrated what successful empires should *not* attempt to be. By 1800 most of enlightened Europe had been persuaded that large-scale overseas settlement of the kind pursued, in their different ways, by Spain, Britain and France in the Americas could ultimately be only destructive to the metropolis itself. They had shown that every immigrant community, no matter what its cultural origins or the degree of self-rule it is able to exercise, will one day come to demand economic self-sufficiency and political autonomy. They had shown, too, that the massive exploitation of forced native – and of imported slave – labour was wasteful of economic resources, and massively destructive of human lives in ways which even the most hardened imperialist could not quite ignore. The ordeal of the British in 1776, the French in the 1790s and the Spanish in the 1820s and 1830s had also come very close to destroying the political systems of the metropolitan powers. By the end of the eighteenth century all the major European states had suffered serious reversals, and their theorists had talked themselves into a position from which no right-thinking person should have been able to contemplate the creation of new empires. Why, then, was it precisely at that moment that the scramble for India and later Africa began?

The answer, as Charles Maurice de Talleyrand, that notable political survivor and Napoleon's foreign minister, had seen in 1797, was that the new colonies which the British had established in India were, in fact, quite unlike the old settlements in America. America had been a place of conquest and expatriation, a place where, in Talleyrand's words, 'individuals without industry without leaders and without morals' had gone precisely in order to escape the constraints of the old world. British India, by contrast, was to be a place not of settlement, but of exploitation. The Europeans in America had made the fatal mistake of handing their colonies over to those who regarded them only as places where they might secure for themselves goods and a way of life which they could never have hoped to acquire at home. They had compounded that mistake by trying to control such peoples by direct rule from a distant metropolis.[13] Their most damaging error, however, had been to cultivate the crops from which the economic wealth of the colonies derived – primarily sugar – in lands where there was no available labour. Bringing vast numbers of human beings halfway across the globe was not merely unacceptably cruel – Talleyrand was not much troubled by that – it was also hugely wasteful, and had led to the creation of societies which, as the uprising in St Domingue on 24 August 1791 had demonstrated, were bound, sooner or later, to collapse in revolt. The British in Bengal had begun to cultivate sugar where there already existed an abundant labour force which could be paid, not enslaved. This, or so Talleyrand supposed, was a policy that would secure the dependence of the native populations without arousing their animosity. In such informal empires administrative costs were low and there was little danger of the development of an independent colonial society. The relationship that existed between colonizer and colonized was also believed to benefit both producer and consumer. A people who lived under the 'tutelage', rather than the rule, of another was clearly likely to prove more cooperative and more productive.[14] France, Talleyrand concluded, should itself now emulate this excellent policy, and, in keeping with this new rational approach to colonization, the traveller-scientists, men like Antoine Bougainville, the 'discoverer' of Tahiti and first Frenchman to circumnavigate the world, should be asked where such future colonies should be established.[14]

British India, as Talleyrand was also aware, had been the creation of an essentially commercial society. Such societies had an abiding suspicion of conquest and the kind of imperial rule which followed conquest. To the 'merchant-adventurer' even the North American 'plantation' seemed to be little more than a relic. As the great Austrian economist Joseph Schumpeter observed, for those modern merchants who were ultimately responsible for the creation of Europe's 'Second empires', imperialism 'fell into that large group of surviving features from an earlier age' which are characteristic of 'every concrete social situation'.[15] It seemed to be merely 'an element that stems from the living conditions, not of the present but of the past'. Entrepreneurs – 'capitalists' in Schumpeter's language – pre-ferred economic gains that could be acquired at low capital expenditure. Conquests, even the conquest of relatively 'primitive' peoples, involved massive initial outlay on both military action and subsequent adminis-tration. As many had argued in the 1770s, the American colonies had cost Britain as much, if not more, than they had provided in either trade or agricultural and manufactured goods. Far better to benefit from the uncoerced labour of others. The exploitation of the Third World by the First had begun.

The new British empire in India may never have been quite as Talleyrand had imagined it. Even within Britain itself there were those, such as the radical dissenter Richard Price, who regarded British India as little more than a replay of the Spanish invasion of America, a place where 'Englishmen, actuated by the love of plunder and the spirit of conquest, have depopulated whole kingdoms and ruined millions of innocent peoples by the most infamous oppression and rapacity'.[16] But Talleyrand was right to assume that this was an empire which had, in the first instance, been intended to be based not upon settlement but upon the enjoyment of a 'surplus' produced by a willing, if lowly paid, native population. He was right, too, in assuming that, at least at this formative stage, every effort had been made to prevent the emergence of a settler society which might one day follow the example of the Thirteen Colonies.

The British in India and later in Africa also avoided the wholesale destruction, physical as well as cultural, of the indigenous populations. This is not to say that the killing was not intense, nor that there were not many colonial administrators who seriously considered the possibility of genocide. After the 1870s apparently similar patterns of invasion and settlement to those which the Spaniards had pursued in America were being followed enthusiastically by the British, the French, the Belgians and the Germans in Africa. But the long-term effects of these were never so disastrous as the colonization of the Americas had been. India and Africa today are, very largely, populated by Indians and Africans, whereas in America the autochthonous people, though now on the increase, are a largely disenfranchised minority, with limited cultural rights, but no significant political or economic role in a predominantly Creole community. This can in part be attributed to the fact that most Asian and African peoples were militarily more robust than the Native Americans had been, and the Asian cultures more like those which Europeans were prepared to recognize as civil societies. But it was also a self-conscious policy. The doctrine of 'indirect rule', which was to become an ideological feature of subsequent British imperialism, may have been in great measure expedient, but it was also believed to benefit both colonized and colonizer alike, and it made for the creation of a wide and flexible trading base.

But by the mid-nineteenth century many of the political and economic features of British rule which Talleyrand had so admired had disappeared. In their place there had emerged a belligerent militarism which borrowed its rhetorical style, and its political culture if not its colonial policies, from the same Roman imperial imagery which had driven the earlier European empires.

This resurgence of the earlier methods of colonization does not, however, presuppose the revival of earlier ideological objectives. The European empires in America had been created in the shadow of an ancient and medieval legacy of universalism, of a presumed right of lordship over the entire world. Even the British, whose common-law traditions had insulated them to a certain degree from this predominantly Roman-law patrimony, could never quite escape the ambition to create for themselves a true *Imperium britannicum*. By the end of the eighteenth century, the European empires in America had become very different kinds of polities, but in their links with their respective 'mother countries' *nationalism > Roman universalism* [handwritten annotation]

they could never fully escape the terms of their creation. This is why when their hold over their American colonies finally began to weaken in the eighteenth century, the 'mother countries' responded with a desperate bid to reassert the older traditional ties. The semi-federalist solutions to the impending dissolution of their nations' empires which, as we shall see in Chapter 7, were offered to their respective governments by the Count of Aranda, Adam Smith and Anne Robert Turgot, were all attempts to formulate entirely new principles for any future colonial relations, ones which were precisely conceived on Greek rather than Roman models.

The British empire in India and Africa, although outwardly a neo-classical one, was largely untouched by Roman universalism. Instead it was, as C.A. Bayly has recently argued, the child of that other, more sinister legacy of the Enlightenment: nationalism. The assumption by the British crown\of direct rule over India in 1858 constituted precisely the *1858* [margin annotation] seizure of power by a centralized bureaucratic state from the 'aristocratic republicans' of the East India Company, who, in the attempt to safeguard their privileges, had fallen back upon the same language of country-party opposition which the American Revolutionaries had used seventy years before. Victoria's coronation as 'Empress of India' was the most fully elaborated attempt the modern world has ever witnessed to recreate the ancient Roman *imperium*. But it was meant largely for home consumption, an attempt by Disraeli to enhance the faltering status of the monarchy. Similarly Lord Cornwallis's 'viceregal pageantry', which combined images of Roman triumphalism with the now transfigured image of 'imperial benevolence', was intended to enforce the concept of loyalty to the king in the face of working-class radicalism.[17] In France, too, although the French overseas empire had never fed to the same degree on Roman imperial imagery as either the Spanish or the British, the new imperialism was the product of the nationalism which had followed the collapse of the Napoleonic empire, the last of the great unifying projects, whose inspiration had originally been a republican one.

Whatever the realities of their political organisation or economic objectives, the 'second' European empires clearly saw themselves as quite distinct from the first. The claim once made by the English historian J.R. Seeley that the British empire had been acquired in a fit of absentmindedness is patently absurd, if not actually meaningless. But it does contain *bi* [margin annotation] one significant insight, for an empire which could, by Seeley's day, have come to *believe* that it had been acquired in this way could clearly not be, whatever else it might with time become, one sustained by any larger, cohesive cultural, political or juridical purpose. Insofar as the new European imperialists possessed any declared ideological objectives, these were supposedly limited to the quest for a world-wide civilization based upon European political and social principles. *vr. before?* [handwritten annotation]

It is here, in the domain of political and cultural self-imagining – the domain, to use Lacan's now familiar term, of the *imaginaire* – that the most enduring historical link between the first and second empires is to be found. For the languages in which the nineteenth-century empires sought to frame themselves were the transfigured products of their early-modern forebears. They were the transfiguration, however, not of the languages of empire but instead of the critique which the enemies of imperialism had levelled against them in the closing years of the eighteenth century. This had insisted that the inescapable legacy of all forms of colonialism could only be human and material waste followed by moral degeneracy. Europe's relationship with the non-European world should, in future, be limited to a programme of harmonious exchange. As commerce had replaced conquest, so enlightenment would replace evangelization and the crasser forms of cultural domination. Condorcet's programme for the 'Future progress of the human spirit' (*Esquisse d'un tableau historique des progrès de l'esprit humain*), a text which was to have a considerable influence on later conceptions of empire, transposes the arbiters of the old world order, the 'tyrants, priests and hypocrites', with the enlightened scientists of the new, and replaces conquest, physical and spiritual, by enlightened instruction. For, or so Condorcet believed, the peoples of America, Africa, Asia and other 'distant countries', 'seem to be waiting only to be civilized and to receive from us the means to be so, and find brothers among the Europeans to become their friends and disciples'.[18] The conception of a world imperial base, generating enlightenment and technology, and laced with a certain amount of Christianity which constituted the 'white man's burden', was perfectly in keeping with the late eighteenth-century notions of empire. If the empires of the nineteenth century possessed no larger vision of themselves which they were prepared to articulate with any force, if they were, as Marx and others supposed, merely the necessary expression of a certain kind of economic system, this was, in part at least, because their ideological groundwork had already been laid out. The older providentialist languages of imperialism had been transformed into a pretence to enlightened rationalism. It is with the origins and development of these languages that this book is concerned.

CHAPTER ONE

The Legacy of Rome

Haec est in gremium victos quae sola recepit humanumque genus communi nomine fovit matris, non dominae ritu, civesque vocavit quos domnuit nexuque pio longinqua revinxit.

Claudian, *De Consulatu Stilichonis*, III, 150–4

I

The late fifteenth century, enthused the Scottish historian William Robertson in his *History of America* of 1777, had been the period

> when Providence decreed that men were to pass the limits within which they had been so long confined, and open themselves to a more ample field wherein to display their talents, their enterprise and courage.[1]

Robertson's was a common sentiment, expressed by his contemporaries, David Hume and Adam Smith in Britain, by the abbé Raynal (whom we shall meet again in Chapter 6) in France, and by the historiographer royal and Robertson's associate Juan Bautista Múñoz in Spain. In structural, political and economic terms, the colonies which first Portugal and Spain, then France and Britain, and finally, if also only fitfully, Holland, Sweden and Denmark had established in America were, as all these writers recognized, unquestionably new. Unlike their ancient predecessors, they were remote and ruled across great distances. They had been created out of a seemingly insatiable European need for precious metals, and an ambition, which the Ancients could scarcely have understood, to change the religious beliefs of their autochthonous inhabitants.

Yet for all their apparent, and much discussed, novelty the theoretical roots of the modern European overseas empires reached back into the empires of the Ancient World. It was, above all, Rome which provided the ideologues of the colonial systems of Spain, Britain and France with the language and political models they required, for the *Imperium romanum* has always had a unique place in the political imagination of western Europe. Not only was it believed to have been the largest and most powerful

11

political community on earth, it had also been endowed by a succession of writers with a distinct, sometimes divinely inspired, purpose.

To understand the meaning of this imaginative dependence of the new upon the old, I shall begin by sketching in what I take to have been the determining features of the Roman empire as it came to be understood by its medieval and later by its modern commentators. I do not intend, however, to offer an account of what either the Roman or the medieval empire was like, or even how it was seen by those who actually lived in it. It is rather an attempt to capture those features which by the early sixteenth century had come to dominate the discursive practices of all who were driven to ask themselves what sort of thing an empire was, what it should be, and whether or not its existence could be justified. These features will, in one way or another, dominate the discourse until the late eighteenth century.

II

The word 'empire' is itself an elusive one, whose signification, and the contexts in which it could be employed, shifted constantly until it acquired its modern meaning in the early eighteenth century. This semantic map is still also a muddled one, and what follows is an attempt to find only one path across it.

In the first instance the Latin term 'empire', *imperium*, described the sphere of executive authority possessed by the Roman magistrates, and like everything in the Roman state it had marked sacral overtones, which would survive well into the modern period.[2] It was frequently employed, particularly in the various humanistic discourses of the late fifteenth and sixteenth centuries, which borrowed their etymologies from Cicero, in the somewhat indeterminate sense which would later be captured by the word 'sovereignty'. The first sentence of Machiavelli's *The Prince*, for instance, begins: 'All the states and dominions which have had and have empire over men . . .' ('che hanno avuto et hanno imperio sopra gli uomini . . .'). The term was also used in the more limited context, of the non-subordinate power exercised within what the Aristotelians called a 'perfect community' ('perfecta communitas').[3] This is the sense in which it is used in the often-repeated phrase of the canonists, and later of the French jurists that, whatever the status of the emperor might be, each ruler was also an 'Emperor in his own Kingdom' – *rex imperator in regno suo*.[4] As Francesco Galasso has written, this phrase 'had from the beginning meant simply this: that those powers which were recognized in this period as belonging to the Emperor as "dominus mundi", should also be recognized as those of every free king within the limits of his own kingdom'.[5] 'All those powers', runs the famous law code of Alfonso X of Castile, the *Siete Partidas* (Seven

Parts), 'which . . . Emperors have or should have over the peoples of their empires, those same, the kings must exercise in their own kingdoms' (II. i. 8).

In many instances 'empire' had, by the late sixteenth century at least, become, in effect, synonymous with the earlier meanings of the term *status*, state.[6] Francis Bacon, for instance, spoke of the 'Conditores Imperiorum, Founders of states and commonwealths',[7] a sense which the term retained, especially in the context of the definition of colonial relations, until the late eighteenth century. When Sir Francis Barnard, the Governor of Massachusetts Bay, declared in 1774 that 'the Kingdom of Great Britain is *imperial*', he meant, as he explained, nothing other than that 'it is sovereign and not subordinate to or dependent upon any earthly power'.[8] As Walter Ullmann demonstrated long ago, this is also clearly the sense in which the term was used in the celebrated phrase in the Act in Restraint of Appeals of 1533: 'This Realm of England is an Empire.'[9] 'Empire' could also be used to express the pattern of political relationships which held together groups of peoples in 'an extended system', to use J.G.A. Pocock's words, 'the terms of whose association were not permanently established'.[10] Such a relationship might well describe the *de facto* (and in most cases the *de iure*) relationship between Britain and her colonies. It also described the relationship between the Crowns of England, Wales and Scotland after 1707. As Thomas Pownall, Governor of Massachusetts, explained with characteristic laboriousness,

This modelling of the people into various orders and subordinations of orders, so that it be capable of receiving and communicating any political motion, and acting under that direction as a whole is one which the Romans called by the peculiar word *Imperium*, to express which particular group or idea we have no word in English, but by adopting the word Empire. Tis by this system only that a people become a political body; tis the chain, the bonds of union by which very vague and independent particles cohere.[11]

In this context it is not insignificant that Oliver Goldsmith's *The Present State of the British Empire* of 1768 begins with 200 pages on England, Wales and Scotland.

Already by the first century CE, however, the term had also acquired something of its more familiar modern meaning. The Roman historian Sallust uses the phrase *Imperium romanum* (and he seems to have been the first to do so) to describe the geographical extent of the authority of the Roman people. And when Tacitus spoke of the Roman world as an 'immense body of empire' (*immensum imperii corpus*) he was describing precisely the kind of political, and cultural, unity created out of a diversity of different states widely separated in space, and which Edmund Burke speaking in 1775 of the Spanish and British empires called 'extensive and

EMPIRE 3 STATES

detached empire'.[12] *Imperium*, in this sense, bound together different and formerly independent or 'perfect' states.

Imperium could also create such states where none had previously existed. It was in recognition of this meaning of the term that, from the moment he invaded Lorraine in 869, Charles the Bald, Duke of Burgundy, styled himself 'Emperor and Augustus'. He may only have ruled over two territories, but to rule over more than one was, in effect, to be an 'emperor'. The same assumption lay behind the declaration of Alfonso VI of Castile in 1077 to be 'By the Grace of God Emperor of all Spain'.[13] The actual territorial ambitions of these men may have been limited but both were highly conscious of the extent to which their claims echoed those of the Roman *imperatores*, whose successor they in some sense imagined themselves to be. The greatness of states could be measured by the number and diversity of the nations of which they were constituted. 'A nation extended over vast tracts of land and numbers of people', wrote Sir William Temple, 'arrives in time at that ancient name of kingdom or modern of empire'.[14]

All of these meanings of *imperium* survive, and sometimes combine, throughout the entire period I shall be discussing. It is only with the rise of the nineteenth-century empires, conceived as these were very largely in the aftermath of the collapse of the European colonizing ventures in America, that the term 'empire' becomes limited, as it is today, to Burke's 'extended empire'.

III

Imperium had further, more richly nuanced, meanings still. The root sense of the word is 'order' or 'command'.[15] In the first instance, therefore, an emperor, *imperator*, had been merely one, and generally one among many, who possessed the right to exercise *imperium*. Under the Republic the exercise of *imperium* had been restricted to the Senate, which operated in the name of the Roman people. After the establishment of the Principate, the title became limited to a group of army commanders whose *imperium* derived not, as had that of the Republican magistrature, from the civil sphere (*domi*), but instead from the military (*militiae*). (The division between these two, Edward Gibbon was later to observe, was responsible for the corruption which finally brought the empire to an end.)[16] Augustus, although he paid due deference to the 'empire of the Roman people' (*imperium populi romani*) expected the honour due to the people to be paid to him. And by the first century Roman jurists Gaius and Ulpian had both come to insist that the *imperium* of the 'prince emperor' absorbed that of the *imperium populi Romani*.[17]

Since all empires began with conquest the association of 'empire',

EMPIRE = CONQUEST

understood as extended territorial dominion, with military rule has lasted as long as imperialism itself. But the Roman emperors were not only generals. In time, they also became judges, and although the famous phrase in the *Digest* (1.3.31) that the prince was an 'unfettered legislator' – 'princeps legibus solutus' – had originally only exempted the emperor from certain rules, it came to imply the existence of a supreme legislative authority, and was interpreted in this way by the medieval glossators on the texts of the Roman Law. The emperor may still have had a moral obligation, one which even the most absolute of early-modern monarchs were to retain, to observe his own commands; but there was no legal force which could compel them, even in theory, to do so. It is easy to see how, in time, *imperium* came to donate supreme military and legislative power over widespread and diverse territories. This is why Augustus had considered taking the title Romulus, as the founder of the new Rome, although, according to his biographer, reverence for the ancestors prevented him from doing so, and why in later generations the title Augustus itself became synonymous with absolutism in this extended sense.[18] To claim to be an *imperator* was to claim a degree, and eventually a kind of power, denied to mere kings. And the theocratic dimension which *imperium* acquired during the reign of Augustus, and which was reinforced by the Christian emperors and their apologists, widened still further the distinction between imperial and royal authority.[19]

Such nomenclature of power was, and remained well into the eighteenth century, a matter of profound exegetical concern. In referring to the kings of Europe as *reguli*, Rainald von Dassel, chancellor of the Hohenstaufen empire, was actively denying them the attributes of empire. Petrarch, a man who was more than usually sensitive to the power that words can convey, spoke contemptuously of '*King* Charles [VIII] who by the cognome "The Great" barbarous peoples dare to raise to the level of Alexander and Pompey'.[20] Similarly when in 1625 Charles I declared Virginia, Somers Island and New England to be a part of 'our Royal Empire descended upon us', he could not have been unaware that what he was claiming was more far-reaching than anything which might have been captured by Francis Barnard's 'Kingdom of Great Britain'.[21]

The transformation of the status of the Roman emperor from Augustus to Constantine the Great effectively involved the transformation of a Roman *princeps* into a theocratic Hellenistic monarch, no matter how far removed in historical origins the Roman court might have been from those of the Macedonian monarchy.[22] In the seventh century this understanding of what it was to exercise *imperium* was identified by St Isidore of Seville with the Greek loan-word, 'monarchy'. 'Monarchies', he wrote, 'are those in which the principate belongs to one alone, as Alexander was among the Greeks and Julius among the Romans.'[23] Henceforth – and this will have important consequences, in particular for Spain in the sixteenth century – the term 'monarchy' was frequently used as a synonym for 'empire', to describe a domain composed of a number of different states in which the legislative will of a single ruler was unquestioned, one where not only was the prince 'legibus solutus', but the laws were the expression of the prince's will. In the terms of the *Lex regia*, the body of Roman law which had established the authority of the emperor, 'that which pleases the prince has the force of law': *quod principi placuit legis habet vigorem* (*Digest*, 1.4.1). In this context it is not insignificant that Dante should have chosen to call his defence of the role of the empire in thirteenth-century Europe, *De Monarchia*, 'On Monarchy', rather than *De Imperio*. For, he explained, 'The temporal monarchy, commonly called "Imperium", is that sole principate which is above all other principates in the word, relating to all questions of the temporal order.' 'Imperium', however, could also, as he had explained at greater length in *Il Convivio*, be exercised in spiritual affairs by the Papacy. It was not a fitting description for a purely temporal institution.[24] The term *monarchia*, by contrast, had none of these, for Dante, unfortunate papal associations, yet retained the crucial sense of universal ruler. Similarly the jurist Antonio de Roselli (who in the 1430s found himself engaged in the dispute over the Portuguese claims to the Canary Islands) sought in his *Monarchia* of 1444 to sustain the same imperial claims to the exercise of 'universal lordship' (*dominium universale*) in view of the emperor's status as supreme judge in worldly affairs.[25] When the Spanish Habsburgs referred to their American domains as the 'Kingdoms of the Indies', they were attempting to distinguish them as a separate part of a wider geo-political community now named the *monarchy* of Spain.

It was this identification with empire, understood as a diversity of territories under a single legislative authority, and empire understood as monarchy, which underpins the medieval and early-modern conflict between empire and republic. For, in principle, there was no reason why a true republic – a *respublica* – could not also be an empire, although it clearly could not, at least until Montesquieu shifted the terms of the discussion in the eighteenth century, be a monarchy. Both Athens and Rome had, of course, been republican empires. Mere size, as Alexander Hamilton pointed out in 1788, was no impediment to true republican government, so long as the various parts of the state constituted 'an association of states or a confederacy'.[26] Nor, as Hamilton stressed on more than one occasion, was the fact of its republican constitution any reason for preventing the United Sates from becoming a true empire, 'able to dictate the terms of the connection between the old world and the new'.[27]

The conflict between the political visions of empire and republic is based on the assumption that because all empires are founded upon conquests none, in Hamilton's terms, are in fact ever able to achieve the transition from an extended assembly of states to a true confederacy. Eventually all are destined to be ruled by single individuals exercising supreme, if not arbitrary, power, and so all are ultimately destined to transform themselves into monarchies. The Roman Principate had been responsible not only for greatly enlarging the territorial limits of the Roman *Imperium*, it had also in the process conferred upon it a new political identity, an identity which was a denial of precisely those political values – the participation of all the citizens in the governance of the state – which had been responsible for its creation. As many later commentators observed, only Sparta among the republics of the Ancient World, and Venice among those of the modern, had managed to maintain their political integrity over an extended period of time, and both had achieved this by expressly forbidding all but the most restricted territorial expansion.

Why extension should in this way lead inexorably to one or another mode of absolute rule became one of the great theoretical concerns of modern European political thinking. But whatever the answer, most European commentators had, by at least the early eighteenth century, become convinced that, as the English political and economic theorist Charles Davenant phrased it in 1701, 'while Common wealths thus extend their limits, they are working their own Bane, for all big Empires determine in a single Person'.[28]

IV

All these three senses of the term *imperium* – as limited and independent or 'perfect' rule, as a territory embracing more than one political community, and as the absolute sovereignty of a single individual – survive into the late eighteenth century and sometimes well beyond. All three derived from the discursive practices of the Roman empire, and to a lesser extent the Athenian and Macedonian empires. It was the example of Rome, above all, an empire which had acquired an imaginative identity, a legal and political persona, which reached far beyond the contingencies of the relationship between colony and metropolis, which ensured that all future empires would be closely associated with the institution of monarchy. For by the time of the collapse of the Republic, Rome was already the largest state in the Mediterranean world, and its size, as St Augustine had remarked, was a demonstration of the far-reaching potentiality of the values of the society which had created it.

By the time Constantine the Great launched his massive and intemperate assault on the pagan – but not the Roman – world, this extensiveness had come to be identified with a certain kind of inclusiveness. There might be many kingdoms – but there could be only one empire. In the writings of Cicero, Virgil, Livy, Polybius, Tacitus and Sallust – the authors on whom most subsequent theoreticians of empire from Machiavelli to Adam Smith relied most heavily – the Roman *Imperium* constituted not merely a particular political order but, more significantly, a distinctive kind of society, whose identity was determined by what came to be broadly described as the *civitas*. In the first instance, as with Aristotle's notion of what it is to be a 'political animal' (*zoon politikon*), this involved a life lived in cities. For the Ancients, both Greek and Roman, cities were the only places where virtue could be practised. They were, crucially, communities governed by the rule of law which demanded adherence to a particular kind of life, that of the 'civil society' (*societas civilis*), and which were closely identified with the physical location the citizens happened to inhabit. The *civitas* and the urban centre (*urbs*) were described in most of the literature of the late Republic and the empire as if they were co-extensive. The City of Rome, Horace's *Princeps urbium*,[29] was in the words of the fourth-century poet Claudian, 'mother of arms, who casts *imperium* over all'.[30] Rome, furthermore, was not only the political centre of both Republic and empire, it was also the centre of the state's legislative activities and of most of the state's religious cults. It was the place of custom, *mores*, the collective ethical life of the entire community. It was a finite, bounded space whose walls became an important element of self-promotion during the late Republic. Under Augustus, these came to be seen as a system which provided defence not of the actual structure of the city – that, or so it seemed, was no longer in any danger – but of the traditional Roman *virtus* which having been lost in the final days of the Republic, had now been restored by the empire. 'I have transferred,' Augustus is reported to have said, 'the *res publica* from my power (*potestas*) to the dominion (*arbitrium*) of the Senate and the People of Rome.'[31] The spectacle of the city encircled by great walls transformed Virgil's poetic vision into a reality: *mores*, custom, now went together with *moenia* (walls).[32]

The city is also, of course, the foundational metaphor for the greatest work by a Roman Christian: St Augustine's *De Civitate Dei*, 'The City of God'. And, as such, it was the image which sustained much subsequent thinking about the politics of civil association. It is an image which was to be carefully nurtured by the (real) city states of fifteenth-century Italy, as much as by the architects of the (illusory) 'Cities on the Hill' of Puritan New England. The *civitas*, said Aquinas, is 'the perfect community',[33] and the 'perfecta communitas' is here defined not merely as a politically autonomous society – although it must also be that – but as one which is 'sufficient in providing for life's necessities'.[34] This, too, was a definition which evoked Aristotle's notion of *autarkeia*, or 'self-sufficiency', as the necessary condition of every true community, one which, to return to the language of Cicero, implied a strict adherence to the demands of the 'societas civilis'.[35] But the *civitas* was not only defensive. It was also itself the source of empire, if only because, as Machiavelli pointed out, the city provides both the men for the armies and the source of the authority needed to retain provinces once they have been conquered.[36] As Machiavelli also recognized – a subject about which he was particularly

NB. DC – not the same power in (o many places) imagination

sensitive – for the Romans the greatness of a city was a measure of the greatness of its rulers.[37] Much of this, as we shall see, will survive, or be recreated, in the modern world.

V

citizen ≥ person

For the Roman theorists, Cicero in particular, the *civitas*, as the sole place of human flourishing, was also, and only, the Roman political community.[38] Because of the close identity in all ancient political thought between what it was to be a citizen, and what it was to be a person, the Roman *Imperium*, although it was never defined as such, came to be looked upon not merely as a geographical or political expression but as a source of knowledge. As the Greek historian Polybius – who had no word with which to express *imperium* – phrased it, the 'orbis terrarum' was that part of the globe which had 'fallen under inquiry'.[39]

The gaze of the Roman, Polybius was suggesting, had conferred upon the world an identity, and an identity which, since it was the identity of the *civitas*, was crucially dependent upon the rule of law. 'O Romans,' Anchises ends his famous exhortation to the new race, 'to rule the nations with *imperium*, these shall be your arts – to crown peace with law, to spare the humbled, to tame the proud in war'.[40] 'The imperial majesty,' as Justinian began his *Institutes*, 'should be armed with laws as well as glorified with arms.'[41] It was the Roman Law which shaped every aspect of life within the Roman world. It was the Romans' great intellectual achievement, as moral philosophy and the natural sciences had been the Greeks'. It created not merely political and social order; it also conferred an ethical purpose upon the entire community. Under the late Republic, and then more forcibly under the Principate, the legal formulation of *imperium* merged with a second-century (BCE) Stoic notion of a single universal human race, to use Cicero's phrase, a 'single joint community of gods and men'.[42] Zeno himself, founder of the Stoic School, had taught, or so Plutarch tells us, that

we all should live not in cities and demes (townships), each distinguished by separate rules of justice, but should regard all men as fellow demesmen and fellow citizens; and that there should be one life and order (*koinos*) as of a single flock feeding together on a common pasture.[43]

For Greeks, like Panaetius of Rhodes (*c.*180–109 BCE) teacher and intellectual companion of Scipio Aemilius, whose lost work *On Duty* had a profound influence on Cicero's own *De Officiis*, and for the Roman moralists generally, it was a relatively easy step to think of Zeno's *koinos*, human ⇄ law

and of the Greek *oikumene* in general, as identical with the Roman *Imperium*.[44] As the world (*mundus*) constituted a 'universitas' it could have but one lord to provide it with the *ratio* 'of protection and jurisdiction' (*Digest* 6.1.2).[45] The law of the Roman empire thus became the embodiment of the claim to be what Aristotle had called a *koinos nomos*, a universal law for all mankind.[46] It was not merely a specific set of political arrangements, although equality before the law was a crucial part of what it was to be a *cives*; it was a true *civilization* – even if that word did not acquire its modern meaning until the second half of the eighteenth century.[47]

The civil law itself, which had been created by human reason – *ratio scripta*, in Leibniz's famous phrase – out of an understanding of the natural law, was the human law, the *lex humanus*. Those who lived by it were, by definition, 'humans'; those who did not, were not. But as it was also the Roman people who were responsible for the creation of the law, there was a sense in which only the Romans could be described as human. As Suetonius tells us, the emperor Caligula (37–41 CE) – not perhaps the most impartial witness – spoke of 'the Roman people, or rather, I say, the human race' (*populus Romanus vel dicam humanum genus*).[48] Those who were rational, and thus in some deep sense human, were those who lived within the limits of *the* empire, a set of associations which allowed the Roman jurists, and their medieval commentators, to contrast the 'reason of empire' (*ratio imperii*) with the empire of reason (*rationis imperium*).[49] Roman and subsequently Christian social and political thinking was, and would remain, heavily dependent on the semantics of the Roman Law. Even the term 'civil' itself, which remains central to all our political reflections, was used first to describe a particular kind of law, and was then applied to a particular kind of society. Similarly the verb 'to civilize' meant originally to transfer a case from one branch of the law to another.[50]

Even for Cicero, whose understanding of the concept of the 'republic of all the world' ('respublica totius orbis') changes markedly according to the audience he is addressing and the rhetorical tradition within which he is working, the 'world' was often sharply divided into Romans and 'provincials'. And just as it was politically difficult for him to think of an independent territorial state, so it was difficult for him consistently to accept the existence of independent political or cultural forms.[51] The 'provincials', he said in *De Republica*, are the 'barbarians', rule over whom, he declared emphatically, 'is just precisely because servitude in such men is established for their welfare'.[52]

Cicero also had other, more humane, views on the possible social and political relationship between Romans and barbarians. But his claim that the world might be so radically divided into those whose nature it is to rule and those who are fit only for servitude draws on a real conviction of the Ancient World, one which was to have a profound influence on those who wrote about the nature and legitimacy of later empires.

The most extreme, and the most discussed, expression of that conviction is the one on which Cicero himself was implicitly drawing: Aristotle's theory of natural slavery. The natural slave – as distinct from the rational man who has been enslaved through unfortunate circumstances – is one who is bound *by nature* to a life of perpetual labour. The definition of this anomalous creature was grounded in a distinction between what, in Greek psychology, was called the 'rational' and the 'irrational' souls.[53] In fully developed human males, the rational invariably triumphs over the irrational. This is what it means to possess the capacity for deliberation or moral choice (*prohairesis*). Neither women nor children are, in Aristotle's view, fully rational, since the former lack what he calls 'authority' (*akuron*), while the rational faculty in the latter is only partially formed. The natural slave would seem to be a wholly anomalous creature since he, while being a fully developed adult male, nonetheless has only a share in the faculty of reason, without being in full possession of it. He might be said – conveniently for his would-be enslavers – to be capable of following instructions, yet incapable of issuing them. In Aristotle's own terms, he is capable of understanding (*sunesis*) but incapable of practical wisdom (*phronesis*) for 'practical wisdom issues commands . . . but understanding only judges'.[54] While free he is violating what nature had intended him to be, for his master does his thinking for him, and he is himself almost literally a 'living but separate part of his master's frame'.[55] In practice, however, such creatures would be difficult to identify with certainty. In a crucial passage, Aristotle remarked that they might indeed be identical with the 'barbarians'. This was at best vague, since *barbaroi* was a general term which described all those who did not speak Greek. It would have to include, for instance, the subjects of the Persian monarchy for which, on other occasions, Aristotle had great respect. But it is clear that it is to this passage that Cicero is alluding in his description of the provincials, and that for Cicero the term 'barbarian', or in his rendering 'provincials', possessed some of the more nuanced meanings it has subsequently acquired. 'Barbarians' were those who lacked the necessary qualities for membership of the *civitas*, and anyone who in this way did not share the Greek, and later Roman, view of the nature of the good life was an object of fear and distrust. He was an outsider, and his relationship to those who lived within the civil community could only ever be one of servitude. Being a slave for Aristotle, and sometimes also for Cicero, was thus a necessary identity. Little wonder, then, that the author of the pseudo-Aristotelian *De mirabilibus auscultationibus* believed that even the birds that watched over the temple on the island of Diomedia could distinguish adequately between Greeks and barbarians.[56]

This seemingly stark dichotomy between those who did and those who did not live in 'the world', as defined by Athens or Rome, is perhaps not so very surprising as it might at first seem. The anthropologists have shown us that few peoples have a fully articulate sense of a single undivided genus.

As Lévi-Strauss once observed, 'a very great number of primitive tribes simply refer to themselves by the term for "men" in their language, showing that in their eyes an essential characteristic of man disappears outside the limits of the group'.[57] The Greeks, indeed, seem to have been unusual, if not unique, in possessing a term – *anthropos* – capable of describing the biological species, as distinct from a social category. But if this *anthropos* is taken, as it was in most ancient ethical writing, to be something more than a morphological category, and if membership of any community must ultimately depend upon recognition by that community, then the Greek and later Roman failure to recognize the *barbaroi* or the 'provincials', amounted to a denial of their humanity.

Unlike, however, the 'primitive' tribes described by Lévi-Strauss, or even the Greek *polis*, the Roman *civitas* was crucially a civilization for exportation, something which was already implicit in the myth of the foundation of Latium as a place where, in Virgil's formulation, 'wild races have been gathered together by Saturn and given laws'.[58] In Rome, although not in Athens, a slave could even be manumitted directly into citizenship. Manumission, which was fairly common after the fourth century BCE, involved, in effect, a legal transformation of a person's identity. It constituted, in Bernard Williams's words, 'the most complete metamorphosis one can imagine' from an object to the subject of rights.[59] Where Aristotle's 'barbarians' differed from Cicero's 'provincials' was that whereas the former would seem to be immovable in their slavery – for no amount of instruction in civility could restore a man's capacity for rational understanding – the latter could clearly be educated in the ways of civil society. This is why Cicero himself, always among the most chauvinist of Romans, could nevertheless insist that the Africans, the Spanish and the Gauls were entitled to just rule, despite being 'savage and barbarous nations'.[60] The frontiers between the world of civil men and that of the barbarians was forever dissolving. Potentially at least, the *Imperium* was a culture without limits, which is why Terminus, the god of boundaries, refused to attend the foundation of the city of Rome.

Imperium, in this sense was, as a frequently quoted passage in Seneca's *De Clementia* implied, the *vinculum societatis* – the links in the chain which could bind together the members of widely scattered communities.[61] As the Venetian humanist Paolo Paruta noted in 1599, it had been the sheer diversity of the cultural, ethical and political elements of which it had been composed which had been the true source of the greatness of the Roman Republic. This had, he said, resulted in a society which was 'ruled with such prudence and justice, that it would be almost impossible to form a more perfect royal government'.[62]

Inevitably, however, there existed a tension between a strong sense of inclusiveness, derived from the peculiar importance accorded by the Greeks to the role of the community in human life, and the later Roman insistence that, in order to fulfil the purposes for which that community had been devised it had, in some sense, to include everyone there was in the world – a tension that was to persist in all later European conceptions of empire down to their final demise in the middle of this century. The community – the *civitas* which for the Roman was identical with the *Imperium* – was the only context in which it was possible to achieve one's ends as a person. But the *civitas* also had the power to transform all those who entered it. So long, that is, as you were outside it, a barbarian or a provincial, you were in some sense less than human. Once inside, you would in time become 'civilized'. As James Wilson was to observe in 1790, as he pondered the political significance of the collapse of the British empire in America, 'it might be said, not that the Romans extended themselves over the whole globe, but that the inhabitants of the globe poured themselves upon the Romans'. And this, he added, quite apart from whatever larger moral force it might have, was clearly 'the most secure method of enlarging an empire'.[63]

It is, therefore, unsurprising that by the first century CE this *Imperium* had come to be identified simply with 'the world', the *orbis terrarum* or *orbis terrae*. Cicero spoke in *De Republica* of 'Our own people whose empire now holds the whole world' ('Noster hic populus . . . cuius imperio iam orbis terrae tenetur')[64] and Livy makes Romulus express the wish that *mea Roma caput orbis terrarum sit*: 'my Rome shall be the head of the world'.[65] After the establishment of Augustus' new regime in 27 BCE this became formally expansionist to the point where it developed into what was to be a 'world-state', bounded in Virgil's image only by *Oceanus*[66] – an image with which the later Europeans, the Spaniards in particular, were to use to demonstrate their superiority over the Ancients. This did not mean that the Romans ignored the actual existence of the rest of the globe. Indeed they possessed a lively and sophisticated ethnographical curiosity about the peoples who inhabited the lands beyond the frontiers of the empire. It was that these other worlds, the Chinese for instance or the inhabitants of the Antipodes, had no separate identity as communities – much less as political powers – and that, in the nature of things, they would one day be absorbed into the *Imperium*, *the* world, itself. It was, as Theodore Mommsen in his great history of Roman public law put it, 'a familiar concept to the Romans that they were not only the first power on earth, they were also in a sense, the only one'.[67]

De iure at least, Augustus and his successors had become rulers of the world. It now required only an act of legislation, duly provided by the Emperor Antoninus Pius in the second century in the famous *Lex Rhodia*,[68] to transform the *imperator* into the 'Lord of all the World': 'dominus totius orbis'. The concept of the *orbis terrarum* became in effect the appropriation by the political realm of the Stoic notion of a single human genus. It was, as the French historian Claude Nicolet has said of it, a 'triple achievement: spatial, temporal and political'.[69]

VI

After the triumph of Christianity, these notions of simultaneous singularity and exclusivity were further enforced by the Christian insistence upon the uniqueness both of the truth of the Gospels and of the Church as a source of interpretative authority. Although the secular and sacred authority was formally divided between the Pope and the emperor by Gelasian I in the fifth century,[70] the extension of Christianity remained very largely confined to what was understood to have once been the territory of the Roman world. Christianity was thought of as spatially co-extensive with the *Imperium romanum*.[71] The *orbis terrarum* thus became, in terms of the translation effected by Leo the Great in the fifth century, the 'orbis Christianus', which, in turn, soon developed into the 'Imperium Christianum'. A century later, Gregory the Great would translate this into the 'sancta respublica', a community endowed with the same simultaneous open exclusiveness which had been a feature of the Ciceronian 'respublica totius orbis'.

Underpinning such claims to political and territorial authority was a sense, difficult to track with any precision, that just as the *civitas* had now become conterminous with Christianity, so to be human – to be, that is, one who was 'civil', and who was able to interpret correctly the law of nature – one had now also to be a Christian. By the time that Gregory the Great came to use the term 'barbarus' it had already become synonymous with *paganus*, a sense which it retained in the language of the Curia until at least the fifteenth century. The *pagani* were 'pagans', 'unbelievers', but they were also those who were tainted by 'rusticitas' and who thus, as Peter Brown has characterized it, refused 'to see the world as intelligible'.[72] One clearly did not have to be Christian to be human, but all 'barbari et pagani', for Gregory no less than for Aristotle, hovered on the very edge of inhumanity. For they were those, in the description offered by Albertus Magnus, who confused 'the interrelations (*communicationes*) within society and destroyed the principles of justice which operate in these inter-relations'.[73]

Non-Christians, pagans who were also *barbari*, had to be encouraged to join the 'congregatio fidelium', just as the 'barbarians' had been encouraged to join the Roman *civitas*. Under the terms of the law of nature, furthermore, all men, whether pagan or Christian, had identical political rights. This belief, as we shall see, had important consequences for the subsequent disputes over the legitimacy of the European conquest of what were, in effect, the political domains of non-Christian rulers.

So long as a people remained un-Christian, however, it might still be excluded from the more exacting definition of the term 'world'. Although St Thomas Aquinas and his followers insisted upon the true universality of the law of nature, they were never fully able to obliterate the earlier, more obviously Augustinian, identification of reason with belief. And Augustine himself had given more than a mere hint that he, like Cicero, might be prepared to regard some pagans as slaves by nature.[74] It certainly meant, as Richard Tuck has argued, that those inside 'the world' could legitimately make war on those outside, particularly if those on the outside were not pagans but, like the Ottomans, those – whom Aquinas had termed 'vincibly ignorant' – who had wilfully persisted in their unbelief even after they had heard the Gospel. All too often the *pax christiana* was a peace for Christians only.[75] The sometimes stark difference between the ways in which the two major forms of (western) Christianity – Roman Catholicism, which from the the late fifteenth century was predominantly Thomist, and the various forms of Protestantism, which were all Augustinian in inspiration – approached the question of the beliefs of others, was to have a marked impact on the different histories of the modern European overseas empires.

Christian monotheism helped to enhance this sense of singularity. Unburdened by the notion of a single creator deity, the Romans had seen no reason to confuse the observation of the law with the possession of a specific religious belief, or even the observance of a specific religious cult. For the new Christians, however, the cultural and religious diversity which had been the distinctive feature of the pagan empire was merely symptomatic of the spiritual poverty which had always underpinned the Roman concept, military and essentially secular, of *virtus*. True, Christians, from John of Paris on, allowed for a wide variety of different forms of government, local customs and laws. The 'variety of things' – the *varietas rerum* – had been guaranteed by God's infinite inventiveness, and endorsed by Polybian and later Aristotelian arguments about the psychological significance of climatic variation.[76] Nevertheless all forms of civil association had to be made intelligible within a single system of beliefs. Ultimately, the image of God as father to the human family made the idea of a multiplicity of cultures, and by extension a multiplicity of states within the *Imperium*, difficult to accommodate. In terms of the same trope, if the body politic could have only one head, it could equally only have one voice and, more crucially, one set of beliefs. Christ himself, St Bernard had taught, had left Peter the government of the whole human race.[77] If this were so, if the empire was to be both unique and universal, it had in the Christian imagination also to be sacred.

The medieval empire in the West, as it is conventionally although somewhat misleadingly called, did not employ the term 'sacrum' until it was added by Frederick I in 1157, yet it is clear that in the imaginative refashioning of its own history it had been a holy community from the day of Constantine's conversion. In a wider sense it had always been a holy empire, for classical Rome itself had since its foundation been endowed with both a divine origin and divine status. Virgil's Jupiter bestows upon the new city an empire without limits in either space or time. 'For these [Romans] I set neither bounds nor periods of empire; *Imperium* without end I give',[78] a phrase later echoed by the fourteenth-century jurist Baldus de Ubaldis' definition of the Christian Empire as the 'supreme power without limits'. The concept of 'divinity' within the pagan world was, of course, very different from the Christian one. But in the various (Christian) narratives which sought to link the Ancient to the modern world, the two coincided in a single event. In a culture such as the Christian which gave great eschatological significance to the time and place of birth, the fact that Christ had been born in the reign of Augustus, the architect of the new imperial Rome, identified this as an epochal moment in world history. In Lactantius' formulation the Augustan principate had been a 'Golden Age', the purely human equivalent of the Earthly Paradise. With the *Aeneid*, which under the Emperor Frederick II was read as a semi-sacred poem (as indeed it was by Dante), and the supposed prediction of the birth of Christ in the Fourth Eclogue, it was possible to conceive the *Imperium romanum* not only, as Augustine had done, as God's reward for supreme but secular virtue,[79] but also as God's instrument in the world whose purpose was to prepare the way for its ultimate conversion to Christianity.

The *Lex regia* had been a purely human enactment. For Baldus, however, this human source had acquired divine sanction as a consequence of Christ's endorsement of imperial authority. ('Render unto Caesar that which is Caesar's.') The *Lex regia*, it could then be argued, had been an expression of the will of the people passed on God's behest. If at the time of Christ's birth rulership of the world was in the hands of the Roman people, then this must have been by divine will.[80] No subsequent claim to 'divine right' could quite match the personal endorsement of the Son of God himself. Theocratic emperorship thus became quite unlike theocratic kingship.

For Dante, too, the *Imperium* was the political instrument for the fulfilment of a more enduring human need to create a single community of knowledge, and a single human civilization, bound together by what in *Il Convivio* he called the 'universal religion of the human species'.[81] It could even be argued, on the basis of Matthew 28, 18 – 'all power is given unto me in heaven and in earth', and 1 Corinthians 15, 27: 'for He hath put all things under his feet' – that, as Aquinas among others concluded, it was Christ himself who had been the true 'dominus totius orbis' and Augustus merely his regent.[82] Such a political *ordo* could, therefore, only be, to reverse Voltaire's famous dictum, Holy, Roman and an Empire.

The origin of this unique political order in Jupiter's donation, as recorded by Virgil, also had extensive significance for later generations eager to sustain that, otherwise fragile, continuity between the pagan and Christian empires. For, it was argued, the empire Jupiter had founded and Augustus had re-created had then passed through a succession of political translations to Constantine the Great, and Constantine – at least in the fertile political imagination of the eighth-century Papacy – had bequeathed *imperium* (now conceived as a quasi-hereditary property) to the

Papacy and the Papacy had bestowed it upon a succession of Germanic rulers.[83] In reality this German empire may have been, as Jean Bodin observed in the sixteenth century, one in which the emperor was so in thrall of his own estates that he was not a sovereign at all but, like the Venetian doge, the first citizen of an aristocratic state.[84] But the realities were of little theoretical significance. What mattered, for the other princes of Christendom and for later generations of European rulers, was the historical pedigree of the claims of both the Emperor and the Pope to hold *imperium* over the whole of the Christian world.

The image of the empire as the object of successive 'renovations' over time became, as we shall see, central to the ideological forms which the later European empires were to give to their distinct projects and political identities. It is this which transformed such seemingly absurd seventeenth-century characterizations of universal empire as Tomasso Campanella's *De Monarchia hispanica*, grounded as it was upon prophetic hermeneutics and abstruse astrological calculation, into powerful political ideologies. For the Roman and medieval empires, and all those other future empires which might succeed them, were conceived as being more than simple structures of power. They were also represented as the means which God had placed on this earth for men to use in order to accomplish their ends. In this respect at least they had a strongly Aristotelian identity. The ancient *polis* had made human flourishing – *eudaimonia* – possible. By rendering *eudaimonia* as 'blessedness' *(beatitudo)*, Aristotle's thirteenth-century translator, Robert Grosseteste, had made that a state which it was clearly only possible to achieve within the territorial limits of the Christian *monarchia*. The idea of *monarchia* as a single system embracing the whole of Christendom became, in J.H. Burns's words, 'one of the strongest elements in the political thought of the period'.[85]

VII

Centuries of talk, which privileged in this way the notion of a single exclusive world domain, made the Roman world and its natural successors part of a process of transformation whose origins were those of the human political community itself. *De facto* there might exist other kings in the world, just as *de facto* there existed other belief systems besides Christianity. But *de iure*, there could be only one emperor and only one religion. This vision of exclusiveness is what the fourteenth-century jurist Bartolus de Sassoferato alluded to when he wrote that considered individually there did indeed exist other rulers in the world, whose right to rule he defended fiercely; but when viewed universally, the emperor was, as Antoninus in the second century had claimed to be, 'dominus totius mundi vere'.[86] As Bartolus said elsewhere, shifting significantly the terms he was using, the emperor is *de iure*, 'lord and monarch of all the world' (*dominum et monarcham totius orbis*) and that to deny this – although like all good jurists he was cautious on this point – might be heresy.[87]

This celebrated assertion was dismissed as absurd by later writers, and possibly as blasphemous. But in view of the close association between the empire as a place of human flourishing and the Church's claim to be the unique source of spiritual redemption, the universality of the emperor's jurisdiction was inescapable, and received widespread support from both civilians and canonists alike.[88] The context of Bartolus's remark is also highly significant. Initially he divided the world into five 'genera gentium'. These were then classed as, on the one hand, the 'populus Romanus' and on the other the four species of 'populus extranei'.[89] The former he defined – again with suitable legal caution – as 'almost all those who obey the Holy Mother Church'; the 'populi extranei' as the Turks, the Jews, the Greeks and the Saracens. The emperor would appear to have *de iure* dominion over both categories of person, even if *de facto* he is not undisputed ruler over even the 'populus Romanus'. The effect of Bartolus's ethnic division is once again to limit 'the world' to a distinct cultural, political, and in this case religious, community. And again it places boundaries between what may be counted as the domain of the fully human world, and those others – which because of their rejection of the hegemony of the Western Church now also included the Greeks – who have no place within the *civitas*, and so no certain claim upon the moral considerations of those who do.

The claims to universal *dominium*, which were in the first instance the consequence of a gradually changing view of the identity of the optimal political community, necessarily involved the transfer of a definition of humanity from the moral sphere to the political. This demanded the restriction of the 'human' to a specific political entity which, of necessity, could only have one undisputed ruler whose status came very close to being that of a 'God on Earth'. The translation of the concept of the *civitas* to the Christian world reinforced the sense of the difference between those inside and those outside the Roman universal empire. It is this legacy of universalism, developed over centuries and reinforced by a powerfully articulate learned elite which the European overseas empires, especially that of Spain, could never quite abandon. Compelling, and for many comforting though this sense of uniqueness might have been, it also presented seemingly intractable problems both of legitimation and of representation for political projects which sought to extend the limits of the *orbis terrarum* to the point where the restraining notion offered by Bartolus' two genera of peoples became meaningless.

CHAPTER TWO

Monarchia Universalis

Nos autem, cui mundus est patria velut pisicibus equor . . .
Dante Alighieri, *De vulgari eloquentia*, I vi 3

I

Under the Christian emperors the ancient dream of universality transformed the pagan ambition to civilize the world into the analogous
objective to convert literally all its inhabitants to Christianity. The single
unifying body of law – the *koinos nomos* – thus became a single body of
beliefs. That these beliefs, as re-described by the Latin Fathers from
Augustine to Aquinas, were themselves heavily dependent upon the Stoic
notion of law assured a high degree of theoretical continuity between the
pagan and the Christian empires, and an equally strong sense that
conversion could not be fully or adequately achieved without a corresponding political and cultural transformation.

There was one further component of the founding mythology of the
Roman empire which allowed the classical theory of empire to be
absorbed relatively easily by its Christian successors. For if the *Imperium*
had drawn the legitimacy for its unlimited political power from a unique
moral culture, this was because that culture had been founded in the *pietas*
of which Virgil's Aeneas, 'outstanding in arms and piety' ('pietate insignis
et armis') had been the archetype.[1] *Pietas* denoted loyalty to the family and
more generally to the community, together with the strict observation of
that community's religious laws. It also implied the recognition of the
singularity, and the truthfulness, of a creed, a creed which, in the Roman
case, expressed the complete fusion of the numinous and the political.
Rome, said Cicero, had prospered precisely because of 'our scrupulous
attention to religion and our wise grasp of a single truth'.[2] The *pietas*,
which had been responsible for the foundation of the Roman empire,
claimed Jacobus de Voragine, thirteenth-century author of *The Golden
Legend*, an immensely popular collection of the lives of saints, was to be
understood as humanity. 'What good would it do us,' he asked, employing
a familiar Christian paradox, 'to conqueror barbarians, if we ourselves are

conquered by our own brutality?'[3] To conquer one must first be conquered; to be free one must first be enslaved.

It had been the virtues embodied in this notion of piety, argued Augustine in a much quoted passage in Book V of the *City of God*, which had led God to entrust to the Romans the task of uniting the world prior to the coming of Christ. The Romans, he said, had been given 'excellentissimi imperii' as a reward for

> the virtues by which they pursued the hard road which brought them at last to such glory.... They disregarded private wealth for the sake of the common wealth. They stood firm against avarice, gave advice to their country with an unshakeable mind and were not guilty of any crime against the laws, nor of any unlawful desire.[4]

Pietas, that is, involved the display of *virtus*, the quality of 'manliness', as expressed in the willingness, not merely to die for one's beliefs and one's community but also to value the good of that community, the *utilitas publica*, over one's own personal good, the *utilitas singulorum*. As with the related term, *virtus* which was transformed by the sixth-century Christian philosopher Boethius into the now familiar modern notion of 'virtue', so the translation of the Roman, and by extension imperial, conception of 'piety' to the Christian medieval empire was a relatively simple one. In the final transformation of all mankind into the followers of Christ, it was the empire which would ensure the dissolution of every cultural, political and confessional difference. Livy had made Scipio declare: 'The empire of the Roman people shall be extended to the furthest ends of the earth' ('imperium populi Romani propagaverit in ultimos terrarum fines'),[5] a phrase which found a clear echo in St Jerome's rendering of the Psalm 18:5: 'Their sound has been spread throughout the world and the Word had reached to the end of the Earth.' ('In omnem terram excivit sonus eorum et finis orbis terrae verba eorum.')

Under the aegis of the new order, difference itself would vanish into the brotherhood of the God who was also the Son of Man. This 'new man', St Paul informed the Colossians,

> which is being renewed unto knowledge after the image of him that created him, where there cannot be Greek or Jew, circumcision and uncircumcision, barbarian, Scythian, bondman, freeman: but Christ is all and in all. (3.11)

The Christian emperors had, therefore, not only a duty to uphold and protect Christendom. They had a consequent obligation to extend the empire to those, the non-Christians, who, because of their ignorance, had been denied historical access to the 'congregation of the faithful' (*congregatio fidelium*). The Christian world order whose origins could not be separated from those of the Roman *Imperium* had always, like the empire itself, been thought of as identical *de iure* with the world – the *orbis terrarum* – and thus potentially as a cultural, moral and finally political order with no natural frontiers.

Encouraging outsiders to join the wider Christian world posed serious moral difficulties. Conversion was conceived as essentially a cognitive process, an act of instruction which would lead the convert to join the congregation of the faithful of his or her own free will. Forced conversion, although frequently practised, was, as the great Spanish 'Apostle to the Indians', Bartolomé de Las Casas, later protested so violently in America, void of true significance. The close association in the Christian mind between belief and certain types of social behaviour meant, however, that there were those who were prepared to argue that forced introduction into 'civility' was legitimate as the preliminary and necessary condition of voluntary conversion. Indeed, much colonial legislation in Spanish America, and some in Canada, was directed towards this end.

II

The Christian empire was a secular institution. But the emperor, though no longer a priest in any formal sense, was still the second sword of Christendom. For Dante – who was the most powerful defendant of imperial authority in the Middle Ages – it had been precisely the emperor's role as the secular and politically independent defender of the faith which had made him the possible agent of universal political harmony. This relationship was, however, unstable. Dante himself had famously insisted that 'the authority of the Empire in no way depends upon the Church',[6] and had argued that imperial, which meant of course foreign, rule was the only solution to Italy's internal problems. But for all the persistent and mutual hostility between the empire and the Church which existed until the end of the Thirty Years War in 1648, the Church remained the only body that had the power to confer upon the empire the sacredness it required, *pace* Dante, if its identity as the empire was to be sustained. Ultimately, too, it was only the empire which was able, albeit fitfully, to offer the Church the military protection it so frequently needed. Even after the mutinous troops of one emperor, Charles V, had sacked the city of Rome in 1527, the ancient relationship between the 'Two Swords' of Christendom served to bind European imperialism with the future and the fate of Christianity.

The commitment to a programme of evangelization by the Spaniards, whose sovereign during the period of greatest overseas expansion also bore the title of Holy Roman Emperor, was, in a sense, inescapable. It was reinforced by the fact that the Castilian claim to the American possessions rested in the first instance upon a papal grant. The Bulls (five of them in all) issued by Pope Alexander VI in 1493 conceded to Ferdinand and Isabella the right to occupy a region vaguely defined as 'such islands and lands . . . as you have discovered or are about to discover'.[7] Until the late eighteenth century, these Bulls were represented in the historiography of the Spanish empire as a donation, and as a donation they were looked upon as being, in some sense, analogous with the Donation of Constantine. They may not have provided the Castilian crown with undisputed *dominium* in America, but they did offer a link with the empire in the West, which even those who rejected the Papacy's claim to possess sovereignty over 'all the world' were reluctant to lose. This may explain why so many Spanish writers, from Francisco de Vitoria in the 1530s to the jurist Gregorio López[8] – who rejected most other aspects of Vitoria's works – to Francisco de Ugarte as late as 1655,[9] were prepared to insist upon the authenticity of a document which had been shown to be a forgery as early as 1440.

The association with Constantine is further reflected at two crucial stages in the history of the conquest of Mexico. The first is Hernán Cortés's boast from Mexico in 1519 that he would soon allow Charles to 'call yourself emperor of this kingdom with no less glory than of Germany which your majesty already possesses'.[10] The second is the fictionalized 'donation' by Montezuma of his 'empire' to Charles V, a carefully crafted episode in which the Aztec ruler donates his *imperium* to the Christian monarch in terms which, as John Elliott showed many years ago, are strongly reminiscent of biblical and of medieval Castilian forensic rhetoric.[11] Both served to reinforce the image of the western American empire as a continuation of the older empire in the East. It is perhaps little wonder that Philip II should have considered taking the title of 'Emperor of the Indies' to compensate for the loss of the imperial title itself, or that, by the seventeenth century, the king of Castile was being referred to in semi-official publications as the 'Emperor of America'.[12] The reliance in this kind of political imagery upon a narrative also demanded a constant writing and rewriting of an official history. This is why, as Hakluyt recognized, the Castilians had understood from the beginning the need for a court historiography, something Hakluyt had urged, largely in vain, upon the English crown.[13] The historian and the cosmographer, wrote André Thevet in 1575, who 'by their occular observations render the conquest easy [to grasp]' were the custodians of the imperial imagination.[14]

It would be unwise to place too much emphasis on this. But it was evident that the persistent reliance in circles close to the Castilian court on the papal donation, and its continuing importance in the official historiography of the Spanish empire, served to keep the continuity between the Spanish monarchy and the ancient and subsequent Christian *Imperium romanum* firmly on the agenda.

The Spanish empire in America not only began in this way with the explicit authority of the Papacy. It was also conducted, until the reforms of the 1780s and 1790s altered the nature of the empire altogether, very largely as a Church–State venture. So close was this relationship during the early phase of colonization that between 1516 and 1518 the Island of Hispaniola was governed directly by the Hieronymite order which had itself been a creation of King Alfonso XI of Castile. Despite early attempts by both the *conquistador* elite and the Franciscan and Dominican orders to create a new and independent Church in the New World, the ecclesiastical institutions in Spanish America remained throughout the colonial period under firm royal control. Except for brief periods during the seventeenth and eighteenth centuries, this close relationship between Church and State both shaped the government in America and helped to sustain the ideological presence of the crown as the new colonies slowly developed cultural identities and political aspirations of their own.

In these two respects the Spanish empire in America was unique. The Spaniards were not, however, alone in expressing their initial bid for overseas empire as a mission. The French who, initially at least, had had no papal sanction and, despite continuing bids from Charles VIII to Louis XIV for the imperial title, no immediate link with the older imperial objectives, had since the days of Francis I framed their colonial projects in very much the same terms as the Spaniards.[15] The commission issued on 15 January 1541 to Jean de la Rocque, seigneur de Roberval who followed Cartier's third voyage to North America, expressed the king's desire that he should

> inhabit the aforesaid lands and countries and build there towns and fortresses, temples and churches, in order to impart our Holy Catholic Faith and Catholic Doctrine, to constitute and to establish law and peace, by officers of justice so that they [the Native Americans] may live by reason and civility (*police*).[16]

Half a century later, Henri IV was still insisting that his own colonial ventures in both the Atlantic and the Indian Oceans were merely a continuation of his predecessor's objectives.[17] Some of this, it is true, was intended to ward off complaints from the Spaniards, and the Papacy, that the French were trespassing in the Iberian sphere of influence. Both Francis and Henri rejected on repeated occasions both the validity of Alexander VI's Bulls of Donation and their interpretation by the Castilian crown.[18] Every Christian power, after all, had a duty to evangelize whether this had been made explicit by the Papacy or not. But Francis's claim in the commission granted to Roberval on 15 January 1541 that he had no wish to invade the territories of 'any prince or power allied to us, and especially those of our most dear and beloved brothers the Emperor [Charles V] and the King of Portugal' attests to a certain continuing unease on the subject.[19]

Settling a dispute between rival European states, although a crucial component in the ideological assertions of all three powers in the Atlantic, was not, however, the sole, or even the prime, objective of the French king's ideologues. They were concerned, above all, to settle the royal conscience before God. More murky, though no less urgent, was the need to establish some kind of morally admissible and clearly distinguishable identity for the new colonies. The religious orders had, of course, a vested interest in arguing, as one of them put it in 1691, that the French kings had been moved to create a 'Christian empire, [rather] than to extend the frontiers of a temporal monarchy'.[20] But it was not only they who made such claims. In 1627, when France was no longer in any danger from either of the Iberian kingdoms, Louis XIII, in establishing the first trading company in Canada, the 'Compagnie des Cents Associés pour le Commerce du Canada', returned to what by now had become something of a family tradition. His desire, he claimed, was 'to continue the same desire of the deceased Henry the Great, his father of glorious memory' – a reference to the creation of the colony of Acadia in 1603 – that the French should

> discover in those lands and countries of New France, called Canada, some habitation capable of sustaining colonies, for the purpose of attempting, with divine assistance, to bring the peoples who inhabit them to the knowledge of the true God, to civilize them (*les faire policer*) and to instruct them in the faith and Apostolic, Catholic and Roman religion.

The only means to achieve this end, he continued, was to 'people' these lands with Catholic French nationals who, by their example, might dispose these nations to the Christian religion and the civil life'. Almost as an afterthought, he added that these colonists might also 'derive from the aforesaid newly discovered lands, some commercial advantage for the utility of the King's subjects'.[21] The claim was repeated once again by Louis XIV when he informed the Governor of New France, Daniel de Rémy de Courcelle, that 'The King has two main aims regarding the native Indians. The first is to gain their conversion to the Christian and Catholic Faith as quickly as possible.' The second, which lagged some ideological distance behind, was 'to make these Indians, his subjects, labour usefully for the increase of trade'.[22] Not, of course, that there was any perceived conflict between these objectives. Trade, like the natural resources with which God had blessed the Americas, was viewed as a reward for the efforts of the Europeans to bring the Indians to a knowledge of God. Trade, furthermore, was itself a vehicle for evangelization. 'The advantages of trade,' wrote the Jesuit François du Creux in 1664, 'begins to reach these miserable peoples and with these benefits comes the light of the gospel.'[23] Wherever the merchants' ships went, the priests went too.

The priority given to evangelization was also sustained on behalf of the French crown by the religious orders in the Antilles, although there the indigenous populations had almost ceased to exist before the French arrived. The sole object of the first French colonies – claimed Charles de Rochefort in 1665 in his *Histoire naturelle et morale des Iles Antilles de l'Amérique,* the work which was to provide Rousseau with the data out of which he constructed his 'poor Carib' – had been 'the edification and instruction of the poor barbarians'.[24] Even as late as 1744 the Jesuit historian Pierre Charlevoix was still pretending that the French had been uniquely successful in 'gaining the affection of the Americans', because their colonies, unlike those of either of their two rivals, had been founded principally, if not exclusively, in order to 'establish the Faith among the Barbarians', and, less plausibly, because the French colonists 'had frequently sacrificed their interests to this end'.[25]

Even the English, whose brand of Christianity by detaching itself from the Papacy had simultaneously detached itself from the historical legacy of the medieval empire, made their earliest claim to legitimacy in the name of the seemingly implausible obligation to convert the heathen to the faith. 'Now the Kings and Queens of England have the name of Defenders of the Faith,' claimed Richard Hakluyt in *A Discourse on Western Planting* of 1584, they had incurred an obligation to 'maintain and patronize the faith of Christ, but also to enlarge and advance the same and that this should be the principle and chief of all other [works]'.[26] Similarly the Charter of the Virginia Company in 1609 proclaimed that its purpose was to serve in

propagating of Christian religion to such people, as yet live in darkness and miserable ignorance of the true knowledge and worship of God, and may in time bring the infidels and salvages living in these parts to humane civility and to a settled and quiet government.[27]

Even as late as 1725, by which time the unlikelihood of any successful English mission to the Native Americans should have been obvious, Bishop Berkeley was still calling for the creation of a college for 'propagating the gospel and civil life among the savage nations of America' on the grounds that this had been 'the principal motive which induced the crown to send the first English Colonies thither'. Such a college would, he hoped,

remove the reproach we have so long lain under, that we fall far short of our neighbours of the Romish communion in zeal in propagating religion, as we surpass them in the soundness and purity of it.[28]

For most of the English settlers, however, evangelization – when they considered it at all – was only one part of an enterprise which blurred any real distinction between military glory, God's work and profit. In the

Pamphlet for the Virginia Enterprise written in 1585, Richard Hakluyt had set out the threefold objectives of the new colony as: 'to plant Christian religion, to traffic to conqueror'.[29] The planting of religion, so clearly linked semantically as well as literally to the planting of new European settlements, may have stood as the first priority, but it was virtually inseparable in Hakluyt's mind from the other two. As Edward Winslow noted in 1624, America was a place where 'religion and profit jump together'.[30] The steady link in the English mind between profit and the work of God even made it possible, for someone like John Smith, Governor of the Roanoke colony from 1608 until 1609, to follow the logic of this argument so far as to celebrate the 'unparalleled virtues' of the Spanish and the Portuguese and to attribute 'their mountains of wealth' to the 'plants of their generous endeavours'.[31] What the Scots in the eighteenth century were to refer to with due sarcasm as 'the mitred and booted apostles'[32] were by no means confined to Spain.

These voices are not exceptional; but they are partial. The English colonies in America had been founded by men holding a wide variety of religious beliefs. As the English political economist Sir Josiah Child (1630–99) noted in 1665, the Spaniards had achieved unity between colony and mother country by imposing a rigid code of religious uniformity (although he believed that this had also led to low population growth and excessive indolence among the settler populations), whereas the English who 'vainly endeavour to arrive at a Uniformity of Religion at Home' were prepared to 'allow an Amsterdam of Liberty in our Plantations'.[33] Whatever the nature of these differences, all the British colonists, with the exception of the Catholics in the short-lived settlement of Avalon in Newfoundland, were either Anglicans or Protestants whose religious beliefs might be broadly described as Calvinist. Such men, as Anglicans at home frequently complained, had little real interest in converting Native Americans. 'I would to God,' wrote Richard Eburne in 1624,

> that there were among *Protestants*, that profess and have a better religion than the *Papists*, one half of that zeal and desire to further and dispense our good and sound religion as seems to be among them for furthering theirs.[34]

Like Berkeley, Eburne seems to have misunderstood the profoundly isolationist pull of most of the settlers' beliefs. The views that the majority of these men had on the origin of all civil law in Mosaic Law, and on the dependence of natural law on the divine will – the traditional Wycliffite, and subsequently Calvinist equation of power with grace – was to have a formative influence on the development of a distinctive American theory of political association (not to mention the rituals of political action), a theory which would ultimately be capable of translating religious communities into national ones. 'Whereas the way of God hath always been to gather his churches out of the world,' wrote John Winthrop in 1637, 'now the world or civil state must be raised out of the churches.'[35] For most of these colonists their colonies had been founded for no religious purpose other than their own perfection. The Puritan 'Cities on the Hill' were to be *their* cities. They were to contain no aliens. Charles II's charter to settle Carolina characteristically refers to the Native Americans as 'savages' and places them in the same general category as 'other enemies pirates and robbers': persons who are to be displaced, not incorporated.[36] 'Our first work,' wrote Governor Wyatt in 1623, 'is the expulsion of the savages . . . for it is infinitely better to have no heathen among us, who were at best but as thorns in our sides, than to be at peace and league with them.'[37] As Isaac de Pinto expressed it on the eve of the American Revolution, a revolution which owed a considerable ideological debt to this particular cast of mind, 'it is the temper of Oliver Cromwell which has unhappily taken root and germinated in the wilds of America'.[38]

In time the British dropped all but the most minimal pretence to an overseas mission, although their claim to be exporting their own version of 'civilization' survived well into the nineteenth century. Even the French who, like the Spaniards, maintained a powerful ideological association between Church and monarchy, shifted their ultimate objectives from the cultivation of souls to the cultivation of land and the opportunities for trade. By the second half of the eighteenth century all three empires, even that of Castile, came to be seen by their respective mother countries as predominantly commercial enterprises. Yet for all the economic and political realism which characterizes the discussions over the place and legitimacy of empires by even the late seventeenth century, all three remained powerfully aware that they had begun, and for long had remained, under the lengthened shadow of the transfigured, Christianized *koinos nomos.*

koinos nomos

III

Theoretically the initial shift in the European concept of empire from a *civitas* to a mission introduced quite serious tensions. In the first place it raised some very difficult questions about the degree and the nature of the violence which it might be legitimate to use in bringing about conversion. As James Abercromby shrewdly observed in 1774, the 'Modern nations of Europe' had in effect substituted for the ancient '*Jus Belli* for Dominion' the claim to be extending the 'Dominion of Christ and the Christian Faith, by Conversion of Heathens'. But, he added,

it was clear that our Saviour came not into the World in order to destroy but to save mankind, that Christ's Kingdom was not confined to this or that earthly Kingdom, nor to be advanced by the Arm of Flesh, by Blood and Slaughter.

His remarks were aimed explicitly at the Spaniards, and in particular at the arguments of the seventeenth-century jurist Juan de Solórzano y Pereira (to whom I shall return). But he recognized that although the English 'have been less sanguine' in their exploits, they were clearly not guiltless in this respect.[39] The question of how far military conquest could be identified with religious conversion, and whether religious differences could ever create the conditions necessary for a 'Just War', remained a central concern of all disputes over the legitimacy of empire until well into the eighteenth century.

The identification of empire with the propagation of the Christian faith also demanded, especially after the beginning of the sixteenth century, a re-evaluation of the full significance of the imperial claim to sovereignty over the whole world. As we saw in Chapter 1, the Romans themselves had been prepared to define humanity in terms of membership of a single community. The terms *terra*, *orbis terrarum*, and the later coinage *mundus* had all, however, been highly ambiguous, and while they referred literally to the geographical extent of the entire globe, their political-cultural meaning was commonly far more limited. Even St Augustine says that the term 'orbis terrarum' as it was commonly used in Rome, was only a synecdoche.[40] Later writers tended to be far more literal-minded, and were consequently more troubled by the degree of fit – or evident lack of it – between the Roman world and *the* world itself.

Although Rome's new heirs, from Charles I, Charlemagne to Charles V, or their advisers, spoke with varying degrees of conviction of a Universal Monarchy which would be the true successor state to the *orbis terrae*, they were uncomfortably aware that the 'world' was now composed of a multiplicity of cultures and of independent states, some of which, in particular the Ottoman – the only other polity to be formally described as an empire – and the Chinese, were almost as large in territorial extension, and quite as sophisticated, as any European polity. In the period after 1492 the discovery that there existed an entire continent of which the Ancients had been wholly ignorant effectively excluded the possibility that any ancient emperor could have been literally a world ruler. A new geography – and with it a new cartography and topography which charted the progress of the European empires, and which culminated in Abraham Ortelius's *Theatrum orbis terrarum*, and Georg Braun and Franz Hogenberg's *Civitates orbis terrarum* of 1572–1618 – provided a wholly new and far more immediate image of the 'world' than any that had been available in either antiquity or the Middle Ages.[41] By the mid-sixteenth century, the globe, with the exception of the poles and the Pacific, had come to look very much as it looks today. As the Englishman Charles Davenant, in discussing the various possibilities for a modern world empire, pointed out at the end of the seventeenth century, 'more has been out of their [Rome's] rule than within'.[42] The Romans themselves, he remarked, 'having subdued whatever they thought worth taking in, did at last sit down in quiet'. And where they sat down they deemed to be the end of the world. For the moderns, with their vastly enhanced geographical and anthropological knowledge, to claim to be the ruler of the entire world was, said the Dutch jurist Hugo Grotius in 1625, simply idiotic – 'stultum titulum'. How, asked Grotius – who had played a major role in the protracted seventeenth-century debate about the origin of the American Indians – could any individual ruler claim to exercise a prior authority over 'remote and unknown peoples', many of whom presumably were still waiting to be 'discovered'?[43]

The attempts to combat the new geography were always implausible, and frequently absurd. A coin with the head of Augustus had been found in 'Tierra Firme', argued the humanist historian Lucius Marineus Siculus, thus proving that America, although unrecorded as such, had once formed part of the Roman empire.[44] Gonzalo Fernández de Oviedo, the first royal historiographer of the Indies, claimed that, although Columbus had, indeed, been truly the 'first discoverer' of America, the Native Americans themselves were really the descendants of the survivors of a Visigothic diaspora.[45] Few, if any, of these claims were taken very seriously and none were used to advance any formal argument for jurisdiction in the Americas. But they do expose the desperation that lay behind the need to bind the geographical limits of the old to those of the new empires.

One strategy for salvaging the ancient image of empire from these strategies was to argue, as St Augustine had done, that 'all the world' was indeed nothing more than a synecdoche, and could thus be extended to cover all the newly discovered lands and, for that matter, any lands which might be discovered in the future.[46] Or it could be argued, as Cardinal Bellarmine – best known as the man who tried to persuade Galileo to keep silent about his proof of Copernicus' heliocentrism – later claimed, that 'one can say that these provinces do not belong to the world'.[47] When pressed, however, both arguments collapsed. The claim to total inclusivity was incoherent once examined with any care. The attempt to exclude from the definition of the 'world' all but the three continents known to the Ancients was not only the equivalent of ignoring the evidence of sun spots. It also robbed the empire both of legitimate reason for occupying the Americas, and of its significance as the agent of Christian eschatology.

If nothing more effective could be found to counter the sheer presence of geography, it would seem that the effectively prescriptive claim of the empire to world sovereignty had been irradicably lost. As a subject in political theory it appears to merit no more attention than Grotius had been prepared to give to it. Yet, at one level, the *de facto* occupation by the Spaniards of what, at the time, seemed to be most of the Americas, enhanced that empire until it came to look as though it did indeed encompass the 'whole world'. As early as 1526 Gonzalo Fernández de Oviedo, attentive to his self-imposed role as the creator of a New World historiography, had attempted, much to the disgust of Richard Hakluyt, to integrate the Americas into a Spanish world monarchy as 'universal and sole monarch of the world'.[48] It is little wonder that, by the end of the sixteenth century, millenarian political theorists such as the Calabrian *magus* Tommaso Campanella (1568–1639) and even, in one mood, the more sober Piedmontese failed Jesuit Giovanni Botero, were conjuring with the possibility that America might be merely a stepping stone to Asia, and that soon Columbus's skewed imperial dream would be fulfilled, with Spain as overlord of the former empire of the Great Khan. 'The name *Christophorus*', wrote Campanella, 'should be interpreted to mean "he who carries Christ" [an interpretation which Columbus himself had given to his name] and as *Columbus, Columba*, the Church. And in another place: all the world shall serve you' (Psalm 71:11).[49] By carrying Christ, and with Christ Europe, to America, Columbus, Columba, the 'Christum ferrens', had set in motion a political process which would one day result, in Botero's more ecumenical vision, in a world where, 'as everyone would be subject to a single Prince, one might travel everywhere with a single language and a single currency'.[50]

None of this, of course, had much resonance outside the lands of the Habsburg monarchs in Europe and America. Inside, however, the conception and imaginative fashioning of empire became a constituent of the political cultures of Spain and much of Italy. The Castilians themselves were sufficiently uneasy about Charles V's pretensions and their possible consequences for the place of Castile within the empire to forbid him to use the imperial title on Castilian soil. But it had been a Castilian, Pedro Ruíz de la Mota, Bishop of Palencia, who had drafted Charles's first 'imperialist' utterance (for the meeting of the Cortes of La Coruña in 1520) and it was the Castilians, Pedro de Mexía and Juan Ginés de Sepúlveda, who were to become the emperor's most enthusiastic historians.[51]

By placing the Pillars of Hercules beside the Habsburg arms garlanded with the transfigured Horatian tag 'plus ultra', Charles himself had done more than merely hint that his rule was indeed to be the final fulfilment of Baldus's 'supreme power without limits'.[52] The true architect of Charles's imperial imagery, however, was the Piedmontese Mercurio de Gattinara, the emperor's grand chancellor from 1518 until 1530.[53] Gattinara had been an admirer of Dante's *De Monarchia*, so much indeed that in 1527 he had tried unsuccessfully to persuade Erasmus to prepare a new 'imperial' edition of the work, and in his own *Pro divo Carolo* he made repeated references to Charles's status as the heir to Justinian.[54] In the image-making of the so-called 'Erasmian' intellectuals – men like Juan and Alfonso de Valdés with whom Gattinara had surrounded the emperor – Charles V had been placed on earth by God to fulfil the work begun in the ninth century by Charles I.[55]

Castile itself had also had a long history of expansionist ambitions: first against the Arabs, who had overrun the peninsula in the eighth century, and then against their own Christian neighbours. Limited though this had been, and restrained by a language of 're-conquest' which was dependent upon the initially absurd claim that the petty northern Christian rulers had prior political and property rights in the kingdom of Al-Andalus, it was frequently couched in the terminology of empire. Iberian unity, which remained a central political objective of the Christian kings as they moved south from Leon, found expression in terms of the recovery of the ancient Roman province of Hispania.[56] In 1077 Alfonso VI was already using the title 'imperator constitutus super omnes Ispaniae nationes', and in 1135 his successor Alfonso VII actually had himself crowned 'Hispaniae Imperator'. There was little to match this in either France or England. The English would later point to a pre-American imperial ancestry in their acquisition of Anjou, Aquitaine, Gascony, the islands of Guernsey and Jersey, and later of Ireland and Wales, and both the Valois and the Bourbon monarchy would, like the Habsburg, claim descendancy from Aeneas via Charlemagne.[57] None of this, however, had quite the same shape as the Spanish *Reconquista*. Most of the English possessions, with the exception of Ireland and Wales, had been dynastic acquisitions, whose legitimacy, furthermore, was based embarrassingly on prior conquest not legitimate inheritance, and it was clear, even to Louis XIV, the last French monarch to make a bid for the imperial title, that the legacy of Charlemagne had long since passed *de facto* to France's most powerful enemy.

The Spanish kingdoms were also linked by dynastic succession to the Kingdom of Naples. To this Charles V had added his own claim to the imperial fief of Milan, which had finally been incorporated into the Habsburg patrimony in 1535. Spain thus became part of a wider Italian project for the creation of a European *imperium* which would provide a defence against the Turks without and the menace of the religious conflict offered by the presence of Calvinism within.[58] In this there could be little doubt that the new Carolingian empire provided the same goods as the old Roman one had: protection and the security of the *civitas*, now understood not as civil society under threat from barbarians but as Christianity under threat from unbelievers and heretics. The continuity between the ancient and the modern *imperia* was guaranteed as much by the the translation of power from Augustus to Constantine the Great and from Constantine to Charles V, the *alter Karolus*, via Charlemagne, as it was by the objectives which all these monarchs had pursued. As the imperial historian Pedro de Mexía (1500–52) observed, the history of Rome was the history of an empire which in 'longevity, size and power' was the greatest of all empires because it had begun 'a little less than 2300 years ago and is still alive today'.[59] Neither Charles V nor his advisers were unaware that the Emperor Augustus's claim to sovereignty had rested on his claim to have brought order and stability into a world rent by civil war and threatened by barbarians from the north.[60] To many, indeed, the situation in the late sixteenth century seemed to be remarkably like that of the first century CE. The Roman empire, claimed the Benedictine chronicler Gonzalo Arredondo y Alvarado in 1528, expressing what by then had become a hyperbolic commonplace borrowed from St Augustine, was a moral force, the creation of a people who had – improbably – 'looked not to their own good, but to the common good [of mankind]', and that it was 'by God's hand' that Charles had been granted the 'Empire, kingdoms, dominiums, and lordships, and universal monarchy of all, and by His hand will be guided'. 'My son,' he makes Charles's mother say to him on his coronation in an unmistakable allusion to the *Lex Rhodia*,

> my son, good emperor, the laws call out to you, and name you lord of the world. And this because, as the doctors say, of your position to offer protection, defence and jurisdiction and you are ruler of the whole world *de iure* and after God common father of all.[61]

It was even possible for some enthusiasts to draw a direct analogy between the papal and the imperial election. 'Today,' wrote Alvaro Gutíerrez de Torres in 1523, offering what purported to be an eyewitness account of Charles's election, 'the prince-electors entered into a conclave and by the inspiration of the Holy Spirit have chosen and elected you to be king of the Romans.' This, he added, constituted in effect 'election by the entire world'.[62]

Charles V himself somewhat wearily protested to Pope Paul III in 1536 that 'some say that I wish to be Monarch of the world, but my thoughts and deeds prove that the contrary is true'. That was not, however, the message that his advisers, Spanish, Flemish, German and Italian, gave to the world. To many in the religiously unstable world of the sixteenth century, Spain seemed to be bent upon fulfilling the final prophetic *translatio imperii* of the Book of Daniel. Daniel's vision of four world empires had ended in one which was 'partly iron and partly clay, so the kingdom shall be partly strong and partly brittle'. At this time God

> will set up a kingdom which shall never be destroyed, nor shall its sovereignty be left to other people. It shall break in pieces all these kingdoms and bring them to an end, and it shall stand forever. (Daniel, 2:44)[63]

Christian exegetes were generally agreed in identifying this final world monarchy with Rome. But there was sufficient uncertainty about its possible duration for a number of imperial panegyrists, Campanella among them, to claim that it was the Spanish Habsburgs, as the heirs of Augustus, whom God had chosen to be the agents of the final unification of the world. One contemporary image shows Daniel himself explaining all this to the seated figure of Charles V.[64] 'The Spaniards hold this as a Delphic oracle and most infallible prophesy,' shrilled a mid-seventeenth-century English pamphleteer, in an allusion to Daniel's prophecy 'that the last *Monarchy shall be fixed in Spain'*.[65]

Indeed, for many Castilian writers, Spain, as the new focal point of the empire and the God-appointed scourge of Islam, was now the obvious bearer of the *pietas* that had been the source of the greatness of ancient Rome. For it was not merely their historical position, nor even their obvious military power, which had made the Spaniards the obvious heirs of the *Imperium romanum*, it was also their unique – fanatical, others would say – devotion to the Christian religion. 'The Romans,' observed Bernardo de Vargas Machuca, one of Bartolomé de Las Casas's fiercest enemies, 'had religion as the principal article of their government, and would not tolerate that it should be violated.'[66] So, too, he added, had the Spaniards. Now, wrote Gutíerrez de Torres, with Adrian IV – a Fleming and former regent of Castile – on the papal and Charles on the imperial throne, the two swords of Christendom were united within a single nation – a point that was not lost on either the French or the English.[67]

Spain, with its massive military capabilities and seemingly inexhaustible financial resources, was to remain, even after the abdication of Charles V in 1556 and the formal separation of the *Imperium* from the *Monarchia*, the only viable candidate for a true universal empire. From 1556 until at least the second half of the seventeenth century, the Spanish kings clearly took the full implications of the title 'monarchia' seriously. When Campanella, for instance, wrote his *De monarchia hispanica* during 1600 and 1601, perhaps the most influential, and certainly the most far-reaching of the arguments for Spanish universal empire, he used the term *monarchia* in its literal sense. Similarly, Sebastián de Covarrubias's famous dictionary of 1611, the *Tesoro de la lengua castella o española*, defines 'monarca' as 'absolute lord and sole prince, who acknowledges no other; rather all are beholden to him'. The word 'king' (*rey*), by contrast, appears only in a discussion of chess. By the end of the sixteenth century, by which time the empire itself had shrunk to its earlier Germanic limits, *monarchia universalis* – Universal Monarchy – had, in effect, come to replace *imperium* as a term for the continuing aspiration to supra-national authority. In Giovanni Botero's words, only the Spanish monarchy was uniquely placed to secure that elusive dream of Christian, and ultimately global, unity precisely

> because no monarchy has shewn how much it is worth, and how much it is able to maintain in peace under its obedience, for so many years now, an empire which is not only wide and vast, but is also extended and divided.[68]

To the French and the English, by contrast, Spanish imperialism seemed to offer only the menacing prospect of a Europe under the heel of the narrow bigotry associated with the Spanish version of Catholicism, and represented to the minds of most Europeans by the uniformly gruesome image of the Inquisition. Such an empire, far from being a liberation from external and internal threat and guaranteeing the survival of the *respublica christiana*, seemed to promise only the final and irreversible extinction of the rights of all free men. As Guillaume du Bellay warned the princes of the Protestant Schmalkaldic League in 1535, Charles V's use of the title *Caesar invictissimus* with its sinister military overtones, spelt out for the independent rulers of Germany the emperor's ambition to reduce them all to a condition of slavery.[69]

The sheer size and potential wealth of the Habsburg empire after the conquests of Mexico in 1521 and Peru in 1533 suggested to many European observers that it could really only be a matter of time before Spain seized control of quite literally the whole world. If ultimately they failed to do so, this would be a question of good fortune, or the supposed ineptitude of the priest-ridden Castilians themselves. As William Paterson, first Governor of the Bank of England, observed in 1701, as he proposed to establish a Scottish, Calvinist, colony in the centre of 'Terra Firme',

> it has only been from accident and the unaccountable mismanagement of the Spaniards that any of the nations of Europe worth looking after have been left in a condition to preserve their liberty.[70]

Charles V's universalism was closely associated with the figure of Gattinara. But Gattinara's universalist ambitions did not, as so many historians have claimed, die with him. They did not even die with Charles's abdication of the empire which would seem ultimately to have deprived Philip II and his successors of the one legal claim they had to universality, the imperial title itself. For if one branch of the Habsburg family had succeeded to the old imperial title, it was abundantly clear that it was the other which retained the claim to be 'dominus totius orbis'. On Philip's accession, the structure of power within those territories which he had inherited inevitably changed. The Habsburg lands were now divided into northern and southern blocks and Castile became, and was to remain, the centre of an empire which was now indisputably *Spanish*. As a consequence of this new alignment the overseas possessions became, even more so than they had under Charles, the focal point of the monarchy, while those areas, most crucially the Netherlands, Milan and Naples, which had been central to the older imperial structure, now found themselves on the periphery.

Some parts of this assembly of territories had been acquired through successive dynastic marriages and some – certain regions of the Netherlands and, most significantly, all of the Americas – through conquest, and what the Spanish called 'discovery'. What most troubled Spanish theorists, in particular after Charles's abdication, was how to give both conceptual identity and political legitimacy to this behemoth. By the mid-sixteenth century dynastic claims, even if they continued to be pursued with great vigour, were beginning to look insufficient as a mode of political description if they were unsupported by any larger conception of the purpose, and the potential destiny, of the state. And Spain's dynastic rights in some of her more important European dominions were, after 1556, very slender indeed. Milan and much of the Netherlands had, after all, been imperial not Habsburg fiefs and should by right have passed to Ferdinand along with the empire itself.

By relocating the new Spanish monarchy in Castile, Philip II radically altered the structure – not to say the balance – of power within Europe. In 1581 he also seized the crown of Portugal and from then until 1640 the Portuguese overseas empire was united with the Castilian. Throughout all of his period of ascendancy the 'Spanish monarchy' remained a shifting affair, in constant need of redescription and ideological reassessment.

In both France and Spain reason-of-state theory had, since at least the early sixteenth century, been used to redescribe such archaic dynastic monarchies in more obviously modern terms. Men like the jurist Fernando Vázquez de Menchaca – to whom I shall return – and the diplomat Diego Saavedra Fajardo could argue, along with Botero, that although the current shape of the Spanish monarchy may have been determined by dynastic succession, it could now be defended in terms of its capacity to provide security for its members – or, as Vázquez says, its 'cives et subditi' (citizens and subjects)[71] – which was the recognized function of every modern state.

Although the Spanish monarchy increasingly came to be defined in this humanistic, positive sense, simple defence, even for the humanists, could not, *pace* Grotius and Hobbes, offer sufficient justification for the continuing existence of any state. Ill-articulated though it generally was, the principle which had defined the Holy Roman Empire, which it had inherited from Justinian, and which had then been endorsed by every Spanish monarch down to Philip V (who effectively transformed it into a provincial empire), was the image of the monarchy as the supreme embodiment of a law. It was this image, to which all the Spanish and Italian theoreticians of empire supplied their own, frequently repetitive glosses, which had underpinned Gattinara's frustrated attempts to create a new centre in Italy if only because Italy had always been, in Dante's phrase, 'the garden of the empire'. The concept of a single law, a *ius publicum*, for all the several states within the monarchy also provides a more illuminating context than most for understanding Philip II's insistence on the need for a capital city and for his monarchy to be run from a powerfully constituted centre. 'From Madrid,' as John Elliott has observed, 'it must have seemed that one could rule the whole world.'[72] And, no matter how sceptical they may have been about the possibility or legitimacy of extended empires, it was this image to which most Spanish theoreticians of empire, however realist their assumptions, clung most fiercely.

Since the American possessions were legally a part of the Kingdom of Castile, it was the European states within the Spanish monarchy, which were, and would remain until the War of the Spanish Succession (1701–14), the crucial factor in all considerations of what kind of political community that monarchy was, or should be. The sheer extent of the overseas empire, especially after the conquests of Mexico and Peru, meant, however, that the emperor's, and later the Spanish monarch's, role as *dominus mundi* increasingly came to depend upon the possession of these distant, and seemingly endless, 'Kingdoms of the Indies'. In the years immediately after the discovery and the conquest first of Central and then of South America, the extent of the legitimate authority of the emperor became a crucial component in discussion of the legitimacy of the Spanish conquests. The derisory rejection by English, Dutch and French writers of any historical argument which relied upon an association, other than the simply metaphorical, between the ancient and the modern empires – including their own – is easy enough to understand. None of these nations could claim immediate association with the medieval empire, or any but the most fanciful of humanist associations with the ancient Roman world. What is striking, however, is that some of the fiercest opponents of the idea that the imperial right to 'dominium totius orbis' could be used to validate the acquisition of an overseas empire, were themselves Spaniards, the most important and most outspoken of whom were at the time in the employ of the Castilian crown.

IV

In the period between 1539, when the Dominican theologian Francisco de Vitoria (*c*.1485–1546) delivered his influential lecture on the legitimacy of the fledgling Spanish empire in America – *On the American Indians* (*De Indis*) – and the turn of the century the conquests in America became a subject for discussion in the faculties of theology and of canon and civil law in the Universities of Salamanca and Coimbra. This debate focused on a single, and ultimately insoluble problem, which in Vitoria's formulation could be stated simply as: 'by what right (*ius*) were the barbarians subjected to Spanish rule?'[73]

The legitimacy of the Castilian crown's initial occupation of the Antilles rested, as we have seen, upon the Bulls issued by Pope Alexander VI in 1493. These concessions, however, had been made by the Pope – in his presumed capacity as the spiritual *dominus mundi* – to two sovereigns who could, at this stage, make no claim to be universal rulers. Indeed the main objective of both the Bulls of 1493 and of the closely linked Treaty of Tordesillas of 1494 had been to limit future rivalry between Castile and Portugal. If the Pope could divide up his realm in this fashion, there could be no possibility of one party to the treaty subsequently claiming to be the lord of a world, half of which had already been given away to another ruler. But with the election of Charles V to the empire, the papal donation and the older universal aspirations enshrined in the *Lex Rhodia* became closely associated. Both, however, were rejected, and rejected as firmly – although in a very different language – by the Spaniards as by the English and the French.

The arguments directed against the Bulls by the English and the French depended upon a denial of the Papacy's implicit assumption of jurisdiction in both the spiritual and the temporal sphere, and of Alexander's still more contentious claim to exercise *dominium* over both Christians and pagans, a claim which, as James Otis put it in 1764, had led him to 'grant away the kingdoms of the earth with as little ceremony as a man would leave a sheepcote'.[74] Where was the clause in Adam's will, Francis I is said to have demanded of Charles V, which had bequeathed to him half the world? America belonged, if it belonged to anyone, to its native rulers. The Pope could no more give it away than he could give away the territory of one Christian prince to another. Furthermore, as the British pointed out, even if the donation were held to be legitimate by Catholics, it would not be binding on Protestants.[75]

The neo-Thomist theologians and civil lawyers (though not, unsurprisingly, the canonists) who worked at Salamanca in the sixteenth century – the so-called 'School of Salamanca' – rejected the authority of the Bulls on precisely the same grounds. The Pope was, they recognized, the spiritual ruler of all Christians. But he could exercise no *dominium* in the secular world, nor had he authority of any kind over non-Christians. It is not surprising, given the uneasy relations between the Papacy and the empire under Charles V and later the Castilian monarchy under Philip II, that few Spaniards should have wished to uphold the Papacy's old claim to be the ultimate arbiter in international disputes. They were also hostile to the Augustinian argument which underpinned the canon lawyers' support for the Bulls, that the Pope could deprive infidels of their rights, and effectively even of their property, because they were unbelievers. This they associated less with Augustine himself than with Augustine's deviant followers, Wycliffe, Huss and the 'new heretics' Luther and Calvin. All of these writers had held that power (*potestas*) derived not, as Thomas Aquinas had maintained, from God's Law, but from God's Grace. From this it followed that the ungodly who had no share in Grace could not exercise *dominium*. The more extreme exponents of this view were prepared to argue that any prince who was, in their view, 'ungodly' might legitimately be removed from power by any of his more godly subjects or, indeed, by any other godly prince.[76] The jurists and theologians were acutely aware that any political theory used to legitimize in this way the conquest of the territories of non-Christian rulers could just as easily be used by Christian rulers against each other. This fear was particularly acute at a time when a religious civil war was being conducted in France and a war of containment, which was also divided ideologically along confessional lines, was being fought in the Netherlands. The arguments deployed by both the Huguenots in France and the followers of William the Silent in the Low Countries rested precisely on the claim that the kings of France and Spain had demonstrated themselves to be 'ungodly rulers'. It is also significant that one of the most important contributors to the debate over the legitimacy of the Spanish occupation of America – the Dominican theologian Domingo de Soto (1494–1560) who presided over the famous debate in Valladolid in 1551 between the humanist Juan Ginés de Sepúlveda and Bartolomé de Las Casas – was one of the architects of the policies pursued by the Spanish crown at the Council of Trent.

The success with which writers such as Francisco de Vitoria and Domingo de Soto appear to have defeated the claims of the Caesaro-papalists has generally given the impression that after the end of the sixteenth century the Bulls of Donation were, in effect, a dead letter. This was, however, very far from being the case. Despite the early rejection of the Bulls, by the Salamancan theologians and their immediate successors, what William Paterson contemptuously dismissed as 'certain imaginary mathematical lines between heaven and earth'[77] remained the main point of ideological dispute between Spain and its European rivals in America. There is almost no French or English attack on the claims to Spanish sovereignty overseas which does not begin with a rejection of the validity of both the Bulls and the terms of the Treaty of Tordesillas.

The Castilian crown, too, seems to have insisted upon their significance until the very end of the seventeenth century. They are, for instance, the only explanation for the Spanish presence in America offered by the historiographer royal, Antonio de Herrera in his massive *Décadas* of 1601–15.[78] Even the the Spanish-born judge (*oidor*) of the Court of Appeal (*Audiencia*) of Lima, Juan de Solórzano y Pereira (1575–1654), who, as we shall see in the next chapter, generally preferred the more robust prescriptive argument that no matter how tyrannical the origins of a society it 'becomes in time a perfect and legitimate community',[79] was prepared to endorse the Bulls with the similarly prescriptive claim that although they may subsequently have been shown to be 'insufficient', they had, at the time, provided legitimate grounds for conquest. Retrospective re-evaluation of the original arguments for an act of conquest could not alter the present consequences of that act.

Another, and still more ingenious, attempt to extend the limits of the original donation is to be found in Serafim de Freitas's *De iusto imperio Lusitanorum asiatico* (On the Just Empire of the Portuguese in Asia) written in 1625 at a time when Portugal and the Portuguese possessions in the East still formed part of the Spanish monarchy. The treatise is a reply to Hugo Grotius's *Mare liberum* of 1609 which had argued that the Dutch possessed an equal right with all other nations to trade in waters claimed by the Portuguese, because the ocean was the common property of all mankind.[80] Freitas went to some length to distinguish between three senses in which the Bulls might be interpreted. As a claim to *dominium* they were, he acknowledged, invalid. Similarly the Papacy was in no position to grant to the Portuguese, or to any other Christian power, 'the right to navigate and travel to the Indies considered in the abstract (*de iure abstracto*)'. The Church did, however, possess the right to grant a title to evangelize exclusively to one monarch, for this belonged to the Pope's undisputed (at least by Catholics) power as the spiritual *dominus mundi*. And since evangelization, if it were to be at all effective, necessarily involved both trade and limited conquest, the Portuguese and the Castilian crowns were entitled to enforce their right to exclusion within the zones set down in the Bulls.[81] It was an over-extended argument which, although Solórzano referred to it with approval, no one seems to have been prepared to pursue further.[82] Yet it demonstrates that, however weak the authority of the Papacy in international affairs might have been after the middle of the sixteenth century, the Bulls of Donation offered the Castilians an historical link with the empire as the second sword of Christendom which no argument from natural law could ever provide. And until the Bourbon attempts in the mid-eighteenth century to change the identity of the entire imperial structure, no Spanish monarch was keen to dissociate entirely *monarchia* from *imperium*.

But the Salamancan jurists and theologians were more concerned with the standing of the monarchy in Europe, and with its relationships with the Church, than with the legitimacy of Spain's overseas possessions. In this context, papal claims to sovereignty over non-Christians posed an inescapable threat to their insistence that all *dominium* was dependent upon the law of nature. The claim, however, that the emperor was *dominus mundi* posed no such threat. Their outright rejection of the implications of the *Lex Rhodia* may, therefore, seem odd. Yet there is a strong sense in which the members of the 'School of Salamanca' and their heirs were, as the settlers in America dimly perceived them to be, anti-imperialists. They were so, however, not, as previous historians have imagined, because of their horror at the human suffering which the Spanish colonizers had inflicted upon the colonized – although that horror was real enough – but because of the threat which, in their view, all extended empires posed to what they conceived to be the true nature of the civil community. Discussion over the title of 'dominium totius orbis' thus became a crucial location for a far-reaching and innovative attempt to reverse the overarching intellectual ambitions of the champions of Universal Monarchy.

The first of their objections to extended empire derived from their collective insistence on the Thomist principle that (with the exception of the rule of fathers and husbands) supremacy (*praelatio*), although it belonged to the natural law, had been instituted not by nature itself but by human enactment (*lex*).[83] As Domingo de Soto pointed out,[84] there had been only two divinely appointed rulers, Saul and David. All others had been elected, in one way or another, by men for the preservation of the human political community. So there was no immediate reason why, in Vitoria's menacing conclusion, 'imperial *dominium* should belong to the Spaniards rather than the French'.[85] It was always dangerous, as both Vitoria and Soto knew, to espouse doctrines which your enemies might find as useful as you.

The principle of 'rex imperator in regno suo' was the only one on which relations within the international order could be preserved. A world empire, even if it did possess the kind of force for harmony, civility and religious orthodoxy which the theorists of Universal Monarchy had claimed for it, had still to be limited, *de iure*, to those lands which the emperor ruled, in Vitoria's formulation, 'by livery of seisin (*traditio*)'.[86] In this sense, and in this sense alone, it was true to say, argued Soto, citing the *Lex Rhodia* itself, that 'the order of the world rests upon the tranquillity of the Roman empire'.[87]

So long, that is, as the modern emperor was prepared to limit his ambitions to the frontiers of the ancient Roman *imperium*, there could be no (Roman Law) argument against him. He might not actually be able to conquer France, say, or Britain, and there were very good moral reasons why he should not even try. But the Salamanca theologians were prepared to concede that he had reasonable claims to possess *dominium* in these territories. The problem came when, as in America, any attempt was made by force to translate Bartolus's *de iure* argument for the universality of the emperor's *dominium* into grounds for *de facto* possession of territories which lay unquestionably outside the historical Roman empire.

All the neo-Thomists insisted that civil power could only be transferred by society acting as a single body. To create a truly universal empire it would be necessary, argued Soto, 'for a general assembly to be called of which at least the major part consented to such an election'. No one, however, could possibly imagine a general assembly of literally all the world. Even if, as the pre-history of civil society seemed to require, some such meeting had once been called, the new discoveries would subsequently have nullified its decisions. For, as Soto concluded, 'neither the name nor the fame of the Roman Caesars reached the Antipodes and the islands discovered by us'.[88]

What the Castilian crown was also claiming on the basis of the Papal Bulls – and what it most needed – was not merely jurisdiction in America but also property rights: what was known in the language of neo-

Thomism as *dominium rerum*. The argument proposed by the canon lawyers, which had been advanced most forcefully by the decretalist Hostiensis in the thirteenth century, was that the Pope, as the true heir of the Roman emperors, enjoyed not only sovereignty (*dominium jurisdictionis*) over the whole world but also rights of ownership ('dominium ac proprietatem bonorum omnium'), on the authority of Justinian's decree *Bene a Zenon* (*Codex* VII. 37. 3) which reserves exclusive rights of property in 'the world' to the emperor, and subsequently to the Papacy. This, the canonists believed, permitted the Papacy to distribute that property among its subjects as it so wished. Clearly only the most committed champion of papal supremacy could find any reason for endorsing such a claim. It was, said Soto bluntly, nothing other than a prescription for tyranny. In practice, only the Turks had ever exercised such rights. A Christian prince, by contrast, whose rule was absolute but not arbitrary, could not make use of the goods (*bona*) of his subjects 'except where it is necessary for the defence and government of the community'. Neither was Soto prepared to accept that the dangerously slippery notion of *necessitas*, the master term in the discourse of 'Reason of State', and one which had served all European monarchs as an expedient for suspending the rule of law, could be mobilized to legitimize the conquest in the Americas.[89] In Soto's view, the emperor's sole claim to universal *dominium* was, in effect, the kind of supra-legislative authority which Charles V exercised over the German princes, since this alone could plausibly be said to have been granted by universal consent. And this, too, could, of course, only be exercised within the limits of the ancient *Imperium*.

The only circumstance in which the Castilian monarchy might claim sovereignty *and* property rights in America was if the Native Americans themselves could be said to have surrendered their natural legislative authority to the empire voluntarily. As the fiercest defender of the natural and political rights of the Amerindians, Bartolomé de Las Casas, phrased it, 'the only title that Your Majesty has is this: that all, or the greater part of the Indians, wish voluntarily to be your vassals and hold it an honour to be so', for only this would meet the demands of the Roman Law principle: 'what touches all must be agreed by all' (*quod omnes tangit ab omnibus tractari et approbari debet*).[90] Vitoria himself had made much the same point in *De Indis*. Just as the French had elected Pepin to be their king in 752, so the Indians might 'elect' Charles V to be theirs, for every *respublica* was empowered to 'constitute its own *dominium* with the consensus of the majority'.[91] By the terms of this formulation, the rights that the Castilian crown could now claim in the Indies were similar, not to those it had over the peoples of the peninsula, but to those it had in Milan or Naples. The Native American chieftains, like the Dukes of Milan, ruled over polities which were, in all respects, 'perfect republics' and their subjects were consequently free men with full authority under their own laws. The King of Castile, concluded Las Casas in *De regia potestate* (1544), the last work he ever wrote, could no more parcel out the Amerindians to his Castilian subjects than he could give away the Milanese to the French. Las Casas's lifelong ambition had been to negotiate for the Native Americans a legal guarantee of more humane treatment within the political limits of the Spanish monarchy. As he stressed many times, he never once doubted the legitimacy of the Spanish occupation of the Americas. Only the argument that the Native Americans had surrendered their natural rights to political self-determination of their own free will could leave the political structure of the empire intact while freeing the Indians and their rulers within it. Las Casas was one of the few to endorse, in this way, both the validity of the Papal Bulls and the emperor's claim to universal sovereignty. His emphasis on the precise terms of the Bulls of Donation – that they were principally a charter for evangelization – had, however, the effect of reinforcing the *duty* the Bulls had placed upon the crown to convert the American Indians to Christianity, a duty which the fierce debate over the crown's rights had almost entirely obscured. Las Casas may, indeed, have upheld the political status of the crown in America. But he also deprived it of most of the benefits it had hitherto gained by being there.[92]

Vitoria and Soto's rulings on the Castilian crown's right to sovereignty in America were far less encouraging even than those of Las Casas. Soto went so far as to argue that even those things which the inhabitants of a region hold in common, but do not themselves employ, could not be seized by another 'without the consent of those who live there', an explicit reference to the precious metals which, in his view, the Spaniards had been mining illegally and which logically they should now restore to their rightful owners. Once again the overriding reason for suggesting such a course of action was that any argument which granted the Castilian crown natural mining rights in America could not be limited *to* America. 'For neither,' as Soto pointed out, 'can the French enter into Spain for the same purpose, nor can we enter France without the permission of the French.'[93] If the Salamanca theologians were to protect both the integrity of their own intellectual project, and the status of the empire within Europe – and these were their overriding concerns – they were compelled to reject any claim that sought to extend the emperor's *dominium* beyond the realms he had acquired 'by livery of seisin'.[94] For the Spanish theologians and jurists, as much as for Grotius, it would seem that the imperial title could only ever be, in the words of the Spanish jurist Francisco de Amaya, 'wholly inept and ridiculous'.[95] As we shall see in the following chapter, the Salamancan theologians and their successors all came to recognize that only one natural right could provide the kind of sovereignty their monarch required in America – one, that is, that would allow him to rule without their consent – and that was based on the claim that the conquests of America had been a 'Just War'.

" Just War

V

There were two further Spanish responses to the arguments implied by the claim that the Emperor might be 'lord of all the world' which were to have far-reaching consequences for the future conceptualization of the Spanish monarchy. The first of these came from Domingo de Soto. In the fourth book of his great treatise on rights and justice, *De Iustitia et iure* of 1556, Soto began by pointing out that the claims made first by Augustine and then by the fourteenth-century Thomist, Ptolemy of Lucca, in his hugely influential *De Regimine principum*,[96] that the Roman empire had been a reward from God for the virtue of its members, had been seriously misunderstood. The collective *virtus* of the Romans, Soto argued, had been constituted by purely secular and civil qualities, such as justice and fortitude, which retain their intrinsic merit even when they are pursued for the wrong reasons. The supposition that had underpinned so much Christian thinking about the pagan empire – that because God had allowed it to exist, it must, in some sense, have been divinely ordained – was false. It had been a purely human creation, limited, like all such creations, in both time and space. Soto was prepared to accept that 'the imperial authority . . . surpasses all others, [and] it is the most excellent of all', on the grounds that it involves the rule of more than one people (*natio*). 'But,' he continued, 'it does not follow from this that it is the only one to dominate the world.'[97] Claims to sovereignty that are based upon one historical moment cannot be extended indefinitely through time. The origins of the Christian empire can be traced to the Roman Republic's oath of allegiance to Augustus. From this initial moment its jurisdiction passed to Constantine and thence to the western empire. Thus, by a process of continuing but limited historical transfer there might exist a legitimate emperor of all Christians. A claim to limited sovereignty of this kind could not, however, be extended to the whole world.

> That he [the emperor] should be lord of all the world can be sustained by neither reason nor right (*ius*) since the part over which he ruled was very small in respect of the whole world. Thus this small part could not, in contradiction to natural law, impose a ruler upon its antipodes and other regions.[98]

Furthermore, and this was to become a crucial component of many later arguments against all extended empires, even if the emperor were able to *claim* universal sovereignty, he could not possibly exercise it in practice. And for Soto, as for most of the Roman jurists, *dominium* was for use. 'Those things,' he wrote,

> which do not change, have fixed limits to their size, for an ant cannot reach the height of a man, nor a man the size of an elephant. It

therefore follows that neither can a prince spread his warmth throughout a society (*respublica*) which extends across all regions and all peoples, so that he can know, emend, correct and dispose of what happens in each individual province. . . . Consequently, as power exists in order to be exercised (*potestas sit propter usum*), and its exercise is impossible over such extended territory, it would follow that such an institution is vain. But God and nature never do anything in vain (*nihil fecit frustra*).[99]

Having provided an argument from natural justice for restricting imperial authority to the territorial limits of the former Roman empire, Soto then turned, in what was to become a characteristically humanist move, to examine the possible meanings implicit in the key term in the whole debate: 'world' – *terra.* This, he claimed, had a far more restricted range of uses than the jurists had allowed. It meant, of course, the entire globe, the *orbis terrarum*, but in political and legal discourses it was most often used to describe only a particular and familiar area. In the case of the Roman emperors, this had been merely the territorial limits of their jurisdiction. 'In the same way,' he pointed out, 'and in the same language that we today speak of a New World or a New Earth (*novum orbem, novumque mundum appellamus*) of islands and a continent which encompasses vast spaces'. No one supposed that these places were literally 'new'. They were simply new to *us*. The Romans, argued Soto, citing a line from Lucan – 'Arabs you have come to a world unknown to you' – were themselves fully aware of this usage.[100] Therefore, Soto concluded, in making his initial and seemingly hyperbolic claim, all that the Emperor Antoninus had intended was to reassert his sovereignty over what he already ruled 'by livery of seisin'.

Soto's entire argument lifted the discussion of the possibility of universalism from eschatological to natural time. In Augustine and Ptolemy of Lucca (and, indeed, Aquinas himself) the facts about the Roman empire had not been only facts. They had also been signs, evidence for man of God's ultimate purpose. For these writers the 'world' of the Roman, and subsequently the medieval empire, in both its territorial extent and the time-frame in which it operated, belonged to God's design for the creation. It had to be co-extensive with that creation so that at creation's end it would return to God. For Soto, however, the empire was a natural entity, which, in common with all other human institutions, existed only in chronological time. It could possess none of the divine significance which it had had for both the pagan and the Christian authors of Antiquity. A universal empire which had been a purely human creation (which was *only* a fact) and which existed in natural time was an impossible natural entity. This disjuncture between the domain of the human (and of human conceptions of both chronology and territoriality) and the divine *ordo* became the main device for denying any possible legitimacy to extended empire. In Soto's hands, the *Imperium*, created by the Roman people and sanctioned by Christ himself, had become merely another *respublica*, and like all *respublicae* it had to be limited in extent and driven by the demands of contingency.

The second response came from the canon lawyer Diego Covarrubias y Leyva (1512–67). Unlike most canonists, who could generally be expected to accept the papal claim to secular authority and thus the emperor's claim to world *dominium* as the consequence of the papal coronation, Covarrubias rejected both. He pointed out that Daniel's recognition of the authority of Nebuchadnezzar offered biblical proof that political legitimacy could be accorded to pagan or infidel rulers. This, together with the existence in the modern world of numerous princes, both Christian and non-Christian, who were not subject *de facto* to the empire, made Bartolus's argument for even *de iure dominium totius orbis* very weak indeed.[101] Covarrubias, like most of the civilians, also endorsed Baldus's famous ruling that 'ex facto oritur ius' ('the law has its origin in fact').[102] The law, that is, had to be based on 'the experience of things' and although this did not dissolve the *de iure*/*de facto* distinction, it clearly demanded a far closer relationship between fact and the law than was present in the Bartolist contention that to deny that the emperor was *dominus mundi* amounted to heresy. If the emperor did not actually command the inhabitants of 'all the world' then his claim to do so *de iure* was merely absurd.

But there was something else. Both Covarrubias and Soto pointed out that, as Aristotle had argued,[103] while it would be difficult to govern adequately a large number of cities, it would be impossible to govern the entire world. Government, for Soto and Covarrubias as much as for Aristotle, was a means to achieve the good life. 'The role (*scopum*) of the legislator,' Soto had written, 'is to benefit the citizens and to instill good customs in them.'[104] If the creation of good customs, of a just and harmonious society, were the only possible goals of the true ruler, then an over-extended empire which would clearly be an impediment to that objective could not be a legitimate one. 'By natural law and by its very nature,' concluded Covarrubias, 'the jurisdiction of the entire world has not been given to the Emperor.'[105] This is an early instance of the modern use of an argument which was to play a large role in later criticism of the entire imperial enterprise. For what we are hearing here is a discussion not of rights conferred either by historical precedent or by some version of mediated divine fiat. Instead Covarrubias is making an attack on *any* claim to universality in terms of the capacity of the human community to fulfil the ends for which nature – or God – intended it, and any such argument had clearly to be tied directly to the contingencies, human and geographical, of the particular historical instance.

Both Soto and Covarrubias had successfully restricted the ancient imperial claim to lordship over the entire world to a set of precise, and contained, geo-political realities. The writer who most fully understood the direction the discussion had now taken, and the significance of the changes which Soto and Covarrubias had introduced, was the humanist bureaucrat Fernando Vázquez de Menchaca (1512–69) whose *Controversiarum illustrium aliarumque usu frequentium libri tres*, was first published in Venice in 1564.[106] Vázquez was by training a jurist, and at the time of writing the *Controversiarum illustrium* was a judge (*oidor*) of the Contaduría mayor of the Consejo de Hacienda. In 1561 he accompanied Philip II to the final session of the Council of Trent, and it was there that he seems to have written much of his work. He was, in other words, a prominent member of the royal household and his work, an analysis as the title suggests of 'Famous Controversies', was originally written to defend the claim to pre-eminence of the representatives of the King of Spain over those of the King of France.

From this modest, and somewhat arcane, beginning Vázquez went on to offer what is certainly the most original of all the many sixteenth-century Spanish discussions of political rights, and one which in many ways struck at the ideological basis on which the theoretical power of his royal master depended. It has, however, been almost wholly ignored in modern discussions of what Lewis Hanke long ago called 'The Spanish Struggle for Justice' in the Americas. This may be due, in part, to the curious structure of the book, and in part to the fact that the writings of the 'School of Salamanca' have dominated all previous historical accounts – including my own – of the debates over the legitimacy of the conquest of America.[107] The *Controversiarum illustrium* does engage with the work of the Salamanca School; indeed in a sense it begins where Vitoria, Soto and Covarrubias left off.[108] But it comes to very different conclusions by a very different route, and in certain crucial respects those conclusions constitute a devastating refutation of the main thrust of the arguments for natural rights pursued by both Vitoria and Soto. Its neglect may also be due to the fact that although Vázquez was hostile to the Spanish claims for empire, he was equally dismissive of what he regarded as the illusory natural rights of the American Indians. Yet despite its absence from most contemporary historical scholarship the *Controversiarum illustrium* was to have a massive and sustained influence on Grotius – whose own attack on universalism is little more than a summary of Vázquez's conclusions – and through Grotius on much later discussions of the juridical basis of the relationship between states.[109]

Vázquez begins, in Book II of the *Controversiarum illustrium* (an examination of the Roman law of prescription), with a traditional juridical consideration of the possible meanings of the *Lex Rhodia*.[110] One of these, he claims, is the argument from Aristotle's *Metaphysics* that if there can be only one human good, it follows that there can be only one rule of law. Vázquez shifts the direction of this argument in two quite novel directions. One of these is to claim first, on the authority of Soto, that all civil power depends upon voluntary submission. No other form of 'principate or jurisdiction is legitimate'.[111] This, of course, is the same argument which Vitoria had employed against the possibility of any world empire. But for Vázquez this did not mean, as Soto had supposed, either the acceptance by a people of their magistrates, or the historical moment at which the first men contracted out of what later came to be called the 'state of nature'. It meant, instead, that

> the supreme power of emperor, king, princes and powers, in a word every category of supreme command (*potestas*) is for the exclusive use of the citizens and subjects and not in any sense for their rulers.[112]

In explicit rejection of Soto's distinction between the *respublica* and the purely private citizens (*cives*) of which it is composed, Vázquez insisted that the society of private citizens is all there is. 'Among the citizens,' he wrote, 'there is nothing but a kind of society of good faith contracted . . . to this end that each might thereby the better lead his life in safety, and with every convenience.'[113] In Soto's formulation it is the *consensus* of those about to be ruled which determines who should rule. But because the people gather together in order to submit themselves to some kind of rule, their collective will (as distinct from their reason) is weak. The will of Vázquez's citizen, however, is fully empowered to determine the conditions of rule, in the same way that the will of a testator has the power to determine the ultimate fate of his or her goods. Later, this insistence that the public good is an aggregation of purely private goods will, as we shall see in Chapter 6, be revived, in quite another idiom, to provide what was to be the final and most telling critique of empire.

In common with earlier humanist writers from a broadly republican tradition,[114] Vázquez also came to conceive of *potestas*, imperial or otherwise, as *for* the exclusive benefit of those over whom it is to be exercised. And these are, as he says again and again, to be understood as 'citizens' (*cives*), autonomous rights-bearing political agents, a category which hardly features at all in the earlier juristic or theological literature. A state can never, therefore, be so extended that the ruler is unable to exercise the authority he requires in order to care for the interests of his '*cives et subditi*'. As Annabel Brett has shown in *Nature, Rights and Liberty* which offers a brilliant analysis of this work, Vázquez is concerned to demonstrate not only that the authority of rulers derives from the consent of the members of the community as individuals; but that because societies can only ever be for the good of those same individuals, they can never ever be anything more than *ad hoc* arrangements, with no enduring force. This, as Vázquez knew, had been the inescapable implication of

Covarrubias's claim, but it was an implication Covarrubias himself had been unwilling to make, bound as he was to a far more determinedly Stoic vision of the rule of law.

Like Soto, Vázquez recognized that societies are human and thus historical creations, which must inevitably change over time, and that as they change, so, too, must the languages in which they can be described. Unlike Soto, however, he refused the claim that 'public civil power is a word (*ordinatio*) of God'.[115] Such power belongs only to the realm of human relations, and as such derives its legitimacy not from nature but exclusively from custom. In terms of the crucial distinction in Roman Law, on which the entire argument of the *Controversiarum illustrium* rests, between things which exist *de iure*, and those which exist *de facto*, supremacy (*praelatio*) belongs, not to the realm of *ius*, but to that of fact. *Praelatio*, as Vázquez stressed in the preface to the *Controversiarum illustrium,* 'is a thing of fact, it is not to be believed unless proved'.[116] And as facts change over time so, too, will the laws and the kind of government which they sustain. 'For the law in such things,' he said, 'is for one day only, and on another day it dies.'[117] More significantly still, the right to rule itself, the *ius imperii*, must also alter according to the changes which occur in the real nature of the society to which it applies. For ruling implies, for Vázquez, only one thing – administration: 'Empire (*imperium*) and kingship (*regnum*) are nothing other than jurisdiction.' Like all other political orders, he declared, now citing the poets, Manilius, Virgil, Juvenal, Seneca and Ovid as his authorities, empires are creatures of chance, hence they are mutable and must rise and fall as customs rise and fall: 'For as vicissitudes and customs change daily, therefore, empires must likewise change; for as we have been able to see, empires are linked to customs (*mores imperia insequi*).'[118]

It follows from this that no society can plausibly ground its political authority on an identity based upon indefinite continuity in both time and space, of the kind to which the Roman empire had made claim. It also means that given the huge variety of human beings that actually exists in the world, any society which did extend throughout the globe would be, as Vázquez put it, 'inconvenient, pernicious and noxious'.[119] So

> what is vulgarly said, that the Emperor of the Romans is lord of the world, and is thus superior in dignity to all other princes . . . is to be compared to the tales of children, to the advice of the aged and to the shadows of an unquiet sleep.[120]

The only argument from nature which could be brought to bear upon the problem, he reasoned, was the claim, from Aristotle's *De Anima*, that everything attains to the size that is natural to it.[121] Universal rule was, therefore, not merely a violation of the principles governing the necessary limits on human jurisdiction, it was also contrary to the structure of the natural world. An over-extended empire would, Vázquez said, raising once again the favoured neo-Thomist concern with the ends of nature, be 'vain', in the sense that it would be unable to fulfil its purpose, and God has never created anything which is unable to encompass its ends.[122] If this were the case, then any extended empire could only be, as Charles V's Protestant enemies had declared it to be, not a civil society at all, but a form of slavery.[123]

Like all humanists, Vázquez was very reluctant to admit any degree of *a priori* reasoning. The law which governed human affairs was, he supposed, essentially a set of rules arrived at by agreement among men for their mutual benefit. If anything was to be extended from Europe around the world it could only be – as Vitoria and Soto had tacitly agreed – the civil law. That, of course, was a positive law and so would have to be based upon enactment. Yet it was simply the case that nowhere in what Vázquez calls 'the known facts of human affairs and all written histories' has any such thing as a universal rule ever existed, except, so to speak, in the shadowy interstices of the *de iure/de facto* distinction where Bartolus had located it.

The existence of the New World, 'situated', as Vázquez put it, 'in the most remote and unknown regions which are difficult of access' and which can only be reached by crossing 'immense and tempestuous seas', had made this abundantly clear. 'After the discovery,' he wrote,

it now appears with much greater clarity to be absolutely impossible that the sovereignty (*dominium*) over so many regions, peoples and provinces separated from one another by such enormous distances, could reside with one man.[124]

The possibility, furthermore, that there might exist yet more unknown regions in the world made this clearer still. The term 'mundus', he added (in a consideration of Justinian's crucial exclusion of the sea from the *dominium* of the Roman empire) should be understood in the indefinite mode, as limited in its application to a condition which was still only potential, one which, in the Latinized vocabulary of Aristotelian physics used by Vázquez, was *in habitu* and *in potentia* but not yet 'actual' (*in actu*). Clearly no man can have *dominium* over what is merely potential.[125] Yet, in the light of the contemporary uncertainty about the geography of the world, any claim to *dominium totius orbis* would have to be just that. The claim to universal sovereignty was based upon a tacit assumption that each new society, as it came to light, would have to conform to a rule – the juridical concepts of Western Europe – which had been devised with no prior knowledge of its existence. Furthermore, if such a rule were to be at all legitimate it would also have to be one that had been created for the 'exclusive use' of peoples whose particular needs were as yet unknown to those who had drafted it. And that, concluded Vázquez, would be 'worthy of laughter and mockery'.[126]

Until this point, Vázquez's arguments had consisted very largely of drawing out, to some considerable distance, the implications of Soto and Covarrubias's more guarded observations. His final move, however, relies on a humanistic strategy that had never been fully employed in this context before. Like Soto, he offers a consideration of the natural uses of the terms used in the *Lex Rhodia*, in order to demonstrate that the entire linguistic base on which the arguments of the imperialists had been made to rest was false. For Vázquez, this takes the form of an extended, and highly imaginative, etymology of the term 'mundus' as it appears in the phrase 'dominus mundi'. 'Mundus', he claims, 'means first a woman's dressing table' and was used in this sense in the *Digest*.[127] From this, he continued, it came to be used as a synonym for 'nature', understood as the beauty of the Roman world, a beauty which had been achieved precisely by its high cultural attainments and freedom from barbarism.

This might at first seem, at best, a highly frivolous argument – and the *Controversiarum illustrium* is frequently, although not exactly frivolous, certainly heavily ironical, generally at the expense of the neo-Thomists. It is, however, far more than it might seem. For, in Vázquez's etymology 'mundus' comes to describe not, as the philologically unlettered had supposed, a political domain. It becomes, instead, a cultural one. And although Vázquez leaves it somewhat unclear whether it might be legitimate to export Roman beauty by force, he is quite clear that those who threaten it in any way may be forcibly prevented from so doing. Like a succession of legal humanists from Alberico Gentile to Grotius, Vázquez was quite prepared to accept the claim that the only possible ground for making war on the barbarians was that 'they are our enemies, prejudicial, loathsome and dangerous'.[128] Their customs are sufficiently unlike ours to constitute a menace to ours. Their very existence is a threat to the inherent beauty of the *mundus* which 'we' have created. The paradox is that, on Vázquez's account, such barbarians may be conquered to prevent them causing any further damage, but their conquerors cannot, in the nature of things, exercise true *dominium* over them.

This was radical enough, but Vázquez's next move was even more striking. Up to now most of his claims, unorthodox though they were, had been based very largely upon the traditional authorities. Having established that no extended *imperium* could be legitimate because no such polity could possibly be in the interests of all its members, he now, in a characteristically humanist move, brought in the poets to counter the 'Philosopher', the theologians and the jurists. Horace and Claudian had maintained that navigation and long sea journeys are contrary to nature, for nature had placed the seas where they were precisely to keep men apart. But man, with his capacity for creation – his *ingenium* – and his *audacia*, is capable of breaking the bounds which nature has established in the world.[129] 'The first who dared to cleave the deep sea with a ship constructed by his own hand and with his crude oars stirred the waters,' wrote Claudianus, had violated that natural frontier, and the gods had given sailors a hard time ever since. All extended empires depended for their existence upon this wilful and perverse use of man's exceptional mental faculties, this 'forbidden and unholy crime', as Horace had described it. 'A single man cannot be lord of all the world,' wrote Vázquez,

> even in those things which refer only to jurisdiction and defence, without obliging the subjects and magistrates who come to him very often to cross extensive seas. It therefore follows that no such extended empire can belong *de iure* to one man.[130]

This was a rich, if also deeply ambiguous, literary tradition in which Vázquez had chosen to situate his argument. His insistence that the only true civil society was one which was small enough to be governed without the need for extensive journeys was more than a practical consideration, although it was that too. It was grounded in a powerful conviction, as much Greek as Roman in origin, that the true community was a body of persons in communication with one another, sharing a common language and living out their lives according to a common set of customs.

In Christian Europe, however, the assumption that all modes of human flourishing could only be conducted in settled communities conflicted with an equally powerful recognition that men were, in St Francis's phrase, *homines viatores*, that European societies could never be endogamous, that the total immobility which Plato had urged upon the inhabitants of his ideal *polis* was for most humans simply not an option. It conflicted, too, with the image of the *mundus* or *orbis terrarum* as another kind of community, a universal *civitas*, governed by a universal body of custom, the natural law. In terms of this image travel and communication – and later commerce – become indispensable for human interaction. 'The sea links all nations,' wrote Diego Saavedra Fajardo in the seventeenth century, 'which would be uncivilized and savage (*fieras*) without the communication provided by navigation.'[131] This is why for the Thomists, the right of access to all nations, the *ius perigrinandi*, was held to be a right in nature. One of the few arguments which Vitoria, and some at least of his successors, was prepared to accept for the conquest of America was that by resisting the Spaniards' supposedly legitimate wish to 'travel' over their lands, the Native Americans had violated the 'right of society and natural communication', and might therefore be punished by conquest.[132]

All the European empires lay at the centre of these contrary imaginings. They had, by definition, been the creation of armed and acquisitive travellers. 'The *inhospitable* conduct of the civilized states of our continent,' Kant was later to protest, 'the injustice which they display in *visiting* foreign countries and peoples (which in their case is the same as *conquering* them) seems appallingly great.'[133] Yet the same 'visitors' had not merely been responsible for conquest and the human carnage that had followed conquest. They had also opened the trade routes between the Old World and the New, and it had been these routes, as Kant himself had argued, which were the only possible means to create the truly cosmopolitan world order, and only such an order would be able, finally, to put an end to all human conflict.[134]

By claiming that the *mundus* could only be conceived as a particular kind of culture, and by insisting that travel, which was a necessary condition of all empires, was unnatural, Vázquez de Menchaca had, in ways which would not be repeated until the late eighteenth century, shifted the argument over the legitimacy of the conquest and colonization of the Americas away from the stark concern with rights – although rights are what he is discussing – to a concern with the calculation of purely human benefits. By doing this he had also, as had Soto before him, focused attention on the origins and the particular conditions of empire in a way which would henceforth be inescapable. It is the most crucial of those – conquest and settlement – that I now wish to consider.

CHAPTER THREE

Conquest and Settlement

Extensive conquests when pursued, must be the ruin of every free government; and of the more perfect governments sooner than of the imperfect; because of the very advantages which the former possess above the latter.

David Hume, 'On the Idea of a Perfect Commonwealth'

Q. or defense against each other in Eur. ?? eg. France 17thc.

I

Joseph Schumpeter once described imperialism as the 'objectiveless disposition on the part of the state to unlimited forcible expansion'. Every aspect of this sentence can be faulted. Neither the New World empires, nor I suspect any other world empires, were objectiveless; their expansion was neither unlimited nor consistently forcible; nor were any of them, at least in the first instance, the creation of the state. But it *is* true to say that nearly every European empire began as the formal ideological expression of what Schumpeter elsewhere characterized as 'the purely instinctual inclination towards war and conquest'.[1]

For as all European empires in America were empires of expansion, all, at one stage or another, had been based upon conquest and had been conceived and legitimized using the language of warfare. Indeed most government, reflected Andrew Fletcher of Saltoun (1655–1716), a man who had a keen interest in the future of universal monarchies, had been 'framed for conquest'.[2] Belligerence and the desire for territorial expansion, he concluded, were simply an inescapable part of the human condition. Even Sparta and Venice, the most stable republics in the ancient and modern worlds, precisely because their founders had attempted to check future expansion before it had even begun, had ultimately failed; and they had failed because, in Fletcher's view, there was 'nothing even in these constitutions that could sufficiently restrain the desire of enlarging their dominions'.[3] The consequences for both had, of course, been disastrous.

This seemingly inescapable desire for territorial expansion through conquest was also bound by a code of aristocratic values which had played a crucial role in the creation of all the earliest overseas empires. For

(≠ aristocratic code?)

overseas expansion promised to those who engaged in it not only trade and, if they were lucky, precious metals, it also offered the promise of glory, and with glory a kind of social advancement which, before the mid-eighteenth century, could be acquired by almost no other means. This was obviously true of the Spanish, and of the Portuguese at least before 1447[4] when they accepted that, in Africa, trade was both more profitable and far safer than conquest. But it was also true, to a far greater degree than was subsequently acknowledged, of both the English and the French. For the first years or so the English and French voyages to the Americas were conceived very largely as an attempt to imitate Spanish successes. Drake's voyage of 1577, by 'discovering' the still imaginary *Terra australis*, was, declared the English magus John Dee, the beginning of a true *Imperium britannicum*.[5] 'So let the sovereign Empire be increased', wrote George Chapman in 1596,

> And with Iberian Neptune part the stake
> Whose Trident he the triple world would make.[6]

This was why, as the first historian of the American Revolution, David Ramsay, observed in 1789, Henry VII's letters patent to John Cabot of 1496 had echoed exactly the terms of Alexander VI's Bulls of Donation by granting him rights to 'conqueror and possess' for the King any territory not already in Christian hands, as, indeed, had those granted by Elizabeth I to Sir Walter Raleigh in March 1584.[7]

No European nation, furthermore, could ever forget that the Roman empire, the model to which all of them in one manner or another deferred, had been founded as much upon glory as upon *pietas*, nor that, in the Virgilian formulation, honour, piety and arms had always been insepa-rable. 'The honour of our nation is now very great by his Majesty's means,' wrote Robert Johnson in a promotional tract for Virginia, of 1609. But, he went on, the English had, like all martial nations before them, grown idle for want of further opportunity, just as had the Romans, 'who having gotten the Goddess Victoria to Rome, they clipt her wings and set her among the Gods, that they [*sic*] might take her flight no more'.[8] The conquest of new lands in America would, he believed, have the salutary effect of reviving the Englishman's military spirit. 'Up then', Hakluyt urged Walter Raleigh in much the same vein,

> go on as you have begun, leave to prosperity an imperishable monument of your name and fame such as age will never obliterate. For to posterity no greater glory can be handed down than to conquer the barbarian, to recall the savage and the pagan to civility, to draw the ignorant within the orbit of reason.[9]

A similar rhetoric, expressing similar sentiments, can also be found in

France. Like Hakluyt, André Thevet, cosmographer to Henri IV, urged his monarch not to lag behind Spain and Portugal in the rush for empire, if only to provide his towering ego with something to write about. But by the end of the sixteenth century it had already become clear that Raleigh's 'imperishable monument' would have to remain an illusion, for neither the English nor the French would ever have the opportunity or the resources for large-scale overseas conquests. In the eyes of her critics, many of whom by the late seventeenth century were themselves Spaniards, only Spain had been able to carry out sustained and well-publicized conquests, conquests which rapidly became, and have remained to this day, marked down as one of the most appalling chapters in the history of human brutality. Only the Spanish settlers formally styled themselves conquerors, *conquistadores*, and only the native-born Spanish settlers (*criollos*) would, in the end, ground their claims to independence primarily upon their association with an aristocracy of conquest. An empire of this kind had to be an empire based upon people, defeated subjects who could be transformed into a pliant labour force. In America, only the Spaniards, and to a somewhat lesser degree the Portuguese, had found peoples in sufficient numbers whom they were able to overrun in this way. Both the English and the French were, for a number of related causes, driven either to exclude the Native Americans from their colonies, or to incorporate them as trading partners. Despite the abortive attempt by the British to enslave the populations of Carolina, nowhere did they become, as they did throughout Spanish America, 'vassals'.

Castile had, in a sense, been fortunate. It had been the first European power to settle in the Americas and, by geographical chance, had chosen that area in which the Aboriginal peoples had achieved the highest degree of population density and technological expertise. The complexity and – although in the end it proved to be no match for their conquerors – the military organization of Mexica and Inka society also made them relatively easy to rule, once they had been conquered and all serious resistance had been crushed. The tribes which inhabited the eastern seaboard of North America, Canada and the Great Lakes proved far more resilient in the short run. The 'five nations of the Iroquois', as the Governor-General of New France, Philippe de Rigaud de Vaudreuil, wrote to Paris in 1711, 'are more to be feared than the whole of New England'.[10] Feared they may have been but they were also, in the eyes of many Europeans, nomadic or semi-nomadic peoples with (and this was to be crucial) no 'civil' society or agricultural base. Such peoples were not what was known in the language of chivalry as 'worthy enemies', so were clearly unsuited to be true vassals.[11] The crowning by Christopher Newport of the 'Emperor' Powhatan may have been intended to create the image of a North American Atahualpa.[12] (The Privy Council, however, sent a copper crown for the ceremony, thus carefully indicating the inferior status of James I's new tributary ruler.)[13] But in practice the French and English wars of conquest in the Americas, such as they were, were relatively limited affairs generally involving various and mutually hostile Indian groups. Despite such attempts as those by William Strachey to draw a parallel between the settlers in America and the Roman generals who had invaded ancient Britain and 'reduced the conquered parts of our barbarous Island into provinces and established in them colonies of old soldiers building castles and towns in every corner, teaching us even to know the powerful discourse of divine reason',[14] the 'conquest' of Virginia could never be described with any plausibility in the martial terms used to depict the Spanish seizure of Mexico and Peru. The Spanish histories of conquest may have been mendacious, and Cortés's accounts, for instance, of the Mexica capital of Tenochtitlan are very largely fantasy based upon contemporary accounts of Granada, but they were not entirely absurd. There is an abundance of narratives on both the French and English settlement in the Americas. But there is, as has often been remarked, no English or French equivalent of Bernal Díaz del Castillo's account of the conquest of Mexico or Garcilaso de la Vega's evocation of the Inka empire. There is not even anything like the rambling narrative of Antonio de Herrera, who attempted to provide a Spanish version of Livy's great history for the New World. That is so, not, as some have suggested, because of a defect in the historical sensibilities of these nations, but simply because there was nothing which took place in French or British America about which such stories could be told.

II

There was also another, closely associated, difference between the empire of Spain, and those of France and Britain. By the mid-seventeenth century at least, it had become clear to most observers that the British and the French colonies in America were overwhelmingly bases for trade and the production of agricultural produce. Spanish America, by contrast, had been the largely unintended consequence of the need, which by the late fifteenth century had become chronic, for gold and silver. It is misleading to suppose, as so many eighteenth-century French and British critics did, that until the Bourbon reforms of the late eighteenth century, the Spanish crown was wholly indifferent to the potential commercial value of its colonies. As early as 1475 the Portuguese crown had created a government agency, the Casa da Guiné, to deal with the Africa trade, and in 1503 the Casa da India to administer the trade with India. In the same year Spain established a similar institution at Seville, the Casa de Contratación, with sole responsibility for all trade with the American colonies. Throughout the period of the empire trade and manufacture also accounted for a significant portion of the national income. Many *conquistadores*, Hernán Cortés among them, were eager to stress the potentially disastrous conse-quences of the grab-and-run mentality which was shared by most of their kind. The virtual devastation of the Antilles was something few wished to see repeated on the mainland, and laws compelling settlers to settle, to marry and to cultivate the land formed a central part of the Castilian crown's legislation for America.

Yet throughout the history of the Spanish empire in America, the extraction of precious metals continued to be the crown's principal economic concern. Even the Bourbon reforms of the 1770s and 1780s, which were based in part on Colbertian mercantilism and limited free-trade principles, were disproportionately concerned with reinvigorating American silver production.[15] Like France and Britain, metropolitan Spain derived considerable and lasting benefit from trade with its overseas colonies. But until the final demise of the empire in the 1830s, it continued to look upon the importation of specie as the ultimate and only fully reliable source of wealth.

The French and the British by contrast had, in their own national histories at least, always been concerned with commerce and agriculture. This was, wrote Verron de Forbonnais, the author of the long and complex article on 'Colonie' in the *Encyclopédie*, 'the sole reason for the establishment of modern colonies'. It was also what distinguished them from the various categories of ancient colonies whose function had been primarily either defensive or to serve as a deposit for the human detritus of the metropolis.[16] By 1772 this claim looked self-evidently true. But it had not always been so. As with conquest, the first objectives of all the European powers in the Atlantic had been simply to imitate the Spaniards. Jacques Cartier had set out on his first expedition in 1534, just as Columbus had before him, with the aim of 'discovering certain islands and lands where it is said that a great quantity of gold and other rich things might be discovered', although, on examination, all the samples he sent back turned out to be iron pyrites and quartz.[17] Like Columbus, he too returned home with tales of a mysterious land of untold wealth which, undiscovered, would remain a part of the mythology of the French explorations of Canada for decades to come.[18] The expeditions which Martin Frobisher led to Newfoundland in 1576, 1577 and 1578 had all gone in search of precious metals. They, too, returned empty-handed and had to content themselves with rock samples, and a living Eskimo as 'witness of the captain's far and tedious travel'.[19] As late as 1612, however, an ever-optimistic Robert Johnson was still assuring potential settlers in Virginia of the 'undoubted certainty of minerals'.[20] The most famous of the English would-be *conquistadores*, Sir Walter Raleigh, was openly contemptuous of commerce and agriculture as possible objectives of empire. The power of Spain, he wrote, had not been gained from

the trade of sacks of Seville oranges, nor from aught else that Spain, Portugal or any of his other provinces produce. It is his Indian Gold that he endangereth and [that] disturbeth all the nations of Europe.[21]

Raleigh, of course, was no more successful than Cartier or Frobisher had been in locating the New Golden Land he had assured his queen lay somewhere beyond the estuary of the Orinoco, a failure which would lead, inexorably, to his execution.[22]

Neither were the Spaniards the only Europeans to believe that there was an almost eschatological association between gold and godliness. Those, declared Richard Hakluyt, who sought to plead the Gospel in the new-found lands would be rewarded materially for their pains. That, he claimed to believe, was the only reason why God had filled the Indies with such wealth. 'The sound of the Gospel and the Cross,' wrote Joseph Mede to William Twisse in 1635, had drawn a 'group of barbarous nations' across the Bering Strait and down into the New World, where they now awaited the coming of the English, drawn by the promise of infinite riches, to reveal to them the truth of Christianity.[23]

As with conquest the crucial difference between Spain and her rivals was one of chance. Spain, as Adam Smith put it, was alone in having been presented by Fortune with 'something not very unlike that profusion of precious metals which they sought for'.[24] It was only when it became obvious that there was no new Mexico or Peru to be conquered, that both Cartier's 'Saguenay' and Raleigh's 'Large, Rich and Beautiful Empire of Guiana'[25] were fictions, that the British and the French turned, half-reluctantly, to regard their colonies as sources not of mineral or human, but of agricultural and commercial wealth. By the eighteenth century, however, any memory of the earlier objectives which the French crown might have pursued in North America had been erased from the record. Montesquieu, in what was perhaps the most authoritative observation on the subject, declared that although the Spaniards had looked upon the Americas as 'objects of conquest', those who were 'more refined than they, saw them as objects of commerce and as such directed their attention to them'. The goal of these peoples, who probably included the English as much as the French, had clearly *not* been 'the foundation of a town or of a new empire'.[26] They had instead been the peaceful exploitation of commerce and natural resources. 'Riches and conquest, and renown I sing' wrote Robert Chapman in 1596 in the ode 'De Guiana carmen epicum' which was prefixed to Laurence Keymis's narrative of his voyage to America; but, he added, 'Riches with honour, conquest without blood'.

The abandonment of the search for gold and silver by France and Britain quickly changed into a form of triumphalism. The English, who had once seriously demanded what purpose God could have had in giving such natural resources to Spain, soon came – as David Armitage has recently shown – to see the mineral wealth of the Indies as a poisoned chalice.[27] 'Columbus offered gold unto one of your Kings,' wrote James Harrington, 'through whose happy incredulity another prince hath drunk the poison, even unto the consumption of his people.'[28] There were many in Spain who, by the mid-seventeenth century, had come to share the same view. God himself, wrote Diego Saavedra Fajardo, had hidden precious metals in the ground precisely so that there would be no more of them than was required for commercial purposes. Gold and silver, he recognized, were only beneficial if they were used as means to an end. Unlimited wealth of the kind which the Mexican and Peruvian mines had provided for the Castilian crown was bound to diminish a nation's natural human resources. The sailors on a Carthaginian ship, he said, who had seen 'a very rich and wonderful island (which is now believed to have been Hispaniola)' were put to death on their return, so that what they had seen should not harm the *respublica*. The Spanish kings, alas, had not pursued so honourable a policy. 'Who would have believed,' he continued, echoing a famous remark made by the Flemish humanist Justus Lipsius in 1603,

> that with the gold of that world this one would also be conquered? And we see that greater enterprises were undertaken by valour alone than with riches, as Tacitus noted of the time of Vitelius. This same harm which the discovery of the Indies caused [to Spain] was later felt by all the other foreign provinces and kingdoms, for the trust they placed in those riches.[29]

The image of precious metals as inherently corrupting was closely linked to the image of gold in particular, as a semi-miraculous substance, which in Columbus's celebrated phrase could 'drive souls into paradise'. It was also determined by the lingering reliance of the discussion of specie on the language of alchemy.[30] In such a context it was hard to see gold as merely a convenient means of exchange. Adam Smith, who was more than usually sensitive to the nuances of the lexica employed in the languages of economic exchange, had noticed this. 'The same passion,' he wrote,

> which has suggested to many people the absurd idea of the philosopher's stone, has suggested to others the equally absurd one of immense rich mines of gold and silver. They did not consider that the value of those metals has, in all ages and nations, arisen chiefly from their scarcity.[31]

Like the coins they were ultimately used to make, precious metals were only symbols. Their value relied upon an agreement between peoples as to their worth. 'Gold and silver,' argued Montesquieu in a famous passage,

> are a wealth of fiction or of sign. These signs are very durable and almost indestructible by their nature. The more they increase, the more they lose of their worth, because they represent fewer things. When they conquered Mexico and Peru, the Spanish abandoned natural wealth in order to have a wealth of sign which gradually became debased.

Midas

Like Harrington, Montesquieu looked upon Columbus's rejection by the other European monarchs as an unforeseen blessing. Successive Spanish rulers had behaved like Midas, but unlike Midas the Spaniard could find no deity to 'put an end to his destitution'.[32]

The massive inflation which had crippled Castile had not been the only unfortunate consequence of Spain's persistent blindness to the real function of bullion in a world economy. It had, or so Smith believed, resulted in a limited and inflexible domestic economy. It had also had the effect which was sustained at a social, legal and cultural level, of binding the overseas possessions far more tightly to the metropolitan culture than either the French or the English were able, or indeed wished, to attempt. 'The Spanish colonies,' in Smith's words, 'from the moment of their first establishment attracted very much the attention of their mother country; while those of the other European nations were for a long time in great measure neglected.'[33] This was paradoxical, perhaps, since the Spanish conquests had, in the beginning, seemed to guarantee a high degree of political independence on the part of the *conquistadores*. As the marquis de Mirabeau pointed out in 1758, no other group of colonists had had either the ambition or the resources which the *conquistadores* had to establish independent states in America. Yet the failure of the revolt of the Pizarro brothers in 1548 had, he said, 'provided the first example of that dependence of the new world on the old which never diminished'.[34] The effect of this, in Smith's view, had been that the 'Spanish colonies are considered as less populous and thriving than those of almost any other European nation'.[35] What in their different ways Smith, Montesquieu and Mirabeau were claiming was that the over-dependence of the metropolis upon the single staple produced by the colonies had resulted in the suppression of political independence, of the kind enjoyed by the British colonists, and that this combination had had the effect of forcing the metropolitan economy into decline, while preventing growth, either human or economic, within the colonies themselves. As David Hume summarized the whole process in his essay 'Of the balance of power':

1548

> The power of the house of Austria, founded on extensive but divided dominions, and their riches derived chiefly from gold and silver, were more likely to decay of themselves from internal defects, than to overthrow all the bulwarks raised against them.[36]

The continuing importance of bullion also had other and still more insidious consequences. Without the easily mortgageable American silver, Castile would never have been able to sustain its ultimately self-destructive military operations in Europe. As a self-styled 'zealous professor of commerce' explained from Mexico in 1789, the wealth which his ancestors had produced had all gone to finance 'wars in Flanders, wars in France, wars in England'. It had vanished into the pockets of foreign bankers and foreign agents to preserve the dwindling and archaic 'reputation' of the 'Catholic Monarch'.[37] This was, and had been since the outbreak of the Revolt of the Netherlands in the sixteenth century, a common complaint. In 1631, no less a person than the Count Duke of Olivares himself, then virtual master of Spain, told a meeting of the Council of State that, 'if its great conquest have reduced this Monarchy to such a miserable condition, one can reasonably say that it would have been more powerful without that New World'.[38]

What for most enlightened Spaniards was the most damaging consequence of all this spurious wealth was that it had made it possible for Castilians to sustain, long after it had vanished from the other nations of Europe, that military ethos which had been responsible for the creation of the empire. As José de Campillo y Cossío, secretary to the Navy and the Indies between 1741 and 1743, lamented in 1743, mining was indissolubly linked to that 'Spirit of Conquest' which he, like most of Charles III's reforming ministers, saw as the enduring curse of the Spanish imperial system. 'After the conquests,' he wrote

> began the cupidity of the mines. For a time, and so long as the goods which the gold and silver were used to purchase were hers, these yielded great benefits to Spain. Subsequently, however, when we should have adjusted ourselves to the demands of the times, applied ourselves to agriculture and learned how usefully to employ human labour, we have simply continued to draw an infinite quantity of treasure from the ground which has only gone to enrich other nations.[39]

The 'Spirit of Conquest', wrote a despairing Pedro Rodríguez Campomanes (1723–1803), Charles III of Spain's minister of finance, in 1775, had transformed Spain into a 'canal through which the products of her mines and the wealth of the Indies had been emptied over the whole of Europe'. Neighbouring states, in particular Castile's old enemies, England and Holland, had grown and diversified their economies. Spain, shored up by the illusion of an interminable supply of specie, had 'declined under the weight of war which she maintained, almost alone, against the whole of Europe'. By the time Philip II had come to the throne Spain had achieved 'such extended limits' that no ancient or modern monarchy could match her. Philip II, however, had not inherited the burden of *the* empire, but only a divided and heterogeneous set of states. Unlike his father, he was in a position to see the urgent political need to 'abandon the spirit of conquest'. Had he done so, argued Campomanes, had he 'usefully converted the produce of the Indies into augmenting and consolidating the population of Spain, in sustaining its forces through navigation and commerce, and encouraging and advancing its manufactures, wealth and agriculture', Spain could have become as wealthy as its rivals whose initial resources had been negligible. But the cycle had never been broken. The

Philip II

social and political order which the 'spirit of conquest' had imposed upon
Castile in the years after the discovery of America, had rendered it impossible that 'in that political crisis of Europe [the nation] should know its
own interests'.[40] Campomanes had understood, through bitter experience,
what the French and the English had seen through a mixture of pique and
reflective *Schadenfreude*: that the commercial success of the English, the
French and the Dutch could be attributed to their *not* having had ready
supplies of bullion.

It was the unhappy chance of the Mexican and Peruvian mines which
had made Spain's imperial history so unlike that of the other European
powers, not her political system or her religious beliefs. The triumphalist
attitudes which both French and British writers adopted towards the
Spanish monarchy in the eighteenth century, when it was commonly
agreed even in Spain itself that it had been precisely the over-dependence
upon American silver which had devastated the country's economy in the
seventeenth century, were, at best, misplaced. Distracted by what the
English political economist Sir Josiah Child called their 'intense and
singular Industry in their Mines of Gold and Silver', the Spaniards had
never, before the second half of the eighteenth century, been in a position
fully to understand the value of 'Cultivating of the Earth, and producing
Commodities for the Growth thereof'.[41] Furthermore, the poverty of
Castilian industry in the late fifteenth century, and the nation's extensive
dependence upon foreign bankers and foreign merchants, had meant that,
without conquest, it would have been impossible for the Spanish crown,
even if it had wished to, to compete with the other European trading
states. As Campomanes later remarked, in reply to Montesquieu's condemnation of the Spanish preference for conquest over commerce,

> without conquest the country would have passed the commerce of the
> Americas to the more industrious nations who today [1762] are
> conducting it clandestinely. . . . Had things been conducted in any other
> way Spain would have retained nothing of the Indies.[42]

The resulting dependence upon precious metals had, as Child pointed
out, induced a kind of economic blindness, driving the Spaniards to
neglect their domestic agriculture and all forms of manufacturing industry
for the pursuit of specie.[43] The silver imports had not only been responsible for the loss of the political hegemony which Spain had enjoyed in
Europe for most of the sixteenth century. They had also made it impossible
for Spaniards to see their way out of the inflationary trap in which they
had placed themselves. Yet, as Child had recognized, no other European
power which had found itself in the same position would have acted differ-
ently. 'Would you perhaps have despised and abandoned it, had it been
given to *you*,' asked the exiled Jesuit Juan Nuix of the 'philosophising
nations' in 1784.[44] The answer, as Child had seen, could only be no. Even

some of Spain's more hostile observers were sometimes prepared to concede this point. Mining, claimed the Scottish historian William Robertson, was a kind of disease, but it was not one which was peculiar to Spaniards.

> For it is observed that if any person once enter this seducing path, it is almost impossible to return; his ideas alter, he seems to be possessed with another spirit; visions of imaginary wealth are continually before his eyes, and he thinks and speaks and dreams of nothing else.[45]

Unlike the other European nations, Spain had stumbled across the riches of the Americas at an early stage in her history, a stage when, as Arthur Young pointed out in 1772,

> the general importance of every nation's manufacturing for itself was no means so well known as at present. We, at present, have her example to guide our reckoning; she had none by which to frame her conduct: it is therefore no great wonder that the dazzling prospect of immense riches should blind her; and especially when we consider that so great a genius as Sir Walter Raleigh spent so much time, labour and experience, in hunting for gold in Guiana as he did planting tobacco in Virginia.[46]

Because of this blindness, only the Spanish empire in America would continue to identify colonization both with a culture of conquest and with the acquisition of precious metals, until, as we shall see in Chapter 7, in the last two decades of the eighteenth century it, too, like its two main rivals, was transformed into a trading enterprise.

NB or native love of gold too? (Aztec)

III

Expediency, geographical chance, and an unfortunate ignorance of the possible long-term consequences of too much sudden wealth were not the only factors which distinguished Spain's commitment to a policy of continued conquests in America from those of her rivals. Unlike the French and the English, who first settled among the Indian population before they attempted either to integrate them as the French had done or exterminate them like the English, the Spaniards were committed, even by the terms of the capitulations made to Columbus in 1492, to extensive occupation. Ideologically, also, the Spanish conquests in the Americas were unlike the French or British settlements. They had been created by papal concession. Their legitimacy, that is, had been established even before they had come into existence, something which the French and the British generally regarded as absurd. Spain also had had a long, complex history of internal conquest, the *Reconquista* (reconquest) of the peninsula from the Moors. This, too, had been a conquest conducted under papal aegis. Many of the titles, and crucially the kinds of grant, made to the Castilian settlers had their origins in the *Reconquista*, even if they subsequently lost much of their original definition in adaptation to the wholly unfamiliar environment of America. Economically, politically and militarily the conquest of America had more in common with the Spanish wars in Italy than it had with the recovery of the peninsula. But ideologically the struggle against Islam offered a descriptive language which allowed the generally shabby ventures in America to be vested with a seemingly eschatological significance. The substantial Spanish literature of conquest served to enhance this sense of continuity, by redescribing the actions of the most celebrated of the *conquistadores* in the language of the Spanish border ballads. In their own eyes, and in those of their readers, men like Hernán Cortés and Francisco Pizarro were simultaneously the heirs of Caesar and El Cid, the great eleventh-century hero of the *Reconquista*, for whose soul it was customary to dedicate a mass on first reaching the coast of America.[47] And contiguity with the *Reconquista* implied, if not divine sanction, at least divine favour. Few of the *conquistadores* could claim to be executing God's will; but most assumed that God openly favoured their cause. How else could the extraordinary conquests first of Mexico and then of Peru be explained? Little wonder, too, that a disingenuous old soldier like Bernal Díaz could claim to have seen St James of Compostela, the 'Moor-slayer' and patron saint of Castile, fighting alongside him.

Neither the French nor the British could, even if they had wished to, make any similar pretence to quasi-divine inspiration for their colonizing ventures. The historians of the French overseas empire, many of them members of the religious orders, assumed that God had approved their venture, but it was never an approval which favoured conquest, only settlement with the ultimate purpose of peaceful evangelization. The British, during the period of the Commonwealth, took an astonishingly providentialist view of their exploits in the Americas, of which Cromwell's 'Western Design' of 1654–5 (a futile attempt to establish English supremacy in the Caribbean) was the most extreme. The Western Design had been driven by the assumption that the English revolution, and the breed of Calvinism which underpinned it, must have been intended for universal exportation. 'We thank God has not brought us hither where we are,' wrote the Protector, 'but to consider the work that we may do in the world as well as at home.' The English Commonwealth was to become a new Rome in the west, and, as Milton observed after its failure, a new Jerusalem.[48]

As with the more moderate Puritan visions of the City on the Hill, however, this Miltonic republic of virtue was meant to exclude the Native American populations altogether. Yet even the British were aware that some kind of claim to the legitimate possession of the lands of the 'aboriginal peoples' was a necessary condition of successful occupation. But however 'savage', however 'odious' to European sensibilities the Native Americans might appear to be, however extraneous to the objectives of the colonists, few Europeans could accept that they were anything other than human, and as human they clearly possessed both political and territorial rights. The British, even under Cromwell, could make no obvious claim to a divine right of occupation on the basis of the superior faith which God had chosen them to carry to the New World. They were, however, all Protestants of one kind or another, and as David Ramsay later pointed out, although the first settlers might have ridiculed the terms of the papal concession, 'yet they so far adopted the fanciful distinction between the rights of heathen and the rights of Christians, as to make it the foundation of their respective grants'.[49]

This is an allusion to the argument which, as we saw in Chapter 2, the Spanish writers most closely identified with the 'new heretics': that since all *dominium* – that is, property rights and sovereignty – derives from God's grace, not from God's law, no non-Christian, and no 'ungodly' Christian, could be the bearer of rights. For the largely Calvinist settlers in New England, such a claim would, indeed, seem to have been sufficient grounds for dispossession. The Native Americans were infidels. They were therefore denied God's grace, and as a consequence could have no standing under the law. Their properties, and even their persons, were forfeit to the first 'godly' person with the capacity to subdue them. Men, like the dissenting Dean of Gloucester Josiah Tucker, who had a horror of the culture which the English colonists had created on the other side of the Atlantic, believed that this was exactly how the first settlers had attempted to legitimize their actions. 'Our Emigrants to *North-America*,' he wrote to Edmund Burke in 1775,

> were mostly Enthusiasts of a particular Stamp. They were that set of Republicans, who believed, or pretended to believe, that *Dominion was founded in Grace*. Hence they conceived, that they had the best Right in the World, both to *tax* and to *persecute* the *Ungodly*. And they did both, as soon as they got power into their Hands, in the most open and atrocious Manner.[50]

Although the attitudes and the behaviour of the Calvinists frequently seemed to suggest that they did indeed take such a view, few British writers ever employed this argument in any formal sense. Most preferred to believe that it was more of a Catholic aberration than a Protestant one. Since Catholic canon lawyers in their wish to defend papal sovereignty had adopted a position which was not far removed from that of Wycliffe and Huss (if not Luther and Calvin), and since it was precisely this which had underwritten, if only by implication, Alexander VI's Bulls of Donation, this was not an unreasonable assumption.

principles of Nature vs. Grace
(Scot.)   (Spain)

The one instance where this argument might have seemed most attractive was in the abortive Scottish attempt to found a colony on the isthmus of Darien in the 1690s. This, and its subsequent failure, caused widespread controversy over the legitimacy of settlement, and in particular over the legitimacy of establishing colonies in territories already formally occupied by a rival European power.[51] In 1699 the most thoughtful champion of the scheme, Robert Ferguson, argued that the Spanish claims to prior occupation were invalid because they rested, in his view, on the canon lawyers' own version of the Wycliffite principle that 'civil dominion and property [are] founded upon Grace or in the Orthodox Faith'. For Ferguson, however, good Calvinist though he was, as for the Thomists, property rights could only be founded upon 'Principles of Nature'. 'Infidels being rational creatures, as well as other men,' he concluded, 'they are therefore sociable', and consequently in full possession of all the rights due to Christians.[52] It followed that if the native rulers were in true possession of their lands, they could, if they so wished, permit the Scots to settle on them. And this, he believed, they would certainly do immediately the Scots had had the opportunity to explain to them the benefits of having a British colony to defend them against the tyrannical Spaniards.

Ferguson's argument is entirely instrumental, but he could also see, as indeed could most British Protestants, quite as clearly as their Catholic contemporaries, that an argument grounded upon the supposed 'godliness' of individuals – rather than on the natural law – could be used to legitimize any claimant immodest enough to think himself a 'godly ruler'. For this reason, if for no other, it was, as James Otis noted in 1764, a 'madness' which, at least by his day, had been 'pretty generally exploded and hissed off the stage'.[53]

In the absence of sustained argument to right of occupation grounded on the supposed nature of the indigenous inhabitants, the British, and to a somewhat lesser degree the French, were driven to legitimize their settlements in terms of one or another variant on the Roman Law argument known as *res nullius.* This maintained that all 'empty things', which included unoccupied lands, remained the common property of all mankind until they were put to some, generally agricultural, use. The first person to use the land in this way became its owner.[54] The British understanding of what this might involve is captured in what is perhaps the best known, but least discussed, celebration of the possibilities of colonization: Thomas More's *Utopia.* In the second book More explains that when the Utopians founded colonies – which they did in true Greek fashion, when the 'population should happen to swell above the fixed quotas' – they 'join with themselves the natives, if they are willing to dwell with them'. But if these natives should refuse, they make war on them. For

They consider it a most just cause for war when a people which does not use its soil but keeps it idle and waste nevertheless forbids the use and possession of it by others who by the rule of nature ought to be maintained by it.[55]

With very few exceptions this argument was employed by English colonists and their champions from the 1620s on. Argument from conquest, even supposing that it had been historically sustainable, was unlikely to have much force in a political culture such as Britain which, because it had itself been the creation of the Norman Conquest of 1066, was committed to the 'continuity theory' of constitutional law in which the legal and political institutions of the conquered are deemed to survive a conquest.[56] Virginia, argued Richard Bland in 1764, had never been 'conquered': the fact that the Native Americans still possessed 'their native laws and customs, savage as they are, in as full an extent as they did before the English settled upon their continent' was proof enough of that. But even if they had not 'submitted to the English government upon terms of peace and friendship', they could not have been deprived of their 'natural privileges by conquest', for no less a person than Francis Bacon had demonstrated that 'a country gained by conquest hath no right to be governed by English law'.[57]

The *res nullius* argument was also widely used by the French who in many areas were careful, at least at first, to occupy lands which the Native Americans themselves regarded as useless and were unwilling to defend. Settling where the Indians had only hunted, the English and the French had acquired rights of possession. They had made good those rights, however, by 'improving' – a persistent term in the language of the earlier settlers – through agriculture what were frequently described, whatever the realities of the situation, in John Locke's words, as the 'vacant place of America'.[58]

The association between the historical need to press the claim to *res nullius*, and the famous argument in Locke's *Second Treatise on Government* that a man only acquired property rights when he had 'mixed his *Labour* with; and joined to it something that is his own',[59] has recently been made by Jim Tully. The Native Americans, declared Thomas Pownall (1722–1805), Governor of Massachusetts from 1757 until 1760, in allusion to the *Second Treatise*, were 'not landowners, but hunters, not settlers but wanderers, with no idea of property in land, of that property which arises from a man's mixing his labour with it'.[60] By the terms of Locke's argument, if once a settlement had been established the natives attempted to regain the lands they were in violation of nature's laws and might, as Locke phrased it, 'be destroyed as a lion or tiger, one of those savage wild beasts'.[61] When applied to the American case, Locke's argument, in Tully's words, 'bypasses one of the basic principles of Western law, the principle of consent or *quod omnes tangit ab omnibus tractari et approbari debet* [what touches all must be discussed and agreed by all]'. The Spanish had attempted to override this principle by the highly dubious application of the claim that the Papacy possessed the power to impose consent in the propagation of the faith, or with the still more dubious claim that anyone who is capable of knowing, even in retrospect, that something is in his own interest may be said to have consented to it, even when there is no question of his having exercised any freedom of choice.[62] The Native Americans may not have realized at the time that it was in their interest to accept Christianity and the civil order which governed European society, but it was evident that with time, experience and, if necessary, coercion, they would come to see that it had been. They could therefore be said to have consented to their own absorption into the Spanish monarchy. The British had managed a similar move on the grounds that those who could not develop the land God had given them could not be said to be capable of exercising consent at all, at least in those areas where questions of property were concerned. As with so many other differences between legitimizing arguments employed by the two colonizing powers, the Spaniards were overwhelmingly concerned with rights over people, the British with rights in things, in this case land. This is not to say that property rights – the *dominium* exercised over things – was of a lesser kind than the rights exercised over people. Both for the Roman jurists and subsequently for Locke, property was more than the right to possession, since for them it constituted one of the fundamental bases for the development of civil society. Property understood in this broad sense was, as James Madison was later to observe, a 'broad and majestic term', one that 'embraces everything which may have a value to which man may attach a right'.[63] A man who was incapable of performing the acts necessary for him to secure such a right in nature was, therefore, in danger of being held not to be a man at all.

This version of the *res nullius* claim, or the 'agriculturalist argument' as it has sometimes been called, occupied a significant place in Emeric de Vattel's *Le Droit de gens ou principe de la loi naturelle* of 1758 which became the textbook account of the nature of natural rights of property in the second half of the eighteenth century. 'The cultivation of the soil', wrote Vattel,

> not only deserves the attention of a government because of its great utility, but in addition is *an obligation imposed upon man by nature* [emphasis added]. Every nation is therefore bound by natural law to cultivate the land which has fallen to its share. . . . Those peoples such as the Ancient Germans and certain modern Tartars who, though dwelling in fertile countries, disdain the cultivation of the soil and prefer to live by plunder, fail in their duty to themselves, injuring their neighbours, and deserve to be exterminated like wild beasts of prey. . . .Thus while the conquest of the civilized empires of Peru and Mexico was a notorious usurpation, the establishment of various colonies upon the

continent of North America might, if it be done within just limits, be entirely lawful. The people of these vast tracts of land rather roamed over them than inhabited them.[64]

Vattel's argument, like Locke's, drew heavily upon the Roman Law understanding of 'natural' as opposed to 'civil' possession, natural possession of land being that which is clearly evident to those who care to look. Vattel explicitly rejected any argument for conquest or occupation on the basis of a 'civilizing' or evangelizing mission.[65] The state of other peoples' cultures, however deplorable it might be, was not, in itself sufficient grounds for claiming either sovereignty or rights of property over them. For Vattel, however, the cultivation of the land, Locke's 'mingling of labour', is not simply improvement; for him it becomes, in terms of the Aristotelian argument, that a crucial part of what it is to be human is the drive to actualize nature's potentiality, an obligation 'imposed upon man by nature'. Those, by implication all Native Americans other than the Aztecs and the Inka, who fail to fulfil this obligation do not merely choose one, albeit inferior, means of subsistence over another. They fail 'in their duty to themselves' as men, something which, since it clearly constitutes a violation of the law of nature, makes them less than human, creatures who are a threat to the race as a whole and who, in common with Aristotle's natural slaves, may be regarded as indistinguishable from wild animals. Claims which sought in this way to dehumanize hunter-gatherers emerge in a number of eighteenth-century defences of the conquest of America, and were to surface again in the British attempts to legitimize their occupation of Australia. Vattel's argument had the added advantage of reinforcing the French and British assumption that whereas their colonization had been both peaceful and, even when force had been involved, legitimate, that of the Spanish, who had eradicated recognized political communities in pursuit of their ambitions, was not.

The use, by so many English writers of the period, of the terms 'colony and 'plantation' as synonymous became of real legal significance. The Latin word *colonia*, Adam Smith explained, 'signifies simply a plantation'.[66] Both terms were closely tied to the kinds of community the colonies in practice were, and to the arguments for the legitimacy of their existence. Both also assumed a close association between the verb 'to plant' and the 'agriculturalist argument'. 'I like a *Plantation*,' wrote Francis Bacon, 'in a pure soil; that is where People are not displanted to the end, to Plant others. For else it is rather an Extirpation than a Plantation.'[67] Although Bacon allows that it is acceptable to 'Plant where Savages are', this will only be so as long as the Savages themselves do not effectively 'plant'.

The Spanish, by contrast, had founded colonies based not upon 'planting', but upon conquest. These produced not agricultural goods, but semi-sacred precious metals, and were invariably described as 'kingdoms', the 'Kingdoms of the Indies'. Legally these had been a corporate part of the Kingdom of Castile since 1523, but they were very rarely described as such.[68] Even Charles V listed them separately among his titles, and by the seventeenth century America was being described as if it constituted a separate empire. Whatever their legal status they were not, until the second half of the eighteenth century, ever 'colonies', much less 'plantations'.

Any argument from *res nullius*, if it was effectively to be sustained against rival European powers in the same areas, had also to include some claim to prior discovery, since discovery constituted the necessary first step towards effective occupation. The 'right of discovery', as Francisco de Vitoria had pointed out in 1539, had been 'the only title alleged in the beginning, and it was with this pretext alone that Columbus of Genoa set sail'. In the Spanish case, however, it was clear, and generally accepted even by the crown itself, that the Native Americans had been true rulers of their territories before the arrival of the Europeans. Discovery, Vitoria had noted drily, 'of itself provides no support for possession of these lands, any more than it would if they had discovered us'.[69]

The French and the British expended a great deal of effort in a series of claims and counter-claims to property rights over territory they boasted that they had been the first to 'discover'. 'The point of Territorial Right in America,' observed James Abercromby in 1774, 'at first turned totally on the priority of Discovery.'[70] In general such arguments were poorly considered, weakly presented and inconsistently applied. In 1609, when there were only a handful of settlers clinging to the malarial swamps of the St James River, the first royal charter for the Virginia Company solemnly laid claim to all

> territories in America either appertaining unto us, or which are not now actually possessed by any Christian prince or people, situate, lying and being all along the sea coasts between four and thirty degrees of northerly latitude from the equinoctial line and five and forty degrees of the same latitude, and in the main land between the same four and thirty and five and forty degrees, and the islands thereunto adjacent or within one hundred miles of the coast thereof.[71]

No one, it need hardly be said, knew anything about the real extent of these regions, or about the nature of their inhabitants. To match this, the French crown in 1627, at a time when there were only 107 French settlers in Canada, gathered in settlements in Acadia and the St Lawrence and completely isolated from one another, asserted its rights over a territory which reached from Florida to the Arctic Circle, nearly all of which was uncharted, and virtually none of which was in practice either *res nullius* or, given the Spanish presence in the south, 'undiscovered', nor could it possibly have been said to be so even in theory.[72] The struggle which ensued between the British and French over their respective spheres of influence was resolved only by the conclusion of the Seven Years War in 1763 and the final loss of Canada to the British. For most of this time, from the early seventeenth to the late eighteenth century, the struggle for territory was predominantly cartographic. Malachy Postlethwayt's sarcastic observation on Danville's map of 1746, that 'the author has taken upon himself with ink and paper to exercise a considerable part of the British Dominions in North America, and very modestly tacked it to those of his grand monarch', could equally well apply to all of the British and French charts of the period.[73]

The need to sustain claims to prior discovery against those made by rival powers also resulted in some very far-fetched readings of the early history of the European voyages, and a prolonged debate over who had been the first to reach America from Europe. The voyages of a fictional Welshman, Prince Madoc, who supposedly fled civil war in 1170 to what is now Alabama, meant, declared Richard Hakluyt, that 'the West Indies were discovered and inhabited 325 years before Columbus made his first journey'. And if this seemed, at best, a rather weak basis for territorial occupation, he added, somewhat more plausibly, that it had been the Cabots sailing in English ships under English instructions who had 'first discovered Florida for the King of England'.[74] Even as late as 1754, the delegates to the Albany Congress, faced with the prospect of a French invasion, were prepared to state

> That his Majesty's title to the northern continent of America appears founded on the discovery thereof first made, and the possession thereof first taken, in 1497 under a commission from Henry 7th. of England to Sebastian Cabot.[75]

For his part Francis I referred vaguely to a land discovered by the French thirty years before Columbus's first voyage, and even André Thevet – who, without reference to either the English or the Spaniards, renamed the entire American continent 'Antarctic France' – was not above inventing 'some old papers and Pilot books' which, in his view, demonstrated conclusively that Breton sailors had reached America in the reign of Charles VIII.[76]

The trouble with all these stories was not merely their obvious absurdity; it was also the fact that, in law, discovery – even if genuinely 'prior' – constituted only the first step towards legitimate occupation. 'To pass by and eye,' as Francis I icily informed the Spanish ambassador, 'is no title of possession.'[77] Neither, he might have added, were those more formal acts of occupation in which the European colonial powers habitually indulged: setting up a stone cross (known as a *padrão*) as the Portuguese had done all along the coast of West Africa, planting a standard as Columbus had done in the Antilles, or a board, as Bougainville did in Tahiti in 1768. None of these was sufficient, on any terms, to establish either property rights or sovereignty. As Diderot's fictional Tahitian sage says to Bougainville,

> So this land is yours? Why? Because you set foot on it! If a Tahitian should one day land on your shores and engrave on one of your stones or on the bark of one of your trees, *This land belongs to the people of Tahiti*, what would you think then?[78]

Most European jurists would have expressed themselves in much the same way. To 'discover' something in the sense of acquiring rights of possession over it meant, as Grotius argued in 1633, not merely 'to seize it with the eyes *(oculis usurpare)* but to apprehend it'. 'If sailing along a coast can give a right to a country,' remarked Richard Price in 1776, 'then might the people of Japan become, as soon as they please, the proprietors of Britain.'[79] Beneath the heavy sarcasm lay a real legal point: in order to be *rights*, both property rights and sovereignty (*dominium*) have to be exercised. This, as Price pointed out, was also the real theoretical weakness of the arguments set out in the Bulls of Donation. For even if the Pope had been in an undisputed position to make donations of this kind, he would at best only be granting something akin to first refusal. For, Price concluded, 'it is not a donation that grants dominium but consequent delivery of that thing and the subsequent possession thereof'. To be masters of America the English, or the French, would have had to have exercised their mastery – something which clearly they had not done.[80] 'Nothing but possession by a colony, a settlement or a fortress,' wrote Arthur Young,

> is now allowed to give a right from discovery . . . Mr Postlethwayt in his Dictionary talks of the claim we have to California, because Sir Francis Drake was the first discoverer. What absurdity! We made no settlement of any kind whatever; – that is we left it for those who would – which the Spaniards have done, and have therefore a right to the country.[81]

Price and Young sought to uphold what they took to be the natural rights of another European power, in order to reaffirm the claims which the British settlers were making to much of the eastern seaboard and the western hinterland of North America. There were others, however, who were prepared to reject the argument from *res nullius* altogether. For, as many recognized, most of America, and certainly all that the European powers believed worth developing, was by their own criteria, already occupied. Most areas were controlled by societies which possessed at least the minimum necessary features for qualification as 'political societies'.[82] As Jeremiah Dummer pointed out in 1721, the 'claim by *prior discovery or pre-occupancy*' applied only 'to derelict lands, which they [the Americas] were not, being full of inhabitants who undoubtedly had as good a title to their own country as the Europeans have to theirs'. And if the Native Americans had, indeed, been the true owners of 'their' lands, then the only legitimate way in which the colonists could have acquired them was through purchase or 'concession'. There could, Dummer insisted, be

(commercial)

no other right than that in which the honest New-England planters rely on having purchased it with their money. The Indian title, therefore, as much as it is decry'd and undervalued here, seems the only fair and just one.[83]

For Dummer and those who thought like him, it was crucial that the Native Americans should enjoy natural rights of property in their lands since only then could they dispose of them as they wished. No band of wandering hunters devoid of civil institutions would be in a position to make 'concessions' to the colonists – something which the laborious attempt by Thomas Pownall to legitimize the occupation of New England significantly failed to account for.[84]

Claims made on the basis of purchase or concession generally failed to address the point which was made by both Locke and Vattel, and repeated thereafter in nearly every discussion of potential rights over 'unoccupied' land: that mere occupancy does not confer property rights. If the Native Americans had not cultivated their land, it was evidently not theirs to concede. As the Reverend John Bulkley of Colchester, Connecticut, pointed out in 1725, on Locke's own account it was 'such lands only as any of our Aborigines subdued or improved, they had a good right or title to'. The British, for their part, were entitled to 'impropriate all such parts as lay waste or unimproved by the natives'. Since, in his view, there were few or no lands which the Native Americans could be said to have properly 'subdued or improved', this exposed 'that darling principle of many, viz that native right is the only valuable title to any lands in the country', for the absurdity it really was.[85]

Absurd or not, it was a fact, as Bulkley recognized, that in those places where the Native Americans had proved to be too powerful to displace easily both the English and the French had, until the late nineteenth century, to rely upon land purchase or treaty. These agreements, as many historians have pointed out, were often fraudulent even by contemporary legal standards (never stringent) and must have been unintelligible to most Amerindian peoples who had no analogous concept of land ownership. The Royal Proclamation of 1763, whose purpose was to establish principles of government for the lands acquired by the British by the Treaty of Paris, also attempted to limit the damage inflicted in this way upon Native American interests by the colonists. The Proclamation acknowledged that 'great frauds and abuses have been committed in purchasing lands of the Indians, to the great prejudice of our interest, and to the great dissatisfaction of the said Indians'. All further purchases were forbidden unless the initiative came from the Native Americans themselves, and even then all agreements had to be made 'for Us in our name at some public meeting or assembly of the said Indians'.[86] They had, that is, to be a matter of public law rather than private contract. Yet however abusive the specific instances of purchase may have been in the eyes of the Privy Council, purchase indisputably constituted an exchange which was recognized, by the Europeans at least, as a due process of law.

All other claims to legitimacy, argued Arthur Young in his *Essays concerning the Present State of the British Empire* of 1772, 'are fictitious: they will only bear comparison with each other'. Young's point was that even if the Indians could be described, in Lockean terms, as occupying rather than possessing their lands, this was not an argument which would have any meaning for *them*. Since, therefore, they were unlikely to accept the colonists' claims without protest, any attempt to displace them would become *de facto* a conquest. He concluded that 'the only [right] which will bear the least examination . . . is founded upon purchase'.[87] Purchase, as Young conceived it, was also closely associated with the legal arguments grounded upon the notion of 'improvement'. Settlers who had entered peaceably into their property were likely to make better agriculturalists than conquerors, since conquerors' first concern had always been not with agriculture but with the subjugation of people; not with the development of 'God's plenty' but with simple power, and the glory which power conferred. Purchase followed by improvement evidently made for better and more successful colonies than those whose origins had been in 'acts of violence'. Improvement also served to re-enforce a claim to possession on the basis of purchase or exchange. The lands now occupied by settlers from Britain, argued Richard Price in 1776, had both been purchased in the first instance and subsequently developed. 'It is, therefore,' he concluded,

> now on a double account their property, and no power on earth can have any right to disturb them in the possession of it, or to take from them, without their consent, any part of its produce.[88]

Price was a staunch defender of the cause of the American colonists during the War of Independence. His arguments, like Dummer's before him, were not only intended to clear the original settlers of the charge which so many English writers levelled against the Spanish – illicit occupation on the basis of conquest – they were also meant to give greater weight to the argument that the colonies had, in effect, been original and thus effectively independent foundations, over which, in Dummer's words, 'the English king could give . . . nothing more than a bare *right of preemption*'.[89] For the argument from purchase or concession, backed by the claim to have 'improved' the land, also gave added force to the colonists' resistance to a government which had denied them the right of representation in Parliament.

The dispute over the status of the lands which the settlers had attempted to seize from the Native Americans finally resulted in the conferment upon what came to be called the Aboriginal Peoples of America, of a form of ill-defined *de iure* nationhood. The purpose of the Proclamation of 1763 had been to bind Canada more closely to the crown than the original settlements in North America had been. In order to achieve this objective the crown was compelled to grant what it loosely described as 'the several Nations or Tribes of Indians' a large measure of autonomy. It accepted that the Indians had use-rights over 'such Parts of our Dominions and Territories as, not having been ceded to or purchased by Us, are reserved to them, or any of them, as their Hunting Grounds'. It defined all the lands west of the Appalachians as 'under our Sovereign Protection and Dominion for the use of the said Indians'; and it forbade any future settlement there.[90] This injunction reinforced the Treaty of Easton of 1758, which had forbidden settlement west of the Alleghenies. It was unworkable in practice, and later became one of the colonists' grievances against the crown.[91] The Proclamation was not, however, merely an attempt to limit the colonists' powers of acquisition. Nor was it an isolated case. In many ways it can be seen as the final resolution of a legal dispute – to which John Bulkley's *An Inquiry into the Right of the Aboriginal Natives to Land in America* had been a contribution – between the Mohegan nation and the government of Connecticut which had begun in the 1690s. The Mohegans had argued that they were a sovereign nation and, as such, could not be deprived of their lands by the claims that they 'lack such thing as a civil Polity, nor [do they possess] hardly any one of the circumstances essential to the existence of a state'.[92] On 24 August 1705 the Privy Council decided in favour of the Mohegans, and despite fierce lobbying from the colonists, reaffirmed its decision the following year. It was not, however, until 1763 that the matter was decided by a formal royal decree which was intended to be irrevocable.[93]

The Proclamation has also had a long subsequent history. It was incorporated into the Constitution Act of 1867, and still forms the basis for much of the dealing between the Canadian government and the Aboriginal Peoples. As recently as 1982, Lord Denning declared that the Proclamation was as binding today 'as if there had been included in the statute a sentence: "The aboriginal peoples of Canada shall continue to have all their rights and freedoms as recognized by the royal proclamation of 1763".'[94] The Proclamation clearly intended, as successive interpreters have supposed, to grant a measure of legal autonomy to the Native Americans. But the repeated reference in the document to the 'sovereignty', 'protection' and 'dominion' which the British crown claimed to exercise across the whole of America, north of New Spain, Florida and California, makes it clear that this was to be severely limited authority. The Indian 'nations' may have been self-governing communities with rights over their own ancestral lands, but they were certainly not 'perfect communities' and could make no claims to independence from His Majesty. They were, in Bruce Clark's words, 'sovereign in the same way that the colonial government was sovereign – that is vested with a delimited jurisdiction independent of all other governments except as against the imperial government'.[95] And if this were the case, than they also stood – although no British writer ever made this analogy – in the same relationship to the British crown as, on Bartolomé de Las Casas's account, both the 'republics of the Indians' and the states of Milan and Naples stood to the Castilian.[96]

IV

Because both the French and the English arguments for settlements were based in this way upon either one or another variant of the *res nullius*, or on purchase and 'concession', both nations increasingly came to regard conquest as unsustainable in fact, and morally undesirable in theory. '*Conquest*,' Locke had said,

> is as far from setting up any government, as demolishing an House is from building a new one in the place. Indeed it often makes way for a new Frame of a Common-wealth, by destroying the former; but without the Consent of the people, can never erect a new one.[97]

The constitution which he helped to draft for the Carolinas cautions the settlers, with Spanish arguments for conquest in mind, that the Indians' 'idolatry, ignorance or mistakes gives us no right to expel or use them ill'.[98] Conquest, the English believed, could never confer legitimacy and in general, as James Otis pointed out in 1764, had ever been 'in most nations the cause of many severities and heinous breaches of the law of nature'.[99] To rid the English of whatever stain they might still be thought to carry with them from an earlier period of their colonial history, Dummer was even prepared to argue that that most *conquistador*-like of Englishmen, Sir Walter Raleigh, had 'neither conquered nor attempted to conqueror', but merely settled down to peaceful co-existence with the natives.[100] Similarly the French, who had no Raleigh to contend with, were eager to represent themselves to the world as a nation of peaceful settlers. 'I would willingly agree with the Spaniards,' wrote the eighteenth-century Jesuit, Pierre Charlevoix, looking back over more than a century of French colonization, that the French have had no 'conquerors or founders of colonies such as these [Cortés and Pizarro]' who have 'appeared with the greatest *éclat* upon the stage of the New World'.[101]

In terms of their respective national histories, the English and the French had only settled on vacant lands with the consent and enthusiastic cooperation of the native populations, whereas the Spaniards had invaded territories rightly occupied by legitimate, if somewhat primitive, rulers. For such men as Richard Bland, who by the mid eighteenth century were eager to assert the independent nature of the original colonizing project, this meant that the British empire had become something wholly unlike any previous imperial venture. For, declared Bland,

> Planting colonies is but of recent date, and nothing relative to such plantations can be collected from the ancient laws of the kingdoms; neither can we receive any better information, by extending our inquiries into the histories of the colonies established by the several nations in the more early ages of the world.

The Romans had sought to subject 'the whole earth to their empire' through conquest. The English, by contrast, had come to America to 'establish themselves, without any expense to the nations in the uncultivated and almost uninhabited countries'. It was a frequently repeated claim: English colonization had been *sui generis* and, as such, could only be properly understood 'by the law of nature, and those rights of mankind which flow from it'.[102] Bland's conclusions are extreme, and were made in the interests of pressing the case for the legal independence of the American colonies from the metropolitan legislature. But they reflect, nonetheless, a widespread English belief that theirs had been peaceful settlements mutually beneficial to both migrant and native, that they had, indeed, fulfilled some of their much acclaimed ambition to create a new, more virtuous, social order in the New World. The English, wrote Dummer, had no sooner accepted gratefully the lands offered to them by the Native Americans and

> made some necessary provisions for themselves, than they applied their cares for the benefit of the *Indians*, by endeavouring to bring them from their wild manners of life to the civil and polite customs of *Europe*.[103]

The supposedly stark contrast between the behaviour and ideological objectives of the Spaniards and those of the English and the French drew heavily upon a tradition of anti-Spanish and anti-Catholic propaganda which had been fuelled by stories of Spanish atrocities during the Dutch Revolt, and by the wide diffusion of Bartolomé de Las Casas's *Brevíssima relación de la destrución de las Indias* (Short Account of the Destruction of the Indies) after 1583. In the British and French political imagination, Spain not only became an aspirant to Universal Monarchy; it also became a malignant tyrant responsible for the wilful, and entirely pointless, destruction of thousands of innocent persons who, until 1492, had lived in peaceful, if primitive and frequently uncouth, ignorance of their persecutors' very existence. By acting as they had in America, the Spaniards, like the Turks – with whom they became increasingly identified in eighteenth-century Europe – had only destroyed those whose ends they should have been protecting. All government, as Thomas Gordon wrote in his commentaries on Tacitus in 1728, had been instituted for the good of the governed, but 'what Conqueror is there who mends the condition of the conquered?' 'The Spaniard, to secure to himself the possession of America,' declared Gordon,

> destroyed more lives than he had subjects in Europe; and his mighty empire there with its mountain of treasure, bears indeed an awful sound; yet it is allowed that he has lost much more than he got, besides the crying guilt of murdering a large part of the globe.[104]

By the early seventeenth century it had become not uncommon for the English colonists, or at least the more openly evangelical among them, to represent themselves as benevolent settlers helping the benighted Indians to develop God's plenty. The Native Americans were, in Hakluyt's words, a people, 'crying out to us . . . to come and help'. This sentiment was incorporated into the seal of the Massachusetts Bay Company in 1629, on which an Indian is depicted saying 'Come over and Help Us'. Increasingly the British also came to look upon themselves as the Indians' potential saviours not only from paganism and pre-agricultural modes of subsistence, but also from Spanish tyranny.[105] 'And consider,' Robert Johnson had invited the prospective English settlers in Virginia, 'when the great works of freeing the poor Indians from their devourers . . . the children when they come to be saved, will bless the day when first their father saw your faces'.[106] The argument that the British would be welcomed by the Native Americans as liberators, as Raleigh claimed to have been by the inhabitants of Guiana, became a staple of the propaganda war waged against the Spaniards, and on behalf of almost every British colonization project.[107] The Scots, boasted 'Philo-Caledon', the author of a pamphlet in defence of the abortive Darien scheme, would 'peaceably enter upon their new Colony without either Fraud or Force' so as to deliver 'their Brethren, the sons of Adam, from such hellish servitude and oppression'.[108] Just as the English had come to the assistance of the King of Spain's unfortunate subjects in the Netherlands in the name of their natural rights to self-determination, so they might now rescue his subjects in the Americas from *de facto* slavery.

The French were similarly anxious to avoid the charge of usurpation which they, too, levelled so frequently against the Spaniards, although for rather different reasons. The French ambition to create in New France a single state (about which I shall have more to say in the following chapter), however tentative and however, in practice, incomplete, demanded a high level of formal deference, if not practical respect, towards what were seen as Indian rights. The French crown's evident anxiety about its relationship with the Native Americans resulted in extensive legislation, and frequent royal decrees aimed at restraining the potential excesses of the colonists. Louis XIV instructed Daniel de Rémy de Courcelle, the Governor of New France, that the settlers should never be allowed to usurp Indian lands, 'under any pretext that the French find them more convenient and prefer them'. His Majesty's aim was, he said, 'to make them, his subjects, labour usefully for the increase in trade', but 'his intention is that this should be done equitably and that the Indians should come to it of their own free will'.[109] When the French capitulated in September 1760 to Major-General Jeffrey Amherst, the terms of the surrender included a clause which sought to apply the principle that conquest could not deprive a people of the rights they enjoyed under their own laws. This demanded that the Indians 'should be maintained in the lands they inhabit, if they chose to remain there; they should not be molested on any pretence whatsoever ... they shall have, as well as the French, liberty of religion, and shall keep their missionaries',[110] Amherst, who once described the Native Americans as 'the vilest race of beings that ever infested the earth and whose riddance from it must be deemed a meritorious act, for the good of mankind', and whose field commander, a Swiss mercenary called Henri Bouquet, once attempted to 'send the small pox among them' by means of infected hospital blankets, seems reluctantly to have accepted the first of these demands, although, unsurprisingly, he rudely rejected the second.[111]

V

Few if any European titles for original settlement in America would stand much careful scrutiny. As Antoine Bruzen de la Martinière, the French translator of the great Saxon jurist Samuel Pufendorf's *Einleitung zu der Historie der vornehmstem Reiche und Staaten in Europa* (Introduction to the History of the Principal Kingdoms and States in Europe), pointed out in 1732, in the end it was only the continuing fact of their existence which could confer legitimacy on any of the European possessions in the New World.[112] Even some Spaniards, who had invested most in a succession of arguments from conquest and natural rights of occupancy, were prepared to accept that whether in the end their initial claims turned out to be just or unjust, they could only be sustained over time by prolonged occupation. The Roman law of prescription allowed for long-term *de facto* occupation of a particular thing (*praescriptio longi temporis*) to be recognized *de iure* as a case of *dominium*. In terms of this claim, long-term occupation could confirm retrospective rights of property and even – although this was more dubious – of jurisdiction. 'Even a tyranny becomes in time a perfect and legitimate monarchy,' wrote Juan de Solórzano y Pereira in 1629 after a long survey of all the arguments for and against the legitimacy of the Spanish conquests of America. For Solórzano in particular, who was also aware of the role given by sixteenth-century humanist jurists to custom (*consuetudo*) as the means by which prescription could render cases which existed *de facto* into cases *de iure*, it was always the objective condition which conferred legal rights and, in the end, it was legal, not natural rights which were under discussion.[113] A similar historical basis for the acceptance of rights of occupation, and subsequent *dominium*, had, as Solórzano pointed out, been the only claim made by other European maritime states to the seas closest to their shores. No one (except, that is, Grotius, and he was a heretic) had denied the right of Pope Alexander III to grant *dominium* over the Adriatic to Venice, or the right of the Genoese to control of the Ligurian Sea. Turn, he told his readers, to John Selden's *Mare clausum* and there you will find arguments that will do quite as well for the Spanish claims to the land of America, as they do for the English king's claims to sovereignty in the North Sea and the North Atlantic.[114]

Despite the generalized hostility of the common law to the notion of prescription, the British were, in general, willing to accept such arguments. For there had always been one insuperable problem with any simple claim based on *res nullius*. The occupation of lands and moveable goods – or in the language of the Roman Law *dominium rerum* – was distinct from sovereignty or *dominium jurisdictionis*. The British right to occupation 'in consequence of *landed possession*', Thomas Pownall complained in 1765, however incontestable that might be, nevertheless constituted a 'useless, faithless claim to dominion over them', and one which, in Pownall's view, had only resulted in 'our horrid injustice'.[115]

Prescription, however, could be used to resolve this difficulty. Prescription, furthermore, was part of the same essentially existential juridical argument as *res nullius*. The legitimacy of a state or condition depended upon its continual and successful existence. The English, claimed Robert Johnson with suitable vagueness in 1609, had been there 'long since' – in fact a mere two years – 'without any interruption or invasion either of the Savages (the natives of the country) or any other Prince or people'. This in his view was sufficient to grant James I 'rule or Dominion' over all 'those English and Indian people'. And although, like all Englishmen, he rejected the Papal Bulls of Donation, he was willing to concede that this argument could equally be applied to 'their "Nova Hispania"'.[116] Accepting the Spanish presence in the south by 'right of discovery' and subsequent prescription was, as Johnson realized, an inescapable consequence of pressing the English claim in the north. As Robert Ferguson acknowledged in 1699, the only rights which the Spaniards might have had in America derived exclusively from their 'claim and upon the foot of prescription thro' their having inhabited, occupied and inherited them for 200 years without interruption, disseizure or dispossession'.[117] One of the objections to the abortive Darien scheme was precisely that it constituted, in the words of an opponent calling himself

'Britanno sed Dunensi' in 1700, an attempt at 'settling a colony in another man's dominions'. As 'Britanno sed Dunensi' went on to point out, turning Robert Ferguson's argument neatly on its head, the only possible excuse the Scots could have for their invasion of the King of Spain's dominions was 'by Virtue of your Presbyterian tenet viz of Dominions being founded in grace you are the Presumptive Elect, pretended a Divine Right to the Goods of the Wicked', and this – as Ferguson himself had pointed out – was 'unjust and groundless'.[118]

VI

Spanish claims for rights of property, and crucially of sovereignty, in America made no use of the *res nullius*. This was only partly because, as Vitoria pointed out, the lands they had settled in were evidently not unoccupied. It also derived from two further conditions which made the Spanish occupation of America legally quite unlike that of either of its two main rivals. The first was the fact that, because of their origin in a papal charter, the Castilian crown's claims to rights of sovereignty and property in America had been made *prior* to actual occupation. Unlike the *a posteriori* contracts and treaties entered into by the French and the British in America, the Spanish 'titles' did not require any act of concession, or even of more than minimal recognition, on the part of the Native Americans themselves. The only legal relationship, if it can be so called, entered into between the *conquistadores* and the Indians was, therefore, highly peremptory. In the first instance it took the form of a declaration, probably drafted by the jurist Juan López de Palacios Rubios in 1512, appropriately entitled the *Requerimiento*, the 'Requirement'. This document – surely the crassest example of legalism in modern European history – began with a brief history of the world since its creation, laid out the grounds for the Castilian monarchs' claim to be the true rulers of the Americas, and then promised the Native Americans all manner of hideous punishments, including, of course, their enslavement and the seizure of their lands, if they resisted the 'ambassadors' of their new ruler. When he read it, Bartolomé de Las Casas once said, he did not know whether to laugh or cry.[119]

The second reason why Spanish theorists found the *res nullius* argument largely unusable was the fact that the Castilian crown was as much concerned with its potential rights over the Indians themselves as with its rights over their property. The grants made by the crown to settlers in Spanish America – known as *encomiendas* – were precisely not feudatories as they were in Canada and the French Caribbean, nor were they entitlements to semi-independent occupation, as they were in British America.[120] They were titles to labour. The Native Americans were given over (*encomendado*) to their master, who was entitled to the use of their labour in return for a small wage and the duty to protect them and instruct them in the Christian religion. Their land remained, in great part, the property of the crown. There was at least one writer, Juan de Matienzo, who tried to argue that since the *encomendero* was party to a contract with the king, he performed the function of a feudatory even if he did not enjoy the rights of one, and thus must be able to exercise *dominium utile*, which made the *encomienda* a true fief in all but legal title. This, however, was a claim which the crown, eager not to see the creation in the New World of the kind of society it had worked so hard to dismantle in the Old, fiercely rejected. No one knew this better than the *encomenderos* themselves who, from the 1530s until the abolition of the institution in 1720, agitated persistently and sometimes violently for the creation of land grants in perpetuity. Only when they had been transformed into true feudal vassals, Philip II was informed in 1556, would the crown be able to rely upon the full loyalty of the colonists. 'For if they are feudatories they will thus quench the fires of rebellion . . . which until now has not been the case, rather some of them have taken pleasure in these disturbances because they are not holders of perpetual *encomiendas*.'[121]

The Spanish crown required an argument which would reconcile the seizure of the lands and moveable goods of the native peoples whom they overran, with the insistence on their rights to sovereignty over them. These rights, furthermore, had, unlike those supposedly made by prescription, to be *a priori*. The only alternative was the somewhat implausible claim that the Native Americans had themselves willed away their own territories. Since, however, what they must have willingly surrendered in this way was not only their lands but also their natural rights to political autonomy, it could not be claimed that they had done this because, as the British and the French supposed, they could see the advantages of 'conceding' or selling lands to the Europeans. They must have acted as they did in the legally far more significant belief that, in Las Casas's phrase, 'all or the greater part of the Indians wished voluntarily to be vassals [of the King of Spain] and hold it an honour to be so'.[122]

The only alternative to an argument from concession of this kind was the claim that America had been acquired by conquest in pursuit of what its perpetrators claimed to have been a just war. The supposition that rights in America had been acquired through legitimate warfare was far more acceptable to the Spanish political and legal traditions than it was to either the French or the British. Spanish notions of empire had since the eleventh century been inextricably bound in with the language and cultural traditions – as well as the mythology – of the *Reconquista*. From at least 1519, when Hernán Cortés first described the men of his rag-tag army as 'settlers and conquerors' (*pobladores y conquistadores*) the emigrants to America had overwhelmingly thought of themselves as warriors, men whose right to settle, and to manage their own affairs, derived, as had the rights of men like El Cid, from their success in arms. They possessed this land not because they had bought it, or because it was 'unoccupied'. They possessed it because their blood, in that hallowed metaphor, had literally flowed into the ground, and made them and their descendants its true owners *and its true rulers*. To be a *conquistador* you clearly had to have someone to conquer. The occupation of seemingly, or supposedly, unoccupied land, might satisfy the industrious – and Calvinist – English farmer or the French fur-trader; but it had very little appeal for the Spanish hidalgo. Unlike either of their two competitors, the Spaniards had also come to America with the intention of creating European communities which would be wholly dependent upon a native labour force. There is, indeed, some truth in the frequently repeated sneer that, in the marquis de Mirabeau's words, the Spaniard was the 'true Mongul of America', whose 'dignity resides in his idleness'.[123] As Talleyrand scathingly observed in 1797, theirs were not true colonies at all, since the Spaniards had merely invaded 'the first lands they encountered. They wished not to cultivate, but to devastate.'[124] The devastation was certainly not intentional; but Talleyrand was right in claiming that the Spanish had not gone to America, as had both the French and the English, in order to cultivate the land. They had gone to occupy and to benefit, as all good noblemen did, from the labour of others.

It was clear to most Spanish writers, and widely accepted as such by the Castilian crown itself, that ultimately the only argument that could provide all the rights they required was that of the just war. Since both the English and the French were eager to dissociate themselves from the image of conquest, it is hardly surprising – even if we set aside for a moment the other very significant differences between the political cultures of the three nations – that only the Spaniards should have engaged in prolonged disputes over the legitimacy of their overseas empire. Robert Gray's question, in *A Good Speed to Virginia* of 1609, 'by what right or warrant we can enter into the land of these Savages, take away their rightful inheritance from them, and plant ourselves in their place, being unwronged or unprovoked by them' required, as Gray recognized, no answer, since few Englishmen believed that they had entered land belonging to anyone or had deprived anyone of their inheritance, rightful or not – unless, of course, it was some other European power. The English, Gray declared optimistically, had

> no intention to take away from them by force that rightfull inheritance which they have in that country, for they are willing to entertain us, and have offered to yield into our hands on reasonable conditions, more land than we shall be able this long time to plant and manure.[125]

The famous debate over the legitimacy of the English rights in America between John Cotton and Roger Williams, in Massachusetts in the 1630s, although sometimes compared to the famous dispute in 1551 between Las Casas and Juan Ginés de Sepúlveda, was, similarly, limited to the validity and applicability of the *res nullius* argument.[126]

The only major exception to this rule was the much discussed conquest of Virginia. This was intended to be, so far as circumstances allowed, a copy of the conquests of Mexico and Peru. The arguments that legitimized the crown charters to the Virginia Company to invade a legitimate ruler's territory were based, however, upon Sir Edward Coke's disturbing claim supposedly grounded in English common law that all infidels were aliens, *perpetui enemici*, 'perpetual enemies', 'for between them, as with devils, whose subjects they be, and the Christians, there is perpetual hostility, and can be no peace'.[127] This, in Coke's opinion, was a precept not of the canon law, which it so closely resembled, but of the English common law. Few Englishmen were prepared to accept this; still less were they willing to endorse Coke's grander, and bizarre, claim that the common law of the English people was identical with the law of nature. The legitimacy of the conquest of Virginia was never seriously challenged until the eighteenth century. But the settlers soon came to describe themselves as 'improvers' of lands which they had either purchased or which had been 'empty', in much the same way as the inhabitants of the other colonies.

The intellectual battles over the legitimacy of the Spanish occupation, by contrast, depended, in all but a tiny minority of cases, upon the answer to one question: had the wars made on the Native Americans ever been just ones? This was driven in part by a wish to salvage the royal conscience before God, in part because in the sixteenth and seventeenth centuries Spain possessed an obsessively legalistic political culture. But it was driven also by the awareness that if the government of conquered territories were to remain free from internal conflict, its initial act of foundation had to be seen to be legitimate. Sooner or later, wrote Pedro Portocarrero y Guzman (Archbishop of Tyre, *in partibus infidelium*) in 1700, an empire founded on unjust claims was bound, through God's agency or man's folly, to fall. Only the King of Spain, in his view, had 'maintained his conquests, with the same justification with which he began them'. And, he continued,

> we see in those who acquire and conquer with the sword, and govern with reason and the justified motive of their right, that they accompany their valour with prudence, so that the former might win, and the latter preserve.[128]

The need to secure and legitimize the Spanish government in the Americas thus became a crucial part of how the entire future structure of the empire was conceived.

The Augustinian and Wycliffite argument that the Native Americans possessed no natural rights because they were unbelievers was inimical to all but a small group of canon lawyers. Few Christians in early-modern Europe had any doubt that the Christian religion and the European way of living were far superior to anything known to any non-Europeans. Few also doubted that it was the duty of the Europeans to export both religion and civility everywhere and by every possible means. Some were, and had been since at least the days of Tertullian, prepared to accept that almost any price, including slavery, was worth paying for the gift of salvation through Christ. But even this repellent notion could not quite provide a secure justification for war against non-Christians solely on the grounds that they were non-Christians. Expansion, if it were to be achieved by any means other than conversion through rational argument, required, for most at least, a more complex machinery of legitimation than the pious belief that all men would be better off living, and dying, as members of the *congregatio fidelium.* The Romans, though generally less squeamish than their Christian heirs, and unburdened by the belief in a single divine source of justice, had recognized a similar need to legitimize their acts of collective violence. Men, as Cicero had insisted, use language to resolve their differences and resort to violence only when language has failed.[129] Even for the Romans, war was, at least in theory, always looked upon as a means of last resort, and the supposed objective of war had always been to acquire, not cultural and religious transformation, much less territory, but peace and justice. 'War,' St Augustine had told Bonifatius in about 417,

> should be waged only as a necessity, and waged only that God may by it deliver men from necessity and preserve them in peace. For peace is not sought in order to kindle war, but war is waged in order that peace may be secured. . . . So it should be necessity, not desire, that destroys the enemy in battle.[130]

In response to this perceived need for a body of moral precepts governing war, there came into being a doctrine of what came to be – and is still – called the 'Just War'.[131] A just war conferred upon the aggressor a right to wage war – the *ius ad bellum* – and was governed by a set of agreements about how the war should be waged and the benefits which the victor was entitled to derive from it – the *ius in bello*.[132] In general the Roman jurists claimed that war could only be waged defensively, and in pursuit of compensation for some alleged act of aggression against either the Romans themselves or their allies. 'The best state,' as Cicero observed, 'never undertakes war except to keep faith or in defence of its safety.'[133] War was only a means of punishing an aggressor, and of seizing compensation for damages suffered. All wars, furthermore, had to be *wars*, not punitive raids, or acts of pillage. As Cicero, at his most moralistic, had argued:

A fair code of warfare has been drawn up, in full accordance with religious scruple, in the fetial laws of the Roman people. From this we can grasp that no war is just unless waged after a formal demand for restoration.[134]

Most Romans, however, Cicero among them, fully recognized that Rome – like the United States and the Soviet Union in the 1950s and 1960s – had frequently acquired clients with the sole purpose of 'defending' them against enemies, real or imaginary, whose territories they wished to acquire. Cicero himself had also made a somewhat unsettling distinction between wars fought for defence and wars fought for glory and empire. What he defined as 'fighting for empire and seeking glory' clearly constituted a different category of warfare, one which is said to be 'waged less bitterly' than warfare fought for defence and restitution.[135] On this account it would seem that, although in all wars 'just grounds . . . should be wholly present', Rome's own assessment of its needs and goods – glory and booty among them – might be a sufficient ground for belligerence. And, as Richard Tuck has shown, there was a powerful legal humanist tradition from Alberico Gentile (1552–1608) to Hugo Grotius which adopted this view precisely in order to legitimize English and Dutch colonization.[136] Not surprisingly, perhaps, Spaniards such as Vázquez de Menchaca, and the more self-consciously humanist royal counsellor, Sebastiano Fox Morcillo, were prepared to take very much the same line in order to defend the Spanish conquests in America. The king, wrote Fox Morcillo in 1536,

> will likewise send colonies of his citizens to the provinces in order that they . . . not only act as a garrison to the kingdom but also keep the others [i.e. the native inhabitants] always faithful. This was exactly what our countrymen did in the New World when we sent numerous colonies from Spain; and what the Romans did in Egypt, Gaul, Hispania and many other provinces.[137]

Few Christians, in particular Roman Catholic Christians, could bring themselves fully to accept such stark assertions. For them warfare could be made only against someone who was, in some sense, guilty of some crime. Wars, said Augustine, in the most frequently cited passage on the subject, are just

> which revenge the injuries caused when the nation or *civitas* with which war is envisaged has either neglected to make recompense for illegitimate acts committed by its members, or to return what has been injuriously taken.[138]

Simply being in the way of someone else's desires or the satisfaction of their needs was clearly as insufficient a ground for making war on them, as wishing them to share your beliefs and styles of life.

But there were ways in which it was possible to extend the range of this injunction. One, which was frequently employed by Spanish jurists in the American context, was that a prince might go to war in defence of what were called 'the innocent'. If a ruler could be shown to have oppressed his peoples in such a way as to constitute a threat to their lives, then he might legitimately be deposed by another prince. On this ground any people might, by virtue of their predicament, become the *de iure* 'allies' *(socii)* of another. And this would be true even if the oppressed subjects were not aware of their condition, because prolonged habit is capable of obscuring every human being's understanding of the natural law. The American Indians, that is, might not know that to be sacrificed and eaten constituted a violation of their natural rights, they might even defend the rulers who perpetrated such crimes, but it remained the case that any ruler – whether Christian or non-Christian – when confronted by societies such as the Aztec had the duty to depose their rulers (to *tollere principem* or *mutuare principatum*).[139] In such circumstances the victorious prince might be able to send 'ministers' to defend their future interests. There was the further point that in such conditions war becomes defensive – if in the supposed interests of a third party – and might, therefore, be waged to prevent any further deterioration in the status quo. In the view of the great Jesuit metaphysician and theologian, Francisco Suárez (1548–1617) – perhaps the most influential Catholic writer on the justice of war in the seventeenth century – this would, for instance, have constituted a cause for a just war against Henry VIII of England. For England, so Suárez claimed to believe, because of the offences Henry had caused its citizens, was already in disarray and might legitimately be attacked to prevent further collapse.[140] 'War', as Suárez phrased it, 'is permitted so that the state may preserve the integrity of its rights.'[141]

Such arguments, though they were formally deployed to defend the Spanish presence in America, provided no charter for effective colonization. For once the 'integrity of the state' had been established, the invading power should logically withdraw. According to Augustine, however, Cicero had also argued in Book III of *De Republica* that wars might be waged 'in defence of faith'. This clearly widened the possible application of both the Ciceronian and the Augustinian grounds for a *ius ad bellum*. If 'fides' is understood here, as Augustine understood it, to mean religious belief then this again comes out as the familiar and, for the jurists and the theologians, wholly unacceptable claim that Christian princes might make war on pagans because of their paganism. As Suárez observed, it was not man's task to vindicate God. If God wishes to take revenge upon the pagans for their sins, he remarked acidly, 'he is capable of doing so for himself'.[142] But 'fides' could also be interpreted, as Cicero himself would have interpreted it, to stand for a way of life: in this case, of course, the way of life practised within the Roman *civitas*. What extended the possible range of the term still further was Augustine's own universalism, which meant that the *civitas* could effectively be made to embrace the world – the *orbis terrarum* – itself. Thus it might be said that an offensively un-Christian, which meant in effect an offensively non-European, lifestyle – one which, for instance, involved cannibalism, sodomy and human sacrifice – constituted not only a crime against nature, but an offence of such magnitude that it posed a threat to the continuing existence of the *civitas*. The Christian prince might therefore go to war as the defender of the Christian *civitas* on the grounds that Augustine had endorsed elsewhere in the *City of God*, namely that war might be made to 'acquire peace', peace in this context being defined as a 'work of justice' (*opus justitiae*) for the restoration of the 'tranquillity of the order of all things'.[143]

In such circumstances, argued Suárez, 'the natural power and jurisdiction of the human republic' could be mobilized as a 'reason for universal conquest' against all those whose behaviour was so extreme as to constitute a threat to the integrity of humanity.[144] The key term here was the universal force which, as we saw in Chapter 1, it was possible to give to the word 'humanus' in the context of both Thomist natural jurisprudence and the Roman civil law. If we consider that Suárez held that one of the crimes that might legitimize such action was any attempt to 'impede the law of Christ', then the scope of the jurisdiction exercised by the 'human republic' could be very wide indeed.[145] The central passage in Augustine which had been cited by virtually every theorist since Dante, that God had given the empire to the Romans because of their virtue, now served in effect to draw the two idioms – the Thomist and the Augustinian – so close together that on occasions they merged altogether. For by substituting a stylized and imperfectly limited cultural *ordo*, still based upon arguments from the natural law, Suárez was, in effect, providing a justification for war similar to that offered by the canonists and, more perilously, the Calvinists, but without employing the Wycliffite heresy that power was founded by God on grace, not law. Suárez, and such Spanish jurists as Solórzano y Pereira, who employed the same passages from Cicero and Augustine to reach the same translation of religious into cultural values,[146] had effectively provided the Spanish imperial ideologues with what the anti-imperialists of the School of Salamanca, Francisco de Vitoria and Domingo de Soto, had tried so hard to deny them: an argument, grounded somewhere in both Aquinas and the Roman Law, capable of sustaining the intuition which had been so deeply embedded in the whole of Roman and subsequently Christian thinking about the beliefs and behaviour of others – that those who do not share our world-views are our enemies.

In the discussion of what kind of entity a 'human republic' was and how it might legitimately be defended, Suárez, and some of his contemporaries such as Luís de Molina, had in effect come round to a broadly Romanist view of empire as the legitimate agent of a particular – and in their view the only – kind of civilization. It was this set of claims, and this vocabulary, which also underpinned the extended sixteenth- and seventeenth-century debate over the Aristotelian concept of natural slavery. For if the American Indian could be shown to be a natural slave, then it became the duty of those who had discovered him to bring him into the human community. Even in its more robust humanistic form, in which Aristotle's comparison between the capture of such slaves and the hunting of wild animals was made much of, it was clear, as Fox Morcillo pointed out, that the ultimate objective of their servitude was that 'they should be civilised by good customs and education and led to a more human way of life'.[147]

On this account Suárez's argument becomes – at least in so far as its consequences are concerned – barely distinguishable from the purely cultural humanistic arguments. From only a very short distance, Vázquez de Menchaca's radiant 'mundus' and Suárez's 'respublica humana' become virtually interchangeable. The American Indians, said Vázquez, reducing all these arguments to a simple proposition, are 'our enemies, prejudicial, loathsome and dangerous'. Their customs constitute a threat to the necessary beauty of the *mundus*, and this is all we require to justify our going to war against them. *(slavery)*

This argument provided the Spanish crown with the *a priori* right to conquest which it required. It must be stressed, however, that neither Suárez nor Vázquez used it in quite this way. For on their accounts, anything beyond punitive and corrective action would result in precisely the kind of extended empire which, as we saw in Chapter 2, would constitute another kind of threat to the human community. The most any Christianizing or civilizing power could be permitted under such conditions would be to take the 'barbarians' in hand until they had learnt the ways of civility. This indeed – and improbably – was what Sebastiano Fox Morcillo claimed when he wrote that

> the Emperor Charles V recently did so excellently, for the nations of [the New World] once conquered by our countrymen, and instructed in the Christian religion, he granted them their freedom, even though previously they were servile.[148]

An argument for conquest on the basis of a just war fought in defence of the 'human republic' did not, however, provide the kind of special concessions which the Papal Bulls had offered to Spain as the nation chosen by God for the task of bringing the Native Americans into the 'world'. One claim that did was made by the humanist Juan Ginés de Sepúlveda. Sepúlveda is perhaps best known for his celebrated attack upon the natural rights of the Native Americans, the dialogue *Democrates secundus,* which he probably composed in 1544.[149] This provided the grounds for his famous dispute in Valladolid in 1551 with Bartolomé de Las Casas, a dispute which has often been seen as the triumph of Las Casas, and of the School of Salamanca in general, over the more direct and simple-minded of the Castilian crown's imperial ideologues. *Democrates secundus* was not, however, an isolated work, but the final part of a trilogy, each part of which set out to defend what Sepúlveda interpreted as Charles V's struggle against the universal disrupters of the world order. The first work in the trilogy had been *Democrates primus*, an 'Anti-Erasmian' (and also anti-Machiavellian) defence of the sack of Rome, by mutinous imperial troops in 1527, both as a punishment for a lax Church, and as an integral part of the imperial campaign against heresy.[150] The second, *Cohortatio ad Carolum V Imperatorem invictissimum*, composed in 1529, was an exhortation to Charles to make peace among Christians and take up arms against the Turks, precisely in defence of the 'liberty and salvation of the Christian republic'. It is also Sepúlveda who provided the link between these arguments and the more specific arguments for the justice of the conquest of America.

Some time after the completion of *Democrates secundus*, Sepúlveda wrote a treatise on good government for Philip II entitled *De regno et regis officio*, and in this he brought the arguments set out in his trilogy into line with the claim that it was the Spanish monarchy, as the heir to the medieval empire, which God had chosen to bring the 'inhuman' into the sphere of the human. In *De regno* Sepúlveda introduced a modified version of Aristotle's theory of natural slavery to distinguish between three categories of nation: those fitted to exercise 'civil rule'; those capable of managing their own affairs, but neither sufficiently prudent nor intellectually gifted to manage the affairs of others; and those whose public customs violate the natural law in such a way as to render them 'barbarous and inhuman'. The Native Americans, who have so many features in common with the Turks – who had been the subject of detailed vilification in the *Cohortatio* – are, like the Turks, clearly 'inculti' and thus 'inhumani'.[151] They and most other non-European peoples (although Sepúlveda is never very specific about who these might include) clearly belong in the final category. Equally clearly, on the basis of the arguments for a just war which he interprets very much as Suárez did later, these races might be conquered by those who belong in the first category. 'With these rights,' he concluded, 'the Romans, a very civilized people and exalted in virtue, subjected to their rule the barbarian nations.' And just as God had, in more difficult times, chosen the Romans to do his work, so now God's legate, Pope Alexander VI, had chosen the Spanish. In Sepúlveda's reading, what in the text of the Papal Bulls is only an injunction to Christianize has been transformed into a right to conquer in order to civilize.[152] The Spaniards, even if their king is now no longer *de facto* emperor, have been entrusted by the Vicar of Christ with the final execution of the historical role of the *Imperium romanum*.

It might seem that within a political culture so concerned with providentialist explanations as the Castilian, Sepúlveda had offered a reassuring argument for maintaining, and increasing, the Spanish presence in America. Yet it was received with no great enthusiasm. For as Spain visibly went into decline towards the end of the sixteenth century so the Spanish crown became more uneasy about the emphasis given to conquest in its claims to rights in America. The triumphalism which underpinned the whole language of the just war – whose decrees for awarding the victors far exceeded those for protecting the losers – began to wane as Spanish armies suffered defeat after defeat. This may also be why, when in 1598 the Castilian Baltasar Alamos de Barrientos divided the Spanish empire into those states which had been acquired by inheritance, and those which had been acquired through conquest, he placed America, together with Naples, Milan and Sicily, among the hereditary states.[153]

By the mid-seventeenth century the declining Spanish position in Europe, the threat which the *conquistador* elite continued to pose to royal authority in the Americas, and the widespread disapprobation of conquest throughout Europe (to which the Spaniards were by no means as insensitive as they sometimes claimed) led to a number of attempts to diminish the role of conquest in the ideological image of the origins of the Spanish American colonies. In 1680 the *Nueva Recopilación de leyes de los reynos de las Indias* (New Code of the Laws of the Kingdoms of the Indies) required that 'this word conquest be omitted, so that it should not be the case of, or provide an excuse for, force or harm being given to the Indians'.[154] In 1782, in his attempt to meet the challenge of the enlightened critics of colonization, Juan Nuix attempted to distance the whole Spanish colonial process from what he described as the 'thefts, rapes, piracy and usurpation' which had characterized the conquests of the Ancient World. The Indians, he claimed, in a lurid redescription of Las Casas's original argument, had come 'spontaneously to throw themselves at the feet of the Spaniards, pleading with them to receive them as members of a society which made such good and humane men (*hombres tan buenos y humanos*)'.[155]

The American world, he claimed to believe – his vision perhaps heightened as that of so many others of his generation by exile – was now a single community of Europeans and Indians, the heirs of this initial act of obeisance. Nuix's defence of the 'humanity of the Spaniards' is a measure of the degree to which, by the second half of the eighteenth century, even the colonists were prepared to concede that, whatever the original nature of the Castilian crown's claims might have been, they were now there by right of prescription alone. Furthermore, all those involved in the debates accepted that the European empires had been in existence too long to make their withdrawal either possible or humanly desirable. Settler populations had grown up whose members had no place outside the colonies. The 'British Americans', the *criollos* and the *colons* were all, whatever else they might also have been, American. The indigenous populations, what survived of them, had now become not only racially integrated with their invaders, but economically, and to a large degree culturally, dependent upon them. Already by the mid-seventeenth century, America was no longer the place it had been before 1492, and any further discussion over the rights which the Europeans might have there, or even their original purpose in going there, had to take this fact into account.

The prolonged and bitter debates over legitimacy had another dimension. They were not – as they have so often been described – merely struggles, of little long-term consequence in the world of *realpolitik*, over the rights of native peoples. They were also, and more pressingly for the European invaders, discussions about the historical origins, and hence the political and cultural identity, of the settlements themselves. As such they cast a shadow at least as far as independence, and in most cases further. They determined the way in which the theorists of empire considered what kind of future the settler societies were likely to have. The fact that in one way or another all the European empires in America had begun as empires of conquest – however short-lived this might have been in practice – that none appeared able to shed the legacy of the Ancient World, that all ultimately were, even in terms of their own self-description, expansionist, seemed to many observers to condemn them to a certain kind of historical trajectory. This trajectory led them inexorably, and despite the very great differences between them, to the fate which had befallen Rome: persistent and uncontrolled expansion, loss of political control, and, with it, legal and cultural identity. And this in the end could only mean the decline and collapse, not only of the empire, but also of the metropolis itself.

CHAPTER FOUR

Expansion and Preservation

No son las Monarquías diferentes de los vivientes o vegetales. Nacen, viven y mueren como ellos sin edad firme de consistencia. Y así son naturales sus caídos. En su creciendo, descrecen.

Diego Saavedra Fajardo, *Idea de un príncipe politico-cristiano*

I

Since late Antiquity, at least, it had been widely believed that the overwhelming difficulties which faced all empires could be resolved, or at least explained, in terms of the dual question of size and preservation. 'Commonwealths well founded,' wrote Charles Davenant in his *Essay upon Universal Monarchy*, 'would be eternal if they could retain themselves within a reasonable extent of territory.' The dynamics of expansion and consequent collapse would seem, however, to be a contagion which afflicted all peoples who had achieved a degree of military, social and technological success. To this the historical record of Antiquity bore dismal testimony. Their 'most famous law givers', had all, in Davenant's words, 'formed their models of Government rather for Increase than for Preservation'.[1] And despite the examples provided by Athens, by Persia and by Rome, it remained a persistent danger in the modern world. 'Many Empires,' warned Davenant,

> have been driven by too large enlarging their Dominions, and by grasping at too great an extent of territories, so our interests in America may decay, by aiming at more provinces and a greater tract of land than we can either cultivate or defend.[2]

Expansion, ungovernable once it had begun, was perceived as an obvious threat to the stability and continued prosperity of the metropolis, by writers in all three European empires. If limited expansion was, as it seemed to be, impossible, then it was clearly better to concentrate the energies of the people on improving what they already possessed. The wise, the prudent, monarch stayed at home to look after the interests of his

103

pop. control

subjects. In Spain in particular, there were many, the playwright Lopé de Vega among them, who were ready to remind their sovereign of the fate that had befallen King Sebastian of Portugal, fighting a foolish and doomed war of expansion on the African coast in which, in 1578 at Alcacer-Quibir, he had lost his life and ultimately his throne. As even Philip IV's first minister, and virtual ruler of Spain, the Count-Duke of Olivares had come to recognize, by the early seventeenth century the empire was little more than a 'poisoned chalice which had sapped their [the Castilians'] vigour and aggravated their ills'.³

But if expansion posed obvious threats to the continuing welfare of the metropolis, it also seemed to offer some incomparable advantages beyond the wealth or glory it might bring. As the reason-of-state theorists had argued in the sixteenth century, empires could provide an outlet for military, glory-seeking activities which might otherwise lead to internal unrest. They also offered a place in which to dump the increasing numbers of mendicants and criminals who thronged the cities of Europe. Even in Antiquity, noted Samuel Pufendorf in 1688, colonies had been one solution to the problem of what to do with all those who 'wander from want of their daily bread and who harass all whom they meet'.⁴ From the beginning all the European powers seem to have regarded their overseas settlements as either simple deposits for the waste products of the metropolitan society or, more far-sightedly (and more humanely), as a place where the disadvantaged, those whom Richard Hakluyt called the 'superfluous peoples', could create lives for themselves which they would be denied in Europe.⁵

By the eighteenth century, migration to the colonies and, *in extremis*, deportation had come to seem to some to be the only solution to the growing number of the dissatisfied and socially restless beings which every advanced commercial society seemed destined to create. 'Many of those that go to our Plantations,' wrote Sir Josiah Child in 1665,

> if they could not go thither, would and must go into foreign countries, though it were ten times more difficult to go thither than it is; or less, which is worse (as it hath been said), would adventure to be hanged, to prevent begging or starving, as too many have done.

Either that, he believed, or they would have 'sold themselves for soldiers to be knocked on the head'.⁶ The foundation of modern colonies was presented as a providential means of halting what would otherwise have been a crippling social malaise. Migration, thought Hakluyt, was the human equivalent of the swarming of bees.⁷ Even the fact that so many of the migrants from England had been religious dissenters could be seen as part of God's – or nature's – design. The victims of religious persecution, these 'peradventure mistaken and misled People', as Charles Davenant described them in his highly influential reflections 'On the Plantation

Trade', had been provided in America, he believed, with a 'Place of Refuge' by a 'Providence which contrives better for us than we can do for ourselves', so that 'several nations, which in time may grow considerable, have been formed out of what was here thought an excrescence in the body politic'.[8] During the Wars of Religion in France, the absence of extensive overseas colonies in which to dump potentially disruptive populations was thought to be one of the sources of the nation's persistent unrest. 'It is an established fact,' wrote Henri de la Popelinière in 1582, 'that if the Spaniard had not sent to the Indies discovered by Columbus all the rogues in the realm . . . those would have stirred up the country.'[9] They had done so in France for nearly half a century.

Some writers went so far as to suggest that migration of this kind might even turn out to be a stage in the natural growth of all human communities. Once, that is, a society had reached a point at which needs and desire had far outstripped the potential for even minimal satisfaction, then nature would provide new lands. On this account discovery and colonization became a natural impulse, much like the impulse which was supposed to have driven men from the woods on to the plains, to abandon hunting for pastoralism and pastoralism for agriculture. The marquis de Chastellux, for instance – author of a widely read account of a journey through North America in 1782 – argued in his *Discours sur les avantages ou les désavantages qui résultent pour l'Europe de la découverte de l'Amérique* (Discourse on the Advantages and Disadvantages for Europe of the Discovery of America, 1787) that nature might have provided a 'species of rapid rotation', which drew inwards towards its centre all those who are capable of satisfying their needs within their own communities, but flung away 'from its sphere of activity' all those who were not. In this way the 'metropolis is delivered both from their disquieting activities and their despair, which is as dangerous to their compatriots as it is to themselves'.[10]

God or nature could also be relied upon, where necessary, to prepare the new ground for the immigrants. 'It hath generally been observed', wrote Daniel Denton in 1670, with admiration at the symmetry of Providence, 'that where the English come to settle a Divine Hand makes way for them by removing or cutting off the Indians, whether by wars one with the other or by some raging, mortal disease.'[11]

It was, however, by no means certain that Europe did have 'superfluous peoples' it could easily afford to export in this manner. The greatness of states depended, or so it was widely believed, upon the number and the quality of their inhabitants. Sending people overseas, or allowing them to migrate of their own free will, while it might help to free the metropolis of some of its more obviously menacing human elements, also threatened to denude the nation altogether.[12] Underpopulation, as James Harrington had warned in 1656, could lead even the seemingly most powerful nations to 'lose the empire of the world'.[13] This indeed, or so it appeared, was what had happened to Spain. In pursuit of ill-conceived and uncontrolled imperial ambitions, argued the Piedmontese political theorist Giovanni Botero, Spain had sent to the Americas not the superfluous, but 'those who might be useful and even necessary, thereby losing not the excessive or corrupted blood, but that which is pure and healthy, thus draining and weakening the provinces'. A truly successful military nation, like the Romans, had to have a massive population before it could undertake extensive overseas conquests. The Spaniards had never had such resources. Even the *conquistadores* themselves, in Botero's view, had been insufficient for the task, which is why, he claimed, they had had to rely so heavily on dogs, as had the kings of 'Monopotapa' (Zimbabwe) and Finland. They had been able to defeat the Native Americans in battle, as had the French and the English, only because the enemy they faced had been techno- logically and socially so much their inferior. But whereas the conquest of primitive peoples could be managed with relatively slender resources, full-scale colonization could only ever be achieved by mass migration. If the Spaniards were to continue as they had begun, Botero concluded, 'I cannot see how they are to avoid bankruptcy, like banks that pay out great sums and have no income'.[14] As Charles Davenant remarked some hundred years later, Spain had had 'perpetual evacuations and no recruits'.[15]

Migration, which could perhaps be checked, was not the only, or even the most unsettling, danger presented by imperial expansion. Far more serious was the possibility that over-reaching might finally result in the collapse of the metropolis's own political and moral culture, the dissolution of its ethical values, even – the most alarming prospect of all – its final absorption by the very empire it had itself created. For if as each new territory entered the empire, the empire as a whole was compelled to change both its political structure and, in some never very clearly specified sense, its image of what kind of society it was, so the loss or decline of any single part would inevitably result in the decline, and subsequent loss, of the whole. 'For the laws progressively lose their impact as the government increases its range,' wrote Immanuel Kant in 1795 in very much the same vein, 'and a soulless despotism, after crushing the germs of goodness, will finally lapse into anarchy.'[16] This was the true lesson to be gained from the demise of the Roman empire. A prosperous, aggressive, virtuous and Italian (in the sense that it had been confined to the peninsula) republic, which had been among the greatest of all civil creations, had finally been transformed into a luxurious, corrupt, and predominantly German, empire. It was also, as we shall see in Chapter 6, the full force of Montesquieu's realization that you cannot practise tyranny abroad and remain free at home.

In his account of the Roman expedition to Syria in 190 BCE, Livy tells us that the Seleucid emperor Antiochus sent an ambassador, Heraclides of Byzantium, to the commander of the Roman army Publius Scipio in the hope that some peaceful agreement might be reached on the territorial limits of their two domains. Heraclides, at the end of what proved to be a fruitless debate, warned Scipio: 'Let the Romans limit their Empire to Europe, that even this was very large; that it was possible to gain it part by part more easily than to hold the whole.' Scipio was unimpressed. 'What seemed to the ambassador great incentives for conducting peace,' wrote Livy, 'seemed unimportant to the Romans.'[17]

Later European empire-builders, however, were rather more inclined than Scipio had been to listen to what the ambassador had had to say. The meeting between the Roman general and the representative of the Hellenistic Syrian empire became an enduring topos. At the moment of their encounter neither Heraclides nor Scipio could have known how prophetic the former's warning was to be. Sixteenth- and seventeenth-century Europeans, however, did. They knew, from Rome's own example, that as empires expanded they reached an optimum point, beyond which they began to over-reach their capacity both for effective administration and for effective military control. At this point, too, they began progressively to lose their ability to impart a satisfactory legal and cultural definition to ever more extended dominions. 'The interests of the State,' reasoned Pufendorf, after an exhaustive inquiry into the history of every one of them in Europe,

> may be divided into its imaginary and real interests. The former of these, which I take to consist in aiming at Universal Monarchy, and Monopoly and some other things of the like kind, can never be pursued by a Prince without infinite expense and destruction to his subjects; and beside that no solid benefit would arise therefore, if it should succeed.[18]

All empires were of necessity monsters, in Pufendorf's words, 'shapeless, huge and horrifying'.[19] The true imperial state – the 'Universal Monarchy' of Pufendorf's formulation – would, in the end, as Spain had done, be driven to ruin its domestic base in pursuit of the maintenance of its overseas dominions. The larger such conglomerates became, wrote the Spanish diplomat Diego Saavedra Fajardo, who had had direct experience of the problem, the closer they must be to their end.[20] It was, said another Spaniard, Sancho de Moncada, Professor of Sacred Scripture at the University of Toledo in 1619, a common view derived by Botero out of Livy (although he did not himself subscribe to it) that God and nature had placed a limit on all empires beyond which 'they have to return back as do the waves'.[21] The prudent ruler was one who, knowing exactly when he had reached those limits, chose to, in Machiavelli's celebrated phrase, 'maintain his state', by closing its borders. Had the Romans remained within Italy, the empire would have survived for ever. Once, however, the conquest of Syria had begun in the early second century, it had condemned itself to ultimate decline.

II

The preservation of such conglomerates required of the ruler a constant adjustment between internal and external causes. Not only did growth mean increased size, and the administrative and logistical problems which that entailed, especially in early-modern states where communications were invariably slow and poor. It also meant that as each new territory was absorbed, the shape of the whole polity necessarily changed. Empires, in particular overseas empires, could not be governed, as so many European rulers attempted to do, as if they were merely extended provinces of the metropolis. 'Territory,' as Botero phrased it in one of his best-known utterances, 'is acquired a little at a time, but it must be preserved together as a whole.' The consequences of ignoring this observation, Botero warned, could only be the final dissolution of the entire political order. By the end of the sixteenth century this distinction – and Botero's formulation of it – had become the key term in every attempt to understand what seemed to many to be the inevitable progress of all 'extended empire', from that crucial moment when the invading armies, the migrants or the ship-borne settlers left the mother country, to the final collapse of the 'mother country' itself.

In an attempt to reduce what to many seemed, on the basis of the available historical evidence, to be an inevitable inescapable progress it had become common by the mid-seventeenth century for the European colonial monarchies to attempt to set some limit to further expansion. In 1674 Jean Talon, first *intendant* of New France, argued for a southward expansion of the territory to the borders of Mexico and possibly even beyond. To this the finance minister, Jean-Baptiste Colbert, replied that such over-extension would probably lead to the loss not only of the fragile French outposts in southern Canada, but in all probability of the whole of New France. And if New France were to be lost, French prestige both in America and in Europe would be lost with it. It was, he said, far more prudent, and thus likely to prove more honourable, to preserve what one had.[22] Two years later the king himself wrote to the comte de Frontenac, Governor of New France

> You must hold to the maxim that it is far more worthwhile to occupy a smaller area, and have it well populated, than to spread out and have several feeble colonies which could easily be destroyed by all manner of accidents.[23]

By a decree of 1680 the Spanish crown placed a similar restriction on all further 'discoveries' and 'settlements' until those which it already possessed could be 'populated and settled and perpetuated in peace and concord between the two communities [the Spaniards and the Indians]'.[24] The British regarded the attempts to create new colonies west of the

Appalachians with the same misgivings, particularly since it was by no means certain that anyone would wish to develop the new territories, thus making them the potential home of yet more uncontrollable and undesirable human detritus from Europe. 'All those that are willing or able to work in England,' Oliver Goldsmith drily noted in 1761, 'can live happy, and those who are neither able nor willing would starve on the banks of the Ohio, as well as in the streets of St Giles.'[25] To enforce this policy of 'preservation', the crown in 1763 issued the Proclamation which established the western limit of the colonies at the Appalachians. A decade later the Revolutionaries would interpret this as yet another British attempt to restrict their natural right to self-determination.

The tragedy of most empires, however, was that not only did their rulers not know when to stop: in a very real sense they *could* not stop. For, as Charles III's reforming minister, Pedro Rodríguez Campomanes, explained in 1775, the 'spirit of conquest' which provides the 'principle' – to use Montesquieu's term – for all empires, necessarily blinds men to the very fact that every state has limits imposed upon its territorial expansion by nature. 'The unbridled desire to expand,' he wrote of Spain, 'obscured the imagination, so that no-one could see that this expansion was the true cause of [Spain's] ceaseless debilitation'.[26]

It was clear even to Botero that the difficulty with the distinction between 'extension' and 'preservation' was that it could provide no compelling theoretical account of how the forward movement could be stopped. Most sixteenth- and seventeenth-century theorists of empire speak as though all empires were extensions in space only. But they were, of course, also extensive in time. The question then arose: if the empire had begun as one kind of project, at what point in its history, if any, could it transform itself into another? All empires had been created, as Benjamin Constant was later to observe, on the basis of a simple vision of military virtue.[27] And because of the nature of their origins, all European empires had generated, or helped sustain, political cultures with a marked tendency towards tyranny and repression.

It is not simply that the acquisition of empire demands, in the first instance at least, only force, whereas preservation requires acts of legislation, cultural cohesion and the establishment of binding relationships between the various parts of the empire.[28] It is also the case, as Baltasar Alamos de Barrientos noted in his commentary on Tacitus, all empires are committed by their very nature to exponential growth: 'from the natural greed of men to increase their own grows as the greatness of the empire grows'.[29] Immobility, spatial *and* temporal, is no more an option for states than it is for individuals. In 1776, in an attempt to prevent the British from continuing a disastrous war in America, Josiah Tucker made much the same observation. The 'heroic spirit [and] thirst for glory,' he wrote, merely increase exponentially the range of the imperialist's 'desires and artificial wants', and by so doing drain away the 'spirit of industry' from the mother country. It was a process from which, by its very nature, no one could gain. The victors, Tucker concluded, 'in vanquishing others . . . are only preparing a more magnificent tomb for their own interment'.[30]

The 'despotic rule' of all the early-modern European monarchies, which the English regarded with unjustified moral complacency, had been established in this way precisely so as to create the conditions necessary for extended empire. They could not be expected to evolve effectively into polities concerned with preservation without also becoming some other kind of society. In a world in which the honour and glory to be gained from expansion and conquest were the only measurable political goods, the transition to any other form of society did not constitute a shift in direction by the crown. It demanded a change in the self-understanding of the entire society.

As Botero himself had recognized, although he did not attempt a solution to the problem, halting the process of expansion would require an act of reconceptualization of the structure of the whole far greater than that required each time a new territory had to be incorporated into it. Most rulers were simply not wise enough for this task, which is why Lycurgus, the wisest of them, had tried to arrest the whole process at the start.[31] Any attempt to transform the nature of the empire without some such reordering of the political culture which sustained it could only result, as the Spanish example had shown by the end of the seventeenth century, not in the preservation of what already existed, but in the loss of everything. 'Spain fell from her envied situation,' observed Arthur Young in 1772, 'as soon as this invigorating impulse [of expansion] dwindled into the prudence of guarding what was already gained instead of keeping alive for the same purpose that courage which alone won it.'[32]

Defence and consolidation required not only different political virtues to the ones which had been responsible for the creation of the empire – prudence rather than valour, wisdom instead of force – they also required different kinds of ruler, and different concepts of the nature of the states over which they ruled. It was clear, however, that few of those who had given their support to their rulers because they possessed the qualities needed to create great and extensive empires were likely to transfer their allegiance willingly to those who knew when to stop and how to pre-serve. The Romans, observed Botero, had called Fabius Maximus the shield of the Republic, and Marcellus the sword, and, wisely they had 'rated Fabius above Marcellus'. Yet in practice this honour had been purely formal for, he concluded, it is a melancholy truth that people give greater honour to conquerors, just as they 'prefer a tumbling torrent to a calm river'.[33]

As the Spanish royal secretary Pedro Fernández Navarette observed in 1621, when an empire appeared to be successful men were inclined to believe that the wealth and reputation gained by conquest were in themselves sufficient for their own preservation. This was evidently false, but even those who could see that conquest and preservation were two distinct kinds of political goods, and that of the two preservation was the more worthy, 'because it is part of prudence and wisdom, virtues superior to force', were generally compelled to concede that it was force or 'valour' which 'more readily wins the common approval'. In the Spanish case, for instance, it would be wise for the king not merely to cease all further expansion, but even to abandon some of those territories – a clear reference to the Netherlands – which he already had. 'Were it not,' Fernández Navarette sadly concluded, 'that reputation obliges her [Spain] to preserve them.' The ruin of monarchies, he knew only too well, 'usually has its origin in their own greatness'.[34]

In the eighteenth century, as all three of the European empires in America began to fall apart, the degree to which national reputation limited in this way the possibility of purely prudential action became a matter of great urgency. There would, as Josiah Tucker archly noted, be 'time enough for us to consider how far our Glory is concerned with the Recovery of nominal sovereignty over these immense and distant regions'. For in the end, the loss of America to Britain might not be so very different, in terms of its causes and the possible effects it might have on the metropolis, as the loss of the English possessions in France had been in the fifteenth century. By 1776 it was possible – or it was at least for Tucker – to see that throughout the Hundred Years War the English crown had been 'catching at the shadow and losing the substance; – sacrificing the real interests of their own Country to the empty name of foreign acquisitions'.[35] The English crown should now, in Tucker's view, take heed of this example and avoid attempting to repeat it in America.

Honour, however, once acquired could never be quite so easily abandoned as Tucker seemed to suppose. For the maintenance of 'reputation', as the Spanish writers in particular were fully and uneasily aware, was closely associated with the maintenance of power. As early as 1708, John Oldmixon had advised the crown to learn by the fate of the Portuguese. Once the Dutch had driven them out of the East Indies what he called their 'Figure' in Europe had collapsed. This was why, he argued, with an impressive degree of foresight, the Portuguese had subsequently permitted the 'citizens of Goa to sit in the assembly of the Cortes' for fear of losing to internal dissent their remaining colonies in India. If Britain's international reputation were to suffer the same fate, Britain, too, might be driven to make similar concessions. For, Oldmixon concluded, 'if it were asked why our colonies have not their representatives, who could presently give a satisfactory answer?'[36] Even Adam Smith – who in general gave little consideration to the possibility that human beings might wilfully pursue ends which were clearly to their long-term disadvantage – could see all too plainly by the beginning of 1778 that

Tho' this termination of the war [with America] might be really advantageous, it would not, in the eyes of Europe appear honourable to Great Britain; and when her empire was so much curtailed, her power and dignity would be supposed to be proportionately dismissed.[37]

This, he believed, might expose Britain to real threats, particularly from France, which had never entirely abandoned her ambition to regain Canada, lost to the British in 1763. But it was obvious that what was at stake here was not only Britain's security; it was also Britain's self-image, its full Roman, and Machiavellian, sense of its own *grandezza*.[38]

III

For all these theorists the problem of the evolution of empires presented, in its most intractable form, the perennial question of how to sustain certain kinds of cultural value over time. Martial valour, they knew, once it ceased to have anything to act upon, either turned in upon itself, as it had during the Hundred Years War and again during the Wars of Religion in France, or it declined into idleness, vanity and display. Aristotle had taught them that radical cultural change of the kind which the transition from 'expansion' to 'preservation' demanded, the effective transformation of an entire people's ethos, could only be achieved from outside. But to stand outside oneself was rarely, if ever, possible. The age of the great law-givers, who had been great precisely because they possessed this quality, had long since passed. The most that the modern monarchies of Europe could hope for would be to deflect the energies of their would-be conquerors into other analogous but non-destructive activities. And these, too, were likely to prove only a temporary diversion, or the pastimes of men who had grown finally weary of battle. Even Saavedra Fajardo, whose aim was to reconcile Tacitean reason-of-state theory with good Christian principles, and who, on the whole, deplored the idea of possibly unlimited expansion, could, in the end, offer only the somewhat improbable suggestion that the warlike properties which had created the Spanish empire might now be deflected from the possibilities of new conquests into building and science. Augustus, he claimed, had prevented 'his fiery spirit' from becoming 'covered in ashes', by reordering the calendar and calculating the movements of the planets. With the same objectives in mind, Philip II had 'raised up that great work, the Escorial, in which he succeeded in overcoming the wonders of Nature with art, and of demonstrating to the world the greatness of his mind and his piety'.[39] But, as Saavedra Fajardo knew full well, neither of these men had been able to prevent the further expansion of their states, or their ultimate decline.

The only exception to this rule seemed to be China. The Chinese emperors' decision to construct a wall around their domains, argued

Botero in what was perhaps the first such reference to an Asiatic empire in this discussion, provided evidence of the existence of a truly prudential ruler.[40] The famous, and largely illusory, 'immobility' of the Chinese empire, especially after the mid-eighteenth century, appeared to be a refutation of the widely held belief that all empires were doomed by their very nature to eventual extinction. The French physiocrat François Quesnay turned to China as evidence of how a great state might if it were only able to find adequate means to limit the ambitions of its subjects last, as China had lasted, almost for eternity. 'It is a too often generally held belief,' he wrote in *Despotisme de la Chine* in 1767,

> that government and empire can take only transitory forms, that every-thing here below is subject to continual vicissitudes, that empires have their beginning, their progress, their decadence and their end. This view prevails so generally that the irregularity of governments is attributed to the natural order.[41]

In Quesnay's vision of China, only the Chinese had understood that nature's objective was neither honour nor wealth, but prosperity, under-stood as the welfare of all the members of the society. China had managed the cultural, and hence political, transformation the European empires had all failed to achieve and, in most cases, had even failed to understand the need for. Only China had been able to trade military expansion – and the culture which had sustained it – for permanent economic growth. And China had achieved this, so Quesnay believed, by taking the example of Cincinnatus quite literally. In this massive empire, agriculture, not trade or manufacture, had replaced warfare. And in Quesnay's view, only a truly agricultural nation can 'establish fixed and lasting empire under a general invariable government, subject directly to the immutable order of the natural law'. This was why in China the farmer, not the warrior, was the exemplary man – or so at least Quesnay believed. And because the laws of nature – not those of the status hierarchies of the feudal order – were sovereign, farmers could rise to positions of power and eminence unthought of in Europe.

Like many Europeans he was fascinated with the ceremony of *K'eng-chi* in which the emperor himself turned the first furrow and planted the first seed of the season. As Diderot, who shared many of Quesnay's political, if few of his economic, views described it, this was the moment when 'the father of his people, his hand resting on the soil, demonstrates to his people the true riches of the state'.[42] Successful agriculture had made China, because of its immense size, internally self-sufficient. Unlike all European nations which had been forced to depend upon external trade for survival, China required almost none.

Quesnay's image of China, which he shared with Mercier de la Rivière and the other physiocrats, as well as with Diderot, met with fierce resistance. Few, indeed, were prepared to accept that this could ever be a plausible, or even desirable, model for any European empire to imitate. For Gabriel Bonnot de Mably, who in 1768 wrote a critique of *Despotisme de la Chine*, with the title *Doutes proposées aux philosophes économistes sur l'ordre naturel et essentiel des sociétés politiques* – as for Montesquieu before him – China was a society ruled by 'the most puerile of ceremonies', inhabited by 'the most regimented people on earth and the least capable of thought', whose famous meritocracy was selected only on the basis of an exam which never once asked the only important question: 'if that which is done, is that which should be done'. Chinese prosperity was, in his view, an illusion and Chinese stability had been purchased at the price of political and economic stagnation, and secured by a tyranny unparalleled in Europe.[43] Empires which were dynamic rather than 'static', and whose governments allowed their subjects even a minimal degree of liberty, were doomed, for these very reasons, to continue to expand until finally they collapsed, as the Assyrian, Persian, Greek, Roman and Spanish empires had done, under the sheer weight of their own size and cultural and political diversity.

The only modern, dynamic and free state which could hope to evade this melancholy process altogether would have to be a new one created *ex nihilo*, and created by men who recognized the traps into which all the older monarchies of Europe had fallen. In one sense this is what the United Netherlands had been. The Dutch refusal to engage in any war not directed towards the nation's commercial advantage, and to limit their overseas settlements to trading posts, had been responsible for the remarkable economic success of the Republic. After 1776, however, it became clear that the most powerful example was the new United States of America. This was a republic whose origins, as they were understood in Europe, would seem to preclude any ambitions for imperial expansion. Would an independent North America, asked the *philosophe*, and then Comptroller-General of Finances for France, Anne Robert Jacques Turgot in April 1776 – should such a thing come to be – despite the republican idiom in which the Revolutionaries had so far conducted their revolution, 'insinuate in their nascent republic the taste for conquest', if only to secure for themselves long-term commercial opportunities? The answer, he thought, was no. The British colonists, who had themselves been the victims of unreflective, uncontrolled attempts at imperial expansion, who had already witnessed the collapse of the Spanish monarchy in Europe and the loss of New France, were, Turgot believed, alone in a position to understand that prudence should prevent them from embarking on a course which could only lead to the corruption of the principles upon which the new republic had been founded.[44] Franklin, Jefferson and Washington would have agreed with him. It was exactly this desire not to take the road which the ancient Romans had taken which had under-pinned the elevation of Cincinnatus to the position of tutelary hero of the

Conquest ——> commerce

new Republic. The 'Empire of Liberty' which Thomas Jefferson later came to envisage as the potential role for the United States was to be an empire without conquest or expansion. It was to be a union based upon mutual interests and collaboration; a union, not of metropolis and colonies, but of 'sister republics'.[45]

IV

There was one further, and for most eighteenth-century theorists more comforting, answer to the question of how to transform expansion into preservation within existing empires. And this was to exchange conquest for commerce. As we shall see in Chapter 7, commerce came to be viewed, by Diderot and Montesquieu as much as Smith and Hume, as the only agent of a possible solution to Europe's imperial future. This, however, was Montesquieu's *doux commerce*, the source of peaceful exchange between different peoples, and the ultimate check upon the proliferation of modern global warfare. But 'sweet commerce', although it might have the power to transform international relations, would not be able to regenerate the internal structure of the European empires so as to place rational limits on their seemingly innate expansionist tendencies. This could be achieved only through the starker, more determinedly pragmatic, instrument of economics.

In one sense the growing recognition of the place of economics in the organization of states had, by the mid-seventeenth century, demonstrated to all but the most determinedly self-destructive that power could no longer be detached from what Diego Saavedra Fajardo in 1640 called 'economic prudence'.[46] By the time Saavedra Fajardo made this observation, it had already become clear that the future of empires lay not in territorial acquisition but in trade, and trade relied not upon the acquisition of territory, but upon control of the seas. 'The Sea,' declared Andrew Fletcher in 1698, 'is the only Empire which can naturally belong to us. Conquest is not our Interest.'[47] Britain's insular position – and insular political culture – made this an obvious political maxim. 'We have no ways of making ourselves considerable in the world,' wrote John Oldmixon in 1708, 'but by our fleets; and of supporting them by our trade which breeds seamen and brings in wealth to maintain them.'[48] Shipping was the means of rapid international trade, the basis of every nation's true, as opposed to its fictive, wealth. In modern empires, and with modern ships, it also provided the lines of communication which alone could hold widely dispersed political communities together. Oliver Goldsmith concluded *The Present State of the British Empire in Europe, America, Africa and Asia* of 1768 in the optimistic conviction that,

all the parts of our empire are closely connected by means of our navigation, so that we acquire strength by the facility of our conveyance of troops; and while our commerce tends to increase wealth and affluence, it also contributes to our internal strength and security.[49]

Goldsmith's optimism was to prove unfounded. But as Peter Miller has recently shown, by the 1760s the recognition that in the modern world power depended upon maritime commerce had been firmly established.[50] The English and the Dutch, because of the nature of their political regimes, may have been the first to benefit from this recognition, and, as Montesquieu pointed out, they were consequently the first to be in a position to develop 'a navy . . . superior to all other powers, who, because they do not need to use their finances for wars on land, will have more than sufficient for those at sea'.[51] By the mid-seventeenth century, other Europeans from less determinedly maritime cultures had already come to recognize the general theoretical force of such arguments. Even the Spaniards who, although they possessed a massive Atlantic fleet, regarded navies as essentially defensive, had learned from their two most loathed but increasingly successful enemies, the English and the Dutch, that, as Saavedra Fajardo phrased it, in the very mobility of ships, 'the strength of empire consists'.[52] It is not surprising that in the seventeenth century, in an atmosphere of heightened awareness of the place of sea power in the maintenance of empires, the legal and moral discussion of the relationship between states, control of the seas – most strikingly Hugo Grotius's *Mare liberum* (1608) and John Selden's *Mare clausum* (1618) – should come to replace the earlier concerns over the legitimacy of the seizure of land and goods.

It is in this context, too, that towards the end of the seventeenth century both the English and the French began to think quite seriously about what had gone wrong in Spain. Spain had the largest, most powerful, and the longest surviving of all the European empires. If only in sheer territorial extent, as even its enemies were compelled to admit, it was the true modern rival to Rome. Yet as early as the end of the sixteenth century Spain had also become, and was to remain until the final demise of its overseas empire in the 1820s, a model of what an empire should not be. In part this was a picking over by its European rivals of the bones of a culture which had, for so long, been their most hated, most intransigent and most powerful enemy. The Spaniards and the Turks came to be regarded – for instance by Montesquieu – as but two *exempla* of the same type of inflexible, illiberal and ultimately corrupting tyranny. But it was also recognized that an examination of why Spain had declined so dramatically – when its kings had once ruled over an empire on which, in Ariosto's celebrated image, the sun never set, and which had once seemed destined to continue for ever – might also provide useful models for other Europeans following, in many respects, the same political course.

Most such analysts agreed that Spain's mistake had consisted in conceiving greatness in terms of – as no less a person than the Count-Duke of Olivares had expressed it – 'religion and reputation'.[53] Both concerns had seriously hampered the ruler's capacity for effective political action, since as both were static both necessarily limited the possibilities for change over time. What Olivares and few, if any, subsequent ministers before Campomanes and Gaspar de Jovellanos in the second half of the eighteenth century had understood was that it was not the capacity either to sustain international prestige through arms, or to enforce religious conformity of one's subjects, which constituted power in the modern world. It was prosperity.[54] Spain had for long recognized the need in every state for a strong financial base. But successive Spanish monarchs had only ever seen wealth, not as a source of greatness in itself, but as something which could be translated directly into military power.

The forces which had created the Spanish monarchy in the fifteenth century, and the continuing, if erratic, resources of the American mines, had also blinded most Spaniards, and seemingly all Spanish rulers, to the fact that true prosperity could only be acquired through agriculture and trade. And trade demanded the liberality, in particular economic liberality, which, in the opinion of Sir Josiah Child and other English and Dutch writers on economics, the Spaniards and the French, because they were absolutist monarchies, were so reluctant to concede.[55] The Spaniards, in particular, had been destroyed by a tyrannical monarchy determined to place the cause of religious orthodoxy before that of the welfare of its subjects. It was, said Child in 1665, not immigration to America which had reduced Spain's population, and thus her capacity to generate wealth, it was what he called 'contending to uniformity on religion'. This had lost the Castilian crown the 'Moors' (i.e. the Moriscos) and the Jews, and it was this which had driven Philip II to sustain a prolonged war in the Netherlands, a war which had led not only to the depletion of the Castilian treasury and the 'effusion of so much Spanish blood', but had crucially lost to the crown, 'the seven provinces which we now see so prodigious rich, so full of people, while Spain is empty and poor and Flanders thin and weak'.[56] William Paterson, for his part, believed that if the Spaniards had been prepared to grant 'naturalisation, liberty of conscience and a permission to trade to the peoples of all nations on reasonable terms' they might indeed have achieved universal dominance. As it was, 'by their too eager pursuits, instead of overtaking, [they] have quite overrun the game'. The Indies, he concluded, echoing once again Justus Lipsius' famous remark, 'properly speaking . . . may be said to have conquered the Spaniards, rather than having been conquered by them'.[57]

Many Spaniards, at least by the mid-eighteenth century, could see, quite as well as their British critics, the purely economic force of such claims. 'All nations now believe,' wrote Campomanes in 1762, 'that wealth through commerce, navigation and industry is the only source of public happiness.'[58] But the Spaniards also knew, as the British were only dimly aware, that to allow foreigners to settle, or even to grant foreigners trade concessions, in the Americas would be regarded not merely as politically dangerous. It would also be, as Campomanes put it, 'morally [by which he meant culturally] impossible'. Because the Spanish *imperium* had been grounded upon the image of a single, culturally varied political order, ruled according to a codified body of laws and founded upon a unified set of religious beliefs, it had always been a closed society. Free trade meant creating a polity which was potentially open to foreign political influence, and that also meant exposing the colonies, and through the colonies metropolitan Spain itself, to the potential influence of heresy. The Spanish empire under Charles III was in many significant respects a very different society to the one it had been in the reigns of Charles V and Philip II. But even the Bourbon monarchy, even the relatively enlightened Charles III, could not entirely abandon the belief that Spain's greatness, Spain's very survival, depended upon maintaining its political and cultural integrity. Campomanes recognized, even as he attempted to find a theoretical platform for a programme of reform which would meet Child's critique, that to make the changes which the English saw as necessary for the survival of the greatness of the Spanish monarchy would have necessitated its becoming altogether another kind of society. As the Spanish ambassador Alonso Cardenas is said to have told the Earl of Clarendon in 1652, 'to ask a liberty from the inquisition and free sailing in the West Indies, was to ask his master's two eyes'.[59]

The most interesting, and theoretically the most sustained, British reflection upon the significance of the state of the Spanish empire is a curious treatise, entitled *Discorsi delle cose di Spagna* (Discourse on the Affairs of Spain), written in 1698 by Andrew Fletcher and supposedly published in Naples. (In fact it seems to have been printed in Edinburgh.) Although Fletcher begins with the claim that this is not a recipe for Universal Monarchy – 'a government which is so noxious to good customs, and so pernicious for the common happiness of mankind'[60] – the *Discorsi* offered its readers the image, horrific for any Englishman, although not, perhaps, for an often virulently anti-English Scot, of the emergence of a new and vigorous Spanish empire in the wake of the impending crisis over the Spanish succession. It was the image of an empire which had succeeded in transforming the forces of expansion into forces of preservation by diverting its vast military energies into the pursuit of economic gain. The Spanish king, wrote Fletcher, should first follow the advice which foreigners had been giving him for some time. He should introduce religious toleration so as to repopulate both Spain and the Indies from outside, population being, for Fletcher, as much as it had been for Harrington, 'the only foundation capable of supporting great empires'.[61] He should then 'lead these peoples to agriculture, to the mechanical arts and to commerce'. This would, in effect, make the American colonies self-sufficient. Following the example of the English and the Dutch, the Spanish king should then seize command of the seas, a relatively easy task were the Spanish navies not pinned down in the Americas attempting, uselessly, to prevent the contraband trade, 'and with that he might with great ease acquire and conserve the empire of the world'. If this recipe were to be followed, the old universal empire based upon conquest would finally be transformed into a new political society, similarly universal but based now upon the more enduring principles of trade and manufacture. The irony of this proposal for Fletcher was that wealth of this kind would, in its turn, make further conquests where necessary possible, so that the 'remainder of the colonies of Europe in America, Africa and India would, without difficulty, fall into his hands'.[62] Finally, he concluded, with not a little Scots relish, the English and the Dutch 'would become poor and of little importance'.[63] Fletcher's vision was deliberately overstated. It was also harnessed to what he perceived to be a solution to the threat of interminable trade wars within Europe. This (which had been set out most clearly in *An Account of a Conversation concerning the Right Regulation of Governments for the Common Good of Mankind* of 1704) rested upon the creation of a balance of power between ten roughly equal military blocks, a Europe-wide federal system, of which the new Spanish empire would form one part.[64] None of this could ever have constituted a plausible future for Europe in the first decade of the eighteenth century, and some of the details of the plan – which involved France and Spain exchanging large tracts of territory – are too hallucinatory to be intended entirely seriously. Despite his hostility to England, Fletcher's purpose might also have been less to advise the Catholic Spanish than to warn the Protestant English and Dutch. Written in Italian and supposedly published in a city closely associated with the works of Tommaso Campanella,[65] the *Discorsi* might have been intended to offer proof of the potential dangers still lurking in the apparently moribund Spanish empire. The English translator of Campanella's *Della monarchia di Spagna* (On the Monarchy of Spain) had in 1659 used that text to much the same ends.

But whatever Fletcher's purpose, the elements of his project for renewal – above all the emphasis on population expansion, commerce and technical education as means of generating economic growth – if not his understanding of its ultimate purpose, belonged to what was to become a recognizable eighteenth-century idiom. It was an idiom which was taken up in the 1770s and 1780s by the enlightened ministers of Charles III, Bernardo Ward, José del Campillo y Cossío, Campomanes and Jovellanos, in their attempts to find a solution to what Ward, the Irish emigrant who rose to become a minister of 'Commerce and Money', referred to as 'our decadence'.[66] None of these men could have read Fletcher's treatise, nor even been aware of its existence. But in most significant respects their proposals for reform echo Fletcher's principal contentions.

V

One of the most striking and most influential of these was the *Nuevo sistema de gobierno ecónomico para la América* (A New System of Economic Government for America) written by José del Campillo y Cossío, secretary to the Navy and the Indies between 1741 and 1743, which attempted to work out in detail the implications for Spain of the new economics.[67]

Spain, Campillo pointed out, was strong in territorial possessions, but in political and economic terms she was the weakest of the European imperial powers. Trade in the Americas, wrote Campillo – who was fond of medical metaphors – was like the circulation of the blood to the body politic. 'But in America where commerce is a stagnant pool' – he also mixed them – 'it produces only illness and political death.'[68] Spain earned less from her American possessions than Britain and France did from the islands of Barbados and Martinique respectively.[69] In Campillo's view the prime cause of this, to which all others could ultimately be traced, was the fact that Spanish America had been founded upon, and was still run in the interests of, the ubiquitous and malevolent 'spirit of conquest'. In the sixteenth century conquest had been both legitimate and, to a certain degree, profitable for the crown. It had been in keeping both with the martial spirit of the times and with the immediate need to subjugate large numbers of Indians.[70] But those times had passed very rapidly, and the following century which should have been a Golden Age had been instead a 'a century of disgrace and loss', as the Spaniards, rather than consolidating their hold over what they had already gained, and diversifying the colonial economy, had simply gone on conquering.[71] What the *conquistadores* and their heirs, concerned as they were to perpetuate an archaic society based upon martial valour, had failed to grasp was that true political power lay in wealth, and that wealth depends upon a political order directed towards development, not rapine. This was something which the English and the Dutch, and even belatedly the French, had understood but which, as Campillo had hinted in an earlier work, the bitter *Lo que hay de más y de menos en España* (On What There Is More and Less in Spain), few previous Spanish monarchs seemed to have been willing to believe.[72]

Like Campomanes, Campillo knew that the proposals made by Child, Fletcher and others that Spain should open its frontiers and repopulate from without, however desirable in theory, would be unthinkable to any

Spanish monarch. In his *Reflexiones sobre el comercio español a Indias* (Reflections on Spanish Commerce with the Indies) of 1762, which is very largely a reply to Child, Campomanes had argued that if the Spaniards had lost through immigration an indigenous, but in many respects 'superfluous' population, they had acquired, by the same means, a far larger one in America itself. The English, the Danes and the French had all either massacred or driven away the Native Americans in the lands on which they had settled. The Spaniards, by contrast, had transformed theirs into useful subjects. British religious tolerance, he argued, far from being a deliberate policy with predictable, and beneficial, commercial consequences as Child and others had insisted, was merely expedient, and ultimately it had proved to be politically weakening. For,

> If this nation [New England] were to have a single religion, and a zeal for propagating it among the Indians it would be very terrifying, for in this way it would be able to attract to itself all the innumerable peoples who lie between these colonies and the Pacific.[73]

Campillo followed the same track. The Native Americans were, he believed, the only possible source from which a new industrious population might be drawn. Look, he said, at the Great Khan: with less able ministers than the King of Spain and less territory, he nonetheless has a greater income, and, Campillo added, referring to the Native Americans, 'neither are his vassals so oppressed'.[74] The Americas had been laid waste by their European conquerors. What under its 'barbarian rulers' – and Campillo was not inclined to be sentimental about these – had been 'a whole and politic Nation' was now 'so many uncultivated, unpopulated, almost wholly annihilated provinces, which might yet be the richest in the world'.[75] The greatest and most valuable part of the state – its people – had been reduced to a fraction of its previous number and the few Native Americans who still remained had, through tyrannical abuse, been rendered entirely unproductive. It would have been far better, he argued, if the Spaniards had followed the example of the French in Canada and merely traded rather than slaughtering, at enormous cost to themselves, nations from whom they could have derived some economic benefit. Faced as Spain was with a land laid waste, she should now, he argued, 'pursue totally different maxims' and with these turn the corrupt and indolent subjects of the Spanish crown

> towards commerce and the cultivation of those precious fruits [of the land], create a just community among them, and by means of good economic government, reduce the Indians to a civil life, by treating them with kindness and sweetness, and thus encourage them to become industrious, and by this means make them useful vassals, and Spaniards.[76]

But, he ruefully concluded,

> we are always standing with weapons in our hands and the King spends millions in order to sustain an implacable hatred against peoples who, if treated which gentleness and friendship, would render us infinite services.[77]

What both Campillo and Campomanes recognized was that modernizing the Spanish empire was not, as the British supposed, merely a question of economic adjustment. With the end of the War of Succession Spain had finally lost her European possessions, and with them she had lost, too, the basis of her ideological claims to universalism. By the second half of the eighteenth century the need to reform the empire had become far more than the simple quest for an economically productive and politically compliant association of dominions. It had become, as Franco Venturi has rightly observed, a

> quest for a more general need, an insistent search appearing under different forms, for the mission of Spanish life of the past and the future. ... The emphasis was now on revival and on an effort to penetrate more deeply into the nature and history of the nation. The crisis of reform was developing into a crisis of identity.[78]

Like most of her European critics, Campomanes and Campillo believed that Spain was trapped in a mental condition of something we, if not they, might legitimately describe as pre-modernity. Campomanes, in particular, imagined for Castile, much as a number of seventeenth- and eighteenth-century writers had for England,[79] an 'ancient constitution' based upon the liberties (the *fueros*) which the representative assemblies of Castile had supposedly enjoyed before the accession of Charles V. With the defeat of the *comuneros* – the last sustained popular revolt against the monarchy in early-modern Castile – in 1521 these liberties had finally been extinguished. For the enlightened ministers of a Bourbon monarch, the 300 years of Habsburg – *Austrian*, as it then came to be called – rule, and with it the whole dismal *conquistador* inheritance, could be represented as a period of deviance from the true path of Castilian history. This myth was to be the dominant factor in the drafting of the so-called *Sacred Codex* after the Napoleonic invasion in 1813, a crucial moment in the emergence of Spanish liberalism, and it underpinned much of the language of the early independence movements.[80]

The most simple, most effective, means to reverse the deleterious consequences of two centuries of misguided social and economic policies was, argued Campomanes, to pursue the free-trade policies which Sir Josiah Child had advocated in his *A New Discourse on Trade* of 1665. 'All nations believe,' he wrote in his *Reflexiones sobre el comercio español a Indias*, that wealth by means of commerce, navigation and industry is the sole source of public happiness. Today's wars are more concerned with gaining control over trade with the colonies, than they are with dominium.[81]

Although almost a century old by the time he came to reflect on them, Child's observations on the plight of the Spanish 'plantations' were in Campomanes's opinion, together with Montesquieu's remarks in Book XXI of *De l'Esprit des lois*, the most perceptive ever written on the state of Spanish America,[82] and they prompted him into what was, in effect, a far-reaching reconceptualization of the empire. Child had argued for the removal of all the restrictions currently imposed upon the colonies. This, he believed, would not only put an end to the crippling contraband trade, it would also make the colonies themselves more productive as they sought to produce a wider range of goods for hugely increased markets. Above all, it would encourage the colonists to turn away from the simple production of bullion to agriculture which, for Child as for most contemporary political economists, constituted the true source of wealth in all colonial societies. From this process both the colonies and the metropolis would necessarily benefit.

Campomanes, more than any of his contemporaries, could see most clearly the force of these arguments. As he observed with some wonder, New England alone 'has more sailings than the whole Kingdom of Spain and all its vast dominions'.[83] But although it was evidently desirable that Spanish America should emulate British America's astonishing economic output, Campomanes also knew that for all Spaniards there was a seemingly insurmountable obstacle to following Child's advice – quite apart from what, as we have seen, he described as the 'moral' problems involved in transforming a closed society into an open one. The most widely accepted account of the decline of the Spanish economy in the late sixteenth century had been based upon the altogether plausible assumption that an over-dependence upon bullion had led to a decline in manufacturing industries, and consequently to an over-dependence upon foreign goods, foreign supplies and, because of spiralling inflation, foreign bankers. This was an economy which, if never quite so dismal as the portrait Jovellanos, Campomanes himself and others were later to paint of it, was very largely dependent upon staples. It exported agricultural produce and vast quantities of bullion, in exchange for foreign manufactured goods. Furthermore, unlike some staple-dependent economies it produced few, if any, of what Albert Hirschman has called backward and forward linkages.[84] Throughout much of the sixteenth and seventeenth centuries, even the sacks in which Merino wool, one of the mainstays of the Castilian economy, was exported were imported. By the early eighteenth century the policy of restricted trading regulations and tight import controls, which goes under the name of mercantilism, seemed to provide the theoretical possibility of some kind of check on the ceaseless haemorrhage of national resources. To some extent these policies also worked. Public revenue which had stood at a mere 5 million pesos in 1700 had already risen to 18 million pesos by the 1750s, and continued to rise throughout the 1770s and 1780s. To have abandoned this in favour of the *laissez-faire* economic principles which modern, and predominantly French, economic theory demanded seemed to most Spaniards, attracted though they were by the intellectual brilliance of the new economics, merely to be returning to the deregulation and the chaos of the reign of Charles V.

In an attempt to find a solution to this problem Campomanes sought to redescribe the old distinction between the 'Kingdoms of the Indies' and the various dominions within Europe itself. He is one of the first to speak consistently of the American 'colonies', and to treat them not as a distinct although dependent part of Castile, but as communities comparable with the colonies which France and Britain had established in North America, communities which had been created by, and existed very largely in the commercial interests of, the mother country. Campomanes's project for economic regeneration demanded a redeployment of the full economic and political resources of the entire Spanish monarchy. For the mistake, as he understood it, which the Castilian crown had made had not been, as Child had argued, to exclude foreigners, if by foreigners what was meant was those who lived outside the Spanish monarchy. It had, instead, been to limit access to the American trade to Castilians. The monarchy as a whole constituted a vast internal market, and trade should be free to all those who lived within it. Yet in 1596 Philip II had denied the Portuguese (who were at that time subjects of the Castilian crown) any share in the American trade, and in 1634 Philip IV had prevented them from trading in the Philippines.[85] The same limitations had been applied to Flemings, Italians and some Aragonese. The solution, therefore, was to open the American markets to all the subjects of the monarchy and, crucially, to deregulate the trade between them. Such a scheme would not only result in a massive extension of the commercial potential of the monarchy; it would also bring its widely separated, and increasingly dissatisfied, peoples closer together. In this respect, Campomanes's project can be seen as a contribution to the wider political and cultural ambitions of Charles III and Charles IV, to give a new sense of 'union' and 'equality' to the relationship between the various parts of their empire.[86]

The introduction of a free-trade zone which was still confined within the limits of the old Spanish *imperium* was also to be linked to a policy of educational restructuring. Spaniards, all Spaniards, had, in Campomanes's view, to be taught how to be economic beings. This was the aim behind his *Discurso sobre la educación popular* (Discourse on Popular Education) of 1775 and the basis for the suggestions laid out in Jovellanos's *Informe sobre la ley agraria* (Report on the Agrarian Law) of 1793. Campomanes was confident that with the establishment of free trade between all the various far-flung regions of the Spanish empire, the ethos of the commercial society would slowly come to replace the older order of domination.

Campomanes, Jovellanos, Campillo and Ward never fully succeeded in persuading their monarch of the need for economic liberalism. But they did succeed in transforming the political and cultural image of the monarchy itself. The 'Kingdoms of the Indies' were replaced by 'the Ultramarine provinces'. Gone was any notion of a trans-Atlantic community, of a *ius commune* embodied in the legal person of the king. Indeed, the king's advisers, most notably Campomanes and Jovellanos, edged their ruler as close as they dared to the image of a constitutional monarch, of the ruler as magistrate not judge, of one bound by the laws he himself had ratified. And for the first time the Spanish Americans began to be defined in terms which made them clearly part of a periphery.

In urging this transformation, Ward and Campillo, Campomanes and Jovellanos were speaking not just in a clearly modern idiom. They were also speaking in a recognizably European one. If the three European overseas empires had begun in the sixteenth and early seventeenth centuries as different kinds of society with different structures, objectives and ideological matrixes, by the end of the eighteenth century they had converged upon a common set of theoretical concerns. These were overwhelmingly concerned with undoing the deleterious consequences of the 'spirit of conquest' and the military ethos of glory, Machiavellian *grandezza* and, its ecclesiastical counterpart, evangelization and doctrinal orthodoxy. What all of this came to was the quest for an ideology, driven in part by the new languages of moral philosophy and political economy, of a rational, but also humanly rich calculation of the benefits to be gained from empire for all those involved, for the metropolis as for colonies, for the colonized as for the colonizers. Inevitably, this demanded the evolution of a far more complex understanding of the relationship between the colonial societies which had developed in the Americas and their respective 'mother countries'. It is this relationship between colony and metropolis which we must now consider.

CHAPTER FIVE

Metropolis and Colony

Le peuple qui colonise le plus est le premier peuple; s'il ne l'est aujourd'hui, il le sera demain.

Paul Leroy-Beaulieu,
De la colonisation chez les peuples modernes (1874)

I

'Empire,' wrote Talleyrand in 1797, is an art, 'the art of putting men in their place'. It was, he said, 'perhaps the first among the sciences of government', yet surprisingly no one had yet produced a satisfactory account of how it was to be done.[1]

Talleyrand's observation is a measure of the degree to which the whole understanding of the nature of the European overseas empires had shifted since their first creation. During much of the sixteenth and seventeenth centuries, discussions of empire had been conducted in terms of legitimacy, and this meant very largely in the language of rights, principally of the rights to *dominia* through either war or occupation. The conquest and subsequent settlement of America had been described by all three European powers in terms of a universal project, a project which exported Christianity, and the necessary European civilization that accompanied it, to the 'barbarian' regions of the world. In return the mother countries had been granted political and economic control over the peoples and lands of the territories they had occupied.

Talleyrand was not concerned with these things. For him, empire was not a source of honour, or ecclesiastical glory, or mineral wealth, but of commercial and agricultural profit. The French, he argued, should now abandon their remaining colonies in the Caribbean and create new ones after (what he supposed to be) the English model in Bengal, colonies, that is, which were semi-autonomous states and which, crucially, did not involve, as the colonies in the Americas had done, the forced migration of millions of people.[2] Only substantial political independence could ensure the kind of economic growth which, in the end, would benefit both colony and metropolis alike. The French crown, however, had always thought of its imperial ventures in Roman rather than Greek terms. This, in Talleyrand's view, had been its fatal error. For whereas the colonies established by the Greeks, which had been autonomous states of precisely the kind which the British now had in India, had flourished, the Romans whose empire had been based on conquest had, in the end, 'achieved almost nothing'.[3]

Most contemporary British theorists of empire would have agreed. By 1657, English writers within a broadly republican tradition were already claiming – as David Armitage has recently shown – that the English empire was a protectorate of several interests rather than a universal state. The English crown, as James Harrington expressed it – borrowing Cicero's description of the empire of the late Roman Republic – exercised not *imperium* over its various dependencies, but *patrocinium* (protectorate).[4] But the most compelling way of capturing the difference the British perceived between their empire and that of the Spanish, and in some measure the French, was, as Talleyrand had done, in terms of the distinction between the empires of Greece and Rome.

As we saw in Chapter 1, all three senses of the term *imperium* – as limited and independent or 'perfect' rule, as a territory embracing more than one political community, and as the absolute sovereignty of a single individual – derived directly from the discursive practices of the Roman, Athenian and Macedonian empires. The Roman and the Greek empires had, however, been very different kinds of political entity. For the Athenians, unlike the Romans, had established colonies which had always been largely independent partners of the metropolis – children, as Adam Smith described them, but emancipated children.[5] Spain, quite obviously, and France, less certainly, were the true heirs to Rome. Britain's empire, by contrast, as Andrew Fletcher argued in 1704, more closely resembled the Achaean League,[6] a model which was later applied by James Madison and James Wilson to their proposals for a federal structure for the United States.[7] In the terms dictated by this image, the English colonies had been private ventures, unlike both the French and the Spanish settlements which had been very largely engineered by the state. So it could be argued that, like the Greek colonies before them, the British settlements in the New World had been constituted from the beginning as semi-independent political, and possibly even cultural, communities. Each was, in reality, what Kant would later describe as a *civitas hybrida*.[8]

The sharpness of this distinction between a liberal British and despotic French and Spanish metropolitan governments, although frequently endorsed by the French and the Spaniards themselves, fails, perhaps, to capture all the complexities of the relationship between the Spanish and French crowns and their subjects in America. Canada had originally been settled by a private company (albeit one created by a minister of the crown) and although most of the successful Spanish *conquistadores* eventually acquired royal administrative offices, most began as private agents. 'Their Majesties,' noted the official historian of the Indies, Gonzalo Fernández de Oviedo, 'hardly ever contributed to these ventures from either their estates or their purse, but offered only paper and encouraging words.'[9] One important region, what is now Venezuela, was even colonized in the early 1530s by a company financed by a German family, the Welsers. Over time, however, it became clear that these beginnings were of little lasting historical significance. Once the full potential of the Americas, in both mineral and human terms, had been realized, they were fully incorporated into the Spanish monarchy, in ways which the British colonies never were. In French North America and the Caribbean, the same early dependence upon private investment and the corresponding independence from crown, and ecclesiastical, control lasted only a short time, and when it went, all trace of its former political influence went with it. Like the Spanish colonies, the French became, in legal fact, in how they were administered and conceived by both those who lived in them and those who ruled over them, an integral part of the larger French monarchy. In general, the British were right to assume that theirs were the only overseas settlements to have maintained the traditions of autonomy and private venture with which they had begun.

For the British the distinction between their societies in America, and those created by the Catholic monarchs of Spain and France, remained a crucial one in the development of their own cultural and ultimately political identity. It lies at the base of North American exceptionalism, powerfully influenced the concept of 'Manifest Destiny', and still determines North American attitudes, and frequently North American policies, towards the Spanish- and Portuguese-speaking republics in the south. In their historiography, the original English settlers had not only been private persons acting of their own volition and employing their own capital. They had also, because of this, gone to America not to conquer, as their neighbours had; they had gone to 'plant' and they had 'improved'.[10] They had not gone to perpetuate a European society already corrupted by the absolutist (and 'continental') ambitions of the Stuart monarchy; they had gone to build a new, more righteous, and ultimately republican one. Unlike the Spanish and French colonies, which were merely Spain and France transplanted, the British settlements had been Lockean foundations created, quite literally, out of the state of nature.

The Virginian Richard Bland – Jefferson's 'most learned and logical man, profound in constitutional law' – was insistent upon this point. 'When subjects are deprived of their civil rights, or are dissatisfied with the place they hold in the community,' he wrote in 1766,

> they have a natural right to quit the society of which they are members, and to retire into another country. Now when men exercise this right of withdrawing themselves from their country, they recover their natural freedom and independence; the jurisdiction and sovereignty of the states

they have quitted ceases; and if they unite, and by common consent take possession of a new country and form themselves into a political society, they become a sovereign state, independent of the state from which they separated.[11]

Like Jefferson before him – who had used a version of the same argument[12] – Bland was arguing against the crown's right to tax the colonies without true representation in Parliament. The metropolitan power had no authority to limit the freedoms that the originators of these societies had acquired by exercising their right of exit. 'Do those who embark as freemen in Great Britain, disembark slaves in America?' James Wilson had asked in 1774:

Are those who fled from the oppression of regal and ministerial tyranny, now reduced to a state of vassalage to those who, then, equally felt the same oppression? Whence proceeds the fatal change? Is this the return made us for leaving our friends and our country – for braving the danger of the deep – for planting a wilderness, inhabited only by savage men and savage beasts – for extending the dominion of the British crown – for increasing the trade of British merchants – for augmenting the rents of British landlords – for heightening the wages of the British artificers? Britons should blush to make such a claim. Americans would blush to own it.[13]

The understanding of the political origins of British America in a voluntary act of independence could, however, easily be detached from the single issue of taxation.[14] The English, wrote the marquis de Mirabeau in 1758, had been 'the most enlightened of the peoples of Europe in their conduct in the New World'. Although he thought that their conflicting love of liberty and their passion for luxury would finally destroy them, they alone, he recognized, had built their colonies upon 'the laws of Republics, Councils and Parliaments'.[15] Because of this, they alone could hope to survive the fate of all other unreformed empires of the Old World: corruption and ultimate decline. (It was no fault of Mirabeau that he was unable to foresee that it was precisely what Adam Smith described as the 'republican manners' of the English colonists which was to precipitate the final collapse of the empire in America.[16])

Britain had for long had been seen in this way as the paradigmatic modern state: commercial, calculating, and unperturbed by long-term cultural or religious concerns. It had, at least in the eyes of its (predominantly French) admirers, created an empire which was truly like the Achaean League of Fletcher's imagination. All of this, however, seemed to have changed with Britain's victory, and the seizure of Canada at the end of the Seven Years

War in 1763. Britain's increasing intransigence towards its colonies, the insistence that they should contribute more in taxes, and be bound more strictly by the dictates of the central government, without true parliamentary representation, constituted an attempt to exercise something far more like the 'despotic' administration which the Spanish and the French crowns supposedly exercised over their colonies. How, wrote Turgot to the English radical Richard Price in March 1778, could a nation which had achieved so much in the natural sciences – among which he included 'celle du bonheur publique' – have conceived this 'absurd project of subjugating America'?[17] It was, or at least it seemed to be from the far side of the Atlantic (and of the Channel), an attempt, however ill-organized, and ill-conceived in practice, to create something which could plausibly be described as a 'British Empire' in America. Yet as John Adams, later the second President of the United States, had pointed out in 1755, such a concept existed nowhere in either natural or common law. It belonged, he said, solely to 'the language of newspapers and political pamphlets'. The phrase 'the imperial crown of great Britain' had, he insisted, been

> introduced in allusion to the Roman Empire, and intended to insinuate that the prerogative of the imperial crown of England was, like that of the Roman emperor, after the maxim was established, *quod principi placuit legis habet vigorem*, and so far from including the two houses of parliament in the idea of the imperial crown, it was intended to insinuate that the crown was absolute, and had no need of lords or commons to make or dispense with laws.[18]

Britain and its dominions constituted, as Harrington and Fletcher had recognized, not an 'empire' in any generally accepted use of that term, but something far closer to a confederacy of states. The American colonies were not, and never had been, 'part of the realm of England' – as the Spanish, and arguably the French, clearly were; but 'separate and distinct dominions'. As an anonymous contributor to the *Pennsylvania Journal* in March 1766 expressed it:

> In a confederacy of States independent of each other yet united under one head, such as I conceive the British empire at present to be, all the power of legislation may subsist full and complete in each part, and the respective legislatures be absolutely independent of each other.[19]

The consequence of attributing Lockean origins to the colonies was that since they had begun in the state of nature there could be no prior authority among the colonists. This meant either that they were free to establish whatever kind of society – or none at all – they chose, or that authority was vested in the person who had granted them the right to leave the political community into which they had been born. This had been the *person* of the king. It was he who had first granted the colonists, in Bland's words, 'licence to remove under the new country and to settle therein' and it was to the monarch, not to Parliament, that the colonists were therefore subject.[20] The first settlers, added James Wilson pursuing the same line of argument in 1774,

> took possession of the country in the *King's* name: they treated and made war with the Indians by *his* authority; they held the lands under *his* grants and paid *him* the rents reserved upon them: they established governments under the sanction of *his* prerogative, or by virtue of *his* charters.[21]

For these 'English-Americans' the colonies were 'independent nations' or, as some argued, 'distinct states independent of each other, but connected together under the same sovereign'.[22] If this were the case then, as Sir Francis Barnard, Governor of Massachusetts Bay had recognized in 1774 – employing the same Aristotelian and Roman legal terminology the Spaniards had used – all the British colonies in the Americas constituted 'perfect states'.[23]

Barnard's final definition of the status of the British American colonies is identical to the one which Francisco de Vitoria had used in 1539 to describe the relationship between Castile, Aragon, and the Duchy of Milan, and Francisco Suárez employed some years later to characterize that between the crowns of Castile and Portugal.[24] For all of these, too, were *perfectae communitates*, under the universal jurisdiction of a single prince, a condition which granted them unlimited rights to self-determination, except the right to modify the nature of their constitution. Similarly for Barnard, the claim that the British 'dominions' in America were in this way 'perfect' suggested that although they were not, as were the various states which went to make up the Spanish empire, formally kingdoms, their relationship to the mother country might nevertheless be analogous to that of Hanover to the crown of England. This last point was also made by the author of a tract entitled *Candid Observations* which appeared in 1765. The Hanoverians, he pointed out, 'continued to be governed by their own laws under the general superintendence and control of the supreme Magistrate in England and his lawful Deputies and Offices abroad', so 'with respect to the Parliament, and the Power of imposing Taxes', should 'all the Dominions of the Prince . . . be on one and the same footing'.[25] For Vitoria the question had been the right of the princes of such states to wage war without the consent of the 'supreme sovereign'; for Barnard and the author of *Candid Observations* the question was, again, the crucial one of taxation without representation. In both cases what was involved was what had once been called the 'marks' of sovereignty, and both Vitoria and Barnard recognized that in claiming that the rulers of such states possessed the right to declare war or to tax, they were, in fact, granting them complete political autonomy. As Jared Ingersoll commented in 1765, remove the right of taxation from Britain 'and then America is at once a Kingdom of Itself'.[26]

I am not, of course, suggesting any textual or formal relationship between Vitoria and Barnard. Both were drawing on the same Aristotelian, and subsequently Roman legal, vocabulary; both for very different reasons wished to come to precisely the same conclusions. The significance of the similarity of their arguments is rather that it demonstrates the degree to which, in attempting to create a fully centralized empire after 1763, the British crown had driven the 'English-Americans' to redescribe their relationship with the metropolis in the terms in which the Castilians before 1700 had seen their relationship, not with the Americas but with the European states of the empire.

It also serves to focus attention on one crucial aspect of that relationship to which the claims of both Vitoria and Barnard make implicit appeal: its place in a broader legal framework. For the implications of the arguments employed by Barnard, Wilson and others were that if it was the king alone who had granted the first colonists their right to settle, then it was as feudal vassals, not free citizens, that they had come to America. And if this were the case then their relationship to the crown was very similar to both the French and the Spanish.

In legal practice, however, the terms under which the land had been granted in America varied considerably. Despite the persistent British characterization of the Spanish settlement as 'feudal', the Castilian crown created no fiefs in any of its overseas possessions. The notorious *encomienda*, by which the colonists held title to the former territories of Native Americans, were, as we saw in Chapter 3, not grants of lands, but of labour. They carried no formal property rights, and certainly did not entail feudal relationships between the colonizer and the colonized. Only France allowed for large-scale feudatories in its overseas empire. And even these, although they employed the language of feudal obligation, were, in effect, simple land grants. They did not even confer nobility, and although in 1633 most of the seigneuries were in fact in the hands of nobles, by 1763 most were held by commoners.[27] Both France and Spain, however, allowed from the beginning for the possibility of a Creole aristocracy. Locke and Shaftesbury's constitution for Carolina envisaged the establishment of a weird assortment of indigenous titles: barons, landgraves and cassiques. But nothing came of these.[28] As Edmund and William Burke noted in 1757, although 'there is scarce any form of government known that does not prevail in some of our plantations . . . nothing like a pure hereditary aristocracy has ever appeared in any one of them'.[29] One reason why this proved to be so was that, in a sense which the American Revolutionaries were to exploit for their own ends, the English colonies had, in one quite specific way, been feudal foundations, for all the lands in America had originally been granted in 'free and common socage' as of the manor of East Greenwich in Kent.[30] They were, that is, legally part of the royal demesne, and no part of the *terra regis* could be conceived except as constitutively belonging to a royal manor in England. Land in Ireland, for instance, was held as of Carregrotian, or of Trim or of Limerick or of the Castle of Dublin, and when Charles II made over Bombay to the East India Company this, too, was granted in 'free and common socage' of the manor of East Greenwich.[31] Because of this purely legal fiction it was also possible to claim, in matters of taxation and representation, that the colonies were indistinguishable from any English county. Yet if this were so then the colonists should have enjoyed *all* the rights enjoyed by the English. 'What,' asked Benjamin Franklin sarcastically, 'have these inhabitants of East Greenwich in Kent done, that they, more than any other inhabitants of Kent, should be curbed in their manufactures and commerce?'[32]

The fiction that 'New England lies within England' was one reason why those who were eager to assert this semi-feudal dependence of the colony upon the king, rather than Parliament, were similarly eager to avoid the claim that the colonists had merely purchased their lands from the Native Americans. For if it could be demonstrated that the colonists had, in effect, acquired their lands as any European might have done in Europe, then they could hardly claim to hold it independently of Parliament.[33] This is why so seemingly unlikely a person as Thomas Jefferson was prepared to argue that the 'English-Americans' were entitled to self-determination by rights of conquest:

> Their blood was spilt in acquiring land for their settlement; and their fortunes expended in making that settlement effectual; for themselves they fought, for themselves they conquered, and for themselves alone they have the right to hold[34]

As William Strahan, the translator and commentator on Jean Domat's *Les Loix civiles dans leur ordre naturel*, pointed out in 1722, if the American colonies were a part of the royal demesne, this suggested that there was, indeed,

> a very great affinity between them [the English colonies] and the colonies of the Spaniards and other nations, who have made settlements among the Indians of these parts. For the grants made by our King and tracts of land in that country for the planting of colonies and making settlements therein, appear to have been made in imitation of the grants made by the Kings of Spain to the proprietors of lands in the Spanish colonies, upon the very same conditions and in consideration of the same services to be performed by the grantees. So that the government of the Spanish colonies and the right of the proprietors of the lands therein, depending chiefly on the rule of the civil and feudal law, as may be seen by the learned treatise of Solórzano, *De Indiarum iure*, the

knowledge of the said laws must be of service likewise for determining any controversy that may arise touching duties and forfeiture of the property and lands in our English colonies.[35]

James Otis dismissed this claim with the comment that it was 'humbly to be hoped that the British colonists do not hold their lands as well as their liberties by so slippery a tenure as do the Spaniards and the French'.[36]

Strahan's arguments, however, proved to be more uncomfortable than Otis's remark might suggest.[37] The full force of Locke's argument – that no man required anyone's authority to leave civil society if he so wished – was that, if the colonies had indeed been Lockean foundations, then the colonists owed allegiance to no one in whom they had not voluntarily placed their trust. Before the final Declaration of Independence, however, few were prepared to go that far. Despite their use of Locke, most of the more influential colonists were trained lawyers and were generally too respectful of the English common law to be wholly satisfied with arguments based entirely upon abstract principles taken from the law of nature. The colonists might, as John Adams and others insisted, derive their laws 'not from parliament not from common law, but from the law of nature and the compact made with the king in our charters'. But they were equally clear that those charters had been made, in the first instance, *in iure feodali* and rested on the king's common law right to prevent his subjects leaving his kingdom if he so chose: the right of *ne exeat regno*.[38]

As Strahan had apparently noticed, this modified form of the Lockean argument, which retained allegiance to a distant king, came very close in legal terms to being a form of feudal dependency. For if the king had been the sole source of authority for the original foundation, and if legitimacy was to be sought in the historical origins of the colony, then nothing lay between the settlers and the 'frank good will' of the monarch. Strahan's reading of Domat was made even more troublesome by the fact that it was the supposedly feudal origins of the colonies which for many in Britain constituted a powerful component of their claims against the American colonists during the Stamp Act crisis.

Otis's reply to this was that not only had the Spanish and French colonies been established on the basis of (in the Spanish case) sovereignty granted by a Papacy which had 'for ages usurped the most abominable power over princes'; they had also, and consistently, been reliant upon a body of enacted law handed down to them from their respective monarchies. The British colonies in America, by contrast, whatever their nominal dependence on the manor of East Greenwich, had always drafted their own legislation since nearly every colonial charter included the 'liberty of enacting among themselves such laws as they think convenient'[39] – something which could plausibly be interpreted as negating whatever residue of feudal obligation to the English king might have survived the original foundation of the colony. 'The colonies have in reality,' observed John Campbell in 1755, 'in many cases acted as if they thought themselves so many independent states, under their respective charters, rather than as provinces of the same empire.'[40]

The legislative autonomy of the British colonies in America was, indeed, in marked contrast to the close juridical relationships which existed between metropolitan France and Spain and their colonies until the late eighteenth century. The Locke–Shaftesbury constitution for Carolina – although that is a charter for a state which would have looked very unlike contemporary Britain – is the nearest thing to a body of law framed in the metropolis to attempt to determine the structure of the colonial society. And it was never implemented.

In 1799 James Madison, opposing an attempt to create a legal order which would bind all the former colonies within the new United States, pointed out that

> whether it be understood that the original colonists brought the law with them, or made it their law by adoption, it is equally certain that it was the separate law of each colony within its respective limits, and was unknown to them as a law pervading and operating through the whole as one society.

Since, he concluded, there was no common law in any two colonies, 'no common legislature by which a common will could be expressed in the form of law', there could be no possible law which could act as the expression of the entire empire, so that:

> The assertion of Great Britain of a power to make laws for the other members of the empire *in all cases whatsoever*, ended in the discovery that she had a right to make laws for them *in no cases whatsoever*.[41]

On this account, and it was widely shared, the British empire had, as John Adams had claimed, no *legal* existence whatsoever. For the power which each colony possessed to draft its own legislation also determined the nature of the association it enjoyed with the metropolis. 'Different communities forming an empire,' explained Richard Price in 1776, 'have no connexions which produce a necessary reciprocation of interest between them.' And since 'all laws are particular provisions or regulations established by common consent, for gaining protection and safety', they could not, by definition, be drafted and imposed by anyone except their intended beneficiaries. To the question: 'Are there not causes by which one state may acquire a rightful authority over another, though not consolidated by any adequate representation?' he replied unequivocally that 'there are no such causes'.[42] A man who is constrained to live by the laws of others is nothing other than a slave. 'As far,' said Price, as in any instance, the operation of any cause comes in to restrain the power of self-government, so far slavery is introduced. Nor do I think that a preciser idea than this of liberty and slavery can be formed.[43]

On this account what bound the English-Americans to Britain was not a body of law, nor a set of obligations, feudal or otherwise, but rather a common loyalty to a single sovereign.[44] For if the British colonists, as all these arguments indicated, were truly autonomous legal agents, holding their rights of property from their own actions via an initial, but now historically remote, grant from the king, if the relationship between the colonies – such as it was – and each colony's relationship to the metropolitan power was via a purely personal debt to a common sovereign, then as James Otis claimed in 1764, the proper way to understand the relationship between colony and metropolis was as Thucydides and Grotius had understood it, as one based not on the concept of the colonists' legal, much less fiscal obligations, but on their '*reverence* to the city whence they derived their origins'.[45] Reverence, of course, required of the sovereign a high degree of respect. The indignation that characterizes so much of the Revolutionary writing in British America is fired by a sense that the Stamp Acts, and any attempt to deny the colonists their legislative independence, their right to true, not virtual representation, violated their image of the 'British empire' as a modern version of the Achaean League, a collectivity of free states bound together by the will of all its members. It violated that deep community sense that all the subjects of His Majesty, no matter what the nature and origin of their subjection, were, despite the feudal language in which these relationships were still being expressed even in the late eighteenth century, free and equal beings.

II

The legal structures of both the Spanish and the French empires were, in most significant respects, quite unlike the British. The French monarchs, from Henri IV, had conceived of the legal status of their colonies as, to some degree, analogous to those of Spain. Canada had, from the beginning, however, been settled on the basis of feudatories, something which the Spanish crown had explicitly and fiercely avoided, and in administrative practice the relatively small and isolated settlements of which the colony was composed were governed largely by continued negotiation between ministers of the crown and the settlers.[46] All the French overseas colonies, although they always preserved that name, in legal fact and frequently in how they were treated by the metropolis, were, as the lawyer Paul-Ulrich Dubuisson declared in 1785, 'Provinces of the Kingdom of France, as are Normandy, Brittany and Guyenne'.[47] The integration of all the residents of the colonies into the crown of France, and their governance according to a body of local administrative law called the *coutume de Paris* – comparable in its long-term consequences to the incorporation of the Americas into the crown of Castile – determined the ideological shape of the empire until the collapse of the monarchy itself.[48] And like the supposed equality accorded to all members of the Spanish *imperium*, it was to return to haunt the administration in its declining years. 'The people of Saint Domingue,' a group of *colons* informed the National Assembly in 1792, 'form part of the French people constituted by the sovereignty of the French empire.' As such, they pointed out, fearful of the influence already being exerted on the Assembly by the abolitionists, the colonies were inalienable since they were no more the *property* of the National Assembly than they were 'the property of France, nor of the crown, nor can they be ceded to any power whatsoever'.[49]

In Spain the monarchy had always been far more closely bound by Roman Law conceptions of empire than either of its European competitors. Francisco de Vitoria and Sir Francis Barnard had both settled on the Aristotelian notion of the *perfecta communitas* to describe the status of the various parts of their respective empires. But whereas for Barnard the 'supreme sovereign' who bound the British empire together was that convenient legal fiction, the 'King in Parliament', for Vitoria, he was the Holy Roman Emperor. Whereas Barnard was thinking in terms of local conventions between individual monarchies governed by the law of nations, the *ius gentium*, Vitoria was conscious, even if he did not endorse it, of the wider concept of the empire as the embodiment of a *ius*, or, in the language of the Roman Law which had been adopted by the medieval Germanic empire, a *ius publicum*. In contrast, to the British empire, the Spanish monarchy constituted a single legislative body from the Netherlands to Chile. 'Your majesty,' wrote the playwright Lopé de Vega, echoing a common contemporary encomium, 'has an empire of undivided jurisdiction from this to the far hemisphere.'[50] Under the aegis of this empire, the legislation, and the institutions which protected the subjects of the king in Castile, also protected them in Peru. The populations of Spanish America enjoyed the same 'liberties, immunities, privileges and free customs within their provinces' – to hijack some of the terms of the Maryland Assembly of 1648[51] – as anyone born in Castile. The crucial difference here between Spanish and British America was that in the 'Kingdoms of the Indies', as in the kingdoms of the peninsula, those privileges were concessions, not rights.[52] And they had been enacted in Europe, not America.

Of the three European colonial powers, Spain, because it was the only European power to rule over a homogeneous empire with – at least in intention – a single identity, was also the only power to draft an extensive body of legislation for the colonies which at the same time sought to define their relationship with the metropolis: the *Nueva Recopilación de leyes de los reynos de las Indias* promulgated in 1680.[53] As Juan de Solórzano y Pereira, who was responsible for the compilation of the new code, had argued in 1629, distant empires could only survive either on the basis of benign local despots – a course which, as he pointed out, Cicero had considered and rejected – or on the basis of a rigid and secure code of law. The Roman emperors had understood this, which is why he claimed that the decrees (*cédulas*) of the Castilian kings were to be regarded as the 'prescriptions and letters of the Roman Emperors of which there are many texts, and even entire titles in the common law'. And just as the *corpus juris civilis* had been the enactment of the common good – the *salus publici* – of the Roman peoples, so the *leyes de Indias* (which was modelled on the *Digest*) was to provide the *salus publici* for the inhabitants of Spanish America.[54] This close legal association between the mother country and the colonies became, in time, a source of bitter conflict between the settler populations (the *criollos*) and Madrid. 'Our fortune,' Simón Bolívar – 'The Liberator' of much of Central and South America – told the future legislators of Venezuela in 1819, 'is to have always been purely passive, our political existence has always been null . . . we were abstracted, absent from the universe'.[55] The British also attributed the general failure, as they saw it, of the Spanish colonies to make much social or economic progress to the Spanish attempt to pursue, in Sir Josiah Child's words, 'the same policy and government civil and ecclesiastical in these plantations as they do in their mother-kingdom'.[56] The protests of Campomanes, that although this was true in theory, Child had failed to recognize that the legal homogeneity of the empire was rarely observed in practice, failed to address the point that it was legislative autonomy which the Spanish colonies had been denied, and that in the end it was only such autonomy that could allow them to compete with their northern neighbours.[57]

In keeping with the image of its legislative identity, Spain was also the only European power to construct a fully developed imperial administration. The representative institutions of government found in the peninsula – the Castilian *cortes* and the Aragonese *corts* – were never exported overseas in any form to America. Nor was there any suggestion that such local bodies as there were, the *ayuntamientos*, *audiencias* and *cabildos*, should possess any independent legislative authority. Everyone had a right of appeal to the local royal courts, the *audiencias*, over the head of even the viceroy himself. (This included the Native Americans who, swift to adapt to the customs of their masters, had by the end of the sixteenth century begun to be abused as not only lazy, lascivious and idolatrous, but also as litigious.) At the end of his term of office every official was subject to an inquiry – called a *residencia* – which gave everyone else in the colony the opportunity to air their grievances against him. Everything flowed out from and back to Madrid and to the Council of the Indies. It will be clear that the charters by which the British colonies enjoyed, in almost every case, 'the liberty of enacting among themselves such laws as they think convenient', would have been unthinkable in any part of the Spanish monarchy after 1521, since any degree of independent legislative action would have suggested that the common good of America could be separate from that of Castile.

Instead each of the various sectors of the empire was governed from Madrid by a separate council, each of which had equal power beneath the Royal Council. Nothing comparable existed in either Britain or France, for the obvious reason that the colonies of the first were thought of as self-governing entities, and those of the second were legally identical with the city of Paris. Yet no less a person than Charles Davenant, one of the fiercest critics of Spanish expansionism, went so far as to recommend that 'a constitution something like what we call the Council of the Indies in Spain' should be established in Britain. And, if this seemed a curious example to hold up before the British peoples, particularly in the last decade of the seventeenth century, then, he continued, 'whoever considers the laws and political institutions of *Spain*, will find them as well formed, and contrived with as much skill and wisdom, as in any country perhaps in the world'. What had always, in his view, gone so hideously wrong with them was due not to 'a wrong and ill projection, but from the negligent, loose, and unsteady executive of their councils', and this, of course, could be attributed both to their religious beliefs and to the lack of freedom which afflicted all Catholic monarchies.[58]

The conciliar system reflected (as Davenant had, perhaps, failed to grasp) the specific structure of the Spanish monarchy. For at the epicentre of the monarchy's institutional and juridical apparatus was the person of the king himself, whose legislative authority was absolute. The Roman jurist Ulpian's celebrated phrase 'that which pleases the prince has the force of law' (*Quod principi placuit legis habet vigorem*),[59] which all Spanish monarchs endorsed, defined not merely a legislative right; it also described a relationship, and in terms of that relationship what linked the monarch to his peoples was his legal person, his *persona ficta*. 'The fundamental maxim of Spanish jurisprudence with respect to America,' observed the Scottish historian William Robertson, 'is to consider what has been acquired there as vested in the crown, rather than the state.'[60] It was this which compelled the Castilian crown to govern America by means of an Aragonese institution – the viceroyalty – which had originally been intended to sustain the fiction of the king's simultaneous presence in Aragon and Naples. In America, as in Naples, the king's legal persona was constantly on display. When Charles V was buried his obsequies were performed – complete with empty catafalque – in every viceroyalty in the monarchy, with the viceroy doubling for Philip II. Elaborate triumphal ceremonies, meant to suggest a continuity between the viceroy and the Roman consuls, and to sustain the ever-dwindling status of the *conquistadores* who had preceded him, were staged to welcome each new emissary.[61]

Even Adam Smith noted with some disgust the size of the sums spent on these receptions: 'Such ceremonials are not only real taxes paid by the rich colonists upon these particular occasions, they serve to introduce among them the habit of vanity and expense upon all other occasions', he wrote, thus missing completely the political point.[62] When Hernán Cortés's son, Martín, Marqués de la Valle de Oaxaca, rebelled in 1565–8, his first act was to ride around Mexico City carrying the royal standard, and to have a medal cast with his head on one side and Philip's on the other. The viceroy was in no doubt about the meaning of this. Cortés was attempting to appropriate the royal persona for himself. 'The entire fiesta,' as the judges at his trial scathingly described it, 'was meant to indicate that the Marques was to be king of this land.'[63] Nothing remotely like this, it need hardly be said, could possibly have taken place in either French or British America.

Such acts were what Judith Shklar once characterized – although she was describing the processes of democratic elections – as 'consequential rituals', rituals, that is, which serve to 'legitimise and constrain officials and policies', but which also have real political consequences.[64] The imaginative conception which underpinned these rituals, and which sustained the various political communities within the Spanish monarchy, was, in Juan de Solórzano y Pereira's phrase, that 'Kingdoms must be ruled and governed as if the King who held them together was only the King of each one of them.'[65] Solórzano was talking about America; but this much-quoted remark was, significantly, taken word for word from a discussion of the Italian dominions of the Castilian crown by the Milanese Camillo Borello.[66] The same claim was also expressed, in slightly different ways, by both Soto and Suárez and applied to the monarchy as a whole.[67] For all of these writers, this was not merely a plea to the monarch to respect local custom – although it was that too – it was a reaffirmation of the distinction between the king's real and his legal person.

It also pointed to another fact which was to be of enormous consequence in the second half of the eighteenth century. In a multicultural society, all of whose members enjoyed the same notional legal status before the crown, the only distinction between the king's subjects was place of birth. Solórzano's claim that the king must treat each of his domains as if he were the ruler of none other, comes in an argument about the right to appoint to ecclesiastical benefices (an argument which, in various forms, was to have significant repercussions among the *criollo* elite in the eighteenth century). 'Native sons,' he argued, should be preferred, not only because this had always been the custom in the peninsula, but for the obvious reason that 'the descendants of those who inhabited and defended, and with their blood, sweat and labour discovered' the Indies were entitled to the reward of both ecclesiastical and secular office. This argument became for the Spanish settlers the basis of a claim to self-determination.

Solórzano himself, however, was not, as his English readers, in particular

James Abercromby,[68] seemed to have supposed, defending the rights of the *criollos* to administer their own affairs; he was arguing for their almost exactly contrary right to be closer to the legislative person of their king. The pursuit of office was what Solórzano called 'the care of the *respublica*'. Deny that to the *criollos*, he believed, and their pursuit of virtue would vanish. They would be reduced to indolence and vice, and the community as a whole would suffer. The natural rights of the *criollos*, conferred upon them by place of birth, were in all cases, however, only rights to act for the monarch in an executive capacity. Nowhere does Solórzano suggest that place of birth, personal expenditure or participation in conquests, real or imagined, conferred upon the subjects of the monarch any *legislative* power. All they guaranteed was a closer, more intimate dependency on the crown, which Bolívar was later to characterize as the 'active tyranny' enjoyed by the Chinese mandarinate.[69] And behind this claim lay a highly personal, and in that sense truly feudal, vision of the relationship between the sovereign and his subject. It was this which gave force to the secrecy that, in British eyes, had always characterized 'continental' monarchy, the 'secret du roi' and the *arcana imperii* which, as Jefferson noted with disgust, had given the monarch privileged access to a body of law which should by natural justice have been accessible to all.[70]

Although it is easy to find a similar language of personalized dependency, and a similar understanding of vassaldom, in France, nothing could be further from the British conceptualization of the relationship between the king and the colonies. For both the Spanish and the French, the identity of the monarch was one with his power to make and enact laws. For the British, especially after 1688, they were clearly separate. To put it in the neo-Thomist terms employed in Spain (and which Hobbes ridiculed so fiercely), the Castilian monarch wielded both the *potestas* which descends from God alone and the *auctoritas* which is invested in the magistrature by the community. In Britain they were divided between king and Parliament. The American claim that the origin of the colonies had been in a concession granted by the king of England, could be so represented as to eliminate all legal ties between the colonies and the metropolis. Thus when John Adams in 1775 spoke of the British empire as united in the person of the English king, but not the 'King in Parliament', he was precisely denying the king any legal personality.[71] Madison, who had a firm understanding of the theoretical weight carried by the Roman Law notion of perfect community, recognized these differences very clearly. 'The fundamental principle of the Revolution,' he wrote, 'was that the Colonies were co-ordinating members with each other and with Great Britain of an empire united by a common executive sovereign, but not united by a common legislative sovereign.'[72]

Both the Spanish and the British would finally rebel – and the Spaniards had consistently rebelled throughout the sixteenth century – on the grounds that their respective monarchs had violated what it was to be a monarch. But the English crown's close association after 1688 with its own representative institutions, the concept of the 'King in Parliament' as a definition of monarchy itself, made it impossible for the English to plead loyalty to the person of the king while defying the king's agents. The traditional European cry of rebellion, which was repeated by Hidalgo and Morelos in Mexico in 1810, of 'Long Live the King, down with bad government', made no sense when the king was seen as, in Jefferson's words, 'the chief officer of the people, appointed by the laws and circumscribed with definite power', and therefore inferior to what he described as 'the great machinery of government'.[73]

<h1 style="text-align:center">III</h1>

By contrast with both the British and the Spanish, the French settler populations, the *colons*, never sought independence from their mother country. Long before the political or cultural conditions necessary to sustain a prolonged revolt had arisen, the first French overseas empire had all but ceased to exist. With the conclusion of the Treaty of Paris on 10 February 1763, which brought the Seven Years War to an end, the French presence in America had been reduced to the islands in the Caribbean. The most important of these, politically and economically, were Guadeloupe and St Domingue. Unlike Canada they had no native populations with whom the settlers could hope to integrate. These colonies had, by the mid-eighteenth century, developed planter economies very much like those of the British islands in the same region. And like the British colonies they, too, had massive slave populations. Since 1763 the principal political objective of the *colons* had been to procure the abolition of the restrictive laws governing the colonial trade known as *L'Exclusif*,[74] while remaining firmly within the protective limits of the French monarchy. When the Thirteen Colonies rebelled in 1776, the French settlers in the Caribbean, like the British, were concerned only for the potential this might have for generating a massive slave revolt, of the kind which finally came to St Domingue in 1793.[75] Unlike the British, however, in 1789 the French settlers found themselves confronted by a violent and radical transformation of the political culture of the metropolis, a transformation which soon threatened their very survival.

The Revolution evidently weakened the tactical support the colonies could expect to receive from metropolitan France. More significant for the *colons* was the threat posed by the ambitions of the members, Robespierre among them, of the Société des Amis des Noirs to bring about the total emancipation of all slaves in the French colonies.[76] Their fear of what a liberated slave force might do to them was real enough. Slave revolts had been a common event throughout much of the eighteenth century. Their success had been limited, but the *colons* were well aware that their precarious position depended upon the willingness of the metropolitan government to supply them with protection. Introduce the principles of the French Revolution into America and free the slaves, argued Pierre-Victor Malouet, a former commissaire of St Dominque, in a passage of barely suppressed hysteria,

> and the Colonies will exist no longer as workshops of agriculture and commerce. Rather they will be transformed into one vast arsenal of revolution, brigandage and piracy, in which all villains from the four quarters of the globe will find asylum and employment. Doubt not, but that there will come into being societies whose governments will be the enemies of commerce, of navigation and of the entire civilization of Europe. There a population will multiply, fitting to the fertile soil and, for us, unhealthy climate of the Torrid Zone. And there from the Antilles to Mexico and Brazil, from the plains and the mountains of the New World, the philosophy of Marat will carry forth its dogmas, its firebrands and its daggers.[77]

The prolonged and acrimonious disputes over the survival of the French colonies in the Caribbean conducted in the National Assembly between 1790 and 1792 became very largely disputes over the moral, political and economic desirability of slavery. The prime objective of the *colons* was to remain as far as possible within the protective custody of the new French Republic, while continuing to live by an economy based on a practice which violated the political and ethical principles upon which that republic had been created. To achieve this they, and their supporters in the mother country, turned to a legal distinction which the British colonists in America had introduced in an attempt to establish a similar relationship between themselves and the metropolis.

Ever since the seventeenth century, English republican writers had been pressing for a recognized legal separation of the spheres of what James Harrington described as the 'domestic and national', on the one hand, and the 'foreign and provincial' on the other.[78] On this account the legal relationship between the colony and the metropolis was to be determined by a body of laws which were enacted in the metropolis. This would cover the foreign relations, defence and, more contentiously, the commerce of colonies. All matters concerning their internal management were to be regulated by legislation enacted by, and on behalf of, the colonists themselves. The American colonies, wrote Richard Bland in 1766, constituted

> a distinct state, independent as to their *internal* government of the original kingdom, but united with her as to their external policy in the closest and most intimate LEAGUE AND AMITY, under the same allegiance, and enjoying the benefits of a reciprocal intercourse.[79]

As Bernard Bailyn has pointed out, the interpretation of the Stamp Act crisis of 1764–6, as a violation of the distinction between 'internal' and 'external' spheres of legislation – and of taxation – had been placed firmly on the British agenda by Benjamin Franklin's famous three-hour testimony before the House of Commons in February 1776.[80] From then on it was to dictate the terms of every discussion of the competing claims to legislative authority between the colonies and the metropolis.

It was, however, as Franklin and others fully understood, a distinction which made proper legal sense only in the context of the English common law. For the Spanish and the French, at least before 1789, to claim such a division between the spheres of justice when both were recognized as determining in the person of a single ruler would have been legally meaningless. But in France the notion of the absolute sovereignty of the monarch vanished with the Revolution. This made it possible for the French *colons* and their metropolitan supporters, most vocal of whom was Antoine Barnave – it was to be the beginning of his road to the guillotine – to introduce the British differentiation between 'internal' and 'external' legislation, as a means of forcing the new government in Paris to grant them the legislative freedom necessary for them simultaneously to mitigate, if not entirely abolish, Colbert's trade laws, and to ward off any attempt to emancipate the slaves.

The English, as Barnave observed to the National Assembly in 1791, had treated their colonies as 'co-states as far as their internal laws were concerned', whereas they were 'purely subject' with regard to their *régime extérieur*. Had they followed the logic of this arrangement, and therefore accepted that it gave the colonists an inalienable right to representation in Parliament, they would have had their colonies still. Henceforth the French had made no distinction between 'these two classes of laws which should never be confused'.[81] But if the new constitutional French monarchy wished to retain control of its Caribbean possessions, which, as De Curt the deputy for Guadeloupe had pointed out in 1789, had everything to gain and nothing to lose by 'opening its port to all the trading powers of Europe', it would now have to recognize the legitimacy of the colonists' claims to full representation on the newly established *Corps législatif national*.[82] Any further attempt in the new Revolutionary – if not yet republican France – to perpetuate the old legislative order could only lead to an insurgency the French navy would be in no position to control. Even Barnave's great enemy, Brissot, who would have much preferred to see an end to the overseas empire altogether, recognized that the colonists had become part of the revolutionary process, and could not be denied any of the benefits enjoyed by the inhabitants of the metropolis.[83]

Barnave's project for virtual political emancipation of the colonies was not, however, intended to grant the *colons* all the free-trade concessions they demanded since, in his view, 'the laws of commerce and of protection' constituted a part of the external administration of the colonies.[84] But his final concession that in future no law, even in this sphere, 'should be passed by the legislative body except on the precise, formal and spontaneous wish of the colonies', made the colonies virtually independent as far as their legislature was concerned. As a 'M. Blin', the deputy from Nantes pointed out on 1 March 1790, under such an arrangement 'the colonies could in some measure be compared to Ireland, which has its own legislature and a governor with the name of Viceroy [*sic*] who represents the holder of the executive power'.[85] Following this in 1797, when France had ceased altogether to be a monarchy, Pierre-Victor Malouet claimed that the colonies had a natural right 'to resist their own destruction' which necessarily implied a 'right to independence with regard to their internal legislation, and to the mode of their existence'.[86] Unless some such action were taken, the colonies, still thought of as vital to the economic and military life of the nation, would certainly seek their own solution, as the British had earlier sought theirs. 'Rejected like bastards by our common Mother,' warned an anonymous pamphlet *Un mot à l'oreille*, 'they might soon perhaps cease to regard themselves as Children.'[87]

In post-revolutionary France, the old mother–child metaphor which had sustained the relationship between the colonies and their 'mother country', embedded as it always had been in the model of the Roman family which granted parents absolute power over their children, could no longer be sustained. The metropolis itself had voluntarily resigned its role as Roman patriarch. It had become instead a society governed by laws. As Talleyrand knew from experience, all revolutions created in their wake 'a general anxiety in men's minds: a need for movement'.[88] What had taken place in France must inevitably dictate what should now take place in the colonies. Deny the colonies any part of the new legislative order, warned Jean François Merlet, deputy for Maine et Loire, and the empire would collapse. The colonies remained loyal to the metropolis by 'interests, needs, and above all because the links of fraternity bind them strongly'. But none of this would have any purchase if the General Assembly were to exclude a single citizen from the law. 'It is absolutely vital,' he wrote, 'that the French Revolution should produce the same outcome in the colonies, as it has in the metropolis.'[89] Merlet was drawing upon a wholly new language, the language of the law as the expression of the General Will, Rousseau's *volonté générale*. 'The law', wrote Malouet, pondering on the consequences for the colonies of a revolution which he soon came to detest, 'is the result of the general will and of a community.' 'Under an empire with a republican constitution,' wrote another former colonial official, Victor Collot, 'it appears that the political relationship between the metropolis and the colonies should contain no inequalities as far as their respective rights are concerned.'[90]

The French, in their attempt to redescribe the legal relationship between the colonies and the metropolis, had begun with an American reworking of a convenient distinction in the English common law. They had ended with the republican, post-revolutionary language of rights and citizenship. And this, which could make a Caribbean *colon* or even a Huron the legal equal of a Breton, was itself, as Merlet recognized, a mutation of the older idioms of universal membership of the single *civitas*. After the creation of the Republic in 1792 the 'French empire', as it continued to be called, could only survive by pursuing to its conclusion the logic of the edicts which had established the first settlements in Canada at the end of the sixteenth century. Now, however, the king's subjects had been transformed into rights-bearing citizens. Each community within the state had therefore to be permitted to pursue its own independent interests, which meant, in effect, to draft its own laws. The people of France – at least when viewed from the other side of the Atlantic – constituted a single nation with a single body of interests. Yet it was evident that the colonies had, over time, acquired different interests and concerns and must, while remaining beneficiaries of the revolutionary process, be allowed to follow freely their own ways of existence. 'These are men,' wrote Malouet, 'whose laws, whose customs, the sun, the climate, needs, habits and habitations, whose modes of cultivation have made them unlike you.' For this reason, the law which 'is the outcome of the General Will and of a community of interests' had, he concluded, also to be an expression of that difference.[91]

IV

It was not only the weight of contrasting conceptions of legal authority and of the nature of kingship – crucial though these always were – which had produced the very marked differences between the European empires in America. It was also the nature of the metropolitan political cultures themselves. The British empire in America, at least before the outbreak of the Seven Years War with France in 1756, had been grounded upon an image of the king as remote benefactor, not as judge. The degree of control exercised over the colonies was therefore relatively slight. So long as the colonists remained loyal, so long as they served, in some way, the financial and political objectives of the metropolis, they were left to pursue their own ends without interference. Paradoxically, as many historians have observed, the inhabitants of the Thirteen Colonies remained very largely committed to an image of themselves as Englishmen until the behaviour of their king and his government – combined with the colonists' intellectual tendency, in Edmund Burke's words to 'augur misgovernment at a distance and snuff the approach of tyranny in every tainted breeze' – drove them to seek a distinct cultural as well as political identity.[92] Their deference to their monarch in the years before the Stamp Act crisis was generally greater than that of native-born Britons, perhaps, as David Hume suggested, because of their ignorance of the true nature of kingship.[93] If the relatively free and 'liberal' government of the British colonies seems to have encouraged a high degree of cultural dependency upon the mother country, the very reverse was true of French and Spanish America. Both the Spanish *criollos* and the French *colons* seemed to have developed a sense of belonging to an independent cultural world long before they came to think of that world as necessarily an independent nation. Yet both the French and the Spanish monarchies had attempted from the beginning to employ cultural suasion as a means of ensuring the continuing loyalty of their settler populations and, most crucially in the Spanish case, the indigenous peoples they had colonized.

In Benjamin Constant's view, this bid by the metropolis to limit the independent cultural expression of its subject peoples was precisely what distinguished modern from ancient imperialism. For whereas the Ancients had tolerated customary differences within the structure of a single law, and the nominal adhesion to a national 'civil' religion,

> The conquerors of our days wish their empire to present an appearance of uniformity, upon which the proud eye of power may travel without meeting any unevenness that could offend or limit its view. The same code of law, the same measure, the same regulations, and if they could contrive it gradually, the same language, this is what is proclaimed to be the perfect form of social organization.[94]

Constant was speaking of the Napoleonic empire, but his description corresponds, *mutatis mutandis*, to the image which most observers, hostile and friendly, had of the Spanish and, to a lesser degree, the French for a great part of their history. As Kant observed in 1795, the only true cohesion to which any state, whatever its size or ambitions, could aspire had, in the end, to be based not on wealth or military power, but on language and religion, or, to phrase it in more general terms: culture.[95] For Kant, culture was the means by which independent nations would *prevent* any one power from creating a 'universal despotism'. The converse was equally true. As Charles Davenant warned his readers in the late seventeenth century, the kind of empire which Spain in reality was – and which in his view France would very soon become – could be sustained only by a very high level of cultural tyranny. The 'bondage', he warned his readers, imposed by such universal monarchies 'upon our bodies is easy in comparison to that which it would impose upon our minds'.[96] Without the force of custom, which could only be achieved by the manipulation of the cultural and belief systems of the nation, the laws of the state would be ineffective, where no power existed to enforce them; and in the early-modern world such powers, for all their ferocity, were extremely limited. The king of Spain, as the Benedictine Juan de Salazar pointed out in 1619, had three kinds of *imperium* over his subjects: 'that of bodies, that of estates, and that of minds (*entendimientos*)'.[97] And of these the last was always the most powerful.

In *Della Ragion di Stato* (On the Reason of State) of 1589 Giovanni Botero had argued that a true 'monarchia' would also require, in time, a single language – as 'the Romans, the Arabs and the Normans' had had – a single currency, and a single body of customs. In this way, and in this way alone, he argued, 'subjects acquired by conquest may come to resemble natural subjects'.[98] In Botero's view, the supreme example of the success of such cultural strategies was to be found in the Janissary Corps. Non-Turks and non-Muslim in origin, they had been brought up, like the Roman Imperial Guard, to be the most fiercely loyal of the Sultan's troops. The failure to understand that it was only possible to create and to sustain extended empires through such means had cost the French first Sicily and later Naples and Milan, the English France and the Latins Constantinople. For none of these nations, he concluded, had known how to 'govern them so that they felt the interests of the state to be their own'.[99]

The Spaniards themselves were generally highly conscious of the force of such arguments. In 1570 the humanist Benito Arias Montano, Philip II's librarian archivist and book collector, had urged the Duke of Alba to establish a chair of Spanish at the University of Louvain, for, he wrote, 'after the matter of religion, there is nothing which so reconciles the hearts of men from various nations than the unity and conformity of language'. This, he concluded, 'is one of the principal things which the Romans achieved, in order to confirm their empire over the world and reconcile men from every nation'.[100]

Since the would-be world ruler must transform the customs and belief of the peoples over whom he wishes to rule, he must in effect create a new and homogeneous community of knowledge. The prime means of securing this, as Livy had long before made clear, had always been religion. Roman *pietas* had not only been a feature of the empire; it had also been mobilized to sustain it. The Ancients, as one Spaniard, Juan Fernández de Medrano, pointed out, had always 'esteemed [religion and love of country] to the same degree'.[101] Where possible, advised Tommaso Campanella, the world monarch should create a new religion. This, he argued, was what Muhammad had done and Romulus and Pythagoras before him. This, too, had been the good fortune of Charlemagne, and the obvious objective of both Henry VIII of England and of Luther's patron Frederick of Saxony.[102] The Castilian monarch had no such option. But he should, Campanella insisted, impose a rigid orthodoxy throughout his realms, which would identify him, and his authority, with that of the Church. As Campanella's near-contemporary Diego Saavedra Fajardo argued in his *Idea de un principe político-cristiano* (Idea of a Politic-Christian Prince) of 1639, too much free intellectual reflection could lead to 'a variety of sects which is the cause of the fall of empires'. He advised his masters to increase the number of navigators and military tacticians, and to reduce that of scholars.[103] Spanish 'bigotry' of this kind, which for so many English and French critics seemed to have been responsible for the final ruin of the empire, appeared to those within it to be the main instrument of government.

V

Like the Spaniards, the French had established their first colonies with the explicit, if loosely understood, intention of creating a single cultural, as well as legal, and – uniquely in the French case – racial, community. Under the terms of the creation of the Compagnie des Cien Associés, both the French settlers, their descendants and those Native Americans

> who have come to an understanding of the faith and have made a profession thereof, should be supposed and held to be French nationals, and as such might come to live in France whenever they wished.[104]

After 1663, when the Compagnie des Indes Occidentales took over responsibility for the settlements in Canada, Arcadia, Newfoundland and the West Indies, the French settlers were encouraged to intermarry with the Native Americans. Although Colbert described the Iroquois as 'true savages having nothing that is human about them except the appearance of men', he could also, with no apparent sense of contradiction and in the same document, speak of the pressing need to 'oblige the savages to settle among us, and to [learn] our customs and our language'.[105] The act of foundation of the Compagnie des Indes Occidentales, for which Colbert was responsible, granted to all immigrants to America, 'the same liberties and franchises which they had while living in this kingdom'. More strikingly still, it extended the terms made in the *Acte pour l'établissement de la compagnie des cien associés* to

> those who are born of [the colonists] and the savages who have converted to the Catholic Apostolic and Roman Faith, to be registered and counted as denizens and French natives, and as such entitled for all rights of succession, good laws and other dispositions, without being obliged to obtain any letter of naturalization.[106]

It was the hope that the French overseas empire might somehow be able to transcend the evils which had befallen the Spanish, while avoiding the overly liberal colonial policies pursued by the British, which, in 1757, led Antoine de Bougainville, the future discoverer of Tahiti, to propose a plan for a settlement of French and Native Americans in Illinois, which he hoped would be run 'according to what was once the famous system of the Republic of Sparta'.[107]

Colbert's 'Frenchification' scheme had been launched partly because he believed that a massive increase in the population of the American colonies was necessary if they were to survive in the face of English hostility, and also because he believed that this objective could be more easily achieved by this means than by mass migration.[108] It had also, however, been his intention to extend to Canada and the Caribbean Louis XIV's project for an 'état unifié', united in speech, customs, religion, king, and in this case blood, which would later come to seem to many Europeans to be the successor state to the Habsburg 'Universal Monarchy'.

The Spaniards, whose native populations had entered the historiography of the empire as noble, if primitive, warriors, were seen, at least at first, as potential marriage partners, although the crown did nothing to encourage such unions. Some members of the *conquistador* class even attempted liaisons with what they identified as a native aristocracy. Francisco Pizarro's brother Gonzalo, in revolt against the crown, declared that he would marry an Inca princess and thereby make himself king of Peru.[109] He was killed before he had time to put this novel dynastic alliance into action. Such cases, however, were rare, and by the eighteenth century alliance with the Native American aristocracy had been confined to a series of metaphors which preserved, as far as possible, the greatest possible distance between true *criollos*, the now mythologized 'Aztec' and 'Inca' past on the one hand, and the grim realities of the *mestizo* underclass and the still autonomous Amerindian peoples on the other. Racial integration in Spanish America, although it was to result in wholly new groups of peoples with distinctive cultures, and ultimately distinctive political aspirations of their own, played no part in the crown's conception of the empire as a single cultural and political unit.

The English, concerned as they were to domesticate what one of them called the 'wilderness without any comeliness' of America, found the prospect of intermarriage with Native Americans abhorrent.[110] As Sir Josiah Child remarked in 1665, the Spaniards had benefited from having settled in areas where cities and plantations already existed and which had indigenous populations with whom they could interbreed, whereas the British had only 'wild Heathens, with whom they could not, nor ever have been known to mix'.[111] The case of Pocohontas and John Smith had been in many ways so very exceptional, exactly because it was unimaginable for most English settlers in America.

Of all the European powers only the French had attempted to replicate their society in America with a mixed population. Paradoxically Canada was, and remains, more starkly divided between its native and settler populations than any other American community. The long-term effect of Colbert's scheme had been, as Mirabeau caustically noted in 1758, that 'instead of Frenchifying (*franciser*) the savages, these had savagised the French', making them, in his view, 'incapable of that subordination which is the soul of all colonies'.[112] Little wonder that when François Volney, one of the most perceptive observers of the colonial process, passed through the region in 1797 he found it to be largely inhabited by 'Frenchmen of the age of Louis XIV who have become half Indian' together with 'Englishmen of the last century'.[113]

Once, however, the project of full miscegenation was recognized as having failed in America, it was revived in the Pacific. Here, it seemed, was the opportunity for a new kind of colonization, one which would benefit equally the colonizer and the colonized. Charles de Brosses's *Histoire des navigations aux Terres australes* of 1756 conjured up the image of a new America in the Antipodes with peoples similar in culture and disposition to those whom Columbus and his successors had all but destroyed. 'But suppose,' wrote De Brosses,

> a future which is not at all like that which Christopher Columbus secured for our neighbours. . . . Their example would instruct us. For we would avoid the two vices from which the Spaniards then suffered, avarice and cruelty. The former emptied their own country in pursuit of an illusory fortune, something which should never have been attempted. The latter, whose causes were national pride and super-stition, has all but destroyed the human race in America. They massacred disdainfully, and as if they were base and alien beasts, millions of Indians whom they could have made into men. They destroyed to the last man, hundreds of races, as though there was some profit to be had from uninhabited lands.

'Experience, however, has shown,' he continued, 'that in these distant climates, one must trade not conquer, that it is not a question of estab-lishing imaginary kingdoms beyond the equator.' Instead the new French empire of the Pacific would be a network of trading stations, working for the mutual benefit of all those involved with them. They would draw the 'savages' to them from 'the woods' and 'allow them to benefit from the advantages of human and social laws', much as the Jesuits had done in Paraguay. The model for all future French empires should, concluded De Brosses, be not the Spaniards or the Romans but the Phoenicians. For they had created not dependencies or colonies but new nations, and 'what greater objective could a sovereign have' than that?[114]

Bougainville's circumnavigation of the globe between 1766 and 1769, and in particular the account which appeared in his *Voyage autour du monde* of Tahiti, which he named 'La Nouvelle Cythère', seemed to support De Brosses's fantasy. And it was this which underpinned Diderot's hope for a future state based on the image of a racial harmony which would not merely resolve the eighteenth-century anxiety over population decline, and the Enlightenment's horror at the devastation which had followed the European colonists overseas. It would also provide for all humanity the image of a happy state poised, as Diderot phrased it, 'half-way between savagery and civility'.[115]

Even in failure, however, Colbert's vision of a united miscegenated society was, and remains so in what is left of that empire today, an integral part of the self-image of the French empire. If it never succeeded in integrating the colonizer with the colonized, it did identify the settler population more closely with the metropolitan culture than was the case in either Spanish or British America. The French, wrote an admiring Edmund and William Burke in 1757, 'consider the planter as a Frenchman, venturing his life, enduring a species of banishment, and undergoing great hardships for the benefit of his country'. The French, they concluded, alone of all the European colonizing powers, 'advance the intercourse of mankind, the peopling of the earth, and the advantages of their country by wise and effectual regulation'.[116]

VI

'New Cythera' was, and was firmly to remain, an illusion: 'old goods passed off as new,' as the abbé Galiani remarked sardonically in 1769.[117] So, too, was the Spanish vision of a single world order under a single law. The failure of the European colonizers to establish, as the Romans had done so successfully, a universal culture, a world *civitas*, was proof to many that in the modern world extensive overseas empires were doomed to rapid, and generally disastrous, extinction. Over time the settlements established by all three European powers in America developed not a closer harmony with Europe but, sometimes despite themselves, cultural, economic and political identities of their own. By the early eighteenth century it had even become apparent that in the case of Spain the relationship of power between colony and metropolis had not merely changed. It had been inverted. 'The Indies and Spain are two powers under the same master,' observed Montesquieu in 1748, 'but the Indies is the principal one and Spain nothing but an accessory.'[118] With this increased economic and cultural independence, it also became obvious, not only that the colonies might one day seek political autonomy, but that they might also, as Benjamin Franklin had seen, come to replace the mother country as the political and economic centres of their respective empires.[119] (This indeed happened in Brazil when the Portuguese court arrived in Rio de Janeiro in 1808.)

But it was not so much the examples of the Ancient World which dominated the language used to describe the relationship between the colonies and the metropolis, as that of the family.[120] 'Because,' as Gordon Wood has written, 'the image was so powerful, so suggestive of the personal traditional world in which the colonists still lived, almost the entire imperial debate was carried out within its confines.'[121] The parent–child image could also be linked back to a powerful ideological tradition within British political thinking of the seventeenth century: patriarchalism, and in particular the patriarchalism of Sir Robert Filmer. John Locke had written the *Second Treatise on Government*, which was to become a foundational document for North American republicanism, to refute Filmer (or so it was believed), and in the minds of the defenders of colonial autonomy patriarchalism became associated with the older bid by the English crown to achieve absolute, and thus 'Papish', sovereignty over their people. This, presumably, was what Tom Paine was suggesting when in *Common Sense* in 1776 he wrote that:

> The phrase *parent* or *mother country* hath been jesuitically adopted by the king and his parasites, with a low papistical design of gaining an unfair bias in the credulous weakness of our minds.[122]

The language of parenthood, however, could also, if its Filmerian overtones were ignored, be made to work to the colonists' advantage. Final emancipation was implicit in the metaphor of the 'mother country', for as children become adults, so one day the colonies would have to become independent states. The English settlements in America, wrote James Harrington as early as 1656 when the 'British empire' in America barely existed, might still be 'babes that cannot live without sucking the breast of their mother-cities', but, he concluded, 'such as I mistake, if when they come of age they do not wean themselves; which causeth me to wonder at princes that delight to be exhausted in this way'.[123] Patriarchalism adapted the image of the family to the whole of human society, viewed as an entity which, in so far as its relationships of power and authority were concerned, was meant to be unchanging throughout historical time. The mother–child metaphor, by contrast, could *only* be understood historically. 'Supposing, therefore,' wrote Richard Price in 1776,

> that the order of nature in establishing the relationship between parents and children ought to have been the rule of our conduct to the colonies, we should have been gradually relaxing our authority as they grew up.

The British, in the pursuit of their own domestic interests, had, he believed, behaved instead like 'mad parents', and had 'done the contrary', and like mad parents they were soon to lose both the love and respect of their offspring.[124] From the vantage point of the first decade of the nineteenth century, the pamphleteer, adviser to Simón Bolívar, and sometime Napoleonic ambassador, Dominique Dufour de Pradt, in his attempts to summarize the entire colonial process in America, observed that it was precisely because the British had failed to notice this transition that they had lost their colonies. The Spaniards, he warned, were now about to emulate their disastrous example.[125] For as De Pradt, following Montesquieu, pointed out, dependence upon the metropolis clearly demanded that the metropolis be both more powerful and, in some sense, a more developed society than any of its colonies. When this ceased to be the case, emancipation, in all but law, had in effect taken place. Would the British colonies, Richard Price had asked, still be bound to 'acknowledge that supremacy over them which is now claimed', when in

> 50 or 60 years, they will be double our number and form a mighty empire, consisting of a variety of states, all equal or superior to ourselves in all the arts and accomplishments which give dignity and happiness to human life?[126]

The political relationship between Britain and its colonies in America had always been more distant than that between either France or Spain and their American possessions. Although the 'Kingdoms of the Indies' had become independent cultures by the mid-seventeenth century, the Spanish colonists continued to look to Europe as a source of political legitimation until changing political conditions in the metropolis drove them to seek their independence in the early nineteenth century. The British colonists, by contrast, because their societies had been conceived, sometimes from their foundation, as semi-independent communities, had always been acutely aware that it was they alone who had to bring about their own well-being, and that, as a consequence, the 'mighty empire' which in 1759 Jonathan Mayhew dreamed that America might one day become, 'in number little inferior perhaps to the greatest in Europe, and in felicity to none', could only be *their* creation.[127]

Despite this strong sense of their political identity, the British Americans retained until independence cultural affiliations with the mother country far stronger than those of the Spanish *criollos*, and stronger sometimes even than the French *colons*. By the second half of the eighteenth century, however, as the metropolitan power attempted not to loosen but to strengthen the ties between it and the colonies, even the British began to discover that it was no longer possible to sustain the image of America as an England transplanted, improved and purified. Thomas Pownall piously believed that

> the limitations of the capacities, and extent of the necessities of each, all are interwoven into a necessary intercourse of supplies, and all are indissolubly bound in a union and communion of *one general composite interest*

of the whole of the Spaniard, French, Dutch, Danish and British settlements. This is the *natural state* of the European possessions in the Atlantic and in the Americas.[128]

But this was already vain by the time it was written in 1765. One year later, the evident falsity of his claim that 'nothing can eradicate from their hearts their natural, almost mechanical affection to Great Britain which they conceive under no other sense, nor call by any other name, than that of *home*'[129] would be made all too painfully clear.

But if Pownall was wrong about the force of these ancient ties, his sentiments reflected a belief, shared by the French and the Spanish as much as by the British, that in political and cultural terms it was, ultimately, only such ties that could hold extended empires together. Pownall had also seen for himself that this meant that the association between the various parts of any empire had to be conceived, not as one of dependency, but as one of federation. The concept of federation, however, was reliant upon a discourse which sought to calculate the merits of any society in terms of the benefits to be gained by *all* its members. It was also a discourse which had characterized empires, as they had been understood throughout most of modern history, as essentially unworkable political institutions, economically and administratively unmanageable, and humanly intolerable.

CHAPTER SIX

The Calculation of Benefits

Vous avez attaché des peines aux crimes; attachez des récompenses à la vertu; et ne redoutez pour la durée de vos empires, que le laps de temps.

Denis Diderot, *Salon de 1767*

I

'The force that a people needs to keep all others in subjection,' wrote Benjamin Constant in 1813,

is today, more than ever, a privilege that cannot last. The nation that aimed at such an empire would place itself in a more dangerous position than the weakest of tribes. It would become the object of universal horror. Every opinion, every desire, every hatred, would threaten it, and sooner or later those hatreds, those opinions, and those desires would explode and engulf it.[1]

Constant was, of course, writing about the Napoleonic empire, but both the thrust of his essay *De la conquête et de l'usurpation dans leurs rapports avec la civilisation européenne* (The Spirit of Conquest and Usurpation and their Relation to European Civilization) and the range of moral revulsion to which he refers were already securely in place by the early eighteenth century. 'Even when these sons of violence succeed,' Thomas Gordon had written in 1728 of the original founders of the European empires,

they may be fully said to acquire nothing beyond the praise of mischief. What is the occupation and end of Princes and Governors, but to rule men for their good, and to keep them from hurting one another? Now what Conqueror is there who mends the condition of the conquered?[2]

Gordon's question was unanswerable, if only because the European empires had not been based upon a calculation of possible goods, let alone upon the possible goods which might flow from the colonizer to the colonized. They had been founded instead upon the notion that the

156

greatness of the ruler was the measure of the greatness of his people. No matter how poor or weak they might be at home, their collective welfare was believed to have been enhanced by their capacity to command overseas. Outwardly directed in this way, no state could afford to consider too scrupulously the interests of those who might be caught up in its progress.

By the time Gordon came to compose his *Political Discourses* on Tacitus, the related concepts of honour and greatness which had occupied a central place in so much sixteenth- and seventeenth-century political thinking had, as we saw in Chapter 4, come to be seen as restrictive to a nation's economic development, and a threat to any wider understanding of the social good. The empires of Antiquity which had provided, in one shape or another, the models for the first European empires could no longer be sustained in a world which had all but repudiated the values, universal and singular, on which they had been erected. The recognition of the claims of diversity and – although this would not become apparent until the very end of the century – of plurality, had swept them away. As Charles Davenant observed in an essay 'On arbitrary power', 'Those who contemplate nothing but ancient times and the commonwealth of Ancient Greece and Rome are apt . . . to form for themselves schemes for ruling the world of which mankind is no longer capable'.[3]

Davenant's own language, and that of most eighteenth-century political theorists, was directed not, as that of previous generations had been, towards notions either of preservation or of honour and Machiavellian *grandezza*. It was concerned instead with what was widely known as 'public happiness', what we today would call welfare. This was inwardly directed and grounded upon the claim that the interests of the state had primarily to be an expression of the well-being of those *individuals* of whom it was composed. 'The happiness of a community,' wrote George Blewith in 1725,

is nothing but the private happiness of the private individuals who compose it. . . . Are private men the more happy, or the more wealthy, because their sovereign has the glory to be a conqueror? 'Tis highly absurd to call a nation happy and flourishing only because it makes a Figure abroad, and is a terror to its neighbours.[4]

This shift, from honour to public welfare, resulted, as it did in other areas of political discourse, in a shift from the considerations of rights and legitimacy to a concern with interests and benefits: the interests of all those who were members of a community, and the benefits they might expect to derive from their membership. Henceforth societies could only be considered great – and legitimate – in proportion to the degree to which they could make their members happy.[5] 'Machiavellianism,' wrote Isaac de Pinto, somewhat optimistically, 'is no more':

> That atrocious doctrine which at the beginning of this century still
> misled the ministers of a mild and just nation is banished forever.... We
> begin to be sensible that states and sovereigns are only powerful propor-
> tionally as their subjects are happy.

Furthermore, in the terms imposed by this new understanding of the
good, it was neither the statesman, nor the subjects of any one prince, nor
even the dictates of the natural law, which was to act as the final arbiter in
disputes over legitimacy. It was instead an ancient category which had now
been invested with a new power: humanity. In 1776, as he watched what
he knew to be the beginning of the end for the British empire in America,
Richard Price caught something of this shift. 'I wish,' he wrote,

> to have the question brought to a higher test and surer issue. The
> question with all liberal inquiries ought to be, not what jurisdiction
> over these precedents, statutes and charters give, but what reason and
> equity, and the right of humanity give.[6]

In Price's view, over-extended empires were not merely disadvantageous
in the long run, they were humanly impossible, and they were so, not
because of the familiar problems of control and command, not even only
because of the more immediate one of justice. They were so because, in
Price's words, the members of such empires shared none of what he
tellingly called 'the fellow-feeling that takes place between persons in
private life', and because

> the state that governs cannot be a witness to the suffering occasioned by
> its oppressions; or a competent judge of the circumstances and abilities
> of the people who are governed. They must also have in a great degree
> separate interests; and the more the one is loaded the more the other
> may be eased.[7]

Public happiness relied upon the individual's ability to fulfil his (and now,
increasingly, her) individual objectives, so long as these did not conflict
with those of his or her fellow citizens. Such a community had to be one
in which a variety of very diverse objectives could be pursued without the
possibility of conflict. It had to be small, but it also had to exist in a
condition of cultural heterogeneity. Empires, conceived as that of Rome
had been, denied these possibilities. They sought to impose a single end
upon all human desires, and a single conception of what the 'good life'
could be, a conception, furthermore, which lay purposefully beyond the
reach of the concerns of individuals. In pursuit of these ends such empires
had, inevitably, sought to absorb all the space available to human
habitation. An emperor who conceived of himself as Antoninus Pius had

done, could be nothing *other* than *dominus mundi*. It was this image of the Universal Monarchy which had haunted Charles Davenant and others, the image of a state no one could hope to outrun, so that, in Davenant's words, 'he who was oppressed by a Roman emperor could return no where but into the arms of death'.[8]

This concern with reciprocity, with 'public happiness' and with the demands of the private and the particular are some of the dominant features of modernity. They form part of what Charles Taylor has called the 'Affirmation of Ordinary Life'. Taylor locates the origins of this in a development that began in late fifteenth-century humanism,[9] but its major theoretical expression was to be found in radical late seventeenth-century Protestant notions of a society founded upon mutual and reciprocal trust – precisely the kind of society into which Price, the son of a dissenting Welsh minister, had been born. The language of interests and benefits which underpins this notion of the demands of 'ordinary life' does, however, have other antecedents. As I mentioned in Chapter 2, a number of Spanish humanists, and humanist-influenced theologians and jurists, such as Vázquez de Menchaca, Domingo de Soto and Diego de Covarrubias had already, in the late sixteenth century, attempted to demonstrate that the legitimacy of an empire, like the legitimacy of any state, should be judged by the benefits it can bring to *all* those involved. As the argument was expressed by these writers it was grounded upon two claims. The first was that all communities have natural limits. Any vigorous attempt to extend those limits could only result in a violation of the natural law, for the natural law dictated that all communities should serve the good of their members, and over-extended communities could not, by definition, adequately perform that task.

The second was that *overseas* empires, because they necessarily required travel overseas, were in some sense a violation of nature's intention that, once the early nomadic stage of his existence had been completed, man should remain more or less where he was. On this account, there were no reasons for supposing, as the Christian apologists for empire and their ancient predecessors had supposed, either that what is desirable for one community will *necessarily* be desirable for another, or that, even if it were, it would, in the way things are actually constituted, be possible to impose it upon other cultures with other histories and other beliefs. Such constraints, furthermore, would apply with equal force to the attempt by one power to dominate another pre-existent community, as to an attempt by a metropolitan power to impose its will upon a colony. For, as Jefferson argued in *A Summary View of the Rights of the British-Americans* of 1774, all colonies had been the creation of those who had chosen to exercise their natural right

of departing from the country in which chance not choice had placed them; of going in quest of new habitations and of there establishing new societies, under such laws and regulations as to them shall seem most likely to promote public happiness.[10]

This 'public happiness' which they had so created, they had created in their own manner, and whatever form that might take it was highly unlikely to be commensurable with any understanding the metropolis might have of its own shared felicity.

In the sixteenth and seventeenth centuries, once the immediate context of the dispute over the legitimacy of the Spanish empire had collapsed, the force of these claims went largely unrecognized. The first – that the obligation of all rulers was to secure the public happiness of their subjects – although voiced intermittently by the opponents of empire, was similarly neglected. Despite the very real support it received from the neo-Thomists, it was closely identified with a broadly republican tradition which looked upon all members of society as citizens; those, that is, with the right to active participation in the political life of that society. The European monarchies, by contrast, were not accustomed to thinking of themselves in these terms. They provided their *subjects* – persons by definition excluded from active political life – with protection rather than welfare.

The second – the claim that overseas travel was, in some sense, inimical to true civil society – was perhaps too closely associated with a particular literary topos to have much resonance, until in the second half of the eighteenth century that topos reappeared in the context of the debate over slavery.

By the second half of the eighteenth century, however, as all the European empires began visibly to fragment, an argument against empire along the lines suggested by Vázquez and Soto, and echoed later by Grotius, began to reappear, although it did so without any obvious or direct reference to this earlier tradition. What the new enlightened critics of empire – Hume, Diderot, Condorcet and Raynal among others – share in common with these earlier writers are four things: a strong sense of place, a belief in the particularities, and thus the essential incommensurability of all cultural and political forms of life, the conviction that the goods which modern men sought were radically different from those which their ancient or medieval forebears had sought, and finally, that in terms of this set of temporal and spatial calculations, empires always disadvantaged, sometimes lethally, all those who were caught up in them. Founded ultimately upon conquest and the ruthless displacement or exploitation of native peoples, the dedication of all the first European empires to the perpetuation of Caesaro-papal projects for universal Christendom also came to seem not merely outdated, but ruinous in some deeper sense. 'Which way soever we consider great Empires,' wrote Charles Davenant in 1701, whether in their infancy, in their blooming youth, in their manhood and full strength or in their declining age we shall find mankind in all these several periods of time afflicted with wars, famine, bloodshed, thraldom and devastation.[11]

Hume agreed with him. 'Enormous monarchies,' he wrote in his essay 'Of the balance of power' of what he saw as the Habsburg and Bourbon bids for universal monarchy, 'are, probably, destructive to human nature; in their progress, in their continuance, and even in their downfall, which never can be very distant from their establishment.'[12]

At the root of all these anxieties lay the enduring preoccupation with the deleterious consequences of over-extension. As we saw in Chapter 4, this had been a critical component of most discussions of empire since at least the first century CE. In the eighteenth century, however, the concern focused not only on the fact that extended empires were difficult to govern, or that colonies, once they had turned on their 'mother' countries, were ultimately impossible to defeat. It also focused on the seeming impossibility of sustaining any true community in the face of sheer distance. If 'public happiness' was to be determined by the nature of private happiness, and if Price's 'fellow-feeling that takes place between persons in private life' was to be the measure of true political association, then, as Price himself had argued,

a country that is subject to the legislature of another country in which it has no voice, and over which it has no control, cannot be said to be governed by its own will. Such a country, therefore, is in a state of slavery.[13]

Civil society had always, by definition, been urban in origin. The paradigmatic empires – those of Rome and Athens – had been conceived as the extension of single cities, which became, in turn, metonymic for the empires which they had created. Once, however, the metropolis had come to include peoples whose ways of life could never be incorporated into the original community's political culture, an empire became a mere conglomerate, disformed and purposeless. By the eighteenth century the languages which expressed empire in terms of the greatness of cities, Machiavellian *grandezza*, and the programme set out in Botero's *Delle cause della grandezza e magnificenza delle città* (On the Cause of the Greatness and Magnificence of Cities, 1588) had come to be seen as the source of many of the ills which a particular kind of European conception of society had inflicted upon the world. Modern cities, like modern empires, said Diderot, were 'monsters of nature', which nature seeks always to destroy.[14] David Hume's famous outburst to William Strahan in October 1769 that, 'Notwithstanding my age, I hope to see public Bankruptcy, the total revolt of America, the expulsion of the English from the East Indies, the

Diminution of London to less than half',[15] is a list of calamities which an ageing and increasingly embittered critic wished upon a corrupt people and its government. But all of them also represented, like the 'enormous monarchies' he so distrusted, different kinds of over-reaching. Hume's dislike of London reflects in part a country–party distaste for all cities, but it also echoes a far older conviction, reiterated most powerfully in Hume's day by Rousseau, that the limits of the true political community were determined by the range of possible human contact. The creation of large states involved the corruption of this original and, to the minds of many, natural foundation. As Edward Gibbon observed of the final decline of Rome,

> The rise of a city which swelled into an empire, may deserve as a singular prodigy, the reflection of a philosophic mind. But the decline of Rome was the natural and inevitable effect of immoderate greatness. Prosperity ripened the principle of decay; the causes of destruction multiplied with the extent of conquest; and as soon as time, or accident, had removed the artificial supports, the stupendous fabric yielded to the pressure of its own weight.[16]

Modern empires were not merely large. They also embraced a wide variety of different, and generally conflicting, cultures. They had been created, furthermore, through the mass migration of peoples from one side of the globe to another. It was the inherent instability of this particular form of over-reaching – the unnaturalness of persistent displacement – which had served as the basis for both Vázquez and Soto's denial of the imperial title to lordship of all the world. In the course of the European Enlightenment, the fact that the Europeans in America or Africa or India had had to leave the land of their birth and create new hybrid cultures seemed to be the most destructive aspect of the entire colonial process. 'How wonderfully,' exclaimed Kant's most celebrated pupil, Johann Gottfried Herder (1744–1803), in 1791

> [has Nature] separated nations, not only by woods and mountains, seas and deserts, rivers and climates, but most particularly by languages, inclinations and characters, that the work of subjugating despotism might be rendered more difficult, that all the four quarters of the globe might not be crammed into the belly of a wooden horse.[17]

The Trojan horses which seek to subvert this naturally plural world are, of course, the European empires. 'Nothing,' he continued, 'appears so directly opposite to the ends of government as the unnatural enlargement of states, the wild mixture of various races and various nations under one sceptre.' The use of force and economic interest might, he believed, have temporarily 'glued together' the world's empires into 'fragile machines of state', but underneath this apparatus they were all 'destitute of internal unification and sympathy of parts'.[18]

True sociability, it was claimed, could only be maintained within communities of moderate size and homologous beliefs. Empires are, of necessity, societies divided between masters and slaves and, as Diderot who in Russia had witnessed this process at first hand recognized, communities which are so divided are bound one day to erupt into unparalleled violence.[19]

II

Herder's *Ideen zur Philosophie der Geschichte der Menschheit* (Ideas for a Philosophy of the History of Man) is perhaps the fiercest condemnation of the forced deracination of peoples, and the most eloquent defence of the particularity and individual worth of all cultures.[20] But the most sustained of the late Enlightenment critiques of this – and indeed most other – aspects of modern European imperialism was the abbé Thomas Guillaume Raynal's *Histoire philosophique et politique des établissements et du commerce des Européens dans les deux Indes*, to which Herder's own vision owes perhaps more than has generally been recognized.[21]

This first appeared in 1772 (although it was dated 1770) anonymously and with an Amsterdam imprint – thus signalling its possible radicalism. It became an immediate bestseller: more than thirty editions were printed between 1770 and 1787.[22] Napoleon later declared himself to be a 'zealous disciple of Raynal' and, significantly in view of what he did there, took a copy of the book with him to Egypt.[23] The title of the work alone was sufficiently striking to guarantee it a readership. The first part, the claim to be both a philosophical and a political history, made it, as Raynal went to some lengths to explain in the Preface to Book I, unique. 'I have,' he assured his readers, 'interrogated the living and the dead. I have weighed their authority. I have contrasted their testimonies. I have clarified the facts.' From text to text Raynal had travelled the world with the 'august image of truth' always before him as a guide.[24] The second part of his title was equally striking. Here, it claimed, was a history which brought together the two halves of the planet, the East and the West, and the two, hitherto unrelated, spheres of European colonial activity into one work. It was as if the gaze of the European, 'raised above all concerns', so that it might be able to 'glide above the atmosphere', could indeed unite 'the whole world beneath one'.[25]

Raynal – that 'eager inquirer after other men's truths', as John Elliott has nicely characterized him[26] – was a renegade Jesuit and former editor of the *Mercure de France*. He was, however, despite the radicalism of much of the *Histoire*, only a moderate reformer; a man who, in the words of Frederic

Grimm, held views which were 'more in accordance with established politics than with justice'.[27] He also had close, if still little-known, ties with the group around the duc de Choiseul which, after the defeat of the Seven Years War and the loss of Canada, had hoped to reaffirm the French presence in the Caribbean and the Indian Ocean. He was sufficiently concerned about the long-term consequences for Europe of the colonization of America to suggest to the Académie de Lyon in 1782 that they offer a prize for the best essay in answer to the question: 'Has the discovery of America been useful or harmful to mankind?'[28] But he was an unlikely author of what was to become not only the most outspoken condemnation of European colonization, but also one of the most powerful critiques of the *ancien régime* itself,[29] a work which, in the words of one of its fiercest critics, had aroused in all its readers a new brand of fanaticism: 'the fanaticism of liberty'.[30]

The final version of the *Histoire*, which appeared in 1780 in Geneva, was not, however, wholly or even largely Raynal's own work. It contained, in addition to the original 1772 text, extensive contributions by a number of the lesser and greater *philosophes*: Pechmeja, Deleyre, Dubreuil, Valadier, Saint-Lambert, Lagrange and Diderot's future biographer Naigeon, among others. The original text now provided little more than a narrative structure for a series of striking juxtapositions which transformed the work into an *Encyclopédie* on the political, intellectual and social implications for Europe of colonization. The most original, the most radical and sustained of these contributions were by Diderot. These were also far more uncompromising in their anti-colonialism than the more moderate and reconciliatory tones of Raynal's original text.[31] Raynal himself became, in effect, the champion of an anti-colonial movement very much *malgré lui*. Pierre-Victor Malouet, former Governor of Guyana, claimed that the abbé had been bitter about Diderot's reworking of his text and had frequently spoken 'against his own book, or rather against the interpolations of Diderot', complaining that he had 'only turned to Diderot to correct his style', but that Diderot had then taken over and

that the abuse of the confidence which he had placed in him [Diderot], the tyrannical conditions which he had imposed – all or nothing – had been a cause for just reproach, and the only thing that was instructive and important about the work was the part that he had written himself.[32]

In 1785, in collaboration with Malouet, Raynal wrote an *Essai sur l'administration de St Domingue* (Essay on the Administration of St Domingue). In this, he advocated wide-ranging economic reforms for the colony, but on the crucial question of slavery which, as we shall see, plays a central role in the *Histoire* he says only that it is the 'terrible law of the strongest'; but he cautioned against either the emancipation of the slaves or even the abolition of the slave trade.[33] If in the words of Diderot's own riposte to Grimm, Raynal's *Histoire* finally became 'the book which I love and which the kings and their courtiers hate, the book which will give birth to Brutus',[34] this is almost entirely because of Diderot's presence in the text.

III

The *Histoire* is simultaneously a celebration of the humanizing, civilizing effects of international commerce and a condemnation of the European colonizing venture. Far from seeing these as necessarily linked, both Raynal and Diderot regarded them as antithetical. Commerce, as we shall see in Chapter 7, could be redemptive, not only because of the kind of activity it was, but because those who conducted it remained firmly attached to the worlds into which they had been born. The colonist, by contrast, was a terminally deracinated personality. If communities were, as much for Diderot as for Price, the creation of 'the fellow-feeling that takes place between persons in private life' then the dissolute, unlocated, and hence uncivilized, self could only create societies that were fragmentary, unstable and, for all those who were forced into contact with them, ultimately lethal. The target of the *Histoire*'s most eloquent criticism is thus not so much the colonial process itself – although Raynal had much to say about that – as the individual whom that process had created. Behind this stood a thesis, first proposed in 1776 by the great French naturalist Georges Buffon. Buffon had noticed what he assumed to be the existence of species in America which, while recognizably the same as those in Europe, were more fragile and smaller in size. On the basis of this (false) observation he concluded that, because of the ecology of the place, all life in America was smaller, less well formed, sexually less active, and less consistent in purpose than life in Europe. This, furthermore, applied not only to plant and animal life. It also applied to humans, and not merely to those who were indigenous, but also, after a generation or so, to those who had settled there. Buffon's thesis enjoyed wide popularity in Europe, and was repeated in modified forms, by William Robertson, Raynal himself, and most notoriously by the Dutch natural philosopher Cornelius de Pauw, whose *Recherches philosophiques sur les américains* of 1769 painted a hideous picture of a wholly degenerate and irredeemable continent.[35]

The supposed natural inferiority of America itself and the deleterious effects it was believed to have upon all forms of life offered, to those who could believe it, a powerful basis for denying legitimacy to the Creole societies which had developed there. For Diderot, however, the moral decay of the settler populations had been predetermined by the migrants' decision to migrate. If civility could only be attained within settled communities, then those who chose to abandon those communities were necessarily beings with a very uncertain grasp of what it was to be a person. Migration meant the abandonment of the *civitas*, of, in Diderot's own terms, that self-defining, self-creating 'national spirit' which constituted every individual's social identity. Diderot had long been concerned with the fragility of the human personality, a fragility which he consistently expressed in the language of the theatre. We are what the worlds into which we have been born have made us, but we have, at all times, only a tenuous grasp of this selfhood. Detach a person from his or her metropolis and that grasp immediately weakens. 'The greater the distance from the capital,' he wrote in a remarkable evocation of the process of de-personalization,

> the further the mask of the traveller's identity slips from his face. On the frontier it falls away altogether. (Il tombe sur la frontière.) From one hemisphere to another what has he, the traveller, become? Nothing. Once past the equator a man is neither English, nor Dutch, nor French, nor Spanish nor Portuguese. All that he preserves of his homeland are the principles and prejudices which authorize or excuse his conduct.[36]

What he called 'les expéditions de long cours' had, he believed, 'reared a new generation of savage nomads. . . . Those men who visit so many countries that they end by belonging to no one. . . . These amphibians who live on the surface of the waters.'[37] They were the products of civilization's manifold discontents, of the

> tyranny, crime, ambition, misery, curiosity, I know not what restlessness of spirit, the desire to know and the desire to see, boredom, the dislike of familiar pleasures – these things men from all ages have carried abroad (*expatrié*) with them, and will continue to do so.[38]

Such creatures carried 'in the bottom of their hearts the germs of depredation' which under another sky and far from the public gaze had grown 'with inconceivable fury', so that it had finally consumed their entire person.[39] The societies which such creatures had founded could only be societies of the iniquitous. 'Individuals without industry, without leaders and without customs,' as Talleyrand savagely called them, 'and such creatures of vice, ignorance and misery cannot found, they can only destroy.'[40] Even, it would seem, the Dutch, a people whose tolerant and moderate laws, whose republican constitution and dedication to the twin goals of commerce and liberty had made them the envy of Europe, had now been corrupted beyond all hope of recovery by their commitment to overseas empire.[41]

The only possible exception to this dismal rule was the English. The Anglophilia of Raynal's original text was obvious enough for one reader,

Emilien Petit, deputy to the Conseil supérieur des Colonies françaises, to remark sourly that the abbé evidently harboured 'an extreme preference for the British Government and the English nation'.[42] But the image of the North American colonists in the *Histoire*, as the bearers of a new enlightened social order, was largely Diderot's creation. Uniquely, he believed, the English had been driven overseas not by greed, the 'soif d'or' which inevitably brings with it the thirst for blood,[43] nor even by a wish to impose their beliefs upon others. They had gone in pursuit of liberty.[44] Whereas all the other races of Europe had exported the worst, the English had driven out the best, and whereas the Spanish, Portuguese and French Creoles in America had now become, in Diderot's view, 'more or less degenerate',[45] the English-Americans had sustained, and developed, their concern for liberty to the point where it had far outstripped that of their increasingly tyrannical mother country. As the marquis de Chastellux in *De la félicité publique* (On Public Happiness) remarked in 1772, theirs was an America which had been 'peopled under the auspices of liberty and reason'.[46] How different, observed Diderot, was 'the destiny of an empire founded upon virtue' from those which France, Spain and Portugal had founded in America, or which the Dutch, the Portuguese and the British had established in India. Here was virtue without enthusiasm, and in the half-mythical person of the Quaker it was possible, from a distance at least, to see a transitional figure between the ancient republican and the modern merchant. In Diderot's view, no truly good, nor truly evil government had ever existed; but there were those, he believed, which were so much 'more wise in their constitution, more simple in their customs, more limited in their ambitions', than others as to be 'enveloped in a secret well-being', and thus to come as close as was humanly possible to the ideal type. Among such governments was that of Pennsylvania. 'This republic,' he believed,

> without wars, without conquests, without conflicts, without any of those revolutions which astound the passionate and unquiet eyes of the mob, will become a spectacle for the entire universe.[47]

One day, the example of the new Americans might, Diderot hoped, even serve the Europeans as a model from which they might be able to rebuild their own corrupted world. For this reason, he declared, the cause of the American rebels was 'that of the entire human race; it will become ours'. Since for Diderot, prosperity and material success were the necessary products of just government, the Thirteen Colonies were bound to prosper. Pennsylvania itself had already demonstrated, in its own short history, the truth of this conviction. Who, he asked, could not now believe that it was possible, at least with time, for the ancient balance between the old world and the new world to be reversed, that 'Europe will one day find her rulers from among their sons'?[48]

Diderot's vision was, of course, fully in keeping with both the colonists' own image of themselves, and the image generated by their British sympathizers. 'And in America,' Arthur Young had written some years earlier, 'Spain, Portugal and France have planted despotism; only Britain liberty.'[49] It was even possible for Diderot to ignore the Indian massacres and the expropriation of Indian lands which, as others less friendly to the Thirteen Colonies could point out, were every bit as bad as actions committed by other Europeans in other parts of America. In some lights British America would seem to correspond to the colony which, in his attack upon Claude-Adrien Helvétius's excessively mechanistic views of human nature, Diderot had imagined existing, in 'some remote corner of the world', a colony quite unlike any other, which would lie between the condition of the savage and what he referred to sarcastically as 'our wonderful civil state'. Here would be a midway point on man's inexorable and ultimately ruinous progress, a small community 'where the happiness of the species resides,'[50] 'an environment (*milieu*) which would retard the progress of the children of Prometheus . . . and which would fix civilized man between the infancy of the savage and our present decrepitude'.[51] It was a vision which some years earlier Richard Price had seen with similar clarity if much less eloquence. 'Our American colonies,' he wrote in 1776, 'particularly the northern ones have been for some time in the happiest state of society or in the middle state of civilization, between its first rude and its last refined and corrupt state.'[52] The new United States was clearly not Utopia. But then Diderot, like Price, had little time for utopias, and if it was not the ideal society, it was, at least, an attainable optimal society.

IV

In Diderot's view, however, all other Europeans in the Americas, as in India and Asia, had 'shown themselves indistinguishable, throughout all the countries of the New World'.[53] Their restless wanderings had made them not into savages, for savages have access to the virtues of the simple life 'in nature' which civilized man has been compelled to renounce. They have instead become what Diderot had defined elsewhere as 'barbarians', those who have been cursed by 'that sombre disposition which makes man inaccessible to the delights of nature or art and the sweetness of society'.[54] 'Savages' exist only in a particular cultural milieu, but 'barbarians', in common with Hobbes's *homo homini lupus*, are with us always no matter how civilized we may appear to have become. These new barbarians have destroyed, or attempted to destroy, as do all barbarians, the cultures of the peoples among whom they have settled. To this crime the settlers in America have added one which, in Diderot's view, had been still more tragic in its consequences: slavery. If the *Histoire* is at one level a history of commerce, at another – especially in those passages which Diderot contributed to it – it is one of the most powerful contributions to the anti-slavery literature of the late eighteenth century.[55]

To a greater or lesser extent, the European colonies in America were all slave societies, and all those both in America itself or in Europe who were, in some degree or another, hostile to the old colonial order were certain that slave societies were, in their very origins, sources of human corruption. For David Hume, it was precisely the reliance of the otherwise exemplary republics of the Ancient World upon slave labour which made them impossible models for any kind of modern liberty. 'Some passionate admirers of the ancients and zealous partisans of civil liberty,' wrote Hume,

> . . . cannot forbear regretting the loss of this institution; and whilst they brand all submission to the government of a single person with the harsh denomination of slavery, they would gladly reduce the greater part of mankind to real slavery and subjection. But to one who considers coolly on the subject it will appear that human nature, in general, really enjoys more liberty at present, in the most arbitrary government of Europe, than it ever did during the most flourishing period of ancient times. . . . The remains which are found of domestic slavery, in the American colonies and among other European nations, would surely never create a desire of rendering it more universal.[56]

Just as the republics of the Ancient World, for all their apparent virtue, had been corrupted beyond recall by their reliance upon slavery so, as Condorcet claimed, a society such as his own, which tolerated slavery anywhere in the world over which it had some authority, 'would not be a society of men but a band of brigands'.[57] It was for this reason, as Turgot observed to Richard Price in 1778, that even the nascent United States, for all its other manifest virtues, could never become a true *respublica* so long as it relied upon slave labour, for 'slavery is incompatible with a good constitution'.[58]

Modern and ancient slavery were similarly dehumanizing, and involved an identical degree of moral degradation for the slave and ultimately for the master. But they differed in one crucial respect. Modern slavery was not, as its ancient counterpart had been, the response to internal domestic need. It had instead been invented to serve the ends of the new colonial empires. And in order to achieve that it had not only deprived countless thousands of innocent beings of their natural liberty. It had also created a sustained and odious traffic in human merchandise.

The brief history of slavery in the eleventh book of the *Histoire* (probably composed by Jean de Pechmeja) describes how ancient slavery had died out in Europe in the early Middle Ages. This happy event had been the unintended outcome of the wars between the new European monarchies and their feudal nobilities, which had led to such 'ruses' by the monarchs as 'the protection of slaves against the tyranny of their masters', in order 'to sap the power of the nobles by diminishing the number of their subjects'. The pursuit of this 'happy policy' may have been the consequence of the operation of personal interests rather than – as was the modern opposition to slavery – the defence of the 'principles of humanity and benevolence'; but the objective had been the same, and, unlike the modern opposition, it had been successful.[59]

By the early fifteenth century slavery in Europe had almost ceased to exist. What began with the colonization of America, and the realization that for political and social reasons the Native Americans could not successfully be enslaved, was like the discovery itself, a new departure in European history. For the first time, instead of taking slaves in so-called 'just wars', instead of, as the Roman Law of slavery had insisted, 'saving' (one of the etymologies given for the term *servus*) a captive from the death his captor was entitled to inflict on him, men began to buy slaves who were innocent of any act of aggression. Having been bought, they were then transported from one side of the world to another.[60] They became thus doubly dehumanized, deprived of their personal liberty, and forcibly detached from the place, the *domus*, which had provided them, as it provided all persons, with their social identity.

Slavery for Pechmeja, as indeed for Raynal, is an obvious evil because it denies man his one inalienable right, his 'property in himself'. This, which is more than the free capacity for agency, constitutes, after reason itself, 'the distinctive character of man'. As one prominent abolitionist later argued before the Convention nationale, slavery not only 'made of the human race a merchandise', it also valued men precisely for that thing, physical strength, which was the least intrinsic to the human identity, and was thus 'the greatest affront to our nature'.[61] Freedom even to choose one's own modes of human indebtedness – which most clearly distinguished the slave from the European day-labourer with whom his condition was frequently compared – was a mode, as Diderot phrased it, of 'enjoyment in one's own mind' (*esprit*). The slave denied this feature of what it is to be a man was reduced to a level lower even than that of the dogs which the Spaniards had brought with them to America, for the dog is only an automaton, whereas the slave still retains some grasp on what, in the end, nothing can deprive him of: his consciousness.[62] He, or she, alone *knows* that he, or she, is a slave. The possession of a fully developed sense of what it was to be human, while being deprived of humanity, meant that the slave, unlike the free man who may be similarly restricted as far as his real capacity for individual choice is concerned ('most nations,' as Diderot observed, 'live in chains'), can have no cause for hope, no expectation of 'those happy times, those centuries of Enlightenment and of prosperity' which might one day allow even the most miserable labourer to recover his identity to the full.[63]

Slavery, argued Condorcet in the *Réflexions sur l'esclavage des nègres*

(Reflections on the Enslavement of Negroes) – which he printed in 1781 posing as a German pastor called M. Schwartz – since it was governed by the laws of property, constituted a purely private relationship. Even the indentured servant who, in some sense, had sold himself into slavery had, in fact, only sold the right to the use of his labour and in his relationship to his masters was bound by public not private law. The slave, by contrast, was merely a legal thing (a *res*), exactly as he had been under Roman Law, and thus wholly dependent upon 'the caprice of his master'.[64]

For Condorcet slavery was an evil whose abolition it was the duty of every civilized, every enlightened, man to procure. Most of those in the eighteenth century who were in any degree sympathetic to the plight of the Africans wished, however, to maintain a distinction between slavery itself and the slave trade. This allowed many, as Antoine Barnave had done, to support the institution of slavery itself as an as yet irrepressible evil, while venting moral indignation on the system of capture and transportation which had made it possible in the first place. Even such writers as the staunchly pro-colonist lawyer, Michel René Hilliard d'Auberteuil, was willing to concede that whereas the condition of most slaves in the French Caribbean was 'better than that of a European day labourer', to contemplate the slave trade was to experience 'a moment of horror which freezes all the faculties'. If it was not 'dangerous and contrary to public well being' it was certainly, in 'this enlightened century', a threat 'to custom' and a potential moral danger to the metropolitan French.[65] This was why it was advisable, in his view, to leave it in the hands of the English, and others of 'our political enemies', who were in any case better at it.

Diderot, however, had another reason for insisting that the trade was worse than the institution. He in no way attempted to diminish the condition of the slaves once they had reached America, and he shared Condorcet's view that those who argued for a more rigid code of conduct to protect the slaves, in place of full emancipation, merely 'added hypocrisy to barbarism'.[66] But the slave trade was not only a massive violation of the natural rights of countless human individuals. It was also the greatest, and most devastating, forced migration in human history and it had been responsible for the annihilation, literally or culturally, of entire races.[67]

The argument, which ever since the fifteenth century had been used to justify the trade – that the Africans had been seized in a just war 'at home'[68] – was rejected by Diderot, as it had been by Montesquieu, as entirely specious, since, as Diderot pointed out, no state can sell what it cannot own. The Roman Law of slavery which, in one way or another, still sustained modern legislation on the matter had made human beings the objects of the same property laws as inanimate things. But as the Scottish jurist George Wallace – whose denunciation of slavery was partially incorporated by Louis de Jaucourt into his article 'Traite des nègres' in the *Encyclopédie* – phrased it: 'men and their liberty are not *in comercio*.[69] Spurious or not, the claim that warfare was the root cause of slavery conjured up the still more horrific image of African wars fought solely to provide the white men with their labour. 'Such a trade,' bewailed one of the earliest of the English abolitionists, Granville Sharp, in 1776, preyed upon 'the ignorance and brutality of unenlightened nations, who are encouraged to war with each other for this very purpose'.[70] Europe, claimed Condorcet, 'is guilty not only of the crime of making slaves of men, but, on top of that, of all the slaughter committed in Africa in order to prepare for that crime'.[71] The disorders and conflicts within African society which had allowed the slavers to present a widely accepted, if logically incoherent, legal argument, were themselves the creations of Europe's colonial empires. Furthermore, unlike ancient slavery which, however evil, was a function of the kind of society which it sustained, modern slavery, said Diderot, 'is a trade which is based upon injustice and has only luxury as its object' – the twin evils which menaced the well-ordered society of the enlightened imagination.[72] The final outcome of this new and deadly combination of slavery and commerce had been to generate a form of mass involuntary migration. 'In order to people one part of the world which you have devastated,' Diderot accused the 'Féroces Européens', 'you have corrupted and depopulated another.'[73]

V

Depopulation, the spectre which haunted much eighteenth-century social theory, threatened for Diderot, and many of his contemporaries, to make a wasteland not only of America but also of Africa. Because Africa was being emptied of its native populations to meet the 'insatiable greed' of the European settlers in America, because the once populous Native Americans, now decimated by disease and conquest, had proved unwilling and unable to bring their population levels up to anything like their pre-conquest numbers,[74] because the degenerate colonists in America were seemingly unable to breed, and the African slaves would rather destroy their offspring than see them born into slavery,[75] Diderot believed that humanity was faced with the prospect of a rapidly emptying world. 'Free the slaves,' demanded Louis de Jaucourt and 'within a few generations this vast and fertile land will be filled with inhabitants'.[76] Modern slavery was not only a violation of all human rights, an insult to human decency, it was also, as Diderot insisted, 'prejudicial to the interests' of the 'cruel oppressors' themselves. For Diderot the same general rule applied to the relationship between masters and slaves as it did to the far less inhumane relationship between colony and metropolis. A relationship based upon reciprocity, upon benevolence, a recognition of the status of the other, was in the end bound to prove not only morally more desirable but also politically more sustainable and economically more prosperous than any dependent upon repression or coercion. 'Give the slaves a homeland,' he wrote in the *Histoire*,

> a shared set of interests, lands to work, and a form of production in accordance with their tastes, and your colonies will not lack arms. Freed of their chains, they will be both more active and more robust.[77]

Diderot also knew, as indeed had Montesquieu, that one of the features of modern colonization and the new trade routes which it had helped to create, was that the metropolis could never be fully insulated from the consequences of the processes of overseas expansion which it had itself initiated. Colonies in the Ancient World had been, to use Turgot's metaphor, 'like fruit',[78] which had clung to the tree only until they were mature. But modern colonies, created to export and impose a civilization, and sustained for the benefits to be had from trade or mining, had remained attached to their mother countries long after they had reached their maturity. What took place in Miletus or Ephesus could have had no significant moral effect on what happened in Athens. But the behaviour of the American colonists had a constant and frequently devastating impact on what took place in Europe. The vision of a safe, sanitized haven for the potentially destructive forces within European society of the marquis de Chastellux's imagination, ignored the fact that, remote though the Americas were, the European colonies there were still socially, culturally and politically linked to Europe. 'About two centuries after the depopulation of Europe into Asia,' said Diderot, summarizing the entire history of European overseas expansion, 'there came the migration into America. That revolution reduced all things to chaos, and mixed in among us the vices and the corruptions of every climate.'[79]

This had for long been held to be evident in the case of the Spaniards. The Spanish empire, explained Montesquieu, had 'destroyed all to preserve all',[80] and in the process it had destroyed itself. Both the French and the English, in this regard, had had since the beginning self-regarding images of themselves as distinctly more benign than the bigoted Spaniards. 'Neither the French nor the English,' declared the historian Charles de Rochefort in 1665, had followed 'the cruel and barbarous maxims of the Spaniards, nor have they piteously exterminated the original inhabitants of the country.'[81] Such claims may not have been entirely false. By the second half of the eighteenth century, however, neither the English nor the French could afford to be quite so complaisant. Both nations might have had a better record of behaviour towards the Native Americans, although this been almost entirely by circumstance, not design, but both practised slavery and both benefited – as the Spaniards did not – from the slave trade. And by the 1760s this had become a far more pressing moral problem than the extermination of the Amerindians. For as Diderot, Condorcet and others insisted, no one could hope to lead a civilized or enlightened life in a world in which slavery and the slave trade still flourished. If, as was widely believed, slavery made men, even entire races, slavish in their character, so the relationship between masters and slaves would corrupt the masters as inescapably as it dehumanized the slave. Slavery, Montesquieu had said

> is not good by its nature. It is useful neither to the master nor to the slave: not to the latter because he can do nothing from virtue, not to the former because he contracts from his slaves all manner of bad habits; imperceptibly he becomes accustomed to failing in all the moral virtues, as he grows proud, curt, angry, voluptuous and cruel.[82]

Thomas Jefferson, though he famously failed to free his own slaves, fully understood that the owning of slaves would eventually turn the slave master into a tyrant.[83] Enjoying the fruits of the slave's labour, claimed Hilliard d'Auberteuil, was a lamentable but necessary condition of survival for a colonial society based very largely on the production of sugar in climates which white labourers were commonly believed to be unable to endure. It was, in any case, a fact of history and thus a law of nature that 'human society has always demonstrated, and will continue to demonstrate the violence of the strong and the submission of the weak'.[84] But the *colons* among whom he had lived, and whom he supported so fiercely, also appalled him. 'Their tyranny towards their slaves,' he wrote,

> seems to them to be a right, their injustice an act of strength. They take pride in skilful knavery, and they have no [good] customs. Their every action is dominated by an astonishing mixture of avarice, debauchery, and baseness and cruelty.[85]

Contact with such people could, it seemed, erode even the most powerfully seated concern for the welfare of others. This, Brissot believed, was what had overtaken Barnave who, from being a 'firm defender of liberty', had, by consorting with the *colons*, come to embrace the cause, the language and the beliefs of those whose 'habit of commanding slaves, of treating them as if they were domestic animals, has filled them with prejudices which are the most insulting to humanity'.[86]

In Diderot's view, slavery had already in this way closed off the Europeans to a crucial part of their own humanity: their compassion. For a century now, he claimed, Europe had endorsed the 'most sane, the most sublime moral maxims', in which innumerable errors had been 'courageously unmasked'. The fraternity of all mankind has been 'established in the most moving manner in a number of immortal writings'. In the silence of the study, or in the theatre, every conceivable human misery was capable of reducing educated European man and woman to tears. Except one. For the enlightened societies of Europe, the African slave did not exist. 'It is only the fatal destiny of the unhappy negroes,' he lamented, 'which is of no interest to us.'[87] Like the doctor whose constant exposure to the sight of blood and bone will diminish his capacity to be moved by the spectacle of physical pain, so the whole of civilized European society had grown inured to the misery of the African.[88]

The reason for this indifference was not only long familiarity. It was also racial. The Native American, even the 'Hindoo', had excited the European's natural benevolence. But not the African, because unlike these races the African was black. Skin colour, as Médéric Moreau de Saint-Méry, deputy for Martinique in the years immediately following the Revolution, recognized, was a greater barrier between the slave and his master than even the fact of servitude itself.[89] This racism, argued Diderot, like so many of the other ills which afflicted Europe, had been a creation of the Church. 'Theology,' he explained, 'which has attempted to make everything seem marvellous and mysterious so as to reserve the right of explanation to itself' had invented this 'atrocious extravaganza' which is the story of the descendant of Cain.[90] Yet as anyone who had considered the matter had clearly recognized, skin colour and behaviour were unrelated. The slave's undoubtedly slavish behaviour was not a product of his race, it was the consequence of his enslavement. As Brissot claimed in 1776, repeating what had been a commonplace since at least the mid-sixteenth century, 'the ignorant and barbarous slave, born on the banks of the Bosphorus, would be an enlightened Republican had he been born in Philadelphia'.[91] Even an anti-revolutionary and supporter of slavery, such as Malouet, could see that this was true, although for him it was precisely a reason for forbidding slaves to leave their master's home except 'under the gaze of a vigilant police-force'.[92]

Modern slavery, which was entirely a product of modern colonization, had appropriated a primitive Judaic myth to create a race of sub-humans whose moral identity had been crudely assimilated to the colour of their skin so that even so sophisticated and enlightened a man as the marquis de Mirabeau could speak of the Africans as 'a race of men apart distinct and separated from our species'.[93] But for Diderot, the relative ease with which most Europeans had accepted, if only tacitly, these racist arguments, or the arguments from utility – neatly summed up in Barnave's claims that 'each time that one thinks one is doing something for philosophy, you do infinitely more against peace and tranquillity'[94] – was only the inescapable outcome of a process of dehumanization. It was the modern counterpart to the 'luxury' which the Romans had feared so much, and which colonization had inflicted not merely on the colonists themselves, but also on the metropolitan culture.

For the understanding of suffering requires not only the recognition of the humanity the observer shares with the sufferer; it also requires a leap of the imagination. The intrusion of other worlds into the Europeans' imaginative and cognitive space had made this leap possible now only for those enlightened few who could still keep the existence of a universal benevolence firmly within their grasp. For the majority the creation of the European overseas empires had provided the instruments of their own moral destruction. For this reason, Diderot finally came to believe that only a revolution, led by a new 'Black Spartacus', could hope to open the eyes of the European colonial world to the iniquities it had created.

Later Diderot's highly impassioned tribute to this figure came to be interpreted as a prophetic evocation of Toussaint Louverture.[95] Little wonder, perhaps, that Raynal, rather than Rousseau or Condorcet, became the prophet of the new order during Toussaint's rule in St Domingue between 1800 and 1802.[96] But Diderot's new Spartacus is not only an avenger, or even the necessary instrument of political liberation, he is also – as Bartolomé de Las Casas, the sixteenth-century 'Apostle to the Indians' had been before him – the means of redemption for the European.

For the writers of the Enlightenment the European overseas empires were destined for rapid extinction, at the hands of either the colonists or perhaps, in such places as Asia where they still possessed an independent will and the necessary technology, by the native inhabitants themselves. As they stood, these old imperial structures could no longer serve – if they ever had – any humanly acceptable purpose. But Diderot was as aware as Raynal himself had been that the present imperial world was too complex for any single group to dismantle it entirely, without massive loss to all those concerned. After 300 years the colonizers and the colonized in America had become too nearly fused for their distinct interests to be separated with ease. The abolition of the slave trade and the emancipation of the slaves would present no immediate social, moral or political difficulty. But the Europeans could not simply return to Africa the descendants of the Africans whom they had seized, any more than they could abandon to the Native Americans the cities they had created. However much he may have disliked and distrusted them, and the motives that had made them, Diderot recognized that the settler populations of America were now distinct and separate peoples. Anything resembling Herder's belief that what he called the 'full-blown bladders in human shape'[97] would finally become so 'dissipated and consumed' that it would 'not be difficult for the natives to give the finishing strokes to the rotten tree',[98] was merely absurd. Decolonization, although never seriously contemplated by anyone, would necessarily involve far more complex, less intransigent solutions than either simple withdrawal or a belief in the final disappearance of the colonizers. It would require the integration of the unfortunate Creoles into a world which was fully miscegenated and where, as Diderot rather fancifully expressed it, 'through consanguinity the foreigners and the natives of the place would have made a single and common family'. In such a world, he said wistfully, there would 'have been no weapons, no soldiers, only large numbers of many young women for the men, and many young men for the women'.[99] He had even hoped that the Portuguese crown's legislation of 1755 (which had attempted to put an end to the slave trade, and to curb the worst abuses of the colonists) might arouse sufficient confidence in the Indians of Brazil and Paraguay to 'draw them ... from their forests', and that 'a complete confidence might imperceptibly develop between the Americans and the Europeans so that with time they might come to form one people'.[100]

The European powers themselves had also to be compelled to recognize that the societies they had helped to create on the far side of the Atlantic had now become truly independent 'new' worlds, whose futures would no longer run parallel with those of their respective 'mother countries'. This, at least, was one lesson which the French and the Spanish could learn from the outcome of the American Revolution: that by transforming a collection of states linked by political and economic dependence into a federation of independent ones united by a common cultural identity, it might still be possible to preserve from the former European overseas empires some of the benefits to be gained for all those who had been involved.

CHAPTER SEVEN

From Empire to Federation

Les lois de Rome, faites pour gouverner une ville, succombèrent sous le poids du monde entier.

Anne Robert Turgot, *Tableau philosophique des progrès successifs de l'esprit humain*

I

Viewed from one, characteristically eighteenth-century, perspective it was possible to see the trajectory of the European empires as the unhappy outcome of a meeting between cultures at crucial, and unequal, stages in their historical development. Had the first European colonists been less advanced technologically, they would have been driven away from America and Africa and India, or compelled to trade on peaceful and equitable terms with the native inhabitants, as they were in China. Had they been as culturally and philosophically 'enlightened' as their eighteenth-century critics, they would not have embarked on a project of conquest and settlement at all. As it was, wrote Adam Smith, with his vision fixed upon the possibility of a more equitable future balance between nations:

> At the particular time when these discoveries were made, the superiority of force happened to be so great on the side of the Europeans, that they were enabled to commit with impunity every sort of injustice in those remote countries. Hereafter, perhaps the natives of those countries may grow stronger, or those of Europe may grow weaker, and the inhabitants of all the different quarters of the world may arrive at that equality of courage and force which, by inspiring mutual fear, can alone overawe the injustice of independent states into some sort of respect for the rights of one another.

Yet, for all the evil which, even to someone as unsentimental as Smith, colonialism appeared to have bequeathed to the world, it also seemed that it had generated, particularly in France and Britain, the cure for its own malady: *le remède dans le mal*, in Rousseau's perception of a not dissimilar human condition.[1] This was commerce. As we saw in Chapter 4, for many eighteenth-century writers, commerce offered the only mechanism by which it might be possible to transform the older European empires into modern productive and cooperative communities. The arguments of Smith, of Hume, of Turgot, Mirabeau, Campomanes and Ward had all been focused on the economic limits that successful commercial societies imposed upon potentially destructive political choices.

In the historiography of the eighteenth and nineteenth centuries, such trajectories, from the pursuit of mineral wealth, military glory and evangelization, to the quest for wealth through commerce and cultivation, became constitutive of a view of human social development in which warfare, and land-based empires, dependent as they had been upon military virtue for their creation, were regarded as but one phase in the historical development of mankind. 'War then comes before commerce,' wrote Benjamin Constant in 1813. 'The former is all savage impulse, the latter civilized calculation.'[2]

Constant was writing at a time when the collapse of the Napoleonic empire made it seem unthinkable that any European power would embark upon new imperial ventures. But even by the first decade of the eighteenth century, conquest had come to be regarded as a mode of behaviour which corresponded to the aspiration of earlier social forms, determined by the economic constraints experienced by predominantly hunter–gatherer societies. The creation of ancient colonies, wrote the marquis de Mirabeau, in *L'Ami des hommes* of 1758, belonged to that period of human history when warfare had been a form of brigandage, and when what he called the 'level of necessity' within each society had created the 'honour of empires'. Honour fed upon conquest; the 'spirit of conquest', in turn, depended upon terror, and terror, said Mirabeau archly, 'does not have too many neighbours'.[3] What Mirabeau's friend and collaborator, Le Mercier de la Rivière, in 1767 called the 'essential order' of modern societies was no longer based upon physical need, but grouped according to the laws of property and of exchange. And just as this 'essential order' had by the mid-eighteenth century come to be recast in the language used to describe purely private relations, so, too, was the relationship *between* states. In such a world, the only beneficial association between societies, as between individuals within society, had to be based on exchange not appropriation.[4]

Commerce replaces conquest; conversation and the voluntary exchange of goods are substituted for war. Conquering societies are, claimed Le Mercier, possessed by a 'devouring fire which cannot exist without consuming itself; sooner or later it must engulf those who first started it'. This is precisely what had become of the Roman Republic when it came to create 'a system which believed that it was permitted everything which force could acquire'.[5] Modern societies, by contrast, pursued commercial objectives. It was clearly in their interests, however narrowly these might be conceived, not to conquer their neighbours but to ensure their prosperity, for in a commercial world the prosperity of one nation inevitably led to the prosperity of all others. It was 'as a BRITISH subject' that David Hume prayed for 'the flourishing commerce of GERMANY, SPAIN, ITALY and even FRANCE itself'. For 'GREAT BRITAIN, and all those nations would flourish more, did their sovereigns and ministers adopt such enlarged and benevolent sentiments towards each other'.[6]

But there was another, and more far-reaching dimension to the vision these writers had of the consequence of commercial relations. 'Nothing,' wrote Smith, was more likely to bring about the 'equality of courage and force' between nations which he predicted than 'that mutual communication of knowledge and of all sorts of improvements which an extensive commerce from all countries to all countries naturally, or rather necessarily, carries along with it'.[7]

On this understanding, commerce was far more than the simple exchange of commodities. It was, as one of the abbé Raynal's commentators, Paul Ulrich Dubuisson, put it, 'the science of the needs of others'.[8] Ever since Antiquity the exchange of goods, the acquisition of knowledge and the understanding of a common humanity had shared a single vocabulary. Commerce, *commercium*, demanded communication, and communication would finally bring about, not only the end to hostilities between nations, but a deeper human awareness of the identity and singularity of others. From the replacement of a relationship based upon what he called the 'cupidity of conquest' by commerce, everyone, claimed Mirabeau, 'would benefit, foreigners as well as fellow citizens', because everyone would become brothers within a global fraternity called 'humanity'.[9] Commerce, Mirabeau enthused, was the expression at a national and international level of the reciprocity which held individuals together as members of a single family:

> Everything in the universe is commerce because by commerce one must understand all the natural and indispensable relationships of the entire species, which are, and will always be those between one man and another, between one family, one society, one nation and another.[10]

For even more extreme optimists, such as Joseph Mandrillon, Columbus's true destiny had been not to bring the Europeans to America but 'to open new routes across the oceans . . . to create links of fraternity between the two worlds'.[11]

Because it was, as Diderot said, 'the new arm of the moral world',[12] commerce was certain one day to become the agent of a new world order, a new empire, which would be based not upon power and plunder, but upon reciprocity. 'A war among commercial nations,' he wrote in a remarkable passage, is a fire that destroys them all. The time is not far off when the sanctions of rulers will extend to the individual transactions between the subjects of different nations, and when bankruptcy, whose impact can be felt at such immense distances, will become affairs of state . . . and the annals of all peoples will need to be written by commercial philosophers (*commerçans philosophes*) as they were once written by historical orators.[13]

The metaphorical shift from the orator to the philosophically informed commercial historian is significant. For the Ancient World, whose claims to a universal moral authority Diderot distrusted intensely, the limits of the community had been set, as Rousseau insisted, by the range and power of the human voice.[14] The community of the 'commercial historian', by contrast, is global, and the means of communication he has at his command – the written word and the exchange of goods – will be used to construct societies far more complex, and ultimately far more humane, than the constraining oligarchies of Rome or Athens. This would be the truly 'universal society', which, Diderot believed, must

exist for the common interests and the reciprocal interest of all the men of which it is composed. An increase in their happiness should result from their communication with one another. Commerce is the exercise of this precious liberty, in which nature has called all men to place their happiness and even their virtue.[15]

It was a vision shared by most of those who had placed their future hopes, however loosely, in the humanizing power of Montesquieu's 'doux commerce'. Mirabeau's *L'Ami des hommes*, although a treatise on population, is primarily concerned with establishing the possible conditions for a future 'universal Monarchy'. This, however, would be not, as all such monarchies had been in the past, a synonym for 'universal devastation',[16] but instead a common alliance of trading nations. The ruler who promoted such universalism would be the true 'Friend of mankind', *L'Ami des hommes*. A conflict anywhere in the world could easily be resolved by a military alliance between the partners, since every part of this new global federation, united as it would be by what Mirabeau called 'the universal confraternity of trade', would be bound by shared interests and the acknowledgement of a common humanity to work together as a single nation. 'Now supposing,' he wrote,

that that Prince, the Friend of Mankind, whose actions and opinions are all plainly to be seen and whose policies are in full public view, supposing that he might be forced to use the sword to support the common cause of humanity, can it be conceived that such a war would not become the common cause of all the allied powers? And then, once freed by a declaration of war from the shackles of justice which might

> otherwise prevent me even from imposing the yoke of humanity, I [*L'Ami des hommes*] would agree on no treaty except one whose basis was entry into the universal confraternity of trade.

Such 'would be the only yoke which it would be permitted to impose upon one's neighbours and the only empire which it would be useful and practicable to exercise over them'. And, Mirabeau added, anyone who dismissed such projects as nothing other than 'un rechauffé de Platon et de sa république' were sadly in error. 'That extraordinary genius' had merely beaten his wings in the air of metaphysical speculation, whereas 'I speak after considering the facts as they are, and have drawn from them the subsequent arrangements as they must be'.[17]

Such optimism about the potentially beneficial consequences of commercial relations was not shared by all. The more sceptical observers could see that trade itself, or what Hume had identified as 'the Jealousy of Trade',[18] could easily become, not a substitute for but a further cause of war. Hume may indeed have seen, as J.G.A. Pocock has argued, 'commerce and passion as dynamic forces contributing both to the construction of political society and to an active and kinetic history'.[19] But he also recognized that trade wars could become more ferocious than any wars known hitherto. 'Trade has now become,' as Andrew Fletcher had written as early as 1704,

> the golden ball, for which all nations of the world are contending, and the occasion of so great partiality, that not only every nation is endeavouring to possess the trade of the whole world, but every city to draw all to itself.

'And,' he added, 'the English are no less guilty of these partialities than any other trading nation.'[20]

Furthermore, any attentive observer of the political scene of the previous century could hardly fail to notice that the shift in emphasis from conquest to commerce, from military and spiritual honour to economic gain, had never been quite as clean as many eighteenth-century political economists had hoped. It was obvious that the claim of the authors of that most characteristic of eighteenth-century projects, the *Universal History*, that

> the opening of the trade to the Indies which may be truly considered as the main wheel of the great machine of commerce . . . By this means multitudes were brought to devote their time and their labour to cultivating the arts of peace and to the improvement of the countries which they inhabited; instead of placing all their hopes of aggrandizing and enriching themselves by plundering and oppressing their neighbours; and this it was that by degrees, as the many good effects of such a

disposition appeared, gave a new turn to politics and induced princes and their ministers to turn their views to the encouragement of industry as the surest and most effectual means of rendering their subjects, and consequently themselves, rich and powerful . . .

was at best incomplete.[21]

Commerce, as a concept, as a system of exchange, might indeed possess the power, in Montesquieu's celebrated phrase to 'make custom gentle'.[22] But few European observers of contemporary commercial practice had much faith in the merchant class itself as the builders of the new world order. The physiocrats, in particular, made a clear distinction between 'commerce' and the merchant (*commerçan*). Merchants, they knew by experience, were possessed of only short-term interests, and in France they had done all they could to block legislation to free the nation's grain markets. They had none of the larger vision required to place the good of the nation before their own gain, precisely because the interests of all those who lived by profit were, in Smith's words, 'always in some respects different from, and even opposite to, that of the publick'.[23] Many merchants, indeed, seemed to share the same spirit of conquest as their ancestors. It was foolish, wrote Dubuisson, to confuse 'commerce' with 'the merchant', as foolish as it was to confuse the priest with the cult he served. This was so partly, argued Mercier de la Rivière in 1767, because 'commerce' described a complex mode of behaviour involving a range of activities which included not only the trader, but also the producer and the consumer.[24] It was partly, too, because the merchants themselves still lacked what Dubuisson called 'a noble idea of their profession'. Concerned as exclusively with their own interests as the ancient warriors had been with theirs, it was pointless to ask the majority of them to have trust in each other, the trust that was required if the whole system was to function at all. For overseas trade depended, in the first instance, upon settlement, and settlement without conquest might still be a source of honour. Those, wrote Dubuisson, surveying the history of the former French colonies in Canada, who had found themselves compelled to occupy 'open spaces' had, as he scathingly put it, been driven less by needs or the new spirit of commerce than 'agitated by the remnants of the spirit of Chivalry'.[25] Thus, just as the Spanish authorities in America had had difficulty in persuading new arrivals to abandon their aspirations to be knights in favour of farming and trade, so in 1679 the Governor of New France complained to the crown that, although 'the interests of Your Majesty are that the colony should be established in particular for the cultivation and exploitation of land,'[26] the colonists for the most part refused to engage in anything except trade. They were, as Barrin de la Galissonière, Governor of New France between 1747 and 1749, said of them, 'too lazy and too haughty'.[27] This image of the merchant adventurer as the transmogrification of the ancient *noblesse de l'épée* was to haunt much eighteenth-century French discussions of the world-historical significance of the commercial societies which the discovery of America had helped to create.

Because the true 'Spirit of Commerce' – Montesquieu's *doux commerce* – depended upon networks of cooperation and trust, and upon people who could fully understand that in order for any commercial system to function it had to be able to bring benefit to all those involved, it was also thought to be largely confined to those European states whose societies were, if not constitutionally republics, at least republican in spirit. As Bernardo Ward had argued, the republican city-states of Renaissance Italy and the Hanseatic League had been able to afford to pursue commercial gain at the expense of military glory only because in those societies the interests of the private and the public bodies were the same.[28] In monarchies, however, and in the Spanish monarchy in particular, the ethos of individual honour acquired, however notionally, through arms, kept the public and private goods separate. In Ward's analysis this conception of nobility as based upon a code of purely personal honour had served the older feudal order well. But in a modern society, as the Spanish case had demonstrated all too starkly, it ran directly counter to the interests of the state. This is why the noted Spanish mercantilist Jerónomio de Uztáriz (1670–1732), in an attempt to urge similar objectives upon the Spanish crown, had praised Colbert for his attempt to persuade the French aristocracy that trade 'would never prejudice their nobility'.[29]

To some, especially the French physiocrats, it seemed that of all the modern European colonial powers, only Britain had fully succeeded in transforming its ancient military ethos into the spirit of commerce. The British empire, said François Quesnay, had created a 'Carthaginian constitution' where

> not only the colonies, but the provinces of the metropolis itself are subjected to the laws of commerce and carriage, where the laws of maritime commerce pay no heed to the laws of politics, where the interests of the land under cultivation (*glèbe*) in the state are subordinate to the interests of traders (*négociants*), where commerce in agricultural produce, the property in land, and even the state itself, are regarded as accessories to the metropolis, and the metropolis as composed of merchants.[30]

But this vision corresponded less to the perceptible realities of the British system than to the ambition to create the kind of federation which by the end of the eighteenth century most enlightened thinkers were urging upon their respective rulers.[31] At best it was a projection of the wishes of such English mercantilists as Sir Josiah Child (himself of course a merchant); at worst – like Quesnay's depictions of China and Peru – a future project for the Kingdom of France masquerading as a sociological description. Quesnay's argument that the nature of the English system was due to the fact that England was, in all significant respects, a 'mercantile republic' and that in such republics the laws of politics were subordinate to those of commerce whereas in 'monarchical empires, politics and the interests of commerce and carriage are powerfully opposed ... and merchants cannot be seen as anything other than accessories to the metropolis', similarly reflected Montesquieu's characterization of the English constitution, and echoed the claims of innumerable British pamphleteers that it was the liberty of the British government – and its Protestantism – which had given it the lead over the tyrannical, and Catholic, regimes of the south. On this account, as we saw in Chapter 3, the British colonists, once Sir Walter Raleigh's vision of Guiana had faded, had fabricated an image of themselves as peaceful, liberty-loving farmers and merchants. They were not, like their Spanish rivals, archaic *conquistadores*, New World Don Quixotes in rusty armour acting out tales from the romances of chivalry. They had not conquered. They had cultivated lands which they had purchased, and traded with the native peoples among whom they had settled. And it was obvious, to them at least, that only colonial societies which had been built up in this way could hope to achieve long-term commercial prosperity. The Spaniards, by contrast, as Campomanes and Ward often feared, were condemned, by their very origins, to repeat not only Rome's glorious beginnings, but also its ignominious end.

This was not, however, a story which was universally accepted, even within Britain itself. The British may have been able to claim, at least before the move west of the Appalachians, to have conducted themselves with rather less brutality than the Spaniards had done. But, as Richard Price pointed out, at a time when the rhetoric of self-congratulation over the supposedly peaceable nature of the British invasion of America was running high on both sides of the Atlantic, the British had been no less sanguine, no less eager for the glories and the gains offered by conquest than their Catholic neighbours. It was only opportunity they had lacked. 'Turn your eyes to India,' he demanded.

> There more has been done than is now attempted in America. There Englishmen, actuated by the love of plunder and the spirit of conquest, have depopulated whole kingdoms and ruined millions of innocent peoples by the most infamous oppression and rapacity. The justice of the nation has slept over these enormities. Will the justice of heaven sleep? Are we not now execrated on both sides of the globe?[32]

For Price, as for many champions of the cause of the American Revolutionaries, neither the largely mythical 'English constitution', nor the still more illusory British passion for liberty, could be relied upon to guarantee the kind of society of reciprocity and benevolence which he – like Diderot and Condorcet in France and Campomanes and Ward in

Spain – hoped for the future. Like Smith, Diderot and Turgot – and despite Smith's view of him as 'a most superficial Philosopher and by no means an able calculator'[33] – Price could see that this could not be left to such ancient, and localized, cultural constraints. Commerce was an international affair, and the psychologies and customs that made it possible all had to be enacted upon a world stage. They had, that is, to be made an integral part of international relations. Diderot's *commerçans philosophes* had to be allowed to speak for the whole world before any one part of it could hope fully to escape from the grip of the old militarist, aristocratic, monarchic – and murderous – order.

There was little hope, furthermore, that *le doux commerce* could perform this task within the older imperial structures. The only kind of international political order that would allow the market to exercise its natural benevolence was one in which empires had been transmuted into international federations of states, united, not politically or militarily, but by common cultural ties and economic interests.

'The present policy of Europe with respect to America,' wrote the marquis de Mirabeau, had struggled to combine three entirely incompatible 'esprits': that of domination, that of commerce and that of 'population' (i.e. settlement) into 'a new and, I dare to say, monstrous system'.[34] The task which should face all reasonable statesmen was, as he saw it, to separate these elements, to trade ancient domination for the more obviously modern benefits of commerce and population. Like most observers in the 1750s he could see that sooner or later 'the new world will certainly throw off the yoke of the old'. Like Turgot and Smith after him, he also recognized that any attempt to prevent this on the part of those 'little brains' who held power in London, Paris or Madrid would only have the tragic effect of destroying the possibility of transforming 'frequently burdensome subjects' into 'powerful brothers, always ready to assist'.[35] He also knew that this transformation could be achieved only within a new commercial system in which empires would be replaced by free-trade associations between independent nation-states, and the calculation of the benefits to be gained by each party would replace the vain pursuit of honour and glory, or even of Christian salvation. Rome had been destroyed by forces from without. The provinces had overrun the metropolis.[36] The European empires in America, however, had collapsed because of the emergence in their midst of new political cultures, and because, as Benjamin Constant phrased it, the modern concern for pleasure and utility had 'opposed irony to every real or feigned enthusiasm' which had sustained such ancient projects.[37] In the end, the models which had driven the ideologies of empire in all three European monarchies had always been too self-consciously ancient ones, increasingly incapable of explaining the shape of a modern and complex world. As Turgot, reflecting upon what he knew to be the final demise of the first European overseas empires, observed, the 'laws of Rome, which had been made to govern a city', had finally 'succumbed beneath the weight of the entire world'.[38]

II

Something of what this implied had been captured nicely in Andrew Fletcher's *An Account of a Conversation concerning the Right Regulation of the Government for the Common Good of Mankind* of 1704. Here Sir Charles Musgrave offers what is, in effect, a defence of the Grotian argument that the relationship between states should be unhindered by the consideration of anything other than the benefit of one's community, or, as he puts it, 'a citizen in the service of his country ... is not obliged to the same scruples as in his private affairs; and must be true to his public trust and take care that the commonwealth suffer no prejudice,' even if this meant, for instance, defending the gains made in an unjust war. To this Fletcher himself replies:

> Then, said I, no man can be a good citizen of a particular common-wealth and a citizen of the world; no man can be a true friend to his country and to mankind as a whole.[39]

The only way to overcome the human tendency to act 'without any regard to the rest of mankind' was, as Immanuel Kant was to argue in *Perpetual Peace: A Philosophical Sketch* of 1795 (*Zum ewigen Frieden. Ein philosophischer Entwurf*), through the creation of a universal federation bound by common commercial interests. This alone could be the basis for what in *Idea for a Universal History with a Cosmopolitan Purpose* (*Idee zur einer allgemeinen Geschihte in weltburger Abisicht*, 1784) he had called the 'highest purpose of nature, a universal *cosmopolitan existence*', which was to be the 'matrix within which all the original capacities of the human race may develop'.[40]

Fletcher was, of course, no Kantian *avant la lettre* (although as Istvan Hont has pointed out, Kant's *Perpetual Peace* and Fletcher's *Account* do 'run on similar tracks').[41] He was arguing for the desirability of the image of the Achaean League, rather than the Roman *Imperium* – or the unrestrained state of nature – as an image for governing the relationship between the nations of the world.[42] But he, like his more determinedly cosmopolitan French and German successors, was equally concerned that something called 'mankind' should be placed firmly on the agenda. Political theory, what he described as the 'continual scheme of constitutions', had, he complained, always been considered 'with respect only to particular nations for whom they were designed, without regard to the rest of mankind'. Self-interest naturally conditioned men to think solely in terms of their own limited domains:

I think mankind might be best preserved from such convulsions of misery, if instead of framing governments with regard only to a single society, as I believe all legislators have hitherto done, we should constitute such as would be no less advantageous to our neighbours than ourselves.[43]

It was evident to Fletcher that no people could consider themselves in isolation from the rest. If the modern empires were to arrest the process of decline which was the natural consequence of their expansionist origins, they had to transform themselves into something far closer to federations, something like the image – useful rather than accurate – which Fletcher shared with James Wilson of the Achaean League, that 'great masterpiece of human politics', as Wilson called it.[44] Far better, as Fletcher expressed it, a league of 'cities of moderate extent' than 'one great vicious and ungovernable city'.[45]

What all of the theorists of federation, from Fletcher to Wilson, had in mind was not the alliance of semi-independent communities, whose external affairs, fiscal controls and many of whose laws were to be dictated by a central federal government – the kind of society which the United States finally became. Fletcher's vision, like that of the marquis de Mirabeau (and of Benjamin Franklin in the 'Acts of Confederacy and Perpetual Union' of 1775)[46] and, as we shall see, of Kant, was for something at once both looser and far grander, something which was in effect a *confederacy*, as the Amphictyonic Council had been, of independent states, each of which, in James Madison's words, 'retained the character of independent and sovereign states and had equal votes in the federal council'.[47] Only a confederated world system of this kind, divided by climate, culture and language but united in economic and political objectives, would be capable of ensuring world peace and of providing the necessary guarantees for what Fletcher was now able to call 'the general good and interest of mankind'. In the modern world, commercially and politically and culturally pluralist, only a universal consideration could be the ground upon which 'every distinct society depends'.[48] In an unregulated world-system, argued Kant, each state must 'expect from any other precisely the same evils which formerly oppressed individual men [in the State of Nature] and forced them into a law-governed civil state'. The only escape from a world where the large, technically skilled and militarily powerful states were empowered to absorb all others would be

a federation of peoples in which every state, even the smallest, could expect to derive its security and its rights not from its own power or its own legal judgement, but solely from this great federation (*Foedus Amphictyonum*) from a united power and the law-governed decisions of a united will.[49]

The critics of the Enlightenment, from Herder in the late eighteenth century to Adorno and Horkheimer in this, have characterized the expression of such concerns with the welfare of 'humanity' as little more than a thinly disguised re-instantiation of older, cruder imperialist orders.[50] It is true, for instance, that Condorcet's programme for the 'Future progress of the human spirit' – written while in hiding in 1793 from the agents of the Revolutionary present – transposes the arbiters of the old world order, the 'tyrants, priests and hypocrites', with the enlightened scientists of the new, and replaces conquest, physical and spiritual, by enlightened instruction. For, or so Condorcet believed, the peoples of America, Africa, Asia and other 'distant countries' 'seem to be waiting only to be civilized and to receive from us the means to be so, and find brothers among the Europeans to become their friends and disciples'.[51] There are, however, huge differences between such programmes for the inhabitants of the 'distant countries' of the world or, for that matter, Napoleon's for the Egyptians, and say, the older Spanish, French and British plans for the Native Americans.

They may, as their critics claim, share the same foundational assumption: that European, and either secular-republican or monarchical-Christian civilization is an unquestionable good, and that it can successfully be exported. But for Condorcet and Kant – and even possibly for Napoleon – the foundation of that belief is not the rights-based conception of an expanding military culture. It does not suppose that the actual condition of the non-European can confer rights upon the European nor, crucially, does it make any claim that an unwillingness on the part of the non-European to embrace European civilization might legitimize the seizure of the non-European goods or persons. They can be led; but they cannot be pushed. Furthermore, the world in which we all – European and non-European alike – will finally come to live *must* be one in which all parties will benefit equally. You cannot, that is, trade personal servitude for the supposed benefits of Christian redemption, or even, in less extreme cases, for the protection offered by superior technology. The Enlightenment reformulation of empire as confederation sought, as Kant says again and again, to facilitate a process by which peoples would become in the full sense of the term *civilized*.[52]

Such a federation would not be an empire, a 'Universal Monarchy', that 'amalgamation of the separate nations under a single power which has overruled the rest', since linguistic, and what Kant calls 'religious', differences between peoples makes any such world state possible only in the very short run. '*Nature*' – and in this Kant was fully in agreement with Herder – 'wills it otherwise'. The source for the new universalism would not be the result, as the Roman empire had been, of the collapse of republicanism. It would be its natural conclusion. In the new republics which would, Kant was certain, be created in imitation of the French, there would be 'more charity and less strife in lawsuits, more reliability in keeping one's word'. There would, that is, be a higher degree of trust. But it was to be trust not in one's own religious or national kind, but in a law-governed, mutually sustainable community. For Kant, civilization meant the amelioration of all human relations within that order. But he quite specifically rejected the ambition to achieve this, as the older Christian empires had attempted to do, by altering the nature of human beliefs. Sociability for Kant was, famously, the balance of the unsocial forces within human nature, the tension between man's 'inclination to *live in society*', and his 'tendency to *live as an individual*'.[53] What would draw the whole of mankind finally into a single union was not the cessation of difference – for that would have required the restructuring of the individual – but its rationalization. The growth of 'culture', the collective sensibilities of the race, would, he believed, ensure that

> Men gradually move towards greater agreement over their principles, they lead to mutual understanding and peace. And unlike the universal despotism which saps all man's energies and ends in the graveyard of freedom, this peace is created and guaranteed by an equilibrium of forces and a most vigorous rivalry.[54]

In the political culture of trust, which only republics could sustain, it would be possible to extend this notion of competitive cooperation to

> nations in their external relations towards one another up to the realisation of the cosmopolitan society, without the moral foundations of mankind having to be enlarged in the least.[55]

III

Kant's *ius cosmopoliticum*, although he rarely mentions any political order other than the European one, was intended to embrace, quite literally, the whole world. Most of Kant's writings on cosmopolitanism were also composed after the French Revolution seemed to have created some of the external conditions necessary for this transformation.[56] But even if Kantian cosmopolitanism was, as Kant himself fully recognized, unlikely to be realized in present time, by the outbreak of the American War of Independence it had already become clear to the enlightened intellectual elite of all three of the European cultures with which I have been concerned that the creation of stable international relations and of successful commercial networks – both now regarded as the prime moral objectives of government – could only ever be the product of political liberty. Only free states could enter into federation with one another. 'In those places where government is in the hands of the colonists,' wrote

Mirabeau, 'industry, commerce and the arts have been established which are the equal of those in Europe.'[57] Elsewhere, colonial societies had only ever been crude, inefficient and tyrannical simulacra of the cultures of their mother countries. Slaves do not make good producers, and people will always work hardest in pursuit of their own interests. A set of free states in America would hugely enlarge and diversify the world trading base. In purely economic terms the mother countries had nothing to lose, and, since all they would give up was the burden of administration and the cost of defence, everything to gain. For it was already clear, said Turgot, that countries like Switzerland and Austria that had no history of overseas colonization now benefited quite as much from the existence of the American colonies as did the colonies' respective mother countries.[58]

That it should be the English who were the first to have had this truth thrust upon them was an irony which was not lost upon their European rivals. 'The poor English,' wrote Turgot to Pierre Samuel Du Pont in 1776, 'had been thoroughly punished for the all the stupidities (*bêtises*) which they have said about commerce and their political regulations . . . Now they will have to become economists.'[59] But, as the English themselves, most French and not a few Spanish observers had seen, the 'loose' nature of British colonial government had always made it likely that a breakdown in the political relationships between the colony and the metropolis would occur long before a cultural one did. If despotic Spain and France cannot 'maintain their Authority over their American Colonies but very imperfectly,' inquired the Dean of Gloucester, Josiah Tucker, then what hope could there be for 'such Colonies as are the Offspring of a free Constitution'?[60]

'Free Constitution' it may rarely have been, but it was clear to most reflective observers that, in any extended empire, what linked the centre to the periphery had always been not calculated interests but loyalties sustained by a common cultural identity and a common purpose. 'The interests properly understood of two countries,' wrote Talleyrand in Year V of the Revolution, 'is the true link which binds them and this link will be all the more strong if they share a common origin. . . . At a great distance every other form of contact becomes in time illusory.' Canada, he added with prescience, would never cease to be French.[61] The implication of such observations was that if culture was all that linked the colony to the metropolis, then, once again, the way to understand that relationship was not as one of dependence, but as one of protection and free trade; not empire but federation.

In an extensive, and characteristically perceptive, *mémoire* written in April 1776 (although it was only published at the height of the debate over the future of the remaining French colonies in 1791) Turgot had come to much the same conclusions. Empires, as they were currently administered, with restrictive trade laws which favoured the interests of the metropolis, could not hope to survive for long, particularly if the revolution of the

British colonies in America were to succeed. It would, he advised, 'be more advantageous to us to leave them in complete independence rather than wait for the moment when events force us to take our leave'.

Turgot was writing before the outcome of the American war was known, although he was in little doubt as to what it would be, and he had seen what few in France and no one in Spain before the 1780s had seen: that an independent North America would establish in the western hemisphere what he called a 'new state of liberty', which sooner or later would draw the Spanish and then the French colonies into its orbit. The alternative, if by some strange twist of fortune Britain should win the war, would be not dissimilar in its consequences for both France and Spain. The vast resources that the British had poured into America during the war had placed there a huge army which, Turgot believed, could only, in the event of victory, be turned on the remaining French colonies in the region and perhaps even on the Spanish. The vision of a British empire in America reaching from Newfoundland to Panama was, for Turgot, a very real possibility. Or would have been – were it not for the fact that any European nation, even one with the resources of the British, fighting wars in America was doomed to failure. Even success, he pointed out, would ruin Britain. With a vast hinterland into which to retreat, the American colonists could always outrun, if nothing else, a European army. What to Turgot was clear, however, was that whatever the outcome of the war, a new and potentially menacing power was bound to be created, one whose very existence demanded that the two remaining powers in the Americas should now adopt a new conception of their relationship with their colonies. 'Wise and happy,' wrote Turgot, 'would be the nation which, the first to bend its politics to new circumstances, would consent to see its colonies as allied provinces, and not as subjects to the metropolis.'[62]

The Spaniards, he believed – but the same would hold true for the French – should learn to cultivate the 'principles of fraternal liaisons based upon an identity of origins, of language, of customs, without conflict of interests'. The forces – loyalty to a distant monarch, a single body of law, and a centralized administration – which had held the metropolis and the colonies together over the years could not be mobilized to unite them as free members of independent states. The Castilian crown should, he concluded, 'know how to offer liberty as a gift, instead of allowing it to be dragged by force from an empire that can no longer be sustained'.[63]

What Turgot had in mind was the replacement of the existing political and legal ties between the metropolis and its former dependencies by a trading partnership, bound together by a loose and indeterminate political association.[64] Adam Smith agreed. The immediate abandonment of the doomed attempt to hold the British colonies by force would, he claimed, certainly persuade

turbulent   and   factious   subjects,   to   become   our   most   faithful, affectionate and generous allies; and the same sort of parental affection on the one side, and filial respect on the other, might revive between Great Britain and her colonies, which used to subsist between those of ancient Greece and the mother city from which they descended.[65]

In Smith's view, as he expressed it in his 'Thoughts on the state of the contest with America' of February 1788, the American colonies, at least since the 1730s, had only ever been a drain on the nation's resources, finally leading it into two wars – in 1739 and 1755 – which 'were undertaken, the one chiefly, the other altogether on account of the colonies'. From the replacement of colonial dependence by a federal structure, the return of Florida to Spain and Canada to France, 'we should certainly incur', he believed, 'much less expense and might, at the same time, gain as real advantages, as any we have hitherto derived from all the nominal dominion we have ever exercised over them'.[66]

As Smith had seen, it had been precisely the failure of Spain to relinquish total control of the Netherlands after 1609 which had driven the Dutch Republic to persist in its hostility to Spain:

> If all the seventeen provinces of the Netherlands had completely emancipated themselves from the dominion of Spain, their situation, as soon as their independency was acknowledged, would have rendered them the natural enemies of France, and consequently the natural allies of Spain. Spain would have suffered little more than the mortification of losing the dominion of a great country, which, for some years before the revolt, had never paid the expense of its own government. To compensate this mortification, she would have gained the solid advantage of a powerful, and probably a faithful alliance, against the most formidable of her enemies.[67]

To attempt, as the British were doing, to undo their own policies of benevolent cooperation, and to reverse the move towards emancipation, which most saw as not merely inevitable but the final stage in a world-historical process, was, in the opinion of most critical observers, insane. There was simply no possibility of success. Even assuming that the reconquest of America were to be militarily successful, wrote David Hume in February 1776 – and he was certain it would not be, 'unless they break in pieces among themselves' – 'how would they be governed?'[68] In the second half of the eighteenth century it was impossible to imagine how a European power could hope to hold down an overseas colony whose inhabitants belonged to much the same culture and were equipped with precisely the same weapons. Could the British, asked Pierre-Victor Malouet, reflecting in 1810 on the lessons to be gained from the American Revolution, even if they had defeated the colonists, 'have expected to reign peacefully? Reconquest could only have resulted in a perpetual state of war, a huge national debt, [and excessive] taxation'. Eventually it could only have destroyed the entire political edifice, both at home and overseas.[69] As Hume had pointed out, 'it is on opinion that government is founded', not force, if only because, in the end, force would be unlikely, in even the 'most despotic and most military of governments', to secure political compliance for very long.[70] An absolutist power, such as France and Spain, might, he believed, be able to 'extend its oppressive arms to the Antipodes', at least for a time. But a limited government of the kind the British had always maintained in America could 'never be upheld at a distance, even when no disgust has intervened: much less when such violent animosities have taken place'.[71]

In Spain itself the enlightened ministers of Charles III had by the 1780s come to a very similar reading of their nation's imperial history. The loss of the European dominions after the end of the War of the Spanish Succession had effectively transformed the old monarchy into an empire not unlike that which Britain had once possessed in America. This was, however, still ruled according to the now archaic notions of the *ius publicum*. For it to survive the transformation of the political identity both of Spain itself and of the entire American continent, Spanish America had also to change. Failure would ultimately result – as it finally did after 1810 – in a revolution which, like the revolution in the north, could not fail to succeed in the long run, and would bring with it financial and probably also political ruin to the metropolis. 'What is certain,' wrote the Count of Aranda, acquaintance of Voltaire and Raynal, and president of the Council of Castile in August 1778,

> is that we are now faced with the need to change many of the ideas by which we have been guided since the discovery of the New World. For the theatre of that New World is no longer the same, and as a result demands that we change and consolidate our system.[72]

With this end in mind he prepared a memorandum, the celebrated *Exposición del Conde de Aranda al Rey Carlos III sobre la conveniencia de crear reinos independientes en América*[73] on the possible dismemberment of the American colonial system. 'Your Majesty,' he wrote, 'should dispossess himself of all his dominions in both Americas', preserving only the islands of Cuba and Puerto Rico as a basis for Spanish trade. All the rest, he suggested, should be transformed into three independent kingdoms (corresponding to the three viceroyalties) ruled in loose federation not by a Spanish monarch but, as the title had been conceived during the days of Charles V, a Spanish emperor.[74] Such a federation would, Aranda believed, yield more to the Spanish treasury in trade than the colonies now did in taxation. Emigration from Spain, which was still believed to be a drain on the human resources of the metropolis, would cease, and, once united, the three kingdoms would be far more capable, and politically more inclined, to resist the kind of external threat which Aranda, like most Spaniards, believed, not without reason, to be posed to the independence of the southern colonies by the new United States.[75] After the first insurgency in Mexico in 1810, and the outbreak of war in what is now Venezuela two years later, the similarity between the position of the Spaniards then and the situation in which the English had found themselves in 1776 became starkly apparent. 'Spain,' declared Dominque Dufour De Pradt in 1817,

> ought to ask of herself what it will be necessary to do when she can no longer conquer, and no longer keep what she has conquered; whether it would not be as well to make friends of those whom she can no longer have for subjects.[76]

None of these federalist projects, of course, came to anything. For all the obvious benefits they promised, Turgot and Smith, Aranda and Campomanes all recognized that no modern European monarchy would be prepared to surrender short-term political authority for long-term economic and, in some wider general sense, human gain. Monarchies were rarely enlightened agencies. Even the most rational were still driven primarily to the pursuit of honour and 'reputation', and governed by the 'prejudices' which even the English, as Turgot phrased it, 'have long regarded as the source of their grandeur'.[77]

Only in British North America was a former colonial empire successfully transformed into a true federation. But this had, of course, only been achieved by force of arms and in defiance of the intentions of the metropolitan government. The new United States was, or was to become in 1789, a true federal state. But it was not a federation which involved in any way the people of Great Britain, unlike the proposals that Benjamin Franklin had presented to the Albany Congress in 1754 and the English Quaker Thomas Crowley had proposed in the pages of the *Public Advertiser* in October 1768.[78]

IV

The United States was also, as both French and Spanish observers recognized, unique. It was unique in having been the creation of a post-colonial political culture, none of whose leaders had conceived their revolution in federal terms. It was unique, too, in being the ideological beneficiary of a European society which, as Simón Bolívar expressed it, 'was constituted not only by the most brilliant forms of Liberty, but also by solid foundations'.[79] (Because of this, he believed, 'in the course of centuries', the North Americans 'might perhaps become a sole nation, covering the universe – a federation'.[80])

Because of its origins, and because it had succeeded in transforming Thirteen Colonies into a United *States* of America, only the former British colonists were capable of conceiving any continental ambition for the new post-imperial political order they had brought into being. Neither the Spanish Americans nor the French *colons* ever dreamed consistently of more for themselves than the building of independent states. The scattered French settlements in the Caribbean were politically too small, too isolated, to press for anything grander than autonomy, and even that – as Martinique and Guadeloupe which still form part of metropolitan France have shown – was a goal which was always secondary to the desire for freedom to trade. The fissiparous programmes for some larger structure of states – those of Francisco de Miranda's Venezuela and Peru, that of the brief and ineffectual 'Emperor of Mexico', Augustín Iturbide, in the first months of 1822, or of Manuel Belgrano in the Rio de la Plata (later to become Argentina) – all came to nothing, while Bolívar's project for a union of Gran Colombia which would reach from Venezuela to Chile had collapsed even before its creator's death. The crucial difference between Spanish and British America was, in the end, not so much, as both Bolívar and Jefferson supposed, the different political cultures out of which they had grown. It was rather the kinds of republican project which those cultures had led their founders to conceive. As we have seen, such Spaniards as Campomanes and Ward also looked upon free trade as part of a larger, and ultimately transformative, political reform. The white settler elite of Spanish America, the *criollos*, however, had only ever pursued free-trade objectives for the immediate economic benefits they would bring. They had little understanding of the current European faith in commerce as a civilizing agency, and still less ambition to extend its benefits to the whole of mankind. What they, or at least the more educated of their leaders, shared was a belief in the transformative power of a republic founded upon what Bolívar had called 'moral power', a Ciceronian 'well-ordered' *respublica*, which would involve all its citizens in the common project of government and defence.[81]

In the end it was to be this persistently anachronistic vision which both secured their independence and determined their future. Washington was able to disband the Continental Army, because that army had been created to bring into being a society which, for all its outward classicism, had been created out of Locke and Montesquieu, in the image of a self-assuredly commercial, and finally participatory, republic. It was, in the terms of Benjamin Constant's celebrated distinction, a modern, not an ancient republic. The leaders of the Spanish American independence movements, in contrast, were never able to escape from the militarism which was, and remains, an integral part of their political culture. Spanish America, as Bolívar wrote to the people of Nueva Granada in 1812, 'lacks the political virtues which characterizes the true republican', virtues which, he pointed out, 'could not be acquired under absolute governments, in which the rights and the duties of citizens are unknown'.[82] Only force could bring into being a society in which such virtues might flourish. Bolívar had, as he vividly phrased it, to 'constitute men' out of the mixed and politically inexperienced peoples of which the Spanish colonies were composed, before he could hope to transform those men into citizens.[83] The instrument which he, and his successors down to the present day, chose to perform that task was the army. And a standing army, as every good republican knew, posed a persistent threat to true civility. It was a danger which De Pradt himself had warned against in 1825. 'The entire Spirit of a republic,' he wrote, 'must be civil: the military spirit is anti-civil'. Soldiers who begin as citizens within a citizens' army soon come to despise the unarmed citizen. Militarism 'inspires in man a respect and a love for force'. It leads him to be dazzled by the *éclat* of the executive power and 'slowly detaches him from the legislative power'.[84] What Turgot in 1776 had feared for North America – that a culture of militarism generated by prolonged warfare would have the effect of destroying the 'prudence and enlightenment' for which the British colonists had been known – did indeed take place in the South.[85]

The Spanish American republics, all more or less the progeny of Bolívar's powerful, if flawed, political vision of the constitution of Athens, were resolutely ancient. This ancient republicanism became, in the end, modern nationalism. And, like the Roman models it emulated, it had no concern for anything beyond its own territorial limits. The republicanism of Madison, Jefferson and Hamilton, by contrast, which had always been directed towards wide commercial, and ultimately democratic, interests, could afford, even when its own future as a state was still uncertain, to look outwards and forwards. As Turgot had seen, even before the Revolution had been successful, the Anglo-Americans, to protect the principles of free trade, 'would become warriors, not in order to conquer the Sugar Islands, if they preserve some of their wisdom, but to help them to emancipate themselves'.[86] For Turgot, the physiocrat and *philosophe*, the seemingly indomitable love of liberty displayed by the Thirteen Colonies would spread inexorably south, carrying the colonial revolution with it.

Turgot could also see that an independent North America would have every opportunity to transform itself into an American empire. With the British defeated, Canada and the British islands in the Caribbean would be fatally exposed. Once these had been overrun, or merely persuaded to join the union, the French Antilles and even the whole of Spanish America would soon follow. Even as early as July 1775, Benjamin Franklin's proposals for a confederacy of the Thirteen Colonies – to be called 'The United Colonies of North America' – was intended to remain open to all the English-speaking 'colonies' of the Atlantic world, a definition which extended to Ireland, Quebec and the 'East and West Floridas'.[87] It could not, as Turgot recognized, require much further generosity to embrace the entire continent, both north and south.

This fear of the potential consequences for Spanish America of North American independence lasted as long as the empire itself. In 1817, after the initial failure of the first insurgency movements, De Pradt wrote a tract on the *Colonies and the Present American Revolution*, which tried to assess the significance for the rest of humanity of the new configurations of power which were emerging in the Americas. 'If,' he asked,

> the world has had much trouble in bearing the weight of eighteen millions of English, pursuing power in every direction as a means of commerce, and commerce as a means of power, what will the world do under the burden of an indefinite number of Americans, put in motion by similar impulses?[88]

The American conception of freedom offered a yet more powerful threat to the stability of the region than the Continental Army. What, asked Condorcet in 1786, when a pan-American empire was still a distinct possibility, had the European colonists in America to lose by 'uniting themselves with a people who deign to rule over subjects, and wish only to have fellow citizens'?[89] Because of the restrictive trade laws imposed by both the Spanish and the French monarchies in America, free trade meant, in effect, political independence for the colonies. For Turgot, and for Condorcet, the best possible outcome of the War of Independence would have been the emergence of the modern commercial republic which Benjamin Franklin had promised the Paris salons, and which would finally transform the whole of the Americas into a free-trade zone, exporting the new gospel of economic liberalism, as the original colonists had exported their own brand of Christian monotheism.

Of all the former European colonies in America, only the United States could imagine for itself a world role which, while it remained firmly embedded in the ethos of a commercial, democratic society, looked at times – and still looks to many from the South – remarkably like a re-secularized version of the *civitas* which had powered the ideologies of the old Roman empire.

For Alexander Hamilton, indeed, the new United States bore nothing less than an obligation to 'vindicate the honour of the human race', against a Europe which had for too long been able to 'plume herself as mistress of the world and consider the rest of mankind as created for her benefit'. 'Let the Thirteen States,' he concluded,

> bound together in strict and indissoluble Union, concur in erecting one great American system superior to the control of all transatlantic force or influence and able to dictate the terms of the connections between the old world and the new.[90]

Hamilton's vision of pan-American hegemony belonged, he knew, to 'the regions of futurity', was linked to a plea for a strong navy, and had no explicit political content. Jefferson harboured a far more comprehensive project for the future although he, too, knew that the future might still be some time off. 'It is impossible,' he wrote to James Monroe in November 1801,

> not to look forward to distant times, when our rapid multiplication will expand itself beyond those limits and cover the whole northern, if not the southern continent, with a people speaking the same language, governed in similar forms and by similar laws; nor can we contemplate either blot or mixture on this surface.[91]

The nations which would make up this new 'Empire of Liberty' were to be 'sister republics', and the political structure of the whole was envisaged as another kind of federation, not an *imperium*, and certainly not a monarchy. But the doctrine of unity, above all the unshakeable belief in a single vision of a civilization, remained seemingly unaltered.

Jefferson, however, also displayed a marked reluctance actually to export 'liberty' (broadly conceived as participatory republicanism) anywhere. He was inclined to believe that political change had to be effected by those whom it was intended to benefit, and not be imposed from without. This is clear from his attitude towards the one place – Spanish America – whose inhabitants would have welcomed some external interference. As he told Lafayette in 1817, 'our southern brethren', riddled as they were with ignorance and bigotry, were, as yet, 'incapable of self-government'.[92] It was, he said, not the job of the United States to bring enlightenment or political liberty to such places. The Spanish Americans had to find it for themselves. Once, however, they had freed themselves from their dismal monarchical and Catholic legacy, then they would be welcomed within the new empire of liberty.

The modern United States still pursues very much the same political ideology with respect to their relationship with the rest of the world. If the European settlers exported to America one notion of a *civitas*, sustained and enforced by a corresponding vision of a Christian *imperium*, their descendants have created a universal order based upon another, but no less encompassing, conception of civility: democracy, an ideology which is quite as pervasive, and certainly as demanding as its ancient (and its Christian) ancestors. Like the notion of the *civitas*, democracy divides those who live inside it from those who live outside. Like St Augustine's 'Christian Republic' it welcomes all those who wish to enter, but fiercely dehumanizes any who prefer not to. Like both, it cannot really conceive of the existence of any other worlds. Unlike the Roman *civitas*, however, but in common with Condorcet, Diderot and Kant's ideal of a cosmopolitan world order, democracy relies for its civilizing machinery upon an exalted

(self-evident to all...)

vision of commerce. The Christian demand that all men share a single set of beliefs has vanished under the combined weight of scientific scepticism and cultural pluralism. But the price of joining the new world order – now represented by the international monetary institutions – is still the willingness to live by a law whose force is assumed to be not, as is all other legislation, local, but universal. It is marked, too, by the claim that the premises upon which this law are based are self-evident. They require no explanation, much less defence, and they are, by their very nature, applicable to all peoples everywhere. We all internalize our own histories. The history of the European empires in America is one of the reformulation of a constitutive element in European cultural and political thinking: the belief in the possibility of a universal human code of conduct. Today, largely because of the excesses of the nineteenth- and twentieth-century empires, this has grown so attenuated that its indebtedness to the first European imperial projects has been all but obscured. It is, however, still visible. The modern moral, cultural and political worlds we currently inhabit are all, in the first instance, the creation of the Enlightenment, and the Enlightenment was, perhaps more than has been recognized, the product of a world which was in the process of ridding itself of its first – although by no means, alas, its last – imperial legacy.

Notes

Introduction

1 For a discussion of the uses of this term see Harlow, 1952, I, 4 and Bayly 1989.

2 Letter to Andrew Millar, Hume, 1932, I, 245, and see Armitage, 1995.

3 Letter to Andrew Millar, Hume, 1932, I, 245.

4 Quoted in Pagden, 1993, 93.

5 Blin, 1790, 24.

6 There is now an excellent edition of this hitherto neglected work, edited, with a brilliant introduction, by Guido Abbattista. Anquetil-Duperon, 1993.

7 The version Robertson published in 1777 contained only the account of the Spanish settlements in America. For an account of the original project and why it was never fulfilled see Armitage, 1995.

8 Raynal, 1781, I, 5.

9 See for instance, Canny and Pagden, 1987. For a recent complaint about the lack of any comparison between North and South America, see Maxwell, 1993.

10 See, however, Blackburn, 1988, 35–63.

11 Edward Said, for instance, speaks of the 'age of empire' as 'the period between 1800 and 1870'. Yet the British empire in America, and in particular the settlements in the Caribbean, plays a not insignificant role in his narrative. Said, 1993, 99.

12 See, however, Tucker and Hendrickson, 1982, who use the same term.

13 Talleyrand, 1840, 334–6 He makes the traditional analogy with the distinction between the colonies of Greece and Rome. See pp.127–8.

14 Talleyrand, 1840, 336–7.

15 Schumpeter, 1951, 84.

16 'Observations on the Nature of Civil Liberty, the Principles of Government, and the Justice and Policy of the War with America' in, Price, 1991, 71. And see p.185.

17 Bayly, 1989, 111.

18 Condorcet, 1988, 269. See pp.185–6.

1 The Legacy of Rome

1 Robertson, 1800, I, 55. On Robertson and Hume's view of the fifteenth century as the beginning of modernity see Armitage, 1995.

2 For a brief account of *imperium* – and a far longer one of 'imperialism' – see Rudolf Walther, *Imperialismus* in Brunner *et al.*, 1972–92, III, 171–88.

3 For the later uses of this concept see pp.130–32.

4 Versions of this phrase were employed by Ugo de Fleury in the twelfth century to challenege the claims of Pope Gregory VII (see Paradisi, 1983, 250) and by Innocent III in the decretal 'Per venerabilem' in 1202, against the claims of the German emperors (Calasso, 1957, 403). See Bossuet, 1961 and Kelley, 1991, 78. The concept was also employed by the Spanish and the English. See in general Walther, 1976, 65–111.

5 Calasso, 1957, 22–3.

6 Machiavelli, for instance, speaks of the Venetians and the Florentines as having 'cresciuto l'imperio loro' (*Principe* xii). Machiavelli, 1960, 55.

7 'On Honour and Reputation' in

Bacon, 1857–74, VI, 505.

8 Barnard, 1774, 71.

9 Ullmann, 1979.

10 Pocock, 1988, 68.

11 Pownall, 1752, 93–4.

12 Burke, 1775, 35–6.

13 Folz, 1969, 54.

14 'An Essay of the original and nature of government', in Temple, 1720, I, 103.

15 Finley, 1983, 65–6.

16 See Pocock, 1985, 146.

17 Kroebner, 1961, 12–14.

18 As J.S. Richardson (1991, 9) has characterized it, the '*imperium militae*, passed down from the kings through the great individuals of the Republic that had made the *imperium romanum* ...It was the exercise of *imperium* throughout the known world that monarchy had made its return to Rome'.

19 See pp.23–7.

20 Quoted in Yates, 1975, 14. On the Renaissance use of the term *imperium* see Scheller, 1981–2, 12–13.

21 Quoted in Kroebner, 1961, 75.

22 See Millar, 1977, 3.

23 *Etymologiae* 9.3.23. P.L. LXXXI, 345a. '*Monarchae* sunt qui singularem possident principatum, qualis fuit Alexander apud Graecos, et Julius apud Romanos.'

24 'Est ergo temporalis Monarchia, quam dicunt "Imperium", unicus principatus et super omnes in tempore vel in hiis et super hiis qua tempore mensurantur' (I. ii. 3–5) and cf. *Convivio* IV.4.7.

25 Burns, 1991, 100–109. It was, Burns notes, Roselli who was responsible for bringing Dante's 'earlier and more visionary *Monarchia* back into fifteenth-century awareness'. On Roselli's probable involvement with the dispute over the Canaries, see Russell, 1978.

26 *The Federalist*, 9, in Hamilton, *et al.*, 1987, 121–2.

27 *The Federalist*, 11, in ibid. 133–4.

28 'An essay upon universal monarchy' in Davenant, 1771, IV, 3–4.

29 *Odes*, IV, 3, 13.

30 *De Consulatu Stilichonis* III, 135–70.

31 *Res gestae* 34.I. Quoted in Finley, 1983, 25.

32 'Bellum ingens geret Italia, populusque feroces contundet moresque viris et moenia ponet.'
(*Aeneid*, I, 263–4)

33 *Summa Theologiae*, I–II. 90.2.

34 *De Regimine Principum*, I. 1.

35 Aristotle, *Politics*, 1252^{b}28–1253^{a}2, and see Vitoria, 1991, 9, n.18.

36 *Discorsi*, II. 3; Machiavelli, 1960, 285.

37 See Skinner, 1990.

38 *De Officiis*, 1. 124. Cicero spoke of the magistrate as 'assuming the role of the civitas' (*se genere personam civitatis*).

39 Quoted in Blunt, 1978, 168.

40 Tu regere imperio populos, Romane memento
(hae tibi erant artes) pacique imponere morem
parcere subietus et debellare superbos.
(*Aeneid*, VI, 852–3)

41 *Institutes*, Proemium.

42 'Ut iam universus hic mundus it una civitas communis deorum atque hominum existimanda.' *De legibus*, 1. 22–4.

43 Quoted in Barker, 1923, 52.

44 Folz, 1969, 4. Cicero's account of an intellectual circle around Scipio Amelianus which sought to imbue *nobilitas* with the Stoic notion of *humanitas* may indeed, as Strasburger and Finley have shown, be a creation of Cicero's imagination. But his early-modern readers did not know this. See Finley, 1983, 127.

45 See Paradisi, 1983, 308.

46 *Rhetoric*, 1. 12 1373^b, and see Blunt, 1978. The association of Roman Law with Aristotle's *Koinos nomos* was the work of Aelius Aristides. See Oliver, 1953.

47 See 'Le Mot civilisation' in Starobinski, 1989, 15–16.

48 Quoted by Mommsen, 1896, VI, 478–9.

49 Quoted in Aubepin, 1855, 139.

50 'Le Mot civilisation' in Starobinski, 1989, 12, and Kelley, 1991, 72.

51 Mommsen, 1896, VI, 479.

52 Reported by Augustine, *De Civitate Dei*, XIX, 21.

53 For the most compelling modern discussion of Aristotle's views see Williams, 1993, 110–16.

54 *Nichomachean Ethics*, 1143ᵃ11.

55 I have discussed this at greater length in Pagden, 1986, 42–3.

56 *Ibid.*, 16.

57 Lévi-Strauss, 1969, 46.

58 *Aeneid*, VIII, 319–23.

59 Williams, 1993, 108, citing E. Levy. See Finley, 1980, 97.

60 *Epistulae ad Quintum Fratrem*, I. 1–27.

61 Seneca, *De Clementia*, 1.4. See the observations in Azor, 1610–16, 1066ᵇ.

62 Paruta, 1599, 215. Paruta claimed, however, that the collapse of the Roman state was the inevitable outcome of its over-extension in the last days of the Republic. This had led to inequality of property among the members of the *civitas*. Imperial Rome may have been the most perfect *royal* government, but every monarchy was inferior to any republic. On Paruta see Tuck, 1993, 96 and Bouwsma, 1968, 285.

63 'Lectures on law: XI citizens and aliens' (1790–1) in Wilson, 1967, II, 581.

64 *De Republica*, 3.15.24 (I.16).

65 *Historia*, I, XVI.

66 *Aeneid*, I, 286–7. The title of Augustus' official biography was 'Res gestae divi Augusti *quibus orbem terrarum imperii populi Romani subiecit*'. In two denari coins from the seventies BCE, the figure of Roma is depicted with her foot on the globe. For this, and other instances of imperial imagery, see Lintott, 1981.

67 Mommsen, 1896, VI, 478–9.

68 *Digest*, XIV, 2.9. Antoninus, in reply to a complaint from Eudaemon of Nicomedia that he had been robbed by the people of the Cyclades after being shipwrecked, said, 'I am lord of the world, but the law of the sea must be judged by the sea law of the Rhodians when our law does not conflict with it.' Justinian similarly excluded the sea from his jurisdiction (*Institutes*, II, 1.1.), which led to considerable debate in the seventeenth century. Justinian's law, *Bene a Zenone*

(*Codex* VII, 37, 3) which reserves exclusive rights of property to the emperor, and subsequently to the Papacy, was frequently cited together with the *Lex Rhodia*.

69 Nicolet, 1988, 28.

70 Folz, 1969, 9.

71 In the authoritative definition of pagans provided by Tommaso de Vio (Cardinal Cajetan) in his commentary on St Thomas Aquinas's *Summa theologiae*, composed between 1507 and the 1520s, the only category of person which falls uncontentiously under the *dominium* of the Church is constituted by those who live on lands once under Roman imperial rule. Caietanus, 1888–1906, IX, 94, commenting on IIa IIae q.66 art.8.

72 Brown, 1977.

73 Pagden, 1986, 20–1.

74 *De Civitate Dei*, XIX. 21, quoting, with apparent approval, the argument from *De Republica*. See note 12, above.

75 Tuck, forthcoming.

76 Black, 1992, 87–92.

77 See Wilkes, 1964, 412, and, more generally, 411–78.

78 *Aeneid*, I, 277–9, 'His ego nec metas rerum nec tempora pono; imperium sine fine dedi.'

79 See Kantorowicz, 1957, 44–156.

80 See the account in Canning, 1987, 25–8.

81 See the account in Black, 1992, 95–7.

82 See Vitoria, 1991, 255–6 ('On the American Indians', 2.I) for a refutation of this claim.

83 The most thorough accounts of the *translatio imperii* and its significance in the early-modern world are Goez, 1958, and Maffei, 1964.

84 Franklin, 1991, 310–11.

85 Burns, 1992, 100.

86 Bartolus, 1588–9, I, 553, commenting on *Digest*, VI.1.1.

87 *Ibid.*, VI, 637, commenting on *Digest*, XLIX.15.24.

88 In particular from Johannes Teutonicus, a thirteenth-century canonist who, like Bartolus, taught at Bologna. See Kuttner, 1937, I, 93, 99. I am grateful to James Muldoon for allowing me to see an unpublished

paper on 'The concept of empire, 1400–1800: a problem of definition', which stresses the generally neglected role of the canon lawyers in the formation of European universalism.

89   On this see Woolf, 1913, 25–8.

2   *Monarchia Universalis*

1   *Aeneid*, VI, 403.
2   Quoted in Blunt, 1978, 168.
3   Quoted in Folz, 1969, 208.
4   *De Civitate Dei*, V. 15.
5   *History*, XXXVIII, 60.5.
6   See Skinner, 1978, I, 16–17.
7   They did so, however, at least in the terms employed in the first of the two Bulls, only with the purpose of conversion, and they explicitly prevented the Spaniards from inflicting upon the native populations 'hardships or dangers'. Giménez Fernández, 1944, 181. I have followed the text of *Inter cetera* of 3 May.
8   López, 1843, I, 718.
9   Ugarte, 1655, 64.
10   Cortes, 1989, 48.
11   Elliott, 1989, 27–41.
12   Juan Antonio de Vera, Conde de la Roca, dedicated his epic poem *El Fernando* (1622) to Philip as 'Monarch of Spain, Emperor of the Indies'. Fr Joseph Laínez in *El Privado cristiano deducido de las vidas de Joseph y Daniel* (1641) describes Philip IV as 'The Great Catholic King of the Spains, and Emperor of America'. In 1563, the Venetian ambassador reported that Philip II was thinking of officially adopting the title 'Emperor of the Indies', although he never in fact did so. Tanner, 1993, 143. See also Bosbach, 1986, 71, and the observations in Elliott, 1989, 7–8.
13   'Preface' to the *Principal Navigations* [1598] in Hakluyt, 1935, II, 434–5, and see the discussion of this point in Armitage, 1995, 58.
14   Thevet, 1575, I, aij.
15   On the French attempts to win the imperial crown see Zeller, 1934.
16   Printed in Biggar, 1930, 178.
17   *Ordonnances*, 1803–6, II, 4–5.

18   See Trudel, 1973, 11, 34–8. In an effort to reduce the tension between France and Castile, Clement VII told Francis that the Bulls referred only to 'already-known continents and not to lands subsequently discovered by other crowns', a claim which makes nonsense of the wording of the Bulls themselves.
19   Biggar, 1930, 180.
20   Le Clercq, 1691, II, 67. Hamilton, however, argues persuasively that this text was not the work of Le Clercq, but of the abbé Claude Bernou and of the editor of the *Gazette de France*, Eusèbe Renaudot. Hamilton, 1976.
21   *Edits*, 1854–6, I, 5, 8. On the history of the Compagnie see Trudel, 1979.
22   Quoted in Eccles, 1987, 163. Similarly the 'Établissement de la Compagnie des Indes Occidentales', of May 1664, stresses that 'nous regardons dans l'établissement des dites colonies principalement la gloire de Dieu en procurant le salut des Indiens et sauvages, auxquels nous désirons faire connoître la vraie religion'. *Edits*, 1854–6, I, 41.
23   Du Creux, 1951, I, 24.
24   Rochefort, 1665, 283.
25   Charlevoix, 1744, I, vii.
26   Hakluyt, 1935, I, 215.
27   *Charters*, 1957, 2.
28   'A proposal for the better supplying of Churches in our foreign plantations and for converting the savage Americans to Christianity' in Berkeley, 1871, III, 225. With a degree of cynicism rare even among seventeenth-century Anglican divines, Berkeley also warned the planters of the British West Indies that it would be to their advantage to have slaves who should

> obey in all things their masters according to the flesh; not with eye-service as men-pleasers, but in the singleness of heart, as fearing God: that Gospel liberty consists with temporal servitude; and that their slaves would only become better slaves by being Christian. (*Ibid.*, 216)

For the complex history of the

creation of schools for the Native Americans see Axtell, 1985, 179–217.

29   Hakluyt, 1935, I, 332. On the significance of Hakluyt's use here of the verb 'to plant' see pp.79–80.

30   Quoted in Kupperman, 1980, 166.

31   *Ibid.*

32   The phrase is William Paterson's and was wrtten in 1701 in defence of the Scottish colony in Darien. Paterson, 1858, I, 135. On Paterson and the Darien Project see pp.76–7.

33   Child, 1751, 150–51.

34   Eburne, 1624, 4. Bishop Berkeley's college was similarly intended to 'remove the reproach we have so long lain under, that we fall far short of our neighbours of the Romish communion in zeal in propagating religion, as we surpass them in the soundness and purity of it'. 'A proposal for the better supplying of Churches in our foreign plantations and for converting the savage Americans to Christianity', in Berkeley, 1871, III, 225.

35   'A Reply to an answer made to a declaration', in Hutchinson, 1745, 100–101.

36   'The Second Charter granted by Charles II to the Proprietors of Carolina' in *Historical Collection*, 1836, II, 44.

37   Quoted in Vaughan, 1978, 56.

38   Pinto, 1776, 10.

39   Abercromby, 1986, 199. See also Miller, 1994, 196–7.

40   *De Civitate Dei*, V, 25.

41   See Nuti, 1988.

42   'An essay on universal monarchy' in Davenant, 1771, IV, 6.

43   Grotius, 1631, 348. On Grotius's interests in the origins of the Amerindians see Rubiés i Mirabet, 1991.

44   Marineus Siculus, 1579, 959.

45   On this see Gibson, 1977.

46   This, for instance, was the claim of the seventeenth-century Spanish theorist, Francisco de Ugarte. Ugarte de Hermosa y Salcedo, 1655, 62.

47   'Nisi aea provinciae ad mundum non pertinere dicantur', Bellarmino, 1950, 117. The quotation comes from Book V of the *Disputationes de controversiis Christianae fidei*.

48   *A Discourse on Western Planting* [1584] in Hakluyt, 1935, I, 311–12. Oviedo addresses Charles V as 'Vuestra Cesarea Majestad, cuya gloriosa persona largos tiempos nuestro Señor favorezca e dexe gozar de la total monarchia'. Fernández de Oviedo, 1851–5, I, 7; and see Pagden, 1993, 51–87.

49   Campanella, 1633, 87.

50   Botero, 1607, 238.

51   Menéndez Pidal, 1963, 14–16.

52   Later, when Philip II entered the city of Antwerp in 1549, in preparation for his succession, he was greeted by a triumphal arch depicting a large female figure carrying the Pillars of Hercules away altogether. Scribonius, 1550, Hiiii[r].

53   On this see Headley, 1983, 86–113.

54   See *ibid.*, 94–113 for an account of the *Pro divo Carolo*.

55   On the Spanish 'Erasmians' see the classic study by Marcel Bataillon (1966), in particular 364–431. On Charles V as the second Charlemagne see Tanner, 1993, 116, 128.

56   See Maravall, 1954, 261–315.

57   See Zeller, 1934.

58   On this see Pagden, 1990, 37–63, and Tuck, 1993, 65–82.

59   Mexía, 1561, 1[v].

60   See Béranger, 1990, 195. 'Imperium c'est le pouvoir suprême sous lequel Auguste "recueillit le monde fatigué des discordes civiles" (Tacitus, *Annales*, 1 1 1)'.

61   Arredondo y Alvarado, 1528, XXII[r–v], VI[v].

62   Gutíerrez de Torres, 1524 [l7[r–v]].

63   See McGinn, 1979, 11.

64   On the legend of the 'Last World Emperor' see Tanner, 1993, 119–30.

65   *The King of Spain's Cabinet*, 1658, 89.

66   Vargas Machuca, 1599, 10[v].

67   Gutíerrez de Torres, 1524 [L8[r]]. Adrian, however, ruled only from 9 January 1522 until 14 September 1533. By the time Gutíerrez de Torres's book appeared his claim was, therefore, already invalid.

68   Botero, 1607, 236.

69 *Capita orationis Vilhelmi Bellaii Oratoris Regis Gallorum ad Conventum Smalcaldiensem, Dominica quarta Adventus Domini* [19 December 1525] in Bretschneider, 1834, II, 1012–13.

70 Paterson, 1858, I, 132.

71 Vázquez de Menchaca, 1931, II, 23–4.

72 Elliott, 1989, 18.

73 Vitoria, 1991, 233.

74 Otis, 1764, 438.

75 See e.g. 'Philo-Caledon', 1699, 7–8, who claims that the grant was 'amongst Papists themselves but precarious'. 'Philo-Caledon' was one of the champions of the Darien expedition (see pp.76–7).

76 This is the so-called 'Calvinist Theory of Revolution', although both Calvin and Luther themselves insisted that 'ungodly princes' had been placed in power as a punishment by God, and might not, therefore, be resisted. See, in general, Skinner, 1978, II, 189–238.

77 Paterson, 1858, I, 121, and cf. the remarks of Johnson, 1609, Av^{r-v}; Ferguson, 1699, 65; and Hakluyt, *A Discourse on Western Planting* [1584] in Hakluyt, 1935, I, 295–313.

78 See Brading, 1991, 205–10.

79 Quoted in Pagden, 1990, 53.

80 Grotius, 1916, 15, and see Tuck, 1993, 176–9.

81 Freitas, 1960–1, II, 93–4.

82 Solórzano, 1647, I, 37.

83 The common source is Aquinas, *Summa Theologiae*, IIa IIae. 10. 10. On its application to this case see Vitoria, 1991, 254 ('On the American Indians'). On Soto's definition of *dominium*, see Brett, forthcoming, Cap. 5.

84 Soto, 1556, 301.

85 'On the American Indians', in Vitoria, 1991, 254.

86 *Ibid.*

87 'In tranquilitate Romani Imperii totius orbis regularitatem requiescere'. Soto, 1556, 302.

88 *Ibid.*, 304.

89 *Ibid.*, 301.

90 'Sobre el título del dominio del rey de España sobre las personas y tierras de los Indios' [1554], in Las Casas, 1969, 171.

91 Vitoria, 1991, 289.

92 Las Casas, 1969, 33–9, 83–5, and see Pagden, 1990, 32–3.

93 Soto, 1556, 423, and see Las Casas, 1969, 523, who insisted that to deny this was 'to fall into the Heresy of Huss'.

94 See Pagden, 1990, 32.

95 Amaya, 1633, 13.

96 The influence of this work was due to the fact that, throughout the Middle Ages, it had been attributed to St Thomas Aquinas. In fact Aquinas was responsible for only the first and part of the second of the three books. Soto ascribes the entire work to Ptolemy.

97 Soto, 1556, 305.

98 *Ibid.*, 306.

99 *Ibid.* In reply to this argument, royal apologists, such as López de Madera, a member of the Consejo Supremo of Castile, argued that 'lo que dize fray Domingo de Soto de las Republicas y reynos mas extendidas' could not apply to the Spanish monarchy, but only to those 'que no tienen potencia igual para regirse y conservarse, y por ser tan esparcidas quedan algunas partes faltas en la adminstración de justicia y buen gobierno'. López Madera, 1625, 74–5.

100 Soto, 1556, 306.

101 Covarrubias, 1583, 243^{r} and cf. 'On the American Indians' in Vitoria, 1991, 254.

102 On this see Prosdocimi, 1954–5.

103 *Politics*, 7.4 (1326^{a-b}).

104 Soto, 1556, 18.

105 Covarrubias, 1583, 241^{r}, 'iure naturali, et ab ipso natura, non est Imperatori concessa totius orbis'.

106 For a discussion of the various editions of the *Controversiarum illustrium*, see Seelmann, 1979, 30–6.

107 See Pagden, 1986. I would not myself have seen Vázquez's importance if it had not been for the work of Annabel Brett.

108 See in particular Brett, forthcoming, Cap. 5, 245: 'Vázquez should be read neither in isolation from, nor as a continuation of, the School of Salamanca, but rather as a positive

response to its achievements, and particularly to that of Soto'.

109 Grotius, 1916, 11–15.

110 The *Controversiarum* is divided into three books. Vázquez's various arguments against empire occur in Book II, Chapter 20, and are organized under separate, and generally discrete, headings. In order to bring out the force of his overall argument, I have rearranged the ordering of these headings. I have also attempted to locate Vázquez's consideration of the particular problems of empire in the wider context of his discussion of the nature of civil society. As Brett has shown, the twin themes of 'the mutability of civil right' and the argument that 'the ordination of the prince [exists for] the convenience of the people' are both vital 'for a correct understanding of Vázquez's originality, and for saving the integrity of his text'. (Brett, forthcoming, Cap. 5).

111 Vázquez de Menchaca, 1931, II, 26.

112 *Ibid.*, 23–4. On the distinction which Vázquez makes between *potestas* – which is the power conceded by the citizens to the ruler so that he may be able to look after their own good, and is limited by law – and what he calls *potentia*, which, as Brett puts it, 'signals that purely *de facto* power which has nothing to do with law or right, and everything to do with sheer might', see Brett, forthcoming, Cap. 5.

113 Vázquez de Menchaca, 1931, I, 276 and quoted by Brett, forthcoming, Cap. 5.

114 E.g. Paolo Paruta. See Tuck, 1993, 96. '[Paruta's] account of the danger to republics posed by imperial expansion was readily open to recasting in terms of the *interests* of the people involved'.

115 Soto, 1556, 302.

116 Vázquez de Menchaca, 1931, I, 20 (Praefatio n. 25) and quoted in Brett, forthcoming, Cap. 5.

117 Vázquez de Menchaca, 1931, I, 18.

118 *Ibid.*, II, 31. Cf. Brett, 'Vázquez' imaginative genius . . . maps Roman poetry unto Roman law, to create a moral dynamic of human history

which can serve both to legitimate and to lament the practice of his own day'. Brett, forthcoming, Cap. 5.

119 Vázquez de Menchaca, 1931, II, 23–4.

120 *Ibid.*, I, 17.

121 *Ibid.*, II, 33–4.

122 On this point see Pagden, 1986, 228.

123 Vázquez de Menchaca, 1931, II, 26–7.

124 *Ibid.*, 25.

125 *Ibid.*, 30.

126 *Ibid.*, 29.

127 *Ibid.* *Mundus* probably derived from an Etruscan word meaning decoration. The Greek term 'cosmos' was derived, in a similar way, from 'ornamentation'.

128 Vázquez de Menchaca, 1931, II, 84–5.

129 See Brett, forthcoming, Cap. 5.

130 Vázquez de Menchaca, 1931, II, 23–4.

131 Saavedra Fajardo, 1976, II, 664.

132 See Pagden, 1990, 23–4.

133 *Perpetual Peace, a Philosophical Sketch* in Kant, 1970, 106.

134 See pp.189–90.

3   Conquest and Settlement

1 Schumpeter, 1951, 7, 83. Cf. 'Expansion for its own sake always requires, among other things, concrete objects if it is to reach the action stage and maintain itself, but this does not constitute its meaning. Such expansion is, in absence its own "object", and the truth is that it has no adequate object beyond itself' (Schumpeter, 1951, 7).

2 See pp.118–20.

3 'An Account of a Conversation concerning the Right Regulation of Governments for the Common Good of Mankind', in Fletcher, 1737, 437.

4 Gomes Eanes de Zurara ended his *Crónica de Guiné* on that date because, 'depois deste ano avante, sempre se os feitos daquelas partes trataram mais por tratos e avenças de mercadaria que por fortaleza nem trabalho das armas'. Zurara, 1973, 409 (Cap. XCVI).

5 Kroebner, 1961, 62.

6 *De Guiana carmen epicum*, 14–15.

7 Ramsay, 1789, I, 2. Cabot, quoted in Finley, 1976, 180.

8   Johnson, 1609, C2^v.
9   Hakluyt, 1935, II, 368.
10 Quoted in Eccles, 1987, 168 n.74.
11 On the concept of 'worthy enemies', see Greenblatt, 1988.
12 Powhatan's coronation is described by John Smith, in Smith, 1986, I, 237.
13 On Powhatan's legal status in the eyes of the British crown see Williams, 1990, 206–12.
14 Strachey, 1953, 24. I am grateful to David Armitage for drawing my attention to this text.
15 New mining techniques and a more systematic approach to the production of silver resulted in a huge increase in output in the 1790s. On this see Brading, 1971, 33–92.
16 *Encyclopédie*, 1772, III, 649–50.
17 Biggar, 1930, 128, and see Trudel, 1973, 48–50 and Eccles, 1987, 159.
18 Trudel, 1973, 19–20. This was 'Saguenay'. A land identified as Cibola (the territory of the Zuni between the Little Colorado and the Rio Grande) appears in La Salle's commission as late as 1678, although by then its wealth was said, more plausibly, to consist in furs rather than minerals. Eccles, 1964, 106.
19 Frobisher, 1867, 74–5. And see the comments in Greenblatt, 1991, 109–18.
20 Johnson, 1612, f.[E4^v]–G3^v.
21 Raleigh, 1848, xiv.
22 See Fuller, 1991.
23 Mede, 1677, 980–1.
24 Smith, 1976, II, 563–4.
25 Trudel, 1973, 190–2. Raleigh, 1848, 9, and for an analysis of Raleigh's language in *The Discoverie of Guiana* see Fuller, 1991.
26 *De L'Esprit des lois*, XXI, 21, in Montesquieu, 1949–51, II, 643. For the influence of Montesquieu's observations on Colbert see Tarrade, 1972, I, 87.
27 Armitage, forthcoming.
28 Harrington, 1977, 332.
29 Saavedra Fajardo, 1976, II, 681. 'Conquered by you,' wrote Lipsius to a Spanish friend, 'the New World has conquered you in turn, and has weakened and exhausted your ancient

vigour.' Quoted in Elliott, 1989, 25.
30 On this see Pagden, 1993, 18–20.
31 Smith, 1976, II, 563.
32 *De L'Esprit des lois*, XXI, 22, in Montesquieu, 1949–51, II, 645–6.
33 Smith, 1976, II, 568.
34 Mirabeau, 1758, III, 180.
35 Smith, 1976, II, 568.
36 Hume, 1985, 338.
37 'Reflexiones sobre el comercio libre de América, que produce el amor público de un zeloso profesor de comercio. Año 1789'. British Library, Add. Ms. 13,984, ff. 135–67, at f.136v.
38 Quoted in Elliott, 1989, 25.
39 Campillo, 1789, 17.
40 Campomanes, 1775, 411–12.
41 Child, 1751, 153.
42 Campomanes, 1988, 360.
43 See pp.123–5 for Campomanes's reply to this argument.
44 Nuix, 1782, 66.
45 Robertson, 1800, IV, 66.
46 Young, 1772, 438.
47 See Schwartz, 1978, 35.
48 Armitage, 1992, 536–7.
49 Ramsay, 1789, 3.
50 Tucker, 1775, 18–20, and quoted in Pocock, 'Josiah Tucker on Burke, Locke, and Price. A study in the varieties of eighteenth-century conservatism', in Pocock, 1985, 164.
51 For a wider account of the origins of the scheme see David Armitage, 'The Scottish vision of empire: intellectual origins of the Darien venture', in Robertson, forthcoming.
52 Ferguson, 1699, 74–5.
53 Otis, 1764, 422.
54 The most commonly cited source is *Digest* XLI 1. and the law *Ferae bestiae*, Justinian, *Institutes*, II. 1. 2. 'Natural reason admits the title of the first occupant to that which previously had no owner.'
55 More, 1965, 137, and see the observations in Finley, 1976, 179.
56 See Tully, 1993b, 257–8 and Pocock, 1987, 237–8.
57 Bland, 1764, 319.
58 *Second Treatise* 36 in Locke, 1967, 311. This was one of the motives which prompted the crown to impose formal obligations upon French immigrants

to Canada to develop their land. By a decree of 1711, Louis XIV required colonial governors to suppress seigneuries which failed to do this. Neither was this an idle threat. Eighteen such fiefs were suppressed for this reason in 1741 alone. Trudel, 1971, 20.

59 *Second Treatise* 27 in Locke, 1967, 306.

60 Pownall, 1765, 157.

61 Tully, 1993a, 264. *Second Treatise* 36–7 in Locke, 1967, 310–12.

62 See Pagden, 1986, 105.

63 'Essay on Property', in Madison, 1900–10, VI, 101, 103.

64 Vattel, 1916, III, 37–8, and see the observations in Tully, 1993a, 168–9 and Pagden, 1990, 29.

65 On this point see Green and Dickason, 1989, 73–8.

66 Smith, 1976, II, 558. In Moses Finley's definition, a colony in the Ancient World 'was a plantation of men, a place to which men emigrated and settled'. Finley, 1976, 171.

67 'Of Plantations' in Bacon, 1857–74, VI, 457.

68 On this point see Manzano Manzano, 1951–2.

69 Vitoria, 1991, 264–5.

70 Abercromby, 1986, 200.

71 10 April 1609. *Charters*, 1957, 1.

72 Trudel, 1973, 163. In 1627, even the population of the Dutch colony of New Holland on the Hudson river was twice as numerous as that of New France. The ordinance establishing the Compagnie des Indes Occidentales in 1664 similarly speaks of 'la terre ferme de l'Amérique, autrement appelée France equinoctiale'. *Edits*, 1854–6, I, 40.

73 Postlethwayt, 1751–5, I, 373.

74 *A Discourse on Western Planting*, in Hakluyt, 1935, II, 292–5. The English were still resorting to the right of prior discovery in claiming Hudson's Bay in 1670. Eccles, 1964, 111. On the Madoc voyage see Armitage, 1995.

75 'Representation of the Present State of the Colonies', in Franklin, 1959–93, V, 368.

76 Trudel, 1973, 38 and Thevet, 1575, II, 964ᵛ–965.

77 Quoted in Trudel, 1973, 38.

78 Diderot, *Supplément au voyage de Bougainville*, in Diderot, 1992, 421.

79 'Observations on the nature of civil liberty, the principles of government, and the justice and policy of the war with America', in Price, 1991, 40.

80 Grotius, 1916, 15.

81 Young, 1772, 472. The dictionary to which he refers is Postlethwayt, 1751–5.

82 See Tully, 1993a.

83 Dummer, 1721, 14. In his *Plain Facts* of 1781, Samuel Wharton argued that Locke's natural rights to the means of preservation did in fact mean that the Indians had a right to their land, since it constituted their means of subsistence. Wharton, however, had a clear interest in maintaining the validity of this argument since his land speculation companies claimed substantial areas of the state of Virginia on grounds of 'concession'. Tully, 1993a, 268.

84 Pownall, 1765, 161–2.

85 Bulkley, 1725, lii–lv. The treatise is an attempt to deny the Mohegans any right to their traditional tribal lands. On Bulkley and his reliance on Locke see Tully, 1993a, 166–7.

86 The Proclamation is printed in Kennedy, 1918, at pp. 20–21, and see Tully, 1993a, 172.

87 Young, 1772, 472.

88 'Observations on the nature of civil liberty, the principles of government, and the justice and policy of the war with America', in Price, 1991, 40.

89 Dummer, 1721, 13.

90 Kennedy, 1918, 20.

91 See Jones, 1982, 41–5, who points out that the Proclamation Line was in practice unworkable not least of all because it was innacurate. The Iroquois, the Cherokee and the Creek all had ancestral lands to the east of the line, while by 1763 there were already settlements from Virginia to the west.

92 Smith, 1950, 434.

93 The texts of the case are to be found in Smith, 1950, 417–22. For a more sustained acccount of the dispute over the status of the Indian nations see

94 Quoted in Clark, 1990, 84.

95 *Ibid.*, 41n. As John Pocock has pointed out, it was only by assuming that the United States had acquired the imperial authority formerly exercised by the crown that Lord Chief Justice Marshall was able, in 1832, to make his famous, and still authoritative, ruling that the Native American peoples constituted nations. Pocock, 1993b, 420.

96 See pp. 130–32.

97 *Second Treatise* 2.175, in Locke, 1967, 403.

98 *The First Set of Fundamental Constitutions of South Carolina as compiled by Mr John Locke* [March 1669]. Act XCVII, in *Historical Collection*, 1836, II, 386.

99 Otis, 1764, 452.

100 Dummer, 1721, 13.

101 Charlevoix, 1744, I, 2. On Charlevoix's *Histoire et description générale de la Nouvelle-France* – 'the first serious study of Canadian history' – see Trigger, 1986.

102 Bland, 1769, 11–13.

103 Dummer, 1721, 20–1.

104 Gordon, 1728, I, 123.

105 Axtell, 1985, 133, and more generally on the evangelical programme, 131–78.

106 Johnson, 1609, C2^v.

107 See Kupperman, 1993, 93–4.

108 'Philo-Caledon', 1699, 24. This tract is sometimes falsely attributed to Fletcher.

109 Quoted in Eccles, 1987, 163.

110 Articles of the Capitulation of Montreal, 8 September 1760, in Kennedy, 1918, 12. On the principle of continuity see p. 77.

111 Eccles, 1987, 176–9.

112 La Martinière, 1732, I, 136–7.

113 The most important source for the significance of prescription to such cases – and the one cited by Solórzano – was Bartolus's discussion (*repetitio*) on the law *Quominus*, under the title *De fluminibus* (*Digest* 43. 12.2) discussing the possibility of acquiring rights over a public river. See Brett, forthcoming, Cap. 5.

114 See Pagden, 1990, 34–5. Bartolus had raised similar questions with regard to the rights of the Venetians and the Genoese to restrict sailing within their respective gulfs. See Brett, forthcoming, Cap. 5.

115 Pownall, 1765, 163.

116 Johnson, 1609, B2r–v.

117 Ferguson, 1699, 72–3. He went on, however, to argue that, as the Spaniards' first incursions had been based on a conquest which, in his opinion, was nothing other than a case of 'Fraud, Violence and Usurpation', these, too, were invalid, which suggests a curious understanding of prescription.

118 'Britanno sed Dunensi', 1700, 'Epistle dedicatory'.

119 It was not, however, legally as vacuous as the response of Las Casas and others might suggest. See the observations of Seed, 1993, 125–7.

120 See Matienzo, 1580, 295^v.

121 'Parecer acerca de la perpetuydad delas ecomiendas de indios delos Reynos del Piru que hizieron los tres comisarios iuezes que el dicho Reyno embió al Rey Don Felipe II nuestro señor el año 56', quoted in Canny and Pagden, 1987, 53.

122 Quoted in Pagden, 1990, 32.

123 Mirabeau, 1758, III, 213.

124 Talleyrand, 1840, 330.

125 Gray, 1609, C3^v–[C4^r].

126 See Tuck, forthcoming.

127 Quoted in Williams, 1990, 200.

128 Portocarrero y Guzmán, 1700, 97–9.

129 Cf. Cicero, *De officiis*, 1.34–5. 'There are two types of conflict: the one proceeds by debate, the other by force. Since the former is the proper concern of man, but the latter of beasts, one should only resort to the latter if one may not employ the former.'

130 Epist. 189.6 *Patrologia latina*, XXXIII, col. 856.

131 See Russell, 1975.

132 See in general Albert, 1980.

133 *De republica*, 3.34. See Barnes, 1986.

134 *De officiis*, 1.36.

135 *Ibid.*, 1.35, 38. Cf. 2.26–7.

136 Tuck, forthcoming.

137 Fox Morcillo, 1536 [L7 $^{r-v}$]. For Fox

Morcillo's views on kingship see Tuck, 1993, 33–5.

138 *Quaestionum in Heptateuchem*, VI. X. *Patrologia latina*, XXXIV, col. 781.
139 Pagden, 1990, 22.
140 See *ibid.*, 31.
141 Suárez, 1954, 126–7.
142 *Ibid.*, 149–52.
143 *De Civitate Dei*, XIX, 13.
144 Suárez, 1954, 238.
145 *Ibid.*, 158–61.
146 Solórzano, 1647, I, 39–40. On Solórzano see pp.89–90 and 140–41.
147 Fox Morcillo, 1566, 252.
148 *Ibid.*, 1566, 253.
149 On this see Pagden, 1986, 109–18.
150 See Mechoulan, 1974. For Sepúlveda's attack on Machiavelli see Coroleu, 1992.
151 *De regno et regis officio, ad philippum Hisp. regem*, in Sepúlveda, 1780, IV, 99.
152 *Ibid.*, 100.
153 Alamos de Barrientos, 1867, 13–14. Navarre, however, which was occupied by Ferdinand the Catholic in 1512, is classified as a conquered state.
154 Book 4, Tit. I, Ley 6, *Recopilación*, 1791, II, 4.
155 Nuix, 1782, 155–6.

4   Expansion and Preservation

1 'An Essay upon Universal Monarchy' in Davenant, 1771, IV, 4.
2 'On the Plantation Trade', *ibid.*, II, 26. And see the observations in Miller, 1994, 155–9.
3 Quoted in Elliott, 1989, 25–6.
4 Pufendorf, 1934, II, 1355, quoting a remark made by Isocrates to Philip of Macedon.
5 Preface to *Divers Voyages* in Hakluyt, 1935, I, 175–6.
6 Child, 1751, 138.
7 Preface to *Divers Voyages* in Hakluyt, 1935, I, 176.
8 Davenant, 1771, II, 4–5.
9 Quoted in Elliott, 1989, 12.
10 Chastellux, 1787, 60–1.
11 Denton, 1670, 7.
12 The colonies themselves were corre-spondingly anxious to expand the size of their settler populations. People, explained Louis XIV on accepting the demise of the Compagnie des Cien Associés, were the substance of all colonies, and in order to ensure that his increased in number, he forbade the immigration of all 'priests, monks and nuns', and in 1669 the Sovereign Council of Canada offered a pension of 300 *livres* to 'any inhabitant having, in legitimate marriage, ten children not priests'. Quoted in Diamond, 1961, 10.
13 *The Commonwealth of Oceana*, in Harrington, 1977, 332.
14 Botero, 1956, 156–7.
15 'An Essay upon Universal Monarchy', in Davenant, 1771, IV, 14.
16 *Perpetual Peace, a Philosophical Sketch* in Kant, 1970, 113
17 Livy, *History*, XXXVII, 35.
18 Pufendorf, 1764, I, ix.
19 Quoted in Pocock, 1988, 67.
20 'Tienen sus periodos los imperios. El que más dura, mas cerca está de su fin.' Saavedra-Fajardo, 1976, II, 822.
21 Moncada, 1619, 1^r–v.
22 Quoted in Eccles, 1964, 163–4.
23 Quoted in *Ibid.*, 105–6.
24 *Recopilación*, 1791, II, 1. Lib. IV, Tit. I, ley i.
25 'Thoughts upon the present situation of affairs' [October 1791] in Goldsmith, 1927, 95.
26 Campomanes, 1775, 411.
27 *The Spirit of Conquest and Usurpation and their Relation to European Civilization*, in Constant, 1988, 52–3.
28 See pp.156–7.
29 Alamos de Barrientos, 1987, 129.
30 'The case of going to war for the sake of trade considered in a new light; being the fragment of a greater work', in Tucker, 1776, 65–75.
31 Botero, 1956, 6.
32 Young, 1772, 478.
33 Botero, 1956, 6–7.
34 Fernández Navarette, 1626, 60–5.
35 Tucker, 1782, 83, 88–9.
36 Oldmixon, 1741, I, xxvii.
37 'Thoughts on the state of the contest with America', in Smith, 1977, 383.
38 See Tucker and Hendrickson, 1982,

196. 'Above all it [the need to preserve the colonies] must be found in the equation of sovereignty with the preservation of those interests that were considered indispensable to Britain's status as a great power.'

39 Saavedra Fajardo, 1976, II, 604–5.

40 Botero, 1956, 293. On Botero's conception of *prudenza* see Borelli, 1993, 63–94. For the Jesuit sinologist Domingo Fernández Navarette, however, the Great Wall was proof of the 'little valour and spirit of the Chinese'. Fernández Navarette, 1676, 31.

41 *Despotisme de la Chine* [March–June 1767] in Quesnay, 1888, 660.

42 Raynal, 1781, I, 104.

43 Mably, 1768, 132–7.

44 Turgot, 1791, 18.

45 See Tucker and Hendrickson, 1990, 160–68.

46 Saavedra Fajardo, 1976, II, 673.

47 'A Discourse on government with relation to militias', in Fletcher, 1737, 66.

48 Oldmixon, 1741, I, xvii. And cf. Thomas Sprat, 'It is now rightly understood that English greatness will never be supported or increased in this age by any other wars than those at sea' (1734, 404).

49 Goldsmith, 1768, 486.

50 Miller, 1994, 150–9.

51 *De l'esprit des lois*, XIX, 27, in Montesquieu, 1949–51, II, 579.

52 Saavedra Fajardo, 1976, II, 664. Cf. Alberto Struzzi who told the king in 1629, 'Cosa es asentada que el que será señor del la mar será de la tierra'. Quoted in Echevarría Bacigalupe, 1988, 927.

53 Quoted in Parker, 1979, 45–63.

54 On this point see Viner, 1965, who argues that all mercantilists – and Campomanes can be considered a neo-mercantilist – would have subscribed to four propositions: (1) wealth is the absolute and essential means to power, whether for security or for aggression; (2) power is essential or valuable as a means to the acquisition and retention of wealth; (3) wealth and power are each proper

ultimate ends of national policy; (4) there is a long-term harmony between these ends.

55 Child, 1751, 149.

56 *Ibid.*, 142.

57 Paterson, 1858, I, 128–9. This was a common theme throughout the eighteenth century. 'Had he kept the industrious Moors,' observed Thomas Gordon in 1728, 'and expelled the barbarous inquisitors; encouraged liberty and trade and consequently liberty of conscience, Spain would have been a more powerful nation and consequently a greater king, than all his wishes of guilty conquests had made him' (Gordon, 1728, I, 123).

58 Campomanes, 1988, 11–12.

59 Quoted by Armitage, 1992, 536.

60 Fletcher, 1737, 183.

61 *Ibid.*, 333.

62 *Ibid.*, 334–7.

63 *Ibid.*, 340. See Robertson, 1994, 239, who describes the *Discorsi* as a 'transparently ironical demonstration afforded by a new Spanish succession to establish a Universal Monarchy'.

64 See pp.187–8.

65 On this see Robertson, 1987, and on the links between the *Discorsi* and the Darien scheme, Armitage, 1995.

66 Ward, 1799, 122. Ward was minister for the Real Junta de Comercio y Moneda.

67 Campillo, 1789. Although it was only printed in 1798, the *Nuevo sistema* circulated widely in administrative and court circles before that date. A version of the text, in most places word for word, also appeared as the second part of Bernardo Ward's *Proyecto económico en que se proponen varias providencias dirigidas a promover los intereses de España*, first published in Madrid in 1779. Ward's own contribution, which was confined to a discussion of metropolitan Spain, had been composed in 1762. For a discussion of the relationship between the two texts see the introduction by Antonio Elorza to Campillo, 1969, 11–16.

68 Campillo, 1789, 9.

69 *Ibid.*, 2–3.

70 *Ibid.*, 14.
71 *Ibid.*, 6–7.
72 Campillo, 1969.
73 Campomanes, 1988, 238–9, 265.
74 Campillo, 1789, 2.
75 *Ibid.*, 3.
76 *Ibid.*, 15.
77 *Ibid.*, 15–16.
78 Venturi, 1991, I, 237.
79 On this see the classic study by Pocock, 1987.
80 See Pagden, 1990, 141–2.
81 Campomanes, 1988, 11–12.
82 'Juzgo, que de todos los estranjeros, después de Josías Child, es el que con mayor atención ha observado la constitución de nuestras colonias en América y la calidad del comercio que hacemos en ellas.' *Ibid.*, 359.
83 *Ibid.*, 267.
84 Hirschman, 1971.
85 Campomanes, 1988, 62.
86 See Canny and Pagden, 1987, 65.

5 Metropolis and Colony

1 Talleyrand, 1840, 330–31.
2 On this point, see pp.171–3.
3 Talleyrand, 1840, 334.
4 Harrington, 1977, 446. The distinction between *imperium* and *patrocinium* is made by Cicero, *De officiis*, II. 27. And see Kroebner, 1961, 4–11.
5 Smith, 1976, II, 556.
6 'An account of a conversation concerning the regulation of governments for the common good of mankind', in Fletcher, 1737, 436.
7 *Federalist*, 18, in Hamilton *et al.*, 1987, 161–4, and 'Lectures on law: VIII. Of man as a member of a confederacy', in Wilson, 1967, I, 249–55.
8 Kant, 1991, 154–5. The model for this type of relationship which Kant had in mind was, however, Ireland.
9 Fernández de Oviedo, 1851–5, III, 597. The *Nueva Recopilación de leyes de los reynos de las Indias* of 1680 explicitly forbids the use of royal revenue for either exploration or settlement. 'Mandamos que ningún descubrim-
iento, nueva navigación ni población se haga a costa de nuestra hacienda'. *Recopilación*, 1791, II, 7. Lib. IV, Tit. 3, ley 1. Cf. Adam Smith, 'Those adventures were all at the private risk and expense of the adventurers. The government of Spain contributed scarcely anything to any of them.' Smith, 1976, II, 590.
10 See pp.76–9.
11 Bland, 1769, 12.
12 Jefferson, 1774, 4.
13 'Considerations on the nature and extent of the authority of the British Parliament' [17 August 1774], in Wilson, 1967, II, 733.
14 See Greene, 1986, 93–6.
15 Mirabeau, 1758, 213.
16 'There is more equality, therefore, among the English colonists than among the inhabitants of the mother country. Their manners are more republican and their governments, those of three of the provinces of New England in particular, have hitherto been more republican too.' Smith, 1976, II, 585.
17 Turgot, 1913–23, V, 533.
18 Adams, 1819, 30.
19 Quoted in Greene, 1986, 93.
20 Quoted *ibid.*, 94, and see Bailyn, 1965, 135–6 and 709, n.25. The same point is made by Wilson in 'Considerations on the nature and extent of the authority of the British Parliament [1774]' in Wilson, 1967, II, 739–40, who cites Bacon's remarks on sovereignty in Ireland as his authority.
21 'Considerations on the nature and extent of the authority of the British Parliament' [17 August 1774], in Wilson, 1967, II, 742.
22 Quoted in Greene, 1986, 135.
23 Barnard, 1774, 32.
24 'De censuris' (*Disputatio XXXVI 10*) in Suárez, 1856–78, XXVIII, 258.
25 Quoted in Greene, 1986, 94–5. See also the observation of 'Britannus Americanus' in the *Boston Gazette* in the winter of the same year that 'the people of England could have no more political connection with them or power and jurisdiction over them, than they now have with or over the

26 Quoted in Greene, 1986, 102.
27 Trudel, 1971.
28 'The whole of the Carolina Government, so modelled,' wrote James Abercromby, 'proved Abortive and [totally] Ideal.' Abercromby, 1986, 180.
29 Burke, 1757, II, 288–9.
30 Quoted in Barnes, 1923, 178. As in Spain, one fifth of all gold and silver was to be given to the crown.
31 Andrews, 1934–8, I, 86n.
32 'On the tenure of the Manor of East Greenwich' [11 January 1766], in Franklin, 1959–93, XIII, 21.
33 It was for this reason that in 1774 George Mason argued that the colony had been created by prescription on unoccupied lands. Only this could explain the charters, and the fact that Maryland, North Carolina and Pennsylvania had all been created within the charter lines. See Onuf, 1983, 81–2 and on the wider question of land purchase, pp.82–5.
34 Jefferson, 1774, 8.
35 Strahan, 1722, 'The Translator's Preface'. For Solórzano see pp.89–90.
36 Otis, 1764, 438.
37 Which is probably why so much effort was made to refute his claim. See, for instance, Bland, 1769, 11–12.
38 Adams, 1819, 94–8.
39 Greene, 1986, 12.
40 Campbell, 1755, 57 and see Miller, 1994, 160–4.
41 Madison, 1900–10, VII, 373.
42 'Observations on the nature of civil liberty, the principles of government and the justice and policy of the war with America', in Price, 1991, 34, 32.
43 *Ibid.*, 23.
44 *Ibid.*, 34–5.
45 Otis, 1764, 437. For the colonists the law constituted an act of self-imposition, so that, in Wilson's words, 'the only reason why a free and independent man was bound by human laws was this – that he bound himself'. See Bailyn, 1967, 173–4.
46 See Diamond, 1961.
47 Dubuisson, 1785, 13.

48 See Zoltvany, 1971.
49 *Projet* [1792], 98. Precisely the same argument had been used in 1556 by Las Casas against Philip II's proposal to raise money by selling *encomiendas* in perpetuity to their current holders. Las Casas, 1969, 47–65.
50 'Su Majestad tiene imperio que deste al otro hemisferio no parte jurisdicción.' (*Los Españoles en Flandes*, Act XII, 374)
51 Quoted in Greene, 1986, 15.
52 It was also, of course, the case that, as Tucker and Hendrickson have pointed out, 'the privileges of the colonial assembly were merely privileges not rights' (1982, 174–5). But few of the colonists looked upon them as such.
53 On the compilation of this code, and on Solórzano y Pereira's part in it, see García Gallo, 1951–2.
54 Solórzano's *Disputationem de indiarum iure, sive de iusta Indianarum Occidentalium inquisitione, acquisitione et retentione* was first printed in two volumes in 1629. In 1647 he issued a revised and greatly extended Spanish version, and it is this which I have used. Solórzano, 1647, I, 904–6.
55 Bolívar, 1950, III, 677.
56 Child, 1751, 150–1.
57 Campomanes, 1988, 247. On Campomanes's admiration of Child's *A New Discourse on Trade* see p.123.
58 'On the plantation trade', in Davenant, 1771, II, 30–31.
59 *Digest* I, 4, I.
60 Robertson, 1800, IV, 13.
61 On these see Canny and Pagden, 1987, 90–1. Fredrick B. Pike's description of such rituals as a ploy by the crown to distract the *criollo* elite from 'real' politics fails to understand their purpose or to explain why the crown did so much to suppress them. Pike, 1960.
62 Smith, 1976, II, 574.
63 Orozco y Berra, 1853, 59–60. And see Canny and Pagden, 1987, 54–5.
64 Shklar, 1987a, 342.
65 Solórzano, 1647, I, 671.
66 Borello, 1611, 332.
67 Soto, 1556, 11. Suárez, 1971, I, 142 (Book I, Cap.7, n.14).

68 Abercromby, 1986, 70.

69 Bolívar, 1950, I, 176.

70 Jefferson, 1774, vii–viii.

71 Adams, 1819, 95–8, 110–18.

72 'Report on the Resolutions' [Philadelphia, 7 February 1799], in Madison, 1900–10, VI, 374.

73 Jefferson, 1774, 16.

74 See in general, Tarrade, 1972, I. Demands for 'liberty of trade' had been constant, however, since the closing years of the reign of Louis XIV. See Rothkrug, 1965, 433, and Schaeper, 1980.

75 On the reluctance of the British Caribbean colonies to support the American Revolution see Jack P. Greene, 'Changing identity in the British Caribbean: Barbados as a case study', in Canny and Pagden, 1987, 241–63.

76 The *Société* had been created, in imitation of its English counterpart, in 1788, and counted among its members Brissot, Condorcet, La Fayette, Mirabeau and Sieyès. See Tarrade, 1989.

77 Malouet, 1797, 8–9.

78 Harrington, 1977, 167.

79 Bland, 1769, 16. Cf. Bland, 1764, 320, 'the legislature of the colony have a right to enact ANY law they shall think necessary for the INTERNAL government'.

80 Bailyn, 1967, 213.

81 Barnave, 1791a, 6–7.

82 De Curt, 1789, 9–10.

83 Brissot, 1790, 14.

84 Barnave, 1791a, 10.

85 Blin, 1790, 23. A similar conceptualization of the relationship between Britain and the American colonies had been suggested by Francis Barnard in 1774. Barnard, 1774, 34–5.

86 Malouet, 1797, 12.

87 Anon., N.D. [2].

88 Talleyrand, 1840, 327.

89 Merlet, N.D., 3–9.

90 Collot, 1800, 7. Collot had been the Governor of Guadeloupe. He believed, however, that with regard to the power of legislation, 'toute discussion devient superflue, la métropole gouverne, et la colonie obéit'.

91 Malouet, 1797, 14–15.

92 Quoted in Wood, 1972, 5. See also Michael Zuckerman, 'Identity in British America: unease in Eden', in Canny and Pagden, 1987, 115–57, Zuckerman, 1977 and Greene, 1970.

93 See the observations in Wood, 1991, 16.

94 *The Spirit of Conquest and Usurpation and their Relation to European Civilization* [1813], in Constant, 1988, 73.

95 *Perpetual Peace, a Philosophical Sketch*, in Kant, 1970, 113–14.

96 'An Essay on Universal Monarchy', in Davenant, 1771, IV, 37.

97 Salazar, 1945, 192.

98 Botero, 1956, 97.

99 *Ibid.*, 95.

100 Quoted in Morales Oliver, 1927, 169.

101 Fernández de Medrano, 1602, 64.

102 See Pagden, 1990, 59.

103 Saavedra Fajardo, 1976, II, 645–6.

104 'Acte pour l'établissement de la compagnie des cien associés pour le commerce du Canada', *Edits*, 1854–6, I, 17.

105 'Mémoire to Jean Talon', 6 April 1607, in *Correspondence*, 1893, I, 201.

106 'Établissement de la Compagnie des Indes Occidentales', May 1664, *Edits*, 1854–6, I, 46.

107 'Mémoire de Bougainville sur l'état de la Nouvelle France, 1757', in Margy, 1867, 42.

108 See, for instance, the terms of the edict to the *intendant* Jean Bochart de Champigny of 24 April 1686. *Edits*, 1854–6, III, 50, and Eccles, 1964, 31.

109 Mentioned in Scammell, 1981, 316.

110 Quoted by Zuckerman, 'Identity in British America: unease in Eden', in Canny and Pagden, 1987, 136.

111 Child, 1751, 153.

112 Mirabeau, 1758, III, 226. And see Delanglez, 1939, 35–65. The analysis offered by this author, himself a Jesuit, of the 'Frenchification' project and its ultimate failure is based on much the same assumptions about the 'atavism of the North-American Indians' (p.38) and their 'centuries-old racial characteristic' (p.64) as were those of contemporary Jesuits.

113 Quoted in Chinard, 1923, 63–6.
114 De Brosses, 1756, I, 17–19.
115 See Pagden, 1993, 168–9.
116 Burke, 1757, II, 44, 46.
117 In a letter to the Neapolitan first minister Bernardo Tanucci. Quoted in Goggi, 1990.
118 *De l'esprit des lois*, XXI, 22, in Montesquieu, 1949–51, II, 648.
119 See Pocock, 'Josiah Tucker on Burke, Locke, and Price. A study in the varieties of eighteenth-century conservatism', in Pocock, 1985, 162.
120 See the comments in Miller, 1994, 222–3.
121 Wood, 1991, 165.
122 Quoted in Wood, 1991, 168.
123 Harrington, 1977, 168–9.
124 'Observations on the nature of civil liberty, the principles of government and the justice and policy of the war with America', in Price, 1991, 39.
125 De Pradt, 1801–1810, I, 19–20.
126 'Observations on the nature of civil liberty, the principles of government and the justice and policy of the war with America', in Price, 1991, 42.
127 Mayhew, 1759, 60–1.
128 Pownall, 1765, 6–7.
129 *Ibid.*, 1765, 28.

6   *The Calculation of Benefits*

1 Constant, 1988, 79.
2 Gordon, 1728, I, 121.
3 Davenant, 1771, IV, 391.
4 Blewith, 1725, 19.
5 Pinto, 1776, 10.
6 'Observations on the nature and civil liberty, the principles of government and the justice and policy of the war with America', in Price, 1991, 36.
7 *Ibid.*, 31.
8 'On the plantation trade', in Davenant, 1771, II, 6.
9 Taylor, 1989, 211–18.
10 Jefferson, 1774, 7.
11 'An Essay upon Universal Monarchy', in Davenant, 1771, IV, 30.
12 Hume, 1985, 340–1.
13 'Observations on the nature and civil liberty, the principles of government and the justice and policy of the war

with America' in Price, 1991, 30.
14 Raynal, 1781, V, 10.
15 Hume, 1932, I, 210.
16 Gibbon 1900–2, IV, 151. *Decline and Fall of the Roman Empire*, Cap. XXXVIII. And see the discussion in Pocock, 1985, 146.
17 Herder, 1800, 224 and cf. 250 where the same image is used again.
18 *Ibid.*, 249.
19 Raynal, 1781, X, 29. See Duchet, 1971, 463–8. It is clear, however, that the same general rule applied to the European empires in America. Cf. Raynal, 1781, I, 308.
20 I have discussed this aspect of Herder's work in Pagden, 1993, 172–88.
21 On the links between Raynal and Herder see *ibid.*, 172–3.
22 For the printing history see Feugère, 1922b, 15–48.
23 Quoted in Wolpe, 1956, 8.
24 Raynal, 1781, I, 3 (I, Introduction).
25 *Ibid.* This section, however, was in fact written by Diderot.
26 Elliott, 1970, 1.
27 Tourneaux, 1877, IX, 487–8 On Raynal's association with Choiseul and the *Bureau des colonies*, see Duchet, 1971, 126, and Benot, 1963, 139.
28 The best account of this prize and of those who entered the competition is Imbruglia, 1983, 378–88.
29 On this aspect of the *Histoire* see Koselleck, 1988, 178–82.
30 Bernard, 1775, 39.
31 I have followed the now definitive reconstruction of Diderot's contributions in Goggi, 1976–7 and Duchet, 1978. See also Yves Benot who, in what is still the only sustained examination of this aspect of Diderot's work, concludes that, in this context, the *Histoire* 'couronne toute son oeuvre de penseur politique', as the '*Neveu de Rameau* achève et synthétise toute sa création littéraire'. Benot, 1970, 259. See also Diderot, 1992, xxvii–xxxi.
32 Malouet, 1868, I, 180. There is an ironical allusion to Diderot's role in the composition of the *Histoire* in the *Supplément au voyage de Bougainville*:

A. Ouvrage excellent et d'un ton si

différent des précédents qu'on a soupçonné l'abbé d'y avoir employé des mains étrangères.

B. C'est un injustice (Diderot, 1955, 38).

33 Raynal, 1785, 13. The text is primarily concerned with the free-trade question. On Malouet's contribution see Feugère, 1922a, 364.

34 'Lettre apologétique de l'abbé Raynal à M. Grimm', in Diderot, 1956, 640.

35 The most detailed account of Buffon's thesis and its subsequent history is Gerbi, 1983.

36 Raynal, 1781, V, 3.

37 *Ibid.*, X, 297.

38 *Ibid.*, V, 16. See Albert Hirschman's observations on this passage in terms of the discontent with the failure of the ever-increasing proliferation of identical goods – of the kind provided by trade with the colonies – to satisfy basic human needs. Hirschman, 1992.

39 Raynal, 1781, V, 138.

40 Talleyrand, 1840, 334.

41 Raynal, 1781, I, 320–3.

42 Petit, 1776, 3.

43 'Sur les cruautés exercées par les espagnols en Amérique', in Diderot, 1875–7, VI, 451–2.

44 Raynal, 1781, VIII, 205–6.

45 *Ibid.*, IX, 107–9.

46 Chastellux, 1772, II, 97.

47 Raynal, 1781, IX, 13.

48 *Ibid.*, IX, 233–4.

49 Young, 1772, 20.

50 Raynal, 1781, V, 15–16. In the *Entretiens sur le fils naturel*, written in 1757, Diderot had even conjured into existence on the island of Lampedusa in the southern Mediterranean, 'far from the land and in the midst of the waves of a sea', just such 'a small band of happy men'. Diderot, 1968, 105–6.

51 'Réfutation suivie d'ouvrage de Helvétius intitulé *l'Homme*', in Diderot, 1875–7, II, 432.

52 'Observations on the nature and civil liberty, the principles of government and the justice and policy of the war with America', in Price, 1991, 56.

53 Raynal, 1781, V, 2.

54 'Discours préliminaire' to his translation of Shaftesbury's *An Inquiry*

concerning *Virtue or Merit* (1745), in Diderot, 1875–7, I, 9.

55 Carminella Biondi (1979, 239) has called it the 'testo chiave degli anni Settanta'.

56 'Of the populousness of ancient nations', in Hume, 1985, 383.

57 Condorcet, 1781, 14.

58 In the famous letter to Richard Price, 22 March 1778 in Turgot, 1913–23, V, 538.

59 Raynal, 1781, VI, 124–5. Adam Smith, who offered a similar explanation for the abolition of slavery in Europe, claimed that the ambition of the clergy to weaken the nobility had also been a factor. 'Thus,' he concluded, 'the influence of the clergy combining with the power of the king hastened the abolition of slavery in the west of Europe. Agreeable to this we find that in countries where neither the king nor the church were very powerful slavery still prevails.' *Lectures on Jurisprudence, Report dated 1766*, Smith, 1978, 454–5.

60 Cf. the comments of Montesquieu, *De l'esprit des lois*, XV, 2 in Montesquieu, 1949–51, II, 491, on this aspect of the Roman Law of slavery which he dismisses as 'senseless', since it supposes 'qu'il soit permis de tuer dans la guerre autrement que dans le cas de nécessité'.

61 Frossard, 1793. Frossard was also the author of a tract entitled, 'La cause des esclaves nègres et des habitans de la Guinée portée au tribunal de la Justice, de la Religion et de la Politique' (Paris 1788).

62 Raynal, 1781, VI, 126.

63 *Ibid.*, 133.

64 Condorcet, 1781, 6–7. The legal status of French slaves under the *Code noir* of 1685 was, in fact, more complex than Condorcet allows. The Code, however, as it was almost entirely based on Roman Law, observed the principle of *partus ventrem sequitur*, which made the offspring of female slaves the property of their master, and thus implied that slaves were 'moveable goods'. See Debtasch, 1967, I, 30–33.

65 Hilliard d'Auberteuil, 1785, 51.

66 Condorcet, 1781, 56. Raynal, 1781, VI, 117.

67 A similar vision of the impact of slavery is offered by Pierre-Victor Malouet. Malouet, 1788, 58–9.

68 Cf. Francisco de Vitoria's observations on this claim, which he also assumed to be fraudulent. Vitoria, 1991, 334.

69 Quoted in Blackburn, 1988, 50.

70 Sharp, 1776, 9.

71 Condorcet, 1781, 9. Raynal, 1781, VI, 130–2.

72 Raynal, 1781, VI, 135.

73 *Ibid.*, 215–16.

74 *Ibid.*, 235. Raynal also repeated the old claim that the number of priests had contributed significantly to the supposed population decline of the *criollo* society because, 'le célibat devint la passion dominante dans un pays désert'. *Ibid.*, 229.

75 Abortion was common in the slave communities. See Père Nicolson, who described the practice as 'une espèce de compassion se joint au plaisir de la vengeance, pour outrager la nature', and laid the blame on the *colons*, 'plus barbares que ces mères homicides'. Nicolson, 1776, 55. Mirabeau took much the same gloomy view of the inability of any of the three groups in America to reproduce with sufficient speed to prevent subsequent depopulation. Mirabeau, 1758, III, 255.

76 *Encyclopédie*, 1772, XVI, 533. There is, however, a marked difference in tone between this article, Jaucourt's article on 'Esclavage' – which is a paraphrase of Book XV of *De l'esprit des lois* – and the essay on 'Nègre' by Boucher d'Assis which, in discussing slavery, limits itself to a commentary on the *Code noir*.

77 Raynal, 1781, VI, 136–7.

78 *Tableau philosophique des progrès successifs de l'esprit humain* [1750] in Turgot, 1913–23, I, 222.

79 Raynal, 1781, X, 287.

80 On this point see Shklar, 1987b, 65.

81 Rochefort, 1665, 282.

82 *De l'esprit des lois*, XV, 1, in Montesquieu, 1949–51, II, 490.

83 Jefferson, 1955, 162. 'The man must be a prodigy,' he wrote, 'who can retain his manners and morals undepraved by such circumstances.' Quoted in Morgan, 1975, 375. And in general on this question see pp. 363–87. Even so staunch, sometimes hysterical, a defender of slavery as Malouet was prepared to recognize that slavery was 'truly for the *colons* a means of corruption and disorder'. Malouet, 1788, 17, and see the observations in Biondi, 1979, 114–15.

84 Hilliard d'Auberteuil, 1785, 5. Cf. Hilliard d'Auberteuil, 1777, I, 131–2, 135. On Hilliard d'Auberteuil and his role in the free–trade debates of 1785 see Tarrade, 1972, II, 563, n.112.

85 Hilliard d'Auberteuil, 1777, II, 34.

86 Brissot de Warville, 1790, 19.

87 Raynal, 1781, VI, 105.

88 'Réfutation suivie d'ouvrage de Helvétius intitulé *l'Homme*', in Diderot, 1875–7, II, 379, and see Lacoué-Laburthe, 1980.

89 Moreau de Saint-Méry, 1789, 20 and see the observations of Mirabeau, 1758, III, 254.

90 Raynal, 1781, VI, 40–41.

91 Brissot de Warville, 1786, 104. On the earlier discussion of the effect of education on the human mind see Pagden, 1986, 99–101.

92 Malouet, 1797, 5–6.

93 Mirabeau, 1758, III, 254.

94 Barnave, 1791b, 26. Although Barnave, in common with most of the Revolutionaries, held slavery to be a moral iniquity he claimed that any attempt to secure the immediate release of the slaves would lead to the loss of the colonies, and that this would amount to placing the well-being of 600,000 men before the 'intérêt national' of the entire French people.

95 Raynal, VI, 127–8. This has been described as a 'rewriting' of a passage in Louis-Sébastien Mercier's *L'An deux mille cent quarante* of 1770. But neither Diderot nor Mercier was alone in predicting an eventual slave revolt of massive proportions. See Biondi, 1979, 250–52.

96 Blackburn, 1988, 243.

97 Herder, 1800, 185.
98 *Ibid.*, 189.
99 Raynal, 1781, V, 4–5.
100 *Ibid.*, V, 69–70.

7 *From Empire to Federation*

1 The phrase itself, however, is from Starobinski discussing Rousseau's account of the perils of civilization. 'Le remède dans le mal: la pensée de Rousseau', in Starobinski, 1989, 169–71.
2 Constant, 1988, 53.
3 Mirabeau, 1758, III, 191. I am grateful to Michael Sonenscher for drawing this aspect of Mirabeau's work to my attention.
4 Mercier de la Rivière, 1767, 355–6.
5 *Ibid.*, 476.
6 'On the jealousy of trade', in Hume, 1985, 331.
7 Smith, 1976, II, 626–7.
8 Dubuisson, 1785, 20–1.
9 Mirabeau, 1758, III, 5.
10 *Ibid.*, 322–3.
11 Mandrillon, 1784, 11.
12 Raynal, 1781, IX, 152.
13 *Ibid.*, III, 205.
14 *Discours sur l'origine de l'inégalité* in Rousseau, 1979–81, III, 146–7.
15 Raynal, 1781, III, 204.
16 Mirabeau, 1758, III, 56.
17 *Ibid.*, 176–7.
18 'On the jealousy of trade', in Hume, 1985, 328–9. 'Nothing is more usual, among states which have made some advances in commerce, than to look on the progress of their neighbours with a suspicious eye, to consider all trading states as their rivals, and to suppose that it is impossible for any of them to flourish, but at their expense.'
19 Pocock, 1975, 497. For Hume's equally dismal view of the relationship between commerce and public debt, see Hont, 1993.
20 'An account of a conversation concerning the right regulation of governments for the common good of mankind', in Fletcher, 1737, 403.
21 Quoted in Miller, 1994, 152–3, n.8.

And see the observations of Thomas Pownall, that commerce had replaced the sword, and in the process had created a 'general composite link' between the colonies and the metropolis. But, he added, it was 'the rise and forming of this commercial interest [which] is what precisely constitutes the present crisis' (Pownall, 1765, 3–5).
22 *De L'Esprit de lois*, XX, 1 in Montesquieu, 1949–51, II, 585.
23 Smith, 1976, I, 267 and cf. I, 434.
24 Mercier de la Rivière, 1767, 355–6. Cf. Dubuisson, 1785, 20–1. For the attribution of this text to Dubuisson see Tarrade, 1972, II, 563.
25 Dubuisson, 1785, 14–15.
26 'Ordonnance de M. Duchesneau qui défend aux engagés de s'absenter de leur service', 2 December 1679. *Archives de la Province de Québec*, 1924, I, 256.
27 Quoted in Lamontagne, 1961, 337.
28 Ward, 1799, 21–2.
29 Uztáriz, 1742, 60–2.
30 'Remarques sur l'opinion de l'auteur de l'*Esprit des lois* concernant les colonies. LIV. XXI, chap. 17' [1766], in Quesnay, 1958, II, 785.
31 See pp. 152–5.
32 'Observations on the nature of civil liberty, the principles of government, and the justice and policy of the war with America', in Price, 1991, 71.
33 Letter to George Chalmers, 22 December 1785, in Smith, 1977, 290.
34 Mirabeau, 1758, III, 233–4.
35 *Ibid.*, 241–2.
36 Cf. the observations in 'Political thought in the English-speaking Atlantic, 1760–1790: (i) The imperial crisis', in Pocock, 1993a, 278.
37 *The Spirit of Conquest and Usurpation and their Relation to European Civilization*, in Constant, 1988, 55.
38 *Tableau philosophique des progrès successifs de l'esprit humain* (1750), in Turgot, 1913–23, I, 226.
39 Fletcher, 1737, 429.
40 *Idea for a Universal History*, in Kant, 1970, 51.
41 Unpublished seminar paper, delivered at the University of Lausanne in 1993.

42 His own solution was also an entirely pragmatic, if also impossible, one. If men as they were could never be fully persuaded of the intrinsic worth of 'curbing that exorbitant inclination' to 'exceed in everything, and draw the advantages to itself', then a balance of power between roughly equal military blocks, constituting federal systems of sovereignty, could be made to do it for them. This project is closely allied to the future structure for the European empires which he drew up in his *Discorsi delle cose di Spagna*, of 1698. See p.118.

43 Fletcher, 1737, 428.

44 'Lectures on law: VIII. Of man as a member of a confederacy', in Wilson, 1967, I, 249–55.

45 '[I] am fully persuaded that all great governments, whether republics or monarchies, not only disturb the world in their rise and fall; but by bringing together such numbers of men and immense riches into one city inevitably corrupt all good manners and make them incapable of order and discipline.' Fletcher, 1737, 420–21.

46 Franklin, 1959–93, XXII, 122–5.

47 *Federalist*, 18 in Hamilton *et al.*, 1987, 159. Madison, however, was fully aware, as indeed was Kant, of the potential weakness of such a system when faced with outside threats, and of its inability to resist the ambitions of its more powerful members. For some interesting observations on the debates over federation, and confederacy in Spanish America, see Chiaramonte, 1993, 24–31.

48 Fletcher, 1737, 436.

49 *Idea for a Universal History*, in Kant, 1970, 47.

50 For instance, Adorno and Horkheimer, 1979, 6–7. 'Enlightenment is Totalitarian' . . . 'In advance the Enlightenment recognizes as being and occurrence only what can be apprehended in unity: its ideal is the system from which all and everything follows.' At this stage in their argument Adorno and Horkheimer conflate confusingly the Enlightenment – as a historical period – and

Enlightenment as a psycho-historical process. It is clear, however, that what implies to the one must, necessarily, apply to the other.

51 Condorcet, 1988, 269.

52 *Idea for a Universal History*, in Kant, 1970, 49.

53 *Ibid.*, 44.

54 *Perpetual Peace: A Philosophical Sketch*, *ibid.*, 113–14.

55 Kant, 1992, 165–6.

56 Only the *Idea for a Universal History with a Cosmopolitan Purpose* (1784) was written before the creation of the French Republic in 1792.

57 Mirabeau, 1758, III, 215.

58 Turgot, 1791, 24–5.

59 Turgot, 1913–23, V, 605.

60 'The True Interest of *Great Britain* set forth in *REGARD* to the *COLONIES*', in Tucker, 1776, 164.

61 Talleyrand, 1840, 335–6.

62 Turgot, 1791, 31–2.

63 *Ibid.*, 34–5.

64 Richard Price had advocated a similar kind of federal structure as a solution to the conflicts within Europe itself. 'Let every state,' he wrote, 'with respect to all its internal concerns, be continued independent of all the rest, and let a general confederacy be formed by the appointment of a senate consisting of representatives from all the different states. Let this senate possess the power of managing all the common concerns of the united states, and of judging and deciding between them, as a common arbiter or umpire, in all disputes; having, at the same time, under its direction the common force of the states to support its decisions. . . . Thus might the scattered force and abilities of a whole continent be gathered into one point, all litigations settled as they rose, universal peace preserved, and nation prevented *from any more uplifting up a sword against nation.*' 'Observations on the nature of civil liberties, the principle of government, and the justice and policy of the war with America' [1776], in Price, 1991, 25.

65 Smith, 1976, II, 617.

66 'Smith's thoughts on the state of

the contest with America, February 1778', in Smith, 1977, 382–3. And see the comments in Winch, 1965, 13–15.

67 'Smith's thoughts . . . February 1778', in Smith, 1977, 384–5.

68 Hume, 1932, II, 307.

69 Malouet, 1810, 54–5.

70 'On the first principles of government', in Hume, 1985, 32–3 Cf. Malouet, 1810, 54: 'les constitutions libres ne se maintiennent que par leur moralité, qui ne permet pas plus l'emploi unique de la force, que sa dégradation'.

71 Hume, 1932, II, 300–301.

72 Quoted in Oltra and Pérez Samper, 1987, 84.

73 There has been some dispute on the authenticity of this manuscript, but there now seems little doubt, not only that it was written by Aranda, but that it develops ideas which he had already presented to the king and the Council. See *ibid.*, 235n.

74 Aranda, 1959, 399–401. The text is undated but must have been written after 1783, when Aranda set out a similar project in a letter to the viceroy of Mexico. See Oltra and Pérez Samper, 1987, 234–5. It is also printed with variations in Rodríguez, 1976, 63–6.

75 On this see the excellent study by Oltra and Pérez Samper, 1987.

76 De Pradt, 1817, 384.

77 Turgot, 1791, 32.

78 See Franklin, 1959–93, V, 368; XV, 238–9 and Franklin, 1950, 72n.

79 'Discurso de Angostura' [15 February 1819], in Bolívar, 1950, III, 685. Bolívar's impressions of the English constitution are largely derived from Montesquieu.

80 'Un pensamiento sobre el Congreso de Panama' [1826], *ibid.*, 756.

81 For a more detailed account of this see Pagden, 1990, 133–53.

82 'Memoria dirigida a los ciudadanos de la Nueva Granada por un caraqueño' [15 December 1812] in Bolívar, 1950, III, 544.

83 'Discurso de Angostura', *ibid.*, 678.

84 De Pradt, 1825, 75.

85 Turgot, 1791, 18.

86 *Ibid.*, 21.

87 Franklin, 1959–93, XXII, 122–5.

88 De Pradt, 1817, 477.

89 *De l'influence de la Révolution Américaine sur l'Europe* [1786], in Condorcet, 1847–9, VIII, 26.

90 *Federalist*, 11 in Hamilton *et al.*, 1987, 133–4.

91 Quoted in Tucker and Hendrickson, 1990, 160–61.

92 Jefferson, 1984, 1408.

Bibliography of Works Cited

For ease of reference, no distinction has been made between manuscripts, printed books or articles, nor between primary and secondary sources

Abercromby, James. 1986. *Magna Charta for America*. James Abercromby's 'An Examination of the Acts of Parliament Relative to the Trade and the Government of our American Colonies' (1752) and '*De Jure et Gubernatione Coloniarum*, or An Inquiry in the Nature, and the Rights of Colonies, Ancient, and Modern' (1774), ed. Jack P.Greene, Charles F. Mullett and Edward C. Papenfuse, Jr. Philadelphia.

Adams, John. 1819. *Novangalus and Massachusettensis: Or Political Essays Published in the Years 1774 and 1775*. Boston.

Adorno, Theodor and Horkheimer, Max. 1979. *Dialectic of Enlightenment* [*Dialektik der Aufklärung*], trans. John Cumming. London.

Alamos de Barrientos, Baltasar. 1867. *Discurso al rey nuestro Señor [Philip II] del estado que tienen sus reinos y señorios, y los de amigos y enemigos con algunas advertencias sobre el modo de proceder y gobernarse con los unos y con los otros* [1598], ed. J. M. Guardi. Paris.

—— 1987. *Aforismos al Tácito español* [1594], ed. J.A. Fernández Santamaria, 2 vols. Madrid.

Albert, S. 1980. *Bellum Iustum* (Frankfurter Althistorische Studien 10). Kallmunz.

Amaya, Francisco de. 1633. *Observationum iuris libri tres*. Geneva.

Andrews, Charles M. 1934–8. *The Colonial Period of American History*, 4 vols. New Haven.

Anon. N.D. 'Un mot à l'oreille', N.P. (but probably St Dominque).

Anquetil-Duperron, Abraham-Hyacinthe. 1993. *Considérations philosophiques historiques et géographiques sur les deux mondes (1780–1804)*, ed. Guido Abbattista. Pisa.

Aranda, Abarca de Bolea, Pedro Pablo, conde de. 1959, 'Exposición del conde de Aranda al rey Carlos III sobre la conveniencia de crear reinos independientes en América' in Andres Muriel, *Gobierno del señor rey Carlos III* [1838], ed. Carlos Seco Serrano, *Biblioteca de Autores Españoles*, 115. Madrid.

Archives de la Province de Québec, 1924. *Archives de la Province de Québec. Ordonnances, commissions, etc. etc. des gouverneurs et intendants de la Nouvelle France, 1639–1706*, ed. Pierre Georges Roy, 2 vols. Beauceville.

Armitage, David. 1992. 'The Cromwellian protectorate and the languages of empire', *The Historical Journal*, 35, 531–55.

—— 1995. 'The New World and British historical thought: from Richard

Hakluyt to William Robertson', in Karen Ordahl Kupperman (ed.) *America in European Consciousness, 1493–1750*. Chapel Hill, 52–75.

——— Forthcoming. *The Ideological Origins of the British Empire*. Cambridge.

Arredondo y Alvarado, Gonzalo. 1528. *Castillo inexpugnable defensorio de la fe. Y concionatorio admirable para vencer a todos enemigos espirituales y corporales*. Burgos.

Aubépin, H. 1855. *De l'influence de Dumoulin sur la législation française*. Paris.

Axtell, James. 1985. *The Invasion Within. The Contest of Cultures in Colonial North America*. New York and Oxford.

Azor, Johannes. 1610–16. *Institutionum moralium in quibus universae quaestiones ad conscientiam recte aut prave factorum pertinentes, breviter tractantur*, 3 vols. Louvain.

Bacon, Francis. 1857–74. *The Works of Francis Bacon*, ed. James Spedding, 14 vols. London.

Bailyn, Bernard, ed., 1965. *Pamphlets of the American Revolution. I 1750–1765*. [no more published]. Cambridge, Mass.

——— 1967. *The Ideological Origins of the American Revolution*. Cambridge, Mass.

Barker, Ernest. 1923. 'The conception of empire', in Cyril Bailey (ed.) *The Legacy of Rome*. Oxford.

Barnard, Sir Francis. 1774. *Select Letters on the Trade and Government of America; and the Principles of Law and Polity, applied to the American Colonies*. London.

Barnave, Antoine. 1791a. 'Rapport fait à l'Assemblée Nationale, sur les colonies, au nom des Comités de Constitution, de Marine, d'Agriculture, de Commerce et des Colonies, le 23 Septembre, 1791' [Paris].

——— 1791b. 'Rapport de M. Barnave sur les colonies, et décret rendu sur cette affaire par l'Assemblée Constituante, le 28 Septembre 1791; sanctionné par le Roi, le 29 du même mois' [Paris].

Barnes, J. 1986. 'Ciceron et la guerre juste', *Bulletin de la société française de philosophie*, 80, 41–80.

Barnes, Viola. 1923. *The Dominion of New England. A Study of British Colonial Policy*. New Haven.

Bartolus of Saxoferrato, 1588–9. *Iuriscon. Coryphaei Bartoli a Saxoferoi Opera quae nunc extant omnia excellentiss. I.C. tam veterum quam recentiorum additionibus illustrata*, 12 vols. Basle.

Bataillon, Marcel, 1966. *Erasmo y España* (2nd Spanish edn). Mexico.

Bayly, C.A. 1989. *Imperial Meridian. The British Empire and the World 1780–1830*. London and New York.

Bellarmino, Roberto. 1950. *Scritti politici*, ed. Carlo Giacon. Bologna.

Benot, Yves. 1963. 'Diderot, Pechmeja, Raynal et l'anticolonialisme', *Europe*, 41, 137–53.

——— 1970. *Diderot de l'athéisme à l'anticolonialisme*. Paris.

Beranger, J. 1990. 'L'expression du pouvoir suprême chez Tacite', in Claude Nicolet (ed.) *Du pouvoir dans l'antiquité: mots et réalités*. (Cahiers du Centre Glotz, 1.) Geneva.

Bernard, F. 1775. *Analyse de l'histoire philosophique et politique*. Leiden.

Berkeley, George. 1871. *The Works of George Berkeley, D.D.*, ed. Alexander Fraser, MA, 4 vols. Oxford.

Biggar, H.P. 1930. *A Collection of Documents Relating to Jacques Cartier and the Sieur de Roberval*. (Publications of the Public Archives of Cananda. No. 14.) Ottawa.

Biondi, Carminella. 1979. *Ces esclaves sont des hommes. Lotta abolizionista e letteratura negrofila nella Francia del Settecento*. Pisa.

Black, Antony. 1992. *Political Thought in Europe 1250–1450*. Cambridge.

Blackburn, Robin. 1988. *The Overthrow of Colonial Slavery 1776–1848*. London.

Bland, Richard. 1764. *The Colonel Dismounted: or The Rector Vindicated* [Williamsburg], in Bernard Bailyn (ed.) *Pamphlets of the American Revolution. I 1750–1765*. Cambridge, Mass., 1965.

—— 1769. *An Enquiry into the Rights of the British Colonies*. London.

Blewith, George. 1725. *An Inquiry whether a general Practice of Virtue tends to the Wealth or Poverty, Benefit or Disadvantage of a People*. London.

Blin. 1790. 'Opinion de M. Blin, député de Nantes' [1 March 1790, Paris].

Blunt, P.A. 1978. 'Laus imperii', in P.A. Garnsey and C.R. Whittaker (eds) *Imperialism in the Ancient World*. Cambridge. 159–91.

Bolívar, Simón. 1950. *Obras completas*, ed. Vicente Lecuna, 2nd edn, 3 vols. Havana.

Borelli, Gianfranco. 1993. *Ragion di stato e leviatano. Conservazione e scambio alle origini della modernità politica*. Bologna.

Borello, Camillo. 1611. *De regis catholici praestantia, eius regalibus, iuribus et praerogatiuis commentari*. Milan.

Bosbach, Franz. 1986. *Monarchia Universalis. Ein politischer Leitbegriff der frühen Neuzeit*. Göttingen.

Bossuet, André. 1961. 'La Formule "Le Roi est empereur en son royaume". Son emploi au XVe. siècle devant le Parlement de Paris', *Revue historique de droit français et étranger*, 371–81.

Botero, Giovanni. 1607. 'Discorso dell'eccelenza della monarchia', in *I Capitani del signor Giovanni Botero Benese*. Turin.

—— 1956. *The Reason of State* [*Della ragion di stato*, 1589], trans. and ed. P.J. and D.P. Waley. London.

Bouwsma, William. 1968. *Venice and the Defence of Republican Liberty*. Berkeley.

Brading, David. 1971. *Miners and Merchants in Bourbon Mexico, 1763–1810*. Cambridge.

—— 1991. *The First America, the Spanish Monarchy, Creole Patriots and the Liberal State, 1492–1867*. Cambridge.

Bretschneider, C.G. 1834. *Corpus reformatorum*, Vol.II, Halle.

Brett, Annabel Sarah. 1994. *Nature, Rights and Liberty*. Forthcoming, Cambridge.

Brissot de Warville, Jacques-Pierre. 1786. *Examen critique des voyages dans l'Amérique septentrionale de M. le Marquis de Chastellux*. London.

—— 1790. *Lettre de J.P. Brissot à M. Barnave*. Paris.

'Britanno sed Dunensi'. 1700. *A Defence of the Scots Abdicating Darien: Including an Answer to the Defence of the Scots Settlement There*. N.P.

Brown, Peter. 1977. *Relics and Social Status in the Age of Gregory of Tours*. Reading.

Brunner, Otto, Conze, Werner and Koselleck, Reinhart (eds) 1972–92. *Geschichtliche Grundbegriffe*, 7 vols. Stuttgart.

Bulkley, John. 1725. [*An Inquiry into the Right of the Aboriginal Natives to Land in America*] printed as the *Preface to Poetical Meditations, being the Improvement of Some Vacant Hours by Roger Wolcott Esq*. New London.

Burke, Edmund. 1775. *Speech of Edmund Burke Esq. on Moving his Resolution for Conciliation with the Colonies* [22 March 1775], 3rd edn. London.

Burke, Edmund and Burke, William. 1757. *An Account of the European Settlements in America*, 2 vols. London.

Burns, J.H. 1991. 'The "Monarchia" of Antonio de' Roselli (1380–1466): text, context and contoversy', in *Proceedings of the Eighth International Congress of Medieval Canon Law, San Diego, 1988*. Vatican City.

—— 1992. *Lordship, Kingship and Empire. The Idea of Monarchy 1400–1525*. Oxford.

Caietanus [Tommaso de Vio]. 1888–1906. *Sancti Thomae Aquinatis doctoris angelica opera cum commentaris Thomae de Vio Caetani* 12 vols. Rome.

Calasso, Francesco. 1957. *I glossatori e la teoria della sovranità. Studio di diritto comune publico* (3rd edn). Milan.

Campanella, Tommaso. 1633. *Monarchia Messiae*, Iesi.

Campbell, John. 1755. *State of the British and French Colonies in North America*. London.

Campillo y Cossío, José de. 1789. *Nuevo sistema de gobierno económico para la América*. Madrid.

—— 1969. *Lo que hay de más y menos en España para que sea lo que debe ser y no lo que es, España despierta* [1741], ed. Antonio Elorza. Madrid.

Campomanes, Pedro Rodríguez. 1775. *Discurso sobre la educación popular de los artesanos y su fomento*. Madrid.

—— 1988. *Reflexiones sobre el comercio español a Indias* [1762], ed. Vicente Llombart Roas. Madrid.

Canning, Joseph. 1987. *The Political Thought of Baldus de Ubaldis*. Cambridge.

Canny, Nicholas and Pagden, Anthony, eds. 1987. *Colonial Identity in the Atlantic World 1500–1800*. Princeton.

Charlevoix, Pierre François-Xavier. 1744. *Histoire et description générale de la Nouvelle-France avec le journal historique d'un voyage fait par ordre du Roi dans l'Amérique Septentrionale*, 3 vols. Paris.

Charters. 1957. *The Three Charters of the Virginia Company of London with Seven Related Documents*, with an introduction by Samuel M. Bemiss. Jamestown 350th Anniversary Historical Booklets. Williamsburg.

Chastellux, François Jean, marquis de. 1772. *De la félicité publique, ou Considérations sur le sort des hommes dans les différentes époques de l'histoire*, 2 vols. Amsterdam.

—— 1787. *Discours sur les avantages ou les désavantages qui résultent pour l'Europe de la découverte de l'Amérique*. London.

Chiaramonte, José Carlos. 1993. 'El mito de los orígenes en la historiografía latinoamericana', *Cuadernos del Instituto Ravignani*, 2.

Child, Sir Josiah. 1751. *A New Discourse on Trade* [1665]. Glasgow.

Chinard, Gilbert. 1923. *Volney et l'Amérique d'après des documents inédits et sa correspondance avec Jefferson*. Paris and Baltimore.

Clark, Bruce. 1990. *Native Liberty, Crown Sovereignty. The Existing Aboriginal Right of Self-government in Canada*. Montreal.

Collot, Victor. 1800. *Mémoire sur la réorganisation de la colonie de Saint-Dominique*. Paris.

Condorcet, Marie-Jean Antoine, marquis de. 1781. *Réflexions sur l'esclavage des nègres*. Neufchâtel.

—— 1847–9. *Oeuvres de Condorcet*, ed. A. Condorcet O'Connor and M.F. Arago, 12 vols. Paris.

—— 1988. *Esquisse d'un tableau historique des progrès de l'esprit humain*, ed. Alain Pons. Paris.

Constant, Benjamin. 1988. *Political Writings*, trans. and ed. Bianca Fontana. Cambridge.

Coroleu, Alejandro. 1992. 'Il "Democrates Primus" di Juan Ginés de Sepúlveda: una nuova prima condanna contro il Machiavelli', *Il Pensiero politico*, 25, 263–8.

Correspondance. 1893. *Correspondance échangée entre les autorités françaises et les gouverneurs et intendants*. Québec.

Cortés, Hernán. 1989. *Letters from Mexico*, trans. and ed. Anthony Pagden. New Haven and London.

Covarrubias y Leyva, Diego de. 1583. *Regulae Peccatum*, in *Didaci Couarrubias a Leyva toletani epsicopi, Opera Omnia*, 2 vols. Frankfurt.

Davenant, Charles. 1771. *The Political and Commercial Works of that Celebrated Writer, Charles D'Avenant LL.D.*, 5 vols. London.

De Brosses, Charles. 1756. *Histoire des navigations aux terres australes*, 2 vols. Paris.

Debtasch, Yvan. 1967. *Couleur et liberté. Le jeu du critère ethnique dans un ordre juridique esclavagiste*, 2 vols. Paris.

De Curt. 1789. 'Motion de M. De Curt, député de la Guadeloupe au nom des colonies réunies'. Paris.

Delanglez, Jean. 1939. *Frontenac and the Jesuits*. Chicago.

Denton, Daniel. 1670. *A Brief Description of New York: Formerly Called New Netherlands*. London.

De Pradt, Dominique Dufour. 1801–10. *Les trois âges des colonies, ou de leur état passé, présent et à venir*, 2 vols. Paris.

—— 1817. *The Colonies and the Present American Revolutions*. London.

—— 1825. *Congrès de Panama*. Paris.

Diamond, Sigmund. 1961. 'An experiment in feudalism: French Canada in the seventeenth century', *William and Mary Quarterly*, 18, 3–34.

Diderot, Denis. 1875–7. *Oeuvres complètes*, ed. Jules Assevat and Maurice Tourneaux, 20 vols. Paris.

—— 1955. *Supplément au voyage de Bougainville* [1773], ed. Herbert Dieckmann. Geneva and Lille.

—— 1956. *Oeuvres philosophiques*, ed. Paul Vernière. Paris.

—— 1968. *Oeuvres esthétiques*, ed. Paul Vernière. Paris.

—— 1992. *Political Writings*, ed. John Hope Mason and Robert Wokler. Cambridge.

Dubuisson, Paul-Ulrich. 1785. *Lettres critiques et politiques sur les colonies et le commerce des villes maritimes de France, adressées à G.T. Raynal par M*******. Geneva.

Duchet, Michèle. 1971. *Anthropologie et histoire au siècle des lumières. Buffon, Voltaire, Helvétius, Diderot*. Paris.

—— 1978. *Diderot et 'l'Histoire de Deux Indes' ou l'écriture fragmentaire*. Paris.

Du Creux, François. 1951. *The History of Canada or New France* [1664], trans. Percy J. Robinson, 2 vols. Toronto.

Dummer, Jeremiah. 1721. *A Defence of the New-England Charters*. London.

Eburne, Richard. 1624. *A Plaine Path Way to Plantations: That is, a Discourse in Generall, concerning the Plantation of our English People in Other Countries*. N.P.

Eccles, W.J. 1964. *Canada under Louis XIV. 1663–1701*. London and New York.

—— 1987. 'Sovereignty association, 1500–1783', in *Essays on New France*. Toronto, 158–81.

Echevarría Bacigalupe, Miguel Angel. 1988. 'Una original contribución al pensamiento antimercantilista: la doctrina Struzzi de 1629', *Hispania*, 47/167, 897–928.

Edits. 1854–6. *Edits, ordonnances royaux, déclarations et arrêts du conseil d'état du Roi concernant le Canada*, 3 vols. Québec.

Elliott, John. 1970. *The Old World and the New 1492–1650*. Cambridge.

—— 1989. *Spain and its World 1500–1700*. New Haven and London.

Encyclopédie. 1772. *Encyclopédie, ou dictionnaire raisonné des sciences, des arts et des métiers*, 28 vols. Geneva.

Ferguson, Robert. 1699. *A Just and Modest Vindication of the Scots Design, for Having Established a Colony at Darien*. N.P.

Fernández de Medrano, Juan. 1602. *De la república mixta*. Madrid.

Fernández de Oviedo y Valdes, Gonzalo. 1851–5. *Historia general y natural de las Indias, islas y tierra-firme del Mar Océano*, ed. José Amador de los Rios, 4 vols. Madrid.

Fernández Navarette, Domingo. 1676. *Tratados históricos, políticos, ethicos y religiosos de la monarchía de China*. Madrid.

Fernández Navarette, Pedro. 1626. *Conservación de monarquías y discursos políticos sobre el gran consulta que el consejo hizo al señor Rey don Felipe Tercero*. Madrid.

Feugère, Anatole. 1922a. *Un précurseur de la Révolution. L'abbé Raynal (1713–1796)*. Paris.

—— 1992b. *Bibliographie critique de l'abbé Raynal*. Angoulême.

Finley, Moses. 1976. 'Colonies – an attempt at a typology', *Transactions of the Royal Historical Society*, 5th series, 26, 167–88.

—— 1980. *Ancient Slavery and Modern Ideology*. London.

—— 1983. *Politics in the Ancient World*. Cambridge.

Fletcher, Andrew. 1737. *The Political Works of Andrew Fletcher*. London.

Folz, Robert. 1969. *The Concept of Empire in Western Europe from the Fifth to the Fourteenth Centuries*. London.

Fox Morcillo, Sebastian. 1536. *De regni regisque institutione*. Antwerp.

—— 1566. *Brevis et perspicua totius ethicae, seu de moribus philosophiae descriptio*. Basle.

Franklin, Benjamin. 1950. *Benjamin Franklin's Letters to the Press, 1758–1775*, ed. Verner W. Crane. Chapel Hill.

Franklin, Benjamin. 1959–93. *The Papers of Benjamin Franklin*, ed. William B. Wilcox, 30 vols [to date]. New Haven and London.

Franklin, Julian H. 1991. 'Sovereignty and the mixed constitution: Bodin and his critics', in J.H. Burns (ed.) *The Cambridge History of Political Thought 1450–1700*. Cambridge, 298–328.

Freitas, Serafim de. 1960–1. *Do justo imperio asiático dos Portugueses (De iusto imperio Lusitanorum Asiatico*, 1625), ed. and trans. Miguel Pinto de Meneses, 2 vols. Lisbon.

Frobisher, Martin. 1867. *The Three Voyages of Martin Frobisher*, ed. Richard Collinson. London.

Frossard, Benjamin. 1793. *Observations sur l'abolition de la traité des nègres présentées à la Convention Nationale*. N.P.

Fuller, Mary. 1991. 'Ralegh's fugitive gold: reference and deferral in *The Discoverie of Guiana*', *Representations*, 33, 40–64.

García Gallo, Alfonso. 1951–2. 'La "Nueva recopilación de las leyes de las Indias" de Solórzano y Pereira', *Anuario de historia del derecho español*, 21–2, 529–606.

Gerbi, Antonello. 1983. *La Disputa del Nuovo Mondo. Storia di una polemica: 1750–1900*. Milan and Naples.

Gibbon, Edward. 1900–2. *The History of the Decline and Fall of the Roman Empire*, ed. J.B. Bury, 2nd edn, 7 vols. London.

Gibson, Charles. 1977. 'Reconquista or conquista', in *Homage to Irving Leonard. Essays on Hispanic Art, History and Literature*, ed. R. Chang-Rodríguez and D.A. Yates. New York, 17–28.

Giménez Fernández, Manuel. 1944. 'Nuevas consideraciones sobre la historia y el sentido de las letras alejandrinas de 1493 referentes a las Indias', *Anuario de estudios américanos*, 1, 173–429.

Goez, Werner. 1958. *Translatio Imperii: ein Beitrag zur Geschichte des Geschichtsdenkens und der politischen Theorien in Mittelalter und in der Neuzeit*. Tübingen.

Goggi, Gianluigi. 1976–7. *Denis Diderot. Pensées détachées. Contributions à 'L'Histoire des Deux Indes'*, 2 vols. Siena.

—— 1990. 'L'Utopia dimidiata', *Intersezioni. Rivista di storia delle idee*, 3, 563–88.

Goldsmith, Oliver. 1768. *The Present State of the British Empire in Europe, America, Africa and Asia*. London.

—— 1927. *New Essays by Oliver Goldsmith*, ed. R.S. Crane. Chicago.

Gordon, Thomas. 1728. *The Works of Tacitus . . . To which are prefixed Political Discourses upon that Author*, 2 vols. London.

Gray, Robert. 1609. *A Good Speed to Virginia*. London.

Green, L. C. and Dickason, Olive P. 1989. *The Law of Nations and the New World*. Alberta.

Greenblatt, Stephen. 1988. 'Murdering peasants: status, genre and the representation of rebellion', in *Representing the English Renaissance*, ed. Stephen Greenblatt. Berkeley.

—— 1991. *Marvellous Possessions. The Wonder of the New World*. Oxford.

Greene, Jack P. 1970. 'Search for identity: an interpretation of of the meaning of selected patterns of social response in eighteenth-century America', *Journal of Social History*, 3, 189–220.

—— 1986. *Peripheries and Center. Constitutional Development in the Extended Polities of the British Empire and the United States 1607–1788*. Athens, Georgia and London.

Grotius, Hugo. 1631. *De iure belli ac pacis*. Amsterdam.

—— 1916. *Mare liberum. The Freedom of the Seas or the Right which Belongs to the Dutch to Take Part in the East India Trade*, trans. with a revision of the Latin text of 1633 by Ralph van Deman Magoffin. Oxford.

Gutíerrez de Torres, Alvaro. 1524. *El Sumario de las maravillosas y espantables cosas que en el mundo han acontecido*. Toledo.

Hakluyt, Richard. 1935. *The Original Writings and Correspondence of the two Richard Hakluyts*, ed. E.G.R. Taylor, 2 vols. London.

Hamilton, Alexander, Madison, James and Jay, John. 1987. *The Federalist Papers*, ed. Isaac Kramnick. Harmondsworth.

Hamilton, Raphael N. 1976. 'Who wrote *Premier Établissement de la Foy dans la Nouvelle France*?', *Canadian Historical Review*, 57, 265–88.

Harlow, Vincent T. 1952. *The Founding of the Second British Empire, 1763–1793*,

2 vols. London.

Harrington, James. 1977. *The Political Works of James Harrington*, ed. J.G.A. Pocock. Cambridge.

Headley, John M. 1983. *The Emperor and his Chancellor. A Study of the Imperial Chancellery under Gattinara*. Cambridge.

Herder, Johann Gottfried. 1800. *Outlines of a Philosophy of the History of Man* [*Ideen zur Philosophie der Geschichte der Menschheit*], trans. T. Churchill. London.

Hilliard d'Auberteuil, Michel René. 1777. *Considérations sur l'état présent de la colonie française de Saint Domingue*, 2 vols. Paris.

—— 1785. *Du commerce des colonies, ses principes et ses loix* [N.P.].

Hirschman, Albert O. 1971. *A Bias for Hope. Essays on Development and Latin America*. New Haven.

—— 1992. 'Industrialization and its manifold discontents: West, East and South', *World Development*, 20, 1225–32.

Historical Collection. 1836. *Historical Collection of South Carolina; Embracing Many Rare and Valuable Pamphlets and Other Documents relating to the State from its First Discovery until its Independence in the Year 1776*, 2 vols. New York. .

Hont, Istvan. 1993. 'The rhapsody of public debt: David Hume and voluntary state bankruptcy', in Nicholas Phillipson and Quentin Skinner (eds) *Political Discourse in Early-Modern Britain*. Cambridge, 321–48.

Hume, David. 1932. *The Letters of David Hume*, ed. J.Y.T. Greig, 2 vols. Oxford.

—— 1985. *Essays, Moral, Political, and Literary* [1777], ed. Eugene F. Miller, with an apparatus of variant readings from the 1889 edition by T.H. Green and T.H. Grose. Indianapolis.

Hutchinson, Aaron. 1745. *A Collection of Original Papers Relating to the History of the Colony of Massachusetts*. Boston.

Imbruglia, Girolamo. 1983. *L'invenzione del Paraguay. Studio sull'idea di communità tra seicento e settecento*. Naples.

Jefferson, Thomas [Tribunus]. 1774. *A Summary View of the Rights of British America*. London.

—— 1955. *Notes on the State of Virginia* [1787], ed. William Peden. Chapel Hill.

—— 1984. *Writings* (Library of America). Cambridge, Mass.

Johnson, Robert. 1609. *Nova Britannia, Offring Most Excellent Fruites by Planting in Virginia*. London.

—— 1612. *The New Life of Virginea: Declaring the Former Successe and Present Estate of that Plantation Being the Second Part of Noua Britannia*. London.

Jones, Dorothy V. 1982. *License for Empire. Colonialism by Treaty in Early America*. Chicago and London.

Kant, Immanuel. 1970. *Kant's Political Writings*, trans. and ed. Hans Reiss and H.B. Nisbet. Cambridge.

—— 1991. *The Metaphysics of Morals* [*Die Metaphysik der Sitten*], trans. and ed. Mary Gregor. Cambridge.

—— 1992. *The Conflict of the Faculties* [*Der Streit der Fakultaten*], trans. and ed. Mary Gregor. Lincoln and London.

Kantorowicz, Ernst. 1957. *Frederick the Second 1194–1250*, trans. E.O. Lorimer. London.

Kelley, Donald R. 1991. 'Law', in J.H. Burns (ed.) *The Cambridge History of Political Thought 1450–1700*. Cambridge, 66–94.

Kennedy, W.P.M. ed. 1918. *Documents of the Canadian Constitution*. Toronto.

King of Spain's Cabinet, The. 1658. *The King of Spain's Cabinet Councel Divulged; or A Discovery of the Prevarications of the Spaniards with all the Princes and States of Europe for Obtaining the Universal Monarchy*. London.

Koselleck, Reinhard. 1988. *Critique and Crisis. Enlightenment and the Pathogenesis of Modern Society* [*Kritik und Krise. Eine Studie zur Pathogenese der bürgerlichen Welt*]. Oxford, New York and Hamburg.

Kroebner, Richard. 1961. *Empire*. Cambridge.

Kupperman, Karen Ordahl. 1980. *Settling with the Indians. The Meeting of English and Indian Cultures in America, 1580–1640*. Totowa.

—— 1993. *Providence Island, 1630–1641. The Other Puritan Colony*. Cambridge.

Kuttner, Stephan. 1937. *Repertorium der Kanonistik (1140–1234)*. Vatican City.

La Martinière, Antoine Augustin Bruzen de, 1732. *Introduction à l'histoire générale et politique de l'univers par Mr. le Baron de Pufendorf*, 7 vols. Amsterdam.

Lamontagne, Roland. 1961. 'Témoignages de Barrin de La Galissonière sur la situation interne de l'Amérique française', *Revue de l'histoire de l'Amérique française*, 15, 333–43.

Lacoué-Laburthe, Philippe. 1980. 'Diderot, le paradoxe et la mimésis', *Poétique, revue de théorie et d'analyse littéraires*, 43, 267–81.

Las Casas, Bartolomé de, 1969. *De regia potestate* [1554], ed. Luciano Perena *et al.* Madrid.

Le Clercq, Chréstien. 1691. *Premier établissement de la foy dans la Nouvelle France*, 2 vols. Paris.

Lévi-Strauss, Claude. 1969. *The Elementary Structures of Kinship*, trans. Harle Bell *et al.* London.

Lintott, Andrew. 1981. 'What was the *Imperium Romanum*?', *Greece and Rome*, 28, 53–67.

Locke, John. 1967. *Locke's Two Treatises of Government*, a critical edition with introduction and notes by Peter Laslett, 2nd edn. Cambridge.

López, Gregorio. 1843. *Las Siete Partidas del Sabio Rey don Alfonso el IX* [1555], ed. Ignacio Sanponts y Barba *et al.*, 4 vols. Barcelona.

López Madera, Gregorio. 1625. *Excelencias de la monarquía y reyno de España* [Madrid].

Mably, Gabriel Bonnot de. 1768. *Doutes proposés aux philosophes économistes sur l'ordre naturel et essentiel des sociétés politiques*. The Hague.

McGinn, Bernard. 1979, *Visions of the End*. New York.

Machiavelli, Niccolò. 1960. *Il Principe e I Discorsi sopra la prima decada di Tito Livio*, ed. Sergio Bertelli. Milan.

Madison, James. 1900–10. *The Writings of James Madison*, ed. Gaillard Hunt, 9 vols. New York.

Maffei, Domenico. 1964. *La Donazione di Constantino nei giuristi medievali*. Milan.

Malouet, Pierre-Victor, baron de. 1788. *Mémoire sur l'esclavage des nègres*. Neufchâtel.

—— 1797. *Examen de cette question: Quel sera pour les colonies de l'Amérique le résultat de la Révolution Française, de la guerre qui en est la suite, et de la Paix que doit le terminer?* London.

—— 1810. *Considérations historiques sur l'empire de la mer chez les anciens et les modernes.* Anvers.

—— 1868. *Mémoires de Malouet publiés par son petit-fils le baron Malouet,* 2 vols. Paris.

Mandrillon, Joseph. 1784. *Le Spectateur américain, ou remarques générales sur l'Amérique septentrionale . . . Suivi de recherches philosophiques sur la découverte de l'Amérique.* Amsterdam.

Manzano Manzano, Juan. 1951–2. 'La adquisición de las Indias por los Reyes Católicos y su incorporación en los reinos castellanos (en torno a una polemica)', *Anuario de historia del derecho español,* 21–2, 1–170.

Maravall, Antonio. 1954. *El concepto de España en la edad media.* Madrid.

Margy, Pierre. 1867. *Relations et mémoires inédits pour servir à l'histoire de la France dans les pays d'outre-mer.* Paris.

Marineus Siculus, Lucius. 1579. *De rebus Hispaniae memorabilibus opus,* in *Rerum Hispanicarum scriptorum,* Vol. II. Frankfurt.

Matienzo, Juan de. 1580. *Commentaria in librum quintum recollectionis legum Hispaniae.* Mantua.

Maxwell, Kenneth. 1993. 'The Atlantic in the eighteenth century: a southern perspective on the need to return to the "big picture"', *Transactions of the Royal Historical Society,* 6th series, 3, 209–36.

Mayhew, Jonathan. 1759. *Two Discourses Delivered, October 25, 1759.* Boston.

Mechoulan, H. 1974. *L'Antihumanisme de J.G. Sepúlveda. Étude critique du 'Democrates Primus'.* Paris.

Mede, Joseph. 1677. *The Works of the Pious and Profoundly-Learned Joseph Mede, Corrected and Enlarged according to the Author's Own Manuscripts.* London.

Ménendez Pidal, Ramón. 1963. *Idea imperial de Carlos Quinto.* Madrid.

Mercier de la Rivière, Pierre Paul. 1767. *L'Ordre naturel et essentiel des sociétés politiques.* London.

Merlet, Jean François. N.D. (but probabaly 1792). 'Opinion de Jean-François Merlet, député du département de Maine et Loire, sur la question de la représentation des colonies dans le corps législatif'. Paris.

Mexía, Pedro de. 1561. *Historia imperial y caesarea, en la qual en suma se contiene las vidas y hechos de todos los caesares emperadores de Roma desde Julio Caesar hasta el Emperador Carlos Quinto.* Antwerp.

Millar, Fergus. 1977. *The Emperor in the Roman World (31 BC – AD 337).* London.

Miller, Peter. 1994. *Defining the Common Good: Empire, religion and philosophy in Eighteenth-century Britain.* Cambridge.

Mirabeau, Victor Riqueti, marquis de. 1758. *L'Ami des hommes, ou traité de la population,* 3 vols. The Hague.

Mommsen, Theodor. 1896. *Le Droit publique romain.* [*Romisches Staatsrecht*], trans. P.F. Girard. 3rd edn, 7 vols. Paris.

Moncada, Sancho de. 1619. *Restauración política de España.* Madrid.

Montesquieu, Charles de Secondat, baron de. 1949–51. *Oeuvres complètes,* ed. Roger Caillois, 2 vols. Paris.

Morales Oliver, Luís. 1927. *Arias Montano.* Madrid.

More, Thomas. 1965. *Utopia,* ed. E. Surtz and J.H. Hexter. New Haven and London.

Moreau de Saint-Méry, Médéric Louis Élie. 1789. *Observations d'un habitant des colonies*. Paris.

Morgan, Edmund S. 1975. *American Slavery, American Freedom. The Ordeal of Colonial Virginia*. New York and London.

Nicolet, Claude. 1988. *L'Inventaire du monde. Géographie et politique aux origines de l'empire romain*. Paris.

Nicolson, Père. 1776. *Essai sur l'histoire naturelle de l'île Saint Dominque*. Paris.

Nuix, Juan. 1782. *Reflexiones imparciales sobre la humanidad de los españoles en las Indias, contra los pretendidos filósofos y políticos. Para ilustrar las historias de MM. Raynal y Robertson*. Madrid.

Nuti, Lucia. 1988. 'The mapped views of Georg Hoefnagel: the merchant's eye, the humanist's eye', *Word and Image*, 4, 545–70.

Oldmixon, John. 1741. *The British Empire in America, containing the History of the Discovery, Settlement, Progress and State of the British Colonies on the Continent and Islands of America* [2nd edn first printed 1708], 2 vols. London.

Oliver, J.H. 1953. 'The ruling power: a study of the Roman empire in the second century after Christ through the Roman orator Aelius Aristides', *Transactions of the American Philosophical Society*, N.S. 43, pt. 4.

Oltra, Joaquín and Samper, Maria Angeles Pérez. 1987. *El conde de Aranda y los Estados Unidos*. Barcelona.

Onuf, Peter S. 1983. *The Origins of the Federal Republic. Jurisdictional controversies in the United States 1775–1787*. Philadelphia.

Ordonnances. 1803–6. *Ordonnances des Intendants et arrêts portant réglement du conseil supérieur de Québec*, 2 vols. Québec.

Orozco y Berra, Mañuel. 1853. *Noticia histórica del la conjuración del Marqués de la Valle*. Mexico City.

Otis, James. 1764. 'The rights of the British Colonies asserted and proved', [Boston] in Bernard Bailyn (ed.) *Pamphlets of the American Revolution. I 1750–1765*. Cambridge, Mass. 1965.

Pagden, Anthony. 1986. *The Fall of Natural Man. The American Indian and the Origins of Comparative Ethnology*, 2nd edn. Cambridge.

—— 1990. *Spanish Imperialism and the Political Imagination*. New Haven and London.

—— 1993. *European Encounters with the New World. From Renaissance to Romanticism*. New Haven and London.

Paradisi, Bruno. 1983. 'Il pensiero politico dei giuristi medievali', in Luigi Firpo (general ed.) *Storia delle idee politiche, economiche e sociali*. Turin, Vol. II, 211–366.

Parker, Geoffrey. 1979. *Spain in the Netherlands, 1559–1659*. London.

Paruta, Paolo. 1599. *Discorsi politici*. Venice.

Paterson, William. 1858. *The Writings of William Paterson, Founder of the Bank of England*, ed. S. Bannister, 2 vols. London.

Petit, Emilien. 1776. *Observation sur plusieurs assertions extraités littéralement de 'l'Histoire Philosophique des Établissements des Européens des deux Indes'*. Paris.

'Philo-Caledon'. 1699. *A Defence of the Scots Settlement in Darien with an Answer to the Spanish Memorial against it*. Edinburgh.

Pike, Fredrick B. 1960. 'The *Cabildo* and colonial loyalty to the Habsburg rulers',

Journal of Inter-American Studies, 2, 405–20.

Pinto, Isaac de. 1776. *Letters on the American Troubles*. London.

Pocock, J.G.A. 1975. *The Machiavellian Moment. Florentine Political Thought and the Atlantic Republican Tradition*. Princeton.

—— 1985. *Virtue, Commerce, and History. Essays on Political Thought and History, Chiefly in the Eighteenth Century*. Cambridge.

—— 1987. *The Ancient Constitution and the Feudal Law, A Reissue with a Retrospect*. Cambridge.

—— 1988. 'States, republics, and empires: the American founding in early-modern perspective', in Terence Ball and J.G.A. Pocock (eds) *Conceptual Change and the Constitution*. Lawrence, Kansas, 55–77.

—— 1993a. ed. with the assistance of Gordon J. Schochet and Lois G. Schwoerer. *The Varieties of British Political Thought, 1500–1800*. Cambridge.

—— 1993b 'A discourse on sovereignty: observations on the work in progress', in Nicholas Phillipson and Quentin Skinner (eds) *Political Discourse in Early-Modern Britain*. Cambridge, 377–428.

Portocarrero y Guzmán, Pedro. 1700. *Theatro monárchico de España que contiene las más puras como cathólicas maximas de estado, por las quales, assí los príncipes, como las repúblicas aumentan . . . sus dominios*. Madrid.

Postlethwayt, Malachy. 1751–55. *The Universal Dictionary of Trade and Commerce, Translated from the French of the Celebrated Monsieur Savary . . . with Large Additions and Improvements upon the Whole Work; which More Particularly Accommodate the Fame and the Trade and Navigation of the Kingdoms*, 2 vols. London.

Pownall, Thomas. 1752. *Principles of Polity, being the Grounds and Reasons of Civil Empire*. London.

—— 1765. *The Administration of the Colonies*, 2nd edn, London.

Price, Richard. 1991. *Political Writings*, ed. D.O. Thomas. Cambridge.

Projet [1792]. *Projet de constitution pour la partie françoise de Saint-Dominque*. Paris.

Prosdocimi, Luigi. 1954–5. '"Ex facto oritur ius". Breve nota di diritti medievale', *Studi senesi*, 66–67, 808–19.

Pufendorf, Samuel. 1764. *An Introduction to the History of the Principal States of Europe*, begun by Baron Pufendorf, continued by Mr. de la Martinière, improved by Joseph Sayer, Serjeant at Law, 2 vols. London.

—— 1934 *De iure naturae et gentium libri octo*, a photographic reproduction of the 1688 edition with a translation by C.H. and W.A. Oldfather, 2 vols. Oxford.

—— 1991. *On the Duty of Man and Citizen*, trans. Michael Silverthorne, ed. James Tully. Cambridge.

Quesnay, François. 1888. *Oeuvres économiques et philosophiques de F. Quesnay*, ed. Auguste Oncken. Paris.

—— 1958. *François Quesnay et la physiocratie*, 2 vols. Paris.

Raleigh, Sir Walter. 1848. *The Discoverie of the Large, Rich and Bewvtiful Empire of Gviana, with a Relation of the Great and Golden City of Manoa (which the Spaniards call El Dorado) and the prouinces of Emeria, Arromaia and other Countries, with their Riuers, Adioyning* [1596], ed. Robert Schomburgk. London.

Ramsay, David. 1789. *The History of the American Revolution*, 2 vols. Philadelphia.

Raynal, Guillaume-Thomas, abbé. 1781. *Histoire philosophique et politique des établissemens et du commerce des Européens dans les deux Indes*, 10 vols. Geneva.

—— 1785. *Essai sur l'administration de St Domingue*. N.P.

Recopilación. 1791. *Nueva Recopilación de leyes de los reynos de las Indias*, 3 vols. Madrid.

Richardson, J.S. 1991. '*Imperium Romanum*: empire and the language of power', *Journal of Roman Studies*, 81, 1–9.

Robertson, John. 1987. 'Andrew Fletcher's vision of union', in Roger A. Mason (ed.) *Scotland and England 1286–1815*. Edinburgh, 216–18.

—— 1994. 'Union state and empire. The Britain of 1707 in its European setting', in Lawrence Stone (ed.) *An Imperial State at War. Britain from 1689–1815*. London, 224–57.

—— Forthcoming. ed. *A Union for Empire: The Union of 1701 in the History of British Political Thought*. Cambridge.

Robertson, William. 1800. *The History of America. Ninth Edition in which is Included the Posthumous Volume Containing the History of Virginia to the Year 1688 and of New England, to the Year 1652*, 4 vols. London.

Rochefort, Charles de. 1665. *Histoire naturelle et morale des Isles Antilles de l'Amérique*. Rotterdam.

Rodriguez, Mario. 1976. *La revolución americana de 1776 y el mundo hispánico. Ensayos y documentos*. Madrid.

Rothkrug, Lionel. 1965. *Opposition to Louis XIV. The Politics and Social Origins of the French Enlightenment*. Princeton.

Rubiés i Mirabet, Joan Pau. 1991. 'Hugo Grotius's dissertation on the origins of the American peoples and the use of comparative methods', *Journal of the History of Ideas*, 52, 221–44.

Russell, Frederick H. 1975. *The Just War in the Middle Ages*. Cambridge.

Russell, Peter. 1978. 'Influencia del descubrimiento de Canarias sobre el debate medieval acerca de los derechos del hombre pagano y de los estados paganos: la documentación portuguesa'. *Revista de historia canaria*, 36, 9–32.

Saavedra Fajardo, Diego. 1976. *Empresas politícas. Idea de un principe polítíco-cristiano* [1639], ed. Q. Aldea Vaquero, 2 vols. Madrid.

Said, Edward. 1993. *Culture and Imperialism*. London.

Salazar, Juan de. 1945. *Política española. Contiene un discurso cerca de su monarquía, materias de estado, aumento i perpetuidad* [1619], ed. Miguel Herrero García. Madrid.

Scammell, G.V. 1981. *The World Encompassed*. London and New York.

Schaeper, Thomas. 1980. 'Colonial trade policies late in the reign of Louis XIV', *Revue française d'histoire d'Outre Mer*, 67, 203–15.

Scheller, Robert W. 1981–2. 'Imperial themes in art and literature of the early French Renaissance: the period of Charles VIII', *Simiolus, Netherlands Quarterly for the History of Art*, 12, 5–69.

Schumpeter, Joseph. 1951. *Imperialism and Social Classes* [*Zur Soziologie der Imperialismen*], trans. Heinz Norden. Oxford.

Schwartz, Stuart B. 1978. 'New World nobility: social aspirations and mobility in the conquest and colonization of Spanish America', in Miriam Usher Chrisman and Otto Grundler (eds) *Social Groups and Religious Ideas in the Sixteenth Century*. Kalmazoo, 23–37.

Scribonius, Cornelius. 1550. *La très admirable, très magnifique, et triumphante entrée, du très hault et très puissant Prince Philipes, Prince d'Espaignes, filz de L'empéreur*

Charles V. Antwerp.

Seed, Patricia. 1993. 'Taking possession and reading texts: establishing authority of overseas empires', in Jerry M. Williams and Robert E. Lewis (eds) *Early Images of the Americas. Transfer and Invention*. Tucson and London, 111–47.

Seelmann, K. 1979. *Die Lehre des Fernando Vázquez de Menchaca vom 'dominium'*. Köln and Graz.

Sepúlveda, Juan Ginés de. 1780. *Johannis Genesii Sepulvedae Opera*, 4 vols. Madrid.

Sharp, Granville. 1776. *An Essay on Slavery proving from SCRIPTURE its Inconsistency with HUMANITY and RELIGION*. London.

Shklar, Judith. 1987a. 'Alexander Hamilton and the language of political science', in Anthony Pagden (ed.) *The Languages of Political Theory in Early-Modern Europe*. Cambridge, 339–55.

—— 1987b. *Montesquieu*. Oxford.

Skinner, Quentin. 1978. *The Foundations of Modern Political Thought*, 2 vols. Cambridge.

—— 1990. 'Machiavelli's *Discorsi* and the pre-humanist origins of republican ideas', in Gisela Bock, Quentin Skinner and Maurizio Viroli (eds) *Machiavelli and Republicanism*. Cambridge, 121–41.

Smith, Adam. 1976. *An Inquiry into the Nature and Causes of the Wealth of Nations* [1776], ed. R.H. Campbell and A.S. Skinner; textual ed. W.B. Todd (Vol. II of the Glasgow Edition of the Works and Correspondence of Adam Smith), 2 vols. Oxford.

—— 1977. *The Correspondence of Adam Smith*, ed. Ernest Campbell Mossner and Ian Simpson Ross (Vol. VI of the Glasgow Edition of the Works and Correspondence of Adam Smith). Oxford.

—— 1978. *Lectures on Jurisprudence*, ed. R.L. Meek, D.D. Raphael and P.G. Stein (Vol. V of the Glasgow Edition of the Works and Correspondence of Adam Smith). Oxford.

Smith, John. 1986. *The Complete Works of Captain John Smith*, ed. Philip J. Barbour, 3 vols. Chapel Hill.

Smith, J.H. 1950. *Appeals to the Privy Council from the American Plantations*. New York.

Solórzano y Pereira, Juan de. 1647. *Política Indiana, sacada en lengua castellana de los dos tomos del derecho i govierno municipal de las Indias occidentales*, 2 vols. Madrid.

Soto, Domingo de. 1556. *De Iustitia et iure*. Salamanca.

Sprat, Thomas. 1734. *History of the Royal Society*. London.

Starobinski, Jean. 1989. *Le remède dans le mal. Critique et légitimation de l'artifice à l'âge des Lumières*. Paris.

Strachey William. 1953. *The Historie of Travell into Virginia Britania* [1612], ed. Louis B. Wright and Virginia Freund. London.

Strahan, William. 1722. *The Civil Law in its Natural Order, together with the Public Law, written in French by Monsieur Domat and translated by William Strahan LL.D.*, 2 vols. London.

Suárez, Francisco. 1856–78. *Opera Omnia*, ed. C. Berton, 28 vols. Paris.

—— 1954. *Disputatio xii. De Bello*, from *Opus de triplice virtute theologica, fide spe et charitate* [Paris, 1621], in Vol. II of Luciano Pereña Vicente, *Teoría de la guerra en Francisco Suárez*, 2 vols. Madrid.

—— 1971. *Tractatus de legibus ac Deo legislatore* [1612], trans. and ed. Luciano Pereña *et al*. Madrid.

Talleyrand-Périgord, Charles Maurice de. 1840. *Essai sur les avantages à retirer des colonies nouvelles dans les circonstances présentes: lu à la séance publique de 15 messidor an V*. Paris.

Tanner, Marie. 1993. *The Last Descendant of Aeneas. The Habsburgs and the Mythic Image of the Emperor*. New Haven and London.

Tarrade, Jean, 1972. *Le commerce colonial de la France à la fin de l'Ancien Régime: l'évolution du régime de 'l'Exclusif' de 1763 à 1789*, 2 vols. Paris .

—— 1989. 'Les colonies et les principes de 1789: les Assemblées révolutionnaires face au problème de l'esclavage', *Revue française d'histoire d'Outre-Mer*, 76, 9–34.

Taylor, Charles. 1989. *Sources of the Self. The Making of the Modern Identity*. Cambridge.

Temple, Sir William. 1720. *The Works of Sir William Temple Bart*, 2 vols. London.

Thevet, André. 1575. *La Cosmographie universelle*, 2 vols. Paris.

Tourneaux, M. 1877. *Correspondance littéraire, philosophique et critique par Grimm, Diderot, Raynal, Meister etc.*, 16 vols. Paris.

Trigger, Bruce G. 1986. 'The historian's Indian: Native-Americans in Canadian historical writing from Charlevoix to the present', *Canadian Historical Review*, 67, 315–42.

Trudel, Marcel. 1971. *The Seigneurial Regime* (Canadian Historical Society Association Historical Booklet no. 6), Ottawa.

—— 1973. *The Beginnings of New France, 1524–1663*, trans. Patricia Claxton. Toronto.

—— 1979. *Histoire de la Nouvelle France II. La seigneurie des Cents Associés 1627–1663*, 2 vols. Montreal.

Tuck, Richard. 1993. *Philosophy and Government 1572–1651*. Cambridge.

—— Forthcoming. *Sorry Comforters: Political Theory and the International Order from Grotius to Kant*.

Tucker, Josiah. 1775. *A Letter to Edmund Burke, Esq., A Member of Parliament for the City of Bristol . . . in Answer to his Printed Speech*. Gloucester.

—— 1776. *Four Treatises on Political and Commercial Subjects*. Gloucester.

—— 1782. *Cui Bono? Or, an Inquiry, What Benefits Can Issue either to the English or the Americans, the French, Spaniards or Dutch, from the Greatest Victories or Successes in the Present War*, 3rd edn. London.

Tucker, Robert W. and Hendrickson, David C. 1982. *The Fall of the First British Empire. The Origins of the War of American Independence*. Baltimore and London.

—— 1990. *Empire of Liberty. The Statescraft of Thomas Jefferson*. Oxford.

Tully, James. 1993a. *An Approach to Political Philosophy: Locke in Contexts*. Cambridge.

—— 1993b. 'Placing the '*Two Treatises*'', in Nicholas Philipson and Quentin Skinner (eds) *Political Discourse in Early-Modern Britain*, Cambridge, 253–80.

—— 1994. 'Aboriginal property and western theory: recovering a middle ground', *Social Philosophy and Policy*, 11, 153–80.

—— Forthcoming. *Strange Multiplicity. Constitutionalism in an Age of Diversity*. Cambridge.

Turgot, Anne Robert Jacques. 1791. *Mémoire sur les colonies américaines, sur leurs relations politiques avec leurs métropoles, et sur la manière dont la France et l'Espagne ont du envisager les suites de l'indépendance des Étas Unis de l'Amérique* [6 April 1776]. Paris.

—— 1913–23. *Oeuvres de Turgot et documents le concernant*, ed. Gustav Schelle, 5 vols. Paris.

Ugarte de Hermosa y Salcedo, Francisco. 1655. *Origen de los goviernos divinos i humanos i forma de su exercicio en lo temporal*. Madrid.
Ullmann, Walter. 1979. '"This Realm of England is an Empire"', *Journal of Ecclesiastical History*, 30, 175–203.
Uztáriz, Gerónimo de. 1742. *Theórica y práctica de comercio y de marina*. Madrid.

Vargas Machuca, Barnardo de. 1599. *Milicia y descripción de las Indias*. Madrid.
Vattel, Emeric de. 1916. *Le droit de gens ou principes de la loi naturelle, appliqués à la conduite et aux affaires des nations et des souverains* [1758], ed. James Brown Scott, 3 vols. Washington.
Vaughan, Alden T. 1978. '"Expulsion of the Savages": English policy and the massacre of 1622', *William and Mary Quarterly*, 3rd series, 35, 57–84.
Vázquez de Menchaca, Fernando. 1931. *Controversiarum illustrium aliarumque usu frequentium, libri tres* [1563], ed. Fidel Rodriguez Alcalde, 3 vols. Valladolid.
Venturi, Franco. 1991. *The End of the Old Regime in Europe, 1776–1798*, trans. R. Burr Litchfield, 2 vols. Princeton [trans. of parts 1 and 2 of Vol.IV of *Settecento riformatore*].
Viner, Jacob. 1965. 'Power versus Plenty as objectives of foreign policy in the seventeenth and eighteenth centuries', in D.C. Coleman (ed.) *Revisions in Mercantilism*. London, 61–91.
Vitoria, Franciso de. 1991. *Political Writings*, ed. Anthony Pagden and Jeremy Lawrance. Cambridge.

Walther, Helmut. 1976. *Imperiales Konigtum. Konziliarismus und Volkssouveranität*. Munich.
Ward, Barnardo. 1799. *Proyecto económico en que se proponen varias providencias, dirigidas a promover los intereses de España, con los medios y fondos para su plantificación* [1762]. Madrid.
Wilkes, Michael. 1964. *The Problem of Sovereignty in the Later Middle Ages. The Papal Monarchy with Augustus Triumphus and the Publicists*. Cambridge.
Williams, Robert A. 1990. *The American Indian in Western Legal Thought. The Discourses of Conquest*. New York and Oxford.
Williams, Bernard. 1993. *Shame and Necessity*. Berkeley, Los Angeles and Oxford.
Wilson, James. 1967. *The Works of James Wilson*, ed. Robert Green McCloskey, 2 vols. Cambridge, Mass.
Winch, Donald. 1965. *Classical Political Economy and Colonies*. London.
Wolpe, Hans. 1956. *Raynal et sa machine de guerre. 'L' Histoire de Deux Indes' et ses perfectionnements*. Paris.
Wood, Gordon. 1972. *The Creation of the American Republic 1776–1787*. New York and London.
—— 1991. *The Radicalism of the American Republic*. New York.
Woolf, C.N.S. 1913. *Bartolus of Sassoferato. His Position in the History of Medieval Political Thought*. Cambridge.

Yates, Frances. 1975. *Astrae. The Imperial Theme in the Sixteenth Century*. London.

Young, Arthur. 1772. *Political Essays Concerning the Present State of the British Empire*. London.

Zeller, G. 1934. 'Les rois de France candidats à l'empire: essai sur l'idéologie impériale en France', *Revue historique*, 173, 273–331; 497–543.

Zoltvany, Yves. 1971. 'Esquisse de la coutume de Paris', *Revue d'histoire de l'Amérique française*, 25, 365–84.

Zuckerman, Michael. 1977. 'The fabrication of identity in early America', *William and Mary Quarterly*, 3rd series, 34, 183–214.

Zurara, Gomes Eanes de. 1973. *Crónica de Guiné*, ed. José de Braganza. Barcelos.

Index of Names

CPSIA information can be obtained at www.ICGtesting.com
Printed in the USA
BVOW06*1759260816

460182BV00004B/26/P